Observing America

*The Commentary of British Visitors
to the United States, 1890–1950*

Robert Frankel

THE UNIVERSITY OF WISCONSIN PRESS

This book was published with the support
of the Anonymous Fund for the Humanities
of the University of Wisconsin–Madison.

The University of Wisconsin Press
1930 Monroe Street
Madison, Wisconsin 53711

www.wisc.edu/wisconsinpress/

3 Henrietta Street
London WC2E 8LU, England

1   3   5   4   2

Printed in the United States of America

Library of Congress Cataloging-in-Publication Data
Frankel, Robert P., 1958–
Observing America : the commentary of British visitors
to the United States, 1890–1950 / Robert P. Frankel.
p.   cm.—(Studies in American thought and culture)
Includes bibliographical references and index.
ISBN 0-299-21880-5 (cloth : alk. paper)
1. United States—Civilization—Foreign public opinion,
British—History—20th century.   2. National characteristics,
American—Foreign public opinion, British.
3. Public opinion—Great Britain—History—20th century.
4. Intellectuals—Great Britain—Attitudes.
5. Intellectuals—Travel—United States.   I. Title.   II. Series.
E169.1.F828   2006
973.91—dc22   2006008622

For my parents

Welcome and thanks, we say, to those visitors we have, and have had, from abroad among us—and may the procession continue! ... Some have come to make money—some for a "good time"—some to help us along and give us advice—and some undoubtedly to investigate, *bona fide*, this great problem, democratic America.

Walt Whitman, "Our Eminent Visitors," *November Boughs* (1888)

Contents

Preface

Despite the shared language, ties of blood, and enduring cultural bonds, the British have always viewed America as a country marked by its own distinctive identity. Since 1776—and even before—they have looked across the Atlantic with a sense of fascination and, inevitably, with their native land as a point of comparison.

To gain an understanding of what British perceptions of the United States have been, the historian could consult many different kinds of evidence. However, the trove of works by Britons devoted specifically to the subject of America may well constitute the most valuable source. Though the authors of these works can by no means be seen as completely representative of the larger society, their collective evaluation of America is more substantial and coherent than the scattered impressions that could be pasted together and characterized as the sentiments of the British people, while at the same time wider in scope and richer in texture than the line on the United States as laid down in Westminster.

The fact is that for many decades—from the early nineteenth century to the mid-twentieth—virtually every Briton with a name and any literary pretensions who visited America would return to publish his or her findings. The travel book dedicated to the trip to America became so commonplace that authors would often apologize at the outset of one of these works for their self-indulgence, while prominent travelers to the United States who refrained from undertaking such an exercise felt obligated to explain why.[1] The British were, arguably, the masters of travel writing—whether their subject be America, Italy, or some far-flung land. Although much of the writing tends to be sketchy or superficial, it can, in the hands of a deft stylist with a keen eye, make for delightful, stimulating reading. In some cases it is also possible to learn as much about the author—his or her beliefs, ideals, and prejudices—as about the country under examination. Scholars have even viewed the travel book as an important literary genre, like the memoir or novel.[2]

Certain British visitors to America, however, qualify as travel writers—they were drawn to many of the same features as their fellow sojourners—but were really far more. Their books are filled with the typical observations of such natural wonders as Niagara Falls, human accomplishments like the New York skyline, and such idiosyncratic customs as the drinking of ice water and the chewing and spitting of tobacco. They were also, however, students and analysts of American society. In their works they did not merely pull the reader from city to city, and from scenic spot to scenic spot, according to the dictates of an itinerary. They described; they commented; but most important, they ventured to form an overarching thesis—to present a point of view on America that would bring a focus and a slant to their observations. Sometimes their writings on America were not connected to any trip at all.

The premier British observers of America—the men and women who wrote the most penetrating and provocative accounts—were not only exceptionally talented, but they possessed more than a fleeting interest in the vast nation across the ocean. To them America was a subject of enduring attraction and, in some cases, even of lifelong passion. While they usually wrote their articles and books against pressing deadlines, and often with an eye toward supplementing profits gained on the lucrative American lecture circuit, they managed to turn out a superior corpus. These writers generally published their commentary on both sides of the Atlantic for a combined Anglo-American readership, though they exerted more of an impact in the New World than the Old.

Reading the best of the British and other foreign observers of the United States was—and is—worthwhile at least in part because they viewed the nation from a different perspective. Americans writing about America were certainly more familiar with the country's customs, social trends, and institutions, but the outsiders approached the same subject from a valuable distance. They, in effect, looked at America with fresh eyes. Furthermore, even when they protested that they were not doing so, they clearly were making their assessments within the context of their native countries and, to an extent, commenting on those countries as well as on America. Long before scholars delved into comparative history, foreign observers of America were making either implicit or explicit comparisons of their own.[3] When Europeans observed America, they used the Old World as their benchmark. They wanted to see what made America distinctive, what made it unique. Social scientists, including historians, have in recent decades devoted considerable attention—sometimes favorable and sometimes not—to the concept of "American exceptionalism," but the foreign observers of the United States were interested in the same concept, without ever using that term, from the birth of the republic.[4] The observers examined American society in all its rich detail, but they also pulled back to look at the larger picture. In fact, they were more prone than Americans themselves to attempt to capture what used to be called the American "character" but is now more commonly referred to as the national "identity."

The greatest of all foreign commentators on American civilization was no doubt the Frenchman Alexis de Tocqueville, author of the monumental *Democracy in America*. But during the nineteenth century, several British writers were also responsible for important works on the United States—most notably Frances Trollope, Harriet Martineau, Charles Dickens, Matthew Arnold, and James Bryce, whose *American Commonwealth* has been compared to *Democracy in America*. These writers shone a light, generally a harsh light, on American society and provoked much controversy as a result.

Bryce may be the most esteemed British observer of America, but he was not the last. There has, however, been a failure to look beyond Bryce, a tendency to see him as the end of a succession. Scholars, and even to some degree a general readership, are familiar with the commentary on America by the grand Victorian observers, but those who followed in Bryce's footsteps have received only minimal attention. From the 1890s to the Second World War, and beyond, British travelers to the United States were still producing thoughtful commentary. If no one work from this period could be deemed a tour de force comparable to *The American Commonwealth*, there was considerable merit in what was published, and as a body of literature it is worthy of examination.

In the final years of the nineteenth century and the first half of the twentieth, profound changes took place in the relationship between Great Britain and America. From Waterloo until the end of Victoria's long reign, Britain was the premier power in the world, while the United States was a relatively insignificant player on the global stage. In fact, America retained something of its colonial status: it provided a prime market for British goods and a ripe investment opportunity for British capital, while it also depended on Britain for much of its cultural sustenance. This was, as well, a time of tension and acrimony between the two nations, despite the many bonds that were maintained on a sub-governmental level.

Yet by the end of the 1800s, Britain's industrial paramountcy was no longer unassailable, challenged, as it was, by formidable American, as well as German, advances, and a half century later the United States had supplanted Britain as the greatest economic power in the world. In this period, one in which the two nations fought as allies in two world wars, American military strength surpassed British to the point that by 1950 no other country could rival the United States. Commensurate with its economic and military development, America gained in political and cultural influence, mainly at the expense of Britain. In short, the years from 1890 to 1950 saw an evolution from a situation in which Britain was the preeminent global power, with the United States dependent upon yet hostile to Britain, to one in which the United States was the dominant force, with Britain closely, amicably linked to America, but distinctly as the junior partner in the "special relationship."

During this era, as both nations grappled with the effects of industrialization, radical political ideologies took root. For the most part, British intellectuals, including the prominent commentators on America, felt disenchanted with the model of society handed down by their Victorian forebears and searched for an alternative, which generally—though by no means always—resulted in their embracing some brand of socialism.

The questions to be confronted are: With so much flux in this period in the relationship between Britain and America, and within each society, what was the British perception of America, at least the perception of those thinkers who fixed their sights on the other side of the Atlantic? How did they differ from their predecessors who wrote during Britain's heyday? How much contemporary recognition was there of the tables being turned, and was there resentment of America, as its fortunes rose while Britain's fell? What did the observers see as the distinguishing characteristics of America, and were these characteristics peculiar to the era or enduring traits? The answers lie in a variety of first-rate books, articles, and diaries that can be culled from the mass of writings that Britons turned out about America in this period.

Four of the most insightful—and dedicated—British observers of America between 1890 and 1950 were W. T. Stead, a flamboyant journalist little known today but a consequential figure in his time; H. G. Wells, the multitalented author whose pronouncements on a variety of

Introduction

The Forebears

The great nineteenth-century British observers of America were tough critics. Conservatively inclined observers were especially harsh in their assessments, which so much dominated the field prior to midcentury that Allan Nevins has called these decades the age of "Tory condescension."[1] The conservative commentators adopted a haughty, disdainful tone in describing a nation they saw as excessively democratic and egalitarian. Devoid of aristocratic leadership and contemptuous of tradition, Americans, in their view, were a crass, ill-mannered people. Throughout the nineteenth century, however, there was an admiration for the United States in British radical circles. America was perceived as the land of freedom and opportunity.[2] Nevertheless, when radicals predisposed to like America actually observed the nation firsthand, the reality they found frequently disappointed them. After confronting such institutions as slavery and the American party machine, they were capable of writing critiques of the United States in many respects as scathing as the Tory assessments. No matter what the political orientation of the writer, America usually fared badly at the hands of British observers, who believed the nation deficient either because of its republican ideals or in spite of those ideals. Only in the late 1880s, with the publication of James Bryce's *American Commonwealth,* did the tide begin to turn.

The most conspicuous—and notorious—of the conservative British observers of America was Frances Trollope, who lived and traveled in the United States for almost three and a half years, beginning at the end of 1827.[3] The extensive notes she compiled resulted in *Domestic Manners of the Americans* (1832), a distinctly unflattering portrait of the United States that caused a sensation on both sides of the Atlantic and established the author's literary reputation.[4]

As she conceded in her book, Mrs. Trollope did not address the American governmental system, except for its effect in shaping the habits and customs of everyday life, her primary focus. In *Domestic Manners* she asserted that Americans were totally lacking in the social graces and showed no appreciation for culture and education either. Furthermore, she maintained that Americans were hypocritical. They would insist, for example, on a certain propriety about keeping the Sabbath or adhering to strict sexual mores, while at the same time holding slaves and treating them brutally. It was also her contention that the Americans were a self-righteous, super-sensitive people who wallowed in patriotism and the conviction that the United States was the best of all possible worlds. They would brook no criticism of their native land yet felt free to hurl all kinds of abuse at the British.

Mrs. Trollope believed that in large part America's shortcomings could be attributed to its rejection of certain long-cherished British traditions and institutions, and the assumptions underpinning them. In her view, American society was deplorable because there was no recognition that humankind naturally organizes itself along hierarchical lines. Thomas Jefferson, among others, had poisoned the American mind with the doctrine of equality. As there was no leisured aristocracy in the United States and all were compelled to work for their livelihood, she wrote, the nation would remain relatively uncivilized.

The tone of American society could have been elevated to some degree, Mrs. Trollope maintained, if the sexes mingled more. She noted how often in the United States, in contrast to Europe, men and women were segregated—commonly dining separately, retreating to different sections on riverboats, and spending their Sundays apart, the women in church rapt by the mesmerizing spell of the preacher and the men off on their own smoking and drinking whiskey. She felt certain that both conversation and etiquette would improve—perhaps even the pervasive spitting by the men would cease—if the sexes were brought into greater contact. But not only was American society not nearly as refined as British,

Trollope observed that the common folk, without the traditional fairs and festivals of the Old World, did not even enjoy themselves as heartily.

Mrs. Trollope openly admitted that she disliked America, and she included precious little in her book of a positive nature—her kind words about a few individuals and her appreciation of the landscape being exceptions. Why she should have found America so distasteful can be explained in various ways. First of all, with her Tory sympathies, it would have been surprising had she returned from her encounter with the radical experiment across the ocean and expressed any considerable enthusiasm. Second, there was a great deal of truth in what she wrote; America was in this nascent period still a raw, unpolished civilization, particularly when judged by European standards. It is especially important to realize that Trollope was exposed first to the western part of the country, landing in New Orleans and then making her way up to Cincinnati, where she spent two years. Though the Ohio city was by this time no frontier outpost, neither was it an established, settled metropolis. When Trollope eventually traveled to the east coast, she found more to her liking—New York she seemed especially to enjoy—but she was not prepared to reassess the general conclusions she had already drawn. Trollope spent so much time in Cincinnati because she had set out for America with the express purpose of establishing a grand store that would help revive the sagging family fortunes, but the lavish, ornate Bazaar failed and she suffered a series of humiliating setbacks, culminating in the sheriff's seizure of her household possessions. Meanwhile, she and her children were struck by debilitating New World diseases. There can be no doubt that the trials she endured while in America colored her view of the nation.[5]

Standing at the opposite end of the political spectrum from Mrs. Trollope was her fellow Englishwoman Harriet Martineau. Born into a well-to-do Unitarian family in Norwich, Martineau developed a radical vision of the world and made her name by writing moralistic tales that popularized the principles of political economy. When she journeyed to America in the mid-1830s, she came with a transatlantic reputation. She also came with preconceived notions about the best approach to take in viewing American society, for it was on board ship as she crossed the ocean that she wrote the first draft of her *How to Observe Manners and Morals* (1838). Martineau's trip to the United States lasted exactly two years, from August 1834 to August 1836, and upon returning she published *Society in America* (1837).[6]

Harriet Martineau was fond of America—the republican ideals upon which it was established and its enduring democratic spirit. In contrast to what Mrs. Trollope had written, she also found the people to be delightful and well-mannered; she even expressed her admiration for the notoriously obstreperous American children. But *Society in America* is by no means a paean to the United States.[7] She placed less emphasis on comparing America with Britain, New World with Old, and focused more on how America was living up to its underlying principles. Martineau revered these, particularly the ideal of equality as enunciated in the Declaration of Independence, and was saddened to see in America a chasm between theory and reality.[8] She pointed to various deficiencies in American society—the conspicuously vulgar and snobbish upper class, the political apathy of the citizenry, and the tendency of the public to conform to prevalent opinion and avoid any kind of conflict. But Martineau was the most critical of the Americans in the areas where she believed they glaringly flouted their own vaunted ideals—most notably in the treatment of women and blacks. She felt that women were actually somewhat worse off in the United States than in Europe and lamented that they had not been brought into the fold of the democratic experiment—that they were not accorded full political rights and equal social and economic opportunities.

Though a strong feminist line of argument can be found running through *Society in America,* an even more pronounced leitmotif—in fact, what Martineau is most remembered for in her treatment of the United States—is her outrage over the institution of slavery. Mrs. Trollope had also condemned slavery, but for Martineau the issue was a driving force. She arrived in America with antislavery sentiments, but through contact with William Lloyd Garrison and his Boston circle, she became a committed abolitionist. Like the English actress Fanny Kemble, she probed into the deep South and observed the "peculiar institution" firsthand.[9] For Martineau the colonization schemes advocated by such worthies as James Madison, John Marshall, and Henry Clay were no answer, and she contended not only that slavery was inhumane, inefficient, and deleterious to Southern society but that blacks were inherently equal in their capacities to whites. Martineau saw the contempt with which abolitionists were treated in both North and South yet chose to be sanguine about the cause. Reflecting her hopefulness for the promise of American civilization, she argued that abolitionism was sweeping the nation.

Charles Dickens believed Martineau's *Society in America* to be the best book on the United States he had ever read.[10] A few years later, he decided that he too would like to travel to America and write a volume based on his own observations, and so at the beginning of 1842 he sailed out of Liverpool bound for Boston. When Dickens embarked on this trip, he was not quite thirty years old, but with such dazzling successes as *Pickwick Papers* and *Oliver Twist* already behind him, he was fabulously famous. In America Dickens was treated by politicians and literati like a visiting head of state, and crowds everywhere mobbed him as if he were a modern-day rock star. Because of this tumultuous welcome and because he was predisposed, as a radical like Martineau, to be sympathetic to the principles underlying the American system, it would not have been unreasonable to expect him to publish a work favorable to the United States. In fact, Dickens himself had intended, before sailing for America, to write just such a book. But the scenario turned out differently. First of all, though he appreciated his warm reception and enjoyed the companionship of such American writers as Washington Irving and Henry Wadsworth Longfellow, the attention he received became overwhelming, particularly when the general public showed no respect for his personal privacy. Second, Dickens was assaulted by the American press when he doggedly and conspicuously, though with much justification, pursued the point that the unwillingness of the United States to sign a copyright agreement with Britain robbed him and other authors of hard-earned royalties as publishers pirated their works at will. But last, and perhaps most important, America simply did not turn out to be the place he thought it would be.[11]

Dickens's *American Notes* (1842) is not as scathing or as uniformly critical as Mrs. Trollope's *Domestic Manners*, but it is decidedly negative and in certain parts reminiscent of Trollope.[12] In this book, however, Dickens was to some extent pulling his punches, because the denunciations of America in the letters he penned while in the United States, which he referred to in writing *American Notes*, are more vivid and explicit.[13] He made no reference at all in this work to the copyright controversy. In fact, despite some interesting descriptions, *American Notes* is not an exceptionally compelling or profound analysis of American life; if its author were not Charles Dickens, it would have been relegated to a dusty library shelf long ago. But because Dickens was Dickens, the book caused a sensation when it was published, and it has remained one of the most familiar critiques of America.

There is no central thesis to *American Notes,* and Dickens offered a minimum of analysis. Most of the book is devoted to the observations he made along the way in regard to specific places, people, and incidents. *American Notes* is a travel book in the most literal sense: a sizable proportion of it is concerned with where Dickens lodged, what he ate, and above all how he was transported from place to place. From an extended account of a nightmarish transatlantic crossing to detailed descriptions of train, riverboat, and stagecoach trips within America, the reader feels as though constantly in motion. Dickens did cover much territory, as he traveled from New England, down to the upper South, into the Midwest, and up through Canada, in only four and a half months. It was in commenting on the manners of the people he observed along his journey that Dickens echoed Mrs. Trollope, for though not as severe as she had been, he was clearly unimpressed by the bulk of the American population. He was horrified by the prevalence of the spittoon and even more so, as slimy boat decks and stained carpeting testified, by the disregard for it. He considered the common Americans he encountered to be dull and joyless and, like Mrs. Trollope, was flabbergasted to discover how his fellow travelers would gobble down their food in complete silence while displaying the most egregious table manners.

Dickens found little to say about the American system of government, though he was received by President John Tyler and leading members of Congress, such as Henry Clay and John Quincy Adams. The major impression he seems to have formed while visiting the capital was that Washington was an unattractive, unhealthy, and uncomfortable city. As he traveled around the country, Dickens, the reformer, not surprisingly occupied himself with observing prisons, asylums, orphanages, hospitals, poor houses, and courts of law. The report card he filled out contains a wide range of marks: he was enthusiastic about the institutions he found in Boston, and he deemed the facilities of Hartford, Connecticut, to be nearly on an equal par, but when he left New England and viewed similar institutions in New York, he was dismayed by what he saw. In his survey of prisons, Dickens was impressed by the Boston House of Corrections but disturbed by New York's legendary Tombs, as well as by the Eastern State Penitentiary of Philadelphia, where a system of strict solitary confinement was enforced.

In the final two chapters of *American Notes,* Dickens cut away from his travel diary format and commented more generally on the United States as a whole. In the penultimate chapter he launched a blistering attack on slavery, and in the concluding chapter he touched on several different themes, each pointing to a flaw in American civilization. He charged that Americans were prone to build people up and then tear them down and assailed what in his view was a national reverence for making money. Furthermore, this journalist waged an attack on the American press by charging that, with a few exceptions, it was mired in hatred, manipulation, and deceit. Dickens also went on to make two points that he had pursued previously in the volume: he asserted that the American people were too practical minded, too lacking in joie de vivre, and turned again to his pet peeve—the Americans' disregard for cleanliness and proper hygiene.

Though he had restrained himself in writing it, Dickens was fully prepared for the adverse reaction his book would engender in the United States. He tried, however, to soften the impact by claiming in the preface that he was a friend of America and that he wished the American people only the best. He had been ready to go to even greater lengths to explain his position but was ultimately afraid of sounding too defensive.[14] Late in life Dickens made one more attempt to take the sting out of the blow he had landed with this book when in 1867–1868 he returned to America for a reading tour. In a speech to members of the New York press, of all bodies, he said that in the past quarter of a century not only had America made great strides but also he had grown since he had written down his impressions of the country as a young man. This speech, he stipulated, should be added as a postscript to *American Notes* and to his novel set in part in America, *Martin Chuzzlewit*.

If Dickens's discussion of the United States in *American Notes* lacks vigor, the same could not be said for his handling of America in *Martin Chuzzlewit*.[15] This novel, which was serialized in 1843–1844, right on the heels of *American Notes,* is probably the most celebrated fictional treatment of the United States by a foreign author, though the American passages make up only a small portion of the book. In these passages, which constitute a self-contained story within the novel, Dickens brilliantly employed satire to make a bold, searing statement about American society. Themes introduced in *American Notes* are fleshed out in *Martin Chuzzlewit*, and, needless to say, the American people were outraged by this book as by Dickens's previous volume.

Martin Chuzzlewit is a novel about greed, and it is filled with scoundrels, on both sides of the Atlantic. The difference is that in England the scoundrels are balanced by certain exemplary figures, whereas in

America virtually everyone is a scoundrel, and a buffoon as well. One of the central figures of the novel, and ultimately one of the most evil, is Mr. Pecksniff, a moralistic, self-righteous Wiltshire man who turns out to be a rapacious schemer. Nearly all of the American characters are, like Pecksniff, overbearing hypocrites. The episodes in America revolve around young Martin Chuzzlewit, a would-be architect who travels to the New World to seek his fortune, and his companion, Mark Tapley, a cheerful, simple villager. Their experiences constitute a tragicomedy, for they land in New York and then head west into the backcountry to settle in the development of Eden, which turns out to be no more than a few ramshackle huts located in the middle of swampland. Not only are the two young Englishmen swindled out of their savings but they both endure near-fatal illnesses before they can find the means to return home.

In the sections on America the reader is confronted with an extraordinary series of colorful, amusing, yet entirely objectionable characters. The first two people Martin meets after landing in New York are Colonel Diver and Jefferson Brick, editor and war correspondent of the *New York Rowdy Journal,* unscrupulous newspapermen who are impressed with their own self-importance and who, like everyone in the United States with whom Martin comes into contact, go on and on about the virtues of America and the faults of Britain. While in New York, Martin is taken to pay a call on the Norris family, who expatiate on American equality while at the same time revealing their own snobbery. On the train westward the two young Englishmen become acquainted with General Choke and LaFayette Kettle, the principals of a group who revel in twisting the British lion's tail by supporting a certain Irish patriot, until they find out that this figure has abolitionist sympathies. General Choke arranges for Martin and Mark to confer with the Eden land agent, one Zephaniah Scadder, who deceives the young men into thinking that Eden is a thriving, established community. Among some of the other characters Martin and Mark meet out west are Mrs. Hominy, a writer whose moral philosophizing makes her an insufferable bore, and Hannibal Chollop, a rough backwoodsman who boasts of the various forms of violence to which he has resorted.

Dickens's writings on America marked the end of a decade in which famous Britons turned out a series of largely negative works about the United States that made an impact on both sides of the Atlantic. Not until the 1880s would British observations of America again elicit so much reaction. In the intervening years Britons continued to write about the United States, but these authors failed to make a comparable splash.[16]

The 1880s witnessed the arrival in America for the first time of the critic and poet Matthew Arnold, whose *Essays in Criticism* (1865) and *Culture and Anarchy* (1869) were well known in educated American circles. He was also recognized as the son of Dr. Arnold of Rugby. Arnold conducted an extensive lecture tour of the United States in 1883–1884 and then returned quietly in 1886 to visit his daughter, who had married a New York lawyer. On the lecture circuit he adhered to a rotation of three different addresses, including one critical of Ralph Waldo Emerson, which he compiled for the volume *Discourses in America* (1885). Arnold's reception in the United States was mixed: in the beginning audiences were disappointed because he was inaudible; Boston took exception to his remarks about Emerson; and he also made some enemies in the press and among America's leading literary figures for his precious, ultra-European ways. Yet his lectures were generally appreciated.[17]

Though he eschewed writing a book about America, Arnold did comment on the nation in a series of short pieces originally published in *Nineteenth Century* and posthumously collected as *Civilization in the United States* (1888).[18] Arnold assessed American society as an outspoken critic of his own country, which he often compared unfavorably to the culture of the Continent. He repeatedly asserted that in England the upper class, middle class, and lower class had been, respectively, "material-ised," "vulgarised," and "brutalised," and reclassified them as the Barbarians, Philistines, and Populace.

Arnold actually wrote "A Word about America" well before he visited the United States. In this article, published in May 1882, he re-sponded to a Boston newspaper which charged that he was contemp-tuous of American society but that if he would only come to the New World and journey beyond the eastern seaboard into the heartland, he would find in the small cities there a civilization of the highest order. Ac-cording to the paper, in each of these towns he would see a significant number of educated, cultivated people pursuing the best in the arts and conducting themselves with exemplary decorum. Arnold answered that he had actually never disparaged the United States but that based on all he had read about the nation, such a picture had to be an illusion. America was a middle-class society, he stated, a society made up wholly of Philistines with no Barbarians and virtually no Populace to speak of.

Like the British middle class, this American middle class could boast of many fine qualities and virtues, particularly a sense of industriousness and a capacity for achievement, but it could not be said that any significant portion of this class was dedicated to and accomplished in the higher, finer things in life. Arnold utilized an eclectic variety of examples to make the case that the American middle class was no more refined—no less vulgar—than its counterpart in Britain or anywhere else. He did concede that it was possible to point to a scattering of exceptional, far-sighted "individuals" in America, though the nation could not claim nearly as many of these valued "gentlemen" as Britain. America, unlike Britain, could not actually speak of a "group" or "class" of such people. The essay concludes on a quintessentially Arnoldean note with the author contending that the key to a better America, and Britain as well, lay in placing greater emphasis on the arts and education.[19]

In "A Word More about America," which appeared in February 1885, Arnold stated that he still stood by the previous piece but realized after visiting the United States that he had not presented a full picture of the country. He argued that America's institutions served the nation admirably, that the democratic federal system of government functioned well, hampered by much less corruption than was often believed. Furthermore, America was a country at social peace, free from the threat of revolution, largely because of the egalitarian, homogeneous character of the population. True, there were extremes of wealth in America, but without the sharp class lines endemic to Britain. He concluded, in short, that the Americans had solved the "political and social problem." From there he went on to say that as a consequence Americans, unlike the British, were able to "think straight and see clear." While America, however, had solved the "political and social problem," it still had not confronted the "human problem."[20]

It was to this "human problem" that Arnold turned his attention in "Civilisation in the United States," which was published in April 1888, three years after "A Word More about America" and only days prior to his death. This apostle of culture's final statement on America was no glowing testimonial; he not only returned to the negativism of his initial "Word about America," but he did so with bitterness. His starting point was the remark by Sir Lepel Griffin that with the exception of Russia, of all so-called civilized countries the United States would be the last in which anyone would want to live.[21] Arnold quickly dismissed Griffin's sentiments as the complaint of one who probably condemned

American civilization simply because it could not supply a level of luxury to which Englishmen of a certain station but of limited means were accustomed. He argued that satisfying creature comforts—particularly for an elite minority—should not be the test of a civilization's worth. The true question to be asked of a civilization should be, simply, is it "interesting"? To be "interesting" a civilization must be possessed of "beauty" and "distinction," and America failed on both counts. Arnold said that America was wanting in "beauty" in its natural landscape, which, at least of what he observed in the East, he compared unfavorably with the English countryside, and in its architecture, which he termed uniformly second-rate. America, he charged, had generated little great art or literature. As for whether the nation had produced men of "distinction," Arnold could point only to Washington and Hamilton, who were raised in the pre-Revolutionary age, and claimed that Lincoln was in many ways admirable, but not marked by "distinction." He stated that "distinction" was difficult to find in a culture that so revered the common man. What especially rankled Arnold was that Americans appeared to be totally unable to see any flaws in their civilization and, on the contrary, were given to endless boasting about the glory of the nation. He ended the essay on a note of sadness by contending that America's failure to see itself realistically would have consequences beyond its borders.[22]

In the same year that *Civilization in the United States* was published, 1888, there appeared arguably the greatest work ever written about America by a Briton, James Bryce's *American Commonwealth*.[23] Bryce was one of those illustrious Victorians with a prodigious mind and seemingly unlimited reserves of energy who excelled in a variety of endeavors. He was born in Belfast into an educated, middle-class family of Scottish Presbyterian background, attended school in Glasgow, and then went up to Oxford, where his academic promise allowed him to remain on a fellowship. But he also began to spend time in London pursuing a profession at the bar and lecturing on legal subjects, and in 1870, though still only in his early thirties, he was appointed to Oxford's Regius Chair of Civil Law. Over the next decade he became involved in politics as well and cast his fortune with the Liberal Party. When William Gladstone, who had taken a personal interest in the brilliant young don, led the Liberals back into power in 1880, Bryce won a seat in the House of Commons and embarked on a long parliamentary career.

It was in 1870, the year he gained his Oxford professorship, that Bryce first traveled to America. In the course of that tour and two subsequent ones he took in the early 1880s, each of which lasted a number of months, Bryce saw and did an incredible amount as he journeyed to virtually every corner of the country. He climbed Mount Washington in the East and Mount Tacoma in the West, observed Tammany Hall in action by attending a New York state Democratic convention in Rochester, and lectured at Harvard and Johns Hopkins. Most striking of all about Bryce's trips to the United States is the number of eminent figures that he mixed with; a list of these personages would read like a "Who's Who" of nineteenth-century American intellectuals.[24]

When Bryce published his three-volume work on the United States, it was so impressive that comparisons were inevitably made to Tocqueville, though *Democracy in America* and *The American Commonwealth,* appearing a half century apart, are very different in nature and scope. The contrast in approaches was perhaps best explained by Bryce himself, who raised Tocqueville's name in the introduction to his book. He wrote that the subject of *Democracy in America* is democracy, not America, and that Tocqueville used the American experience as an example but that his true frame of reference was France. According to Bryce, readers would find *The American Commonwealth* less philosophical, less theoretical, and less speculative and would be in a position, from the wealth of facts presented, to make their own judgments.[25]

In his work Bryce touched on the social, cultural, and intellectual life of the United States but mainly dwelled on political institutions. The book is above all about American government of the late nineteenth century — the constitutional machinery as well as the grease that, unofficially, kept the gears moving. Bryce was a strong champion of the American people, but the dominant theme of his work is that throughout the history of the United States they had been inordinately wary of compromising their sovereignty, at the cost of sacrificing virtuous, efficient government. He never explicitly stated so, but it is clear that Bryce felt that the American political system — though not the social — was inferior to Britain's, particularly the British system in the aftermath of the nineteenth-century reforms.

Although Bryce revered the U.S. Constitution and its framers, he nevertheless asserted that the national government functioned ineffectively. With power divided between the executive and the legislature, and between the two houses of Congress, and then informally even further splintered among the various congressional committees, there was little unity in the government and no way to assign any responsibility. Because the president, as well as members of his cabinet, was forbidden to sit in Congress, it was nearly impossible for him, except during times of crisis—as Lincoln had shown during the Civil War—to take the initiative and provide true leadership. Nor did Bryce find Congress to be a laudable institution, particularly the House of Representatives, which he viewed as an unwieldy body, inferior to the Senate, filled with second-rate men who turned out second-rate legislation. One cause of congressional mediocrity was that all representatives were required to be residents of their districts, thus shutting out many talented men and ensuring that provincialism would prevail. He also questioned the wisdom of holding elections at regularly designated intervals, which added discontinuity to the disunity of national government. But if Bryce was critical of the federal government, he was even tougher on state government, which he thought had been virtually crippled by an excess of democracy.

To Bryce the key to understanding how American government actually worked was to understand the parties, and he believed his treatment of this subject to be the most original and important aspect of his study. Britain, of course, had its parties, but he contended that the American party system was entirely different. In the United States, parties were not used as the basis upon which government was organized, and he argued that by the 1880s they did not even stand for two significantly distinct positions. According to Bryce, the parties had become nothing more than personnel machines, instruments to put up candidates for all of the thousands of elective openings and to fill the even greater number of spots available through patronage. The parties were managed by unscrupulous rings and bosses who, because of the mass of uninformed immigrant voters, were especially successful in controlling city government, which Bryce called the sorriest feature of the American political system.

Mediocre party professionals were able to dominate politics in the United States at least in part because men of greater talents and education tended to shun the political realm, Bryce maintained. In chapters with such titles as "Why Great Men Are Not Chosen Presidents" and "Why the Best Men Do Not Go into Politics," he explained that superior individuals were reluctant to move to a dreary state capital, or even Washington, and at the same time were diverted by the lucrative business opportunities of an expanding nation. Furthermore, even when one of the so-called best men did enter politics, there was no ensuring that he could go far, because the parties sought out candidates, for the presidency and lesser positions, who were the most electable, not necessarily the most qualified. Winning office, and thus controlling patronage, were what counted.

The parties may have kept American government running, but Bryce wrote that in a more general and elusive sense, the whole system was dictated by public opinion. In no other country was public opinion so important, and in no other country was it created in such a diffuse, decentralized manner. Unlike in Europe, setting the tone, direction, and agenda for popular discourse was not the exclusive province of a particular class or of an elite group of metropolitan opinion-shapers. Through the power of election Americans maintained an institutional expression of the public will that could be resorted to at regular, frequent intervals. But the force of mass opinion in the United States was also continuous, as communicated through newspapers, associations, and other channels. Bryce believed in the American people yet thought that the dominance of public opinion in the United States was ultimately deleterious to government. He painted a picture of legislators who served merely as delegates of their constituencies and of public and party officials who were constantly checking to see which way the wind was blowing.

Though Bryce was unsparing in his criticisms of the United States, his approach was measured and balanced, and the American public received the book favorably. In fact, after the turn of the century he would be welcomed back to Washington as his nation's ambassador. *The American Commonwealth* marked a watershed in British observations of the United States, for most of Bryce's fellow countrymen who wrote about America in the decades to come approached their subject in the same constructive spirit.

1

The Plight of the Cities

W. T. Stead and 1890s Urban America

Rarely in American history has a foreign visitor thrust himself onto the domestic scene quite in the way W. T. Stead did in the 1890s. This crusading journalist, one of the most prominent in late-Victorian Britain, possessed a special knack for attracting attention to himself, so it was only appropriate that he would first arrive in America with a bang. His involvement in the effort to reform Chicago made him a conspicuous participant in American affairs, and he left upon the nation his indelible imprint.

Although Stead had developed an affinity for America early in life, when he traveled to the New World in the 1890s he was harshly critical of what he found. After visiting Chicago and New York, he came to the conclusion that American cities were miserable aggregations of humanity plagued by corruption, greed, and callousness. During this period, among the other British travelers to the United States who thought likewise were Rudyard Kipling and Sidney and Beatrice Webb. They too recorded their negative impressions of the cities.

From Stead's encounter with the American metropolises, he also generalized about the nation as a whole. He charged that the republic had come under plutocratic control and that the citizenry had lost faith in one another and in democracy. Despite this blistering assessment of the nation, based upon his experiences in urban America, his devotion to the United States would never diminish. The inconsistency that would come to mark Stead's outlook on America was typical of this paradoxical figure, whose opinions on a range of issues were unpredictable. He was a self-proclaimed imperialist who fought hard for the expansion of the British navy, while he opposed the Boer War and championed the causes of arbitration and world peace. He was a radical who lent his name to an array of progressive causes, but he was a staunch defender of Czarist Russia. And he was a devout Christian, yet he became immersed in spiritualism.

William Thomas Stead was born in 1849 in the north of England, in a small Northumberland village.[1] His father was a Congregationalist minister, and Stead's Nonconformity would be a prime factor in shaping his identity. As a journalist he not only allied himself with the Liberal Party, but the moral causes he took up and the zeal with which he advanced them cast him in the role of a modern-day Puritan. Stead's Nonconformity was also crucial in stimulating his lifelong fascination with America. When he was growing up, his father's library was filled with volumes by such New England–bred preachers as Jonathan Edwards, William Channing, and Henry Ward Beecher. According to Stead, the British Nonconformists were traditionally susceptible to American religious influences and felt closer to the American churches than to the Anglican establishment of their own country.[2] The radicalizing capacity of the Nonconformist sects must have been instrumental, as well, in laying the ground for Stead's favorable view of American republicanism. Concerning his education at Congregationalist Silcoates, he wrote, "I may be said to have acquired three very important things at school, none of which were in the curriculum, viz., Christianity, Cricket and Democracy."[3]

In 1863 Stead left school and became apprenticed at the age of fourteen to a Newcastle merchant. During his apprenticeship he began to read heavily and submitted a prize-winning essay to a boys' magazine on his hero Oliver Cromwell. As part of his award, he selected *The Poetical Works of James Russell Lowell,* a volume that would exert a profound influence on his life. It was Lowell who imbued Stead with the ethos that would drive him for the rest of his days—the idea that being a good Christian meant following the example of Christ and striving to better humanity. When the august New Englander died, Stead wrote, "Mr. Lowell was a Puritan by heredity, and the moral fervour of the men of the *Mayflower* was wrought into the inmost fibre of his being. But his

Puritanism was a living force applied to the living issues of to-day." According to Stead, it was after reading Lowell's "Pious Editor's Creed" that he decided to devote his life to journalism.[4]

Stead embarked on his journalistic mission while still a young clerk in Newcastle. In connection with charitable endeavors he organized in the area, he was prompted to write letters to the newspapers and soon developed a relationship with one particular daily, the Darlington *Northern Echo*. He began to contribute to the paper on a regular basis and made enough of an impact that when the editor's chair became vacant in 1871, the inexperienced, twenty-two-year-old Stead was asked to fill the position. Over the course of the next decade, while at the helm of the *Northern Echo*, he transformed the provincial paper into one of the nation's most influential Liberal organs and established himself as an important editor. Stead was able to achieve this feat primarily as a result of his crucial participation in the Bulgarian Agitation of 1876, through which the "atrocities" committed against the Bulgarians at the hands of the Turks became a cause celebre.[5]

Though he was a true country boy and no devotee of London, it was inevitable that Stead would not remain in Darlington for long. The metropolis beckoned. In 1880 he was asked to serve as the assistant editor of the prestigious *Pall Mall Gazette,* which had just been placed in the hands of John Morley, the Liberal man of letters. Stead accepted the post and moved, with his wife and young children, to London. When Morley left the *PMG* in 1883 to enter the House of Commons, Stead assumed the role of editor and over the next few years became one of the most famous journalists in Britain. He was responsible for developing what Matthew Arnold called the "New Journalism," an approach that appears mild compared to the sensationalism that would follow but at the time represented a break from the drabness of the respectable British press. Stead employed bold headlines, published an unprecedented number of illustrations, and introduced the use of interviews, but even more significant than these technical innovations was the content of his columns, which bespoke a brand of journalism that was startlingly vivid, aggressive, and personalized. His detractors accused him of paving the way for the "Americanization" of the British newspaper.[6]

An essential element of the New Journalism was the idea of the journalist as crusader, which Stead would push to its ultimate limit when in 1886 he enunciated his belief in "Government by Journalism." He argued that the responsibility of governance was being taken out of the hands of the MP and placed within the grasp of the newspaper editor, who was best able to reflect and direct the sentiments of the general public. While editor of the *PMG*, Stead waged a series of journalistic campaigns that yielded substantive results and drew attention to his paper. In 1883 he made the Congregationalist-sponsored pamphlet *The Bitter Cry of Outcast London* the basis for an exposé and denunciation of the terrible living conditions of the city's poor and thus helped to turn the slums into an issue discussed both in and out of the halls of Westminster.[7] The next year Stead's flexing of his editorial muscles produced not triumph but tragedy, when he advocated that the legendary General Charles Gordon lead a military mission to Khartoum, which resulted in the deaths of Gordon and many of his men.[8]

It was, however, the "Maiden Tribute of Modern Babylon" campaign of 1885 that represented the most sensational episode of Stead's flamboyant career and brought him to the high-water mark of his fame. He was enlisted to help rescue the Criminal Law Amendment Bill, a piece of legislation, stalled in Parliament, that was aimed at eradicating juvenile prostitution and the white slave trade. The bill would impose new penalties on those engaged in encouraging or trafficking in these social ills and raise the legal age of consent, then only thirteen. In investigating the matter, Stead as an experiment actually procured a thirteen-year-old girl from her mother for ostensibly illicit purposes. The experience persuaded him that the problem was severe, and as a result he launched his "Maiden Tribute" campaign. For one week, in July 1885, he published a series of articles in the *Pall Mall Gazette* that graphically exposed the world of vice into which young virginal girls were drawn, often, according to Stead, to satisfy the desires of some of London's wealthiest men. Never before had revelations of this sort appeared in a respectable British paper, and many denounced Stead for actually fostering indecency, a charge leveled at him more than once on the floor of the House of Commons. Though W. H. Smith and Son blocked the sale of the *PMG* in English train stations, and it was then also banned within the City of London, Stead could hardly keep up with the demand for the paper as mobs crowded outside his editorial offices to try to purchase copies. Though many obviously wanted to read the paper to satisfy their prurient impulses, Stead's effort was taken seriously and received the support of prominent reformers. In August the Criminal Law Amendment Bill was finally passed, no doubt as a consequence of the stir that Stead had caused. But he felt that the passage of the legislation should not mark the end of his campaign, and later in the same month he led a national conference in St. James's Hall and a massive rally in Hyde Park. This phenomenal chapter in Stead's life concluded with as much fanfare as it began. The mother of the girl he had purchased, now in the care of the Salvation Army in France, came forward to claim that she had been deceived, that she had never intended to sell her daughter into a life of sin and wanted her back. As a consequence, Stead, as well as his accomplices, was brought to trial, and though his admirable intentions were recognized, he was found guilty of having abducted the girl. At the end of 1886, amid a great deal of publicity, Stead began serving a two-month prison sentence.

Stead's controversial activities and radical positions alienated many of the genteel readers of the *Pall Mall Gazette,* and as circulation dropped in the latter half of the 1880s, his relationship with the proprietor deteriorated. In 1890 Stead left the *PMG* when he was invited to edit the *Review of Reviews,* a new monthly, which was to be a digest of the best offerings from other periodicals, while still including original editorial material. Within a few months' time, he gained full ownership of the magazine, and for the rest of his life he used its pages as his main conduit to the public.

Above all, Stead devoted his journal to bolstering the bonds of the British Empire and, just as important, the links between Britain and America. To help realize his dream of establishing unity among the English-speaking peoples, in the spring of 1891 he launched an American edition of the *Review of Reviews.*[9] He appointed as editor Albert Shaw—a Johns Hopkins Ph.D., a municipal reformer, and a veteran journalist—and the magazine eventually flourished. However, Stead was unable to maintain his grip on the American offspring; during the course of the 1890s Shaw managed to wrest editorial control, and even majority ownership, away from Stead. Shaw had no intention of playing the role of vassal to the lord Stead, with whom he repeatedly clashed over matters of journalistic style and substance. One significant point on which the editors differed was that while Shaw took a friendly stance toward Britain, he could not always subscribe to Stead's enthusiasm for English-speaking solidarity. When Stead grew angry at Shaw, he would accuse his American counterpart of betraying the great cause for which the magazine was founded.[10]

In the fall of 1893, Stead would at last get the opportunity to visit America. He had wanted to make a trip in 1892 to study the populist movement, but poor health and his duties in London prevented him. In the summer of 1893, he sent a surrogate, his brother the Reverend Herbert Stead, to report on the Columbian Exposition in Chicago for the *Review of Reviews*. Finally, in October, after a stint of exhausting work, Stead took up Shaw's suggestion that he spend a relaxing vacation in the United States and Canada. When he disembarked in New York, he headed straight for Chicago and reached it just in time to catch the last day of the World's Fair.[11] Stead was now in the position to see for himself the nation that had loomed so prominently in his mind and specifically the city that had recently grabbed his, and the world's, attention.

The Chicago in which Stead arrived in the autumn of 1893 was a city that a half century before had been just a modest Midwestern town and in 1871 had been virtually leveled by a devastating fire, but was now a booming metropolis of over one million, second in population on the North American continent only to New York. The vast majority of Chicago's inhabitants were of non-British stock, those claiming German origins being by far the largest group, followed by the Irish and the Scandinavians, and then by more recent immigrants from Eastern and Southern Europe and by blacks who had migrated from the South. Strategically located between the farm belt and the markets and ports of the East, Chicago had in the previous decades become the center of the grain trade and the meat-packing industry, as well as a major transportation hub. Chicago's most famous citizens were two activist women— Frances Willard, president of the Woman's Christian Temperance Union, and Jane Addams, founder of the legendary Hull House. The city's greatest artistic achievement was embodied in its innovative architecture, namely the skyscraper, and in the realm of education Rockefeller money had made possible in 1892 the establishment of the University of Chicago. Chicago politics were then, as later, turbulent and often sordid, and the year 1893 witnessed two political cataclysms. In June, the newly elected governor, John Peter Altgeld, pardoned the anarchists who had been implicated in the Haymarket bombing of 1886, charging that they and their cohorts who had gone to the gallows had been tried unfairly. Then, in October, just before Stead arrived in the city and the World's Fair closed its gates, the charismatic and popular mayor, Carter Harrison, was assassinated by a mentally disturbed office-seeker.[12]

Stead would write of his first trip to the United States, "For practical purposes, my visit to America was a visit to Chicago." Though he made an excursion into Canada, where he stayed a week with the governor-general in Ottawa, and spent a day or so each in a scattering of American cities, it was Chicago that occupied him for nearly all of his four-month sojourn in the New World. It had not been his original intention to spend so much time in this one city; he had planned to take a quick look at the World's Fair, go on to Canada, and then return home. Furthermore, he had resolved to come to America simply as a tourist, and not as a speaker, reporter, or commentator: "If I made one vow more solemnly than another, it was that during the whole of my stay in America I would not address a meeting or write a line, and would spend my time in learning in silence what the New World had to teach the Old." But Stead's vacation turned out to be a busman's holiday, and by his own estimation he ended up working more furiously than at any time in his life, with the possible exception of during the "Maiden Tribute" campaign.[13]

When Stead arrived in Chicago, he hurried to make a tour of the World's Fair on its last day. He was not particularly impressed by the various displays; they seemed to him no different from what he had observed at previous European expositions. What did excite him was the architecture—the massive neoclassical exhibition halls that together were known as the "White City."[14] Under the general direction of Daniel H. Burnham, these buildings were designed by a group of America's leading architects, but except for the contribution of Louis Sullivan, the structures in no way reflected Chicago's distinctive modernism. However, like Stead, many Americans who visited the Columbian Exposition fell in love with the "White City," which would exert a strong influence on contemporary architectural styles.[15] When Stead discovered that these buildings, which were not constructed to stand permanently, would be destroyed, he appealed for them to be preserved as architectural monuments. They were saved from the wrecker's ball, though ultimately vandalism and fire took a heavy toll. After Stead lent his support for a scheme to relocate the massive Manufactures Building and transform it into a European-style people's palace, he was invited to speak before the Trades and Labor Assembly, and from that point on he became immersed in the burgeoning Chicago reform movement.[16]

The time was ripe for reform when Stead came to Chicago, for the closing of the fair precipitated a dramatic worsening in the city of a depression that had already been severely felt elsewhere in the nation. Because of the money spent during the exposition and because of some bold moves by the city's financial leaders, Chicago for a while had been spared the full brunt of the Panic of 1893. But when the fair shut down at the end of October, bringing an end to the flow of tourists and throwing thousands of exposition workers out of jobs, the depression gripped Chicago with devastating consequences.[17]

When Stead arrived in Chicago, a reform movement to cope with the city's mounting problems was already beginning to develop, but it was a disjointed effort, and the leaders, aware of his commitment to a "Civic Church," appealed to him for help.[18] As an adherent of Christian Socialism, Stead envisioned the "Civic Church" as an organized movement that would work, in London, Chicago, or elsewhere, to ameliorate the living conditions of the poor and downtrodden. Inspired at an early age by Lowell, he was devoted to establishing a truly Christian social order, and based on his activities in Chicago, it could be said that his perception of his cause verged on the messianic. He had answered the call from the Chicago reformers because, in his view, it was his duty: "Nothing was further from my intention than to take any part in local affairs, but whenever it happens that I am on the spot and any one who is fighting a good cause asks me to help him, I do not consider my geographical position, but fall to and do what I can." Being an Englishman in America did not deter him in the least, for he believed his outsider status enabled him to speak in terms that native Chicagoans would not.[19]

The culmination of Stead's participation in the Chicago reform movement came on November 12, 1893, when two mass meetings that he called were held at the Central Music Hall. Attracted to the conferences was an unprecedentedly diverse group of Chicagoans—from clergymen, professors, and labor leaders to saloonkeepers and prostitutes. During the evening session Stead took his ideal of inclusiveness to the limit when he boldly introduced to the assemblage one of the anarchists recently pardoned for the Haymarket bombing. In these meetings Stead preached the gospel of Christian brotherhood, pointed to the social ills besetting the city, and concretely outlined his plan for a "Civic Church" for Chicago.[20] To the afternoon gathering he posed "the question whether, if Christ were to come to Chicago to-day, He would find anything in Chicago that He would wish to have altered." Stead's answer was that he most definitely would. London was not flawless either, Stead conceded, but the European standard was higher, even though the American city had the advantages of youth. If Christ actually were to arrive in Chicago that day, he would perhaps say:

Well, in the Old World, swollen hard with centuries of crime, a world grown grey in misery before I was born, there might be some reason for My failure, but here, in a New World, under new social conditions, here with no curse of crooked alley or soil soaked with sewage, with no kings or aristocracy, here I might expect that My work had achieved some measure of success.[21]

As a consequence of the meetings Stead called in the Central Music Hall, plans were put in motion to establish a Civic Federation based on the concept of a "Civic Church." This federation, officially chartered in February 1894, set about tackling the problems plaguing the city in a variety of areas, and with Lyman J. Gage as president and Bertha Palmer (wife of Potter Palmer) as a vice-president, it could claim the involvement of the cream of Chicago society.[22] The Civic Federation that Stead was so instrumental in establishing became an active and enduring force in Chicago, and soon after its inception, other cities in America followed the example.[23]

The day after the meetings, Stead left Chicago for Canada with the intention of then going back to England. But his time north of the border was marred by poor health and, more important, the disappointing news that his cherished project to start a London daily had fizzled. His sense of despair was so deep that he decided to change his plans, and so instead of sailing home, he returned to Chicago to take up his reform efforts where he had left off. Back in Chicago in early December, Stead once again took to the podium, and in exhorting the city's residents to confront their troubles, particularly the massive unemployment problem, he managed to ruffle quite a few feathers. At no time was this more true than when speaking before a meeting of the Women's Club: he called the well-heeled ladies in attendance, who seemed to him indifferent to the plight of the poor, "some of the most disreputable people in Chicago."[24] He wrote to his friend Henry Demarest Lloyd, the Chicago radical, that his remarks had created "a pretty gabbling outcry."[25] But Stead not only talked; he put himself into action as well. Over the course of the desperate winter of 1893–1894, the Central Relief Association, a creation of the Civic Federation, strove to aid the unemployed by providing food, clothing, and shelter. Able-bodied individuals, however, were supposed to labor for their bread, and so the association instituted an employment program, the major component of which was a crew of three thousand hired to work on the streets, nicknamed "Stead's Brigade." Stead himself made an attempt to work beside the gang, but the task proved to be too strenuous.[26] The efforts undertaken by Stead that winter to roll up his sleeves and directly experience the bleaker side of Chicago life were well captured by Jane Addams when she wrote:

> I can vividly recall his visits to Hull-House, some of them between eleven and twelve o'clock at night, when he would come in wet and hungry from an investigation of the levee district, and, while he was drinking hot chocolate before an open fire, would relate in one of his curious monologues, his experience as an out-of-doors laborer standing in line without an overcoat for two hours in the sleet, that he might have a chance to sweep the streets; or his adventures with a crook, who mistook him for one of his own kind and offered him a place as an agent for a gambling house, which he promptly accepted.[27]

It was such exploits that may have led one Chicago journalist to call Stead the "queerest guest this city ever sheltered."[28] Nevertheless, his various activities during the winter of 1893–1894 all served as grist for the book he was writing. Picking up on the theme that he had introduced at the Central Music Hall, he titled the volume, *If Christ Came to Chicago! A Plea for the Union of All Who Love in the Service of All Who Suffer.* In fact, his original conception of the book was merely to publish the proceedings of the November meetings, but in keeping with every other facet of his trip to America, his plans changed and he ended up creating an entirely original work. Stead was characteristically confident about the importance of his endeavor, telling Lloyd, whose seminal *Wealth against Commonwealth* (1894) was forthcoming, "I think my book will clear the way for your book, as a kind of John the Baptist."[29]

If Christ Came to Chicago is a curious combination of Sunday morning sermon, muckraker's exposé, and social commentary. Stead drew a distinctly unflattering portrait of Chicago and allowed himself to extrapolate and arrive at some conclusions about American civilization in general. Echoing the speeches he made in Chicago, his nostrum for the city's ills was a heavy dose of Christian brotherhood, but he went even further when he called for municipal socialism. The unifying theme of the book is Stead's compelling, repeatedly posed question: what would Christ do if he were to come to Chicago?

In this work Stead described the destitution he observed in the city. He saw "tramps" sleeping packed together in the corridors of the lavish City Hall and on the hard basement floor of the Harrison Street Police Station, only steps away from the lockup for some of the city's toughest criminals. Stead said that these unemployed, homeless men and women, most of whom had apparently held decent jobs but were now down on their luck, would not have been so poorly treated in Britain or even Russia. He also presented a case study of one poor, overcrowded precinct, over half of whose inhabitants were immigrants and blacks. Neighborhood life centered around the saloon, and while houses of prostitution and pawn shops abounded, there was no public lavatory or washing facilities, no library, not even a resident Christian clergyman. According to Stead, "If Christ came to Chicago, it is one of the last precincts into which we should care to take Him. And yet it is probably the first precinct into which He would find His way."[30]

While Stead lamented that the brothel and the saloon had become such prominent features of Chicago life, he in no way pegged the prostitute and the barkeeper as villains. The prostitute was above all a victim, and he reserved his indictment for the society that forced her into her degraded status. A lifelong champion of women, Stead was disillusioned by the treatment they received in America and commented, "Certainly as long as these States persist in leaving defenceless maidenhood without the protection of law, the vaunts about American chivalry and high regard for women and children sound as hollow as did the Declaration of Independence in the old Slave States." Perhaps the most sensational aspect of *If Christ Came to Chicago* was that Stead chose to publish the addresses of several Chicago brothels, as well as the names of the owners of and taxpayers for the establishments.[31]

Although a temperance advocate and an ardent admirer of Frances Willard,[32] the teetotaling Stead was no proponent of an immediate, wholesale abolition of the saloon. In fact, he felt a great deal of respect for many a saloon proprietor. In one of his November addresses at the Central Music Hall, Stead, to the dismay of at least part of his audience, took the Chicago temperance reformers to task for not distinguishing between reputable and disreputable saloons. He told the assemblage that saloonkeepers could be valuable participants in the civic reform movement and that one he had met with that very morning was "nearer the mark in most things than most of your journalists and preachers."[33] In his book, Stead, with new evidence in hand, again displayed his appreciation for saloonkeepers. Because the saloons customarily offered a free lunch, he claimed that they "fed more hungry people this winter in Chicago than all the other agencies, religious, charitable and municipal, put together."[34]

In Chicago, Stead wrote, the saloon and machine politics were inextricably intertwined, with the saloonkeeper often serving as a precinct captain. As in his attitude toward the saloon, Stead placed himself at odds with many a genteel reformer in America in his refusal to condemn the Chicago political system in its entirety. Like these reformers, he was repelled by the widespread corruption that characterized the city's government and the two major parties that vied to control it. A significant portion of *If Christ Came to Chicago* is devoted to detailing these abuses—the selling of franchises by the city aldermen, the extortion of illegal gamblers by the mayor, the undervaluation of select properties by the tax assessors, the purchase of votes by party hacks, and the blackmailing of prostitutes by the police. And the criminal justice system had been so politicized and corrupted that Stead wondered "whether I was really in an American city or whether I had been spirited away and dropped down in some Turkish pashalik."[35]

Yet despite his railing against the "boodling" that had infiltrated virtually every aspect of public life in Chicago, Stead's discussion of the governmental system was not wholly negative. Just as he saw the contributions to community life that the saloon was making, he argued that despite all of its flaws, the political apparatus was to a certain extent serving the needs of the people. In one chapter of his book, he related his conversation inside a saloon with a Chicago Democratic Party operative, one Farmer Jones, who shocked Stead with a series of stories that revealed a complete lack of scruples. Yet amid the tales of vote-buying and intimidating opponents, Stead heard about Jones's experiences aiding his district's residents, many of them immigrants, and this record of service struck a responsive chord in him. Stead wrote that most who would read this chapter would say to themselves, "This . . . is the outcome of Democracy, the latest triumph which Republican institutions have achieved in the New World!" But he argued that his dialogue with Farmer Jones actually instilled in him "a clearer view and a surer hope for the redemption of Chicago" than any other conversation he took part in while in the city.[36]

According to Stead, many prominent citizens of Chicago were so disgusted by the corruption that tainted their government that they were prepared to give up on democracy. He wrote, "'*Vox populi, vox Dei,*' is an old adage not much respected in great American cities, where Lincoln's noble prayer at Gettysburg for the success of the great experiment of government of the people, by the people and for the people, does not seem to elicit a loud 'Amen.'" Stead heard credence given to such schemes as investing the mayor with nearly autocratic powers and allowing Chicago to be governed by a triumvirate appointed from Washington. He believed this kind of thinking was defeatist and argued that the democratic system could work if Chicagoans made it work.[37]

Stead contended that democracy could be made to work in Chicago, and other large American cities, if the most talented and distinguished citizens would step forward and assume leadership roles. He stated, "Few things impress a visitor from England more than the dearth of leaders. Next to the distrust which people have of each other, this phenomenon impresses the stranger most unfavorably." But Stead was optimistic, because he came into contact with two urban leaders whom he felt to be breaking the mold—Hazen Pingree, the Republican mayor of Detroit, and John Patrick Hopkins, the Democrat who succeeded Chicago's late Mayor Harrison. Stead traveled to Detroit to observe the fight Pingree was waging against corruption in that city, and he believed Hopkins, in the short time he had been in office, was beginning to launch a similar campaign in Chicago. Each man started in a humble position in life, and Stead saw young Hopkins's rise to power as Lincolnesque: "To an Englishman the possibility of so sudden a promotion from the ranks to one of the foremost positions in the Republic is one of the few elements of romance and of charm in American politics."[38] Actually, while Pingree was one of the bright lights of the era, Stead's faith in Hopkins was misplaced, for the Chicago mayor turned out to be merely another "boodler."[39]

If Stead was unwilling to blame the ills of Chicago on the saloon or on machine politics, as so many contemporary American reformers did, to what did he attribute the city's troubles? The source of the problem, he felt, was the large concentration of wealth in the hands of an elite group of individuals and corporations. Not only did this accumulation of wealth make possible much of the corruption that stained the city government, but it was at the root of the despair and misery that characterized large sections of the population. Furthermore, he believed that with so much wealth controlled by so few, American republicanism was threatened. Stead wrote, "I came to America to see what Mr. Carnegie described as the Triumph of Democracy. I found instead the Evolution of Plutocracy." The amassing of great fortunes, he stated, "has already destroyed the distinctive glory of the American Republic."[40]

One chapter of *If Christ Came to Chicago* was devoted to three multi-millionaires whom Stead termed the "Chicagoan Trinity"—Marshall Field, Philip Armour, and George Pullman. In a society preoccupied with making money, these three men stood as gods before the reverent multitudes. Stead respected the achievements of these magnates: they had constructed their massive business empires from scratch, while remaining within the bounds of the law, and they each generously contributed to good causes. On the other hand, he could not overlook that Field, with his famous department store, and Armour, in rising to the top of the meatpacking industry, had employed cutthroat business techniques and driven out smaller competitors, while Pullman, in his control over the town he had established for his railroad car workers, had become a dictator. Even more important, Stead lamented that not one of these three talented individuals had offered to use his know-how and clout to address the problems besetting Chicago. They may have donated their money liberally to various private foundations and institutions, but they steered clear of the public sphere; they wanted to have nothing to do with the difficult task of running the city. Stead lamented this abdication of responsibility when he wrote: "Instead of being better the plutocratic system as it prevails even at its best in Chicago is worse than the results obtained by the aristocratic system which prevails in England and Germany."[41]

While Stead could feel a certain admiration for the "Chicagoan Trinity," for these self-made, uncorrupted businessmen who had built thriving enterprises and displayed a certain philanthropic spirit, he was harshly critical of two other groups of millionaires in the city, "the predatory and idle rich." Among the former he placed the infamous Chicago traction magnate Charles T. Yerkes, whom he charged with buying off the aldermen to obtain his streetcar franchises. Yerkes is even featured prominently on the cover of *If Christ Came to Chicago* in an updated depiction of Jesus expelling the money changers from the Temple. But Stead was even more disturbed by the presence of the "idle rich," the children of the great entrepreneurs, who led lives of carefree amusement and felt no sense of duty or obligation. While conceding that "there are social jealousies no doubt as keen between pork butchers and hotel keepers as between dukes and princes of the blood," he was sorry to see such a class of status-conscious pleasure-seekers taking shape in America.[42]

Stead blamed wealthy corporations as well as wealthy individuals for Chicago's plight. He was particularly critical of those corporations that had gained monopolies by obtaining, usually through illegal payoffs, city franchises—Yerkes's streetcar companies, the telephone company, and the companies that made up the gas trust. Instead of providing decent services at reasonable prices, these corporations, he believed, had assumed the license to steal. The most egregious example of corporate irresponsibility observed by Stead was that the railroads constructed their lines into the city on the same level as the streets, with the result that hundreds of Chicagoans were killed every year at the dangerous grade crossings. He likened the rule of the corporations over the city of Chicago to the rule of the Assyrians over the ancient Jews and was shocked that the people so meekly knuckled under. In no country, including Czarist Russia, Stead said, "have I struck more abject submission to a more soulless despotism than that which prevails among the masses of the so-called free American citizens, when they are face to face with the omnipotent power of the corporations." Such behavior, he explained, shattered his conception of the Americans as a people who cherished and guarded their liberty. The reality was that they lived under a system of plutocratic "tyranny."[43]

To remedy the problems of Chicago—the widespread human misery, the corruption, and the crime and vice—and to strike at the root cause of those problems, the concentration of wealth in the hands of the few, Stead offered different proposals. Above all he called for the establishment of the "Civic Church," or, as he put it in the subtitle of the volume, "the union of all who love in the service of all who suffer." Though recognizing the American devotion to the separation of church and state, he argued that there needed to be a "conscience of the community." He maintained, "The Mayflower sailed across the Atlantic not in order to found a free church in a free state, in the sense of a state in which the church had nothing to say, but rather to found a state in which the church should be supreme." Stead, however, was not advocating that any particular sect or denomination be designated as the established church; rather, he was calling for the advent of a spiritual society living by the principles of Christ. In the formation of Chicago's Civic Federation, and similar organizations in other American cities, he detected the beginnings of the "Civic Church" that would lead the way to a more humane civilization.[44]

Stead's ultimate panacea for the ills of Chicago was the establishment of municipal socialism. Rather than turning city services over to the likes of Charles Yerkes, which only allowed the magnates to grow fabulously wealthy at the expense of the ill-treated citizens, the government of Chicago should provide these services itself. Yet Stead went beyond the common late-nineteenth-century call for gas-and-water socialism. In the last full chapter of *If Christ Came to Chicago*, he presented a utopian vision of the city—as of some point in the twentieth century— that embodied municipal socialism in its most extreme form. Not only is the city in control of all of the services that were once franchised out to private corporations, but it also runs the wholesome "New Saloon." Further, the municipality supplies free medical care, and it owns pawnshops, neighborhood circuses and theaters, and even the great Marshall Field department store, which its founder had turned over to the city. Other Chicago millionaires had copied his example and voluntarily forfeited their assets as well. Besides functioning on a socialist basis, Chicago, which is now the "ideal city of the world," is suffused with a spirit of Christian charity and civic pride. This city, with its clean, well-paved streets, lovely parks, and high-rise housing, is headed by an honest, caring government, guided by revitalized churches, and still serviced by the Civic Federation. In fact, Stead made clear that the roots of this golden age for Chicago could be traced back to the reform movement that was instituted in the mid-1890s, following the close of the World's Fair.[45]

His book completed, Stead departed Chicago at the beginning of March 1894. Excerpts were published in the local press immediately, and before he was even back in England, the volume was released in Chicago. Within a few days of its publication, *If Christ Came to Chicago* had sold fifteen thousand copies and was on its way to becoming a spectacular best-seller in America and Europe. There was much negative reaction to the book, particularly among those who thought it wallowed in sensationalism. Reminiscent of the trouble that Stead experienced during the "Maiden Tribute" campaign, the American Union News Company—contending that the title was "blasphemous"—refused to sell the book at train stations. Albert Shaw, Stead's counterpart at the American *Review of Reviews*, despised the work and would not promote it in his magazine.[46]

Shaw was a scholarly, genteel reformer, and the two books he wrote on European municipal government, released in 1895, could not have been more different from Stead's flamboyant work on Chicago.[47] The correspondence between Stead and Shaw over the winter of 1893–1894 reveals a sharp disagreement between the two editors over Stead's campaign. Well before *If Christ Came to Chicago* was completed, Shaw wrote Stead a long, scathing letter chastising him for the activities in which he was immersed and urging him not to stay on in Chicago to edit a daily paper, as Stead was considering. In this letter, Shaw warned that Stead was in danger of damaging his American reputation. It was as an English journalist writing about Old World affairs, Shaw stressed, that Americans had come to respect him, and he was out of his element in the United States. Not only was his pontificating doing harm to the good name of W. T. Stead, and the *Review of Reviews*, it was the height of conceit for Stead to think that his role was indispensable. Shaw said that there were already "plenty of experts" and "plenty of generous people" in the United States addressing the problems Stead was trying to shoulder and that he should have played the "role" of "passing visitor," instead of "responsible citizen." Shaw wrote:

> You have a highly developed sense of humor, my dear Mr. Stead, yet it seems to me you have failed to see that there is really a very humorous aspect about your dropping down unexpectedly upon Chicago and undertaking to reform and regenerate the whole city by the simple process of postponing your homeward sailing.

An exasperated and resentful Shaw also told Stead, "I am afraid you Englishmen are all alike in feeling that your visits must be used most energetically for our edification."[48] When Stead's book was released, Shaw continued to communicate his disdain.[49]

While Shaw's criticism came in private correspondence, Stead was openly taken to task for *If Christ Came to Chicago* in a review of the book by an English historian now transplanted to Canada, Goldwin Smith. His notice in the *Contemporary Review* begins, "No injustice can be done in classing this work with the literature of sensation. So much its very title announces. By most of its readers it will have been bought, not with a view to social instruction or edification, but as a spicy revelation of the scandals of Chicago." Smith argued that Stead exaggerated the problems he saw in Chicago and furthermore that these same problems could be found in British cities too. Such vices as prostitution and gambling were by no means unknown in London, Liverpool, and Birmingham, prompting Smith to state, "There is work, then, for Christ at home." Stead, according to Smith, dwelled on the negative aspects of

Chicago, "it is hard upon a city to be represented by its sewers." "No doubt Chicago has sewers, and possibly they may be fouler than those of Liverpool or of Hamburg," but that was merely the consequence of Chicago's being such a young, developing city. After all, "Venice and Florence no doubt had coarse beginnings." Furthermore, Smith contended that urban Chicago, with its dominant foreign element, could not be taken as representative of the nation. If Stead, or any other visitor, really wanted to get to know America, it was necessary to spend time in the countryside.[50]

When Stead got back to England, he immediately began to defend his Chicago activities and his new book. He wrote that he could have taken the standard traveler's tour of America and seen vast areas of the nation, "but I am certain I should not have gained anything approaching to the insight which my prolonged stay in Chicago gave me into the present perils and future prospects of American institutions." Stead reasoned, "If you wish to study a species you have to confine yourself to a single specimen; if you wish to understand the constitution of a liquid you take an infinitesimal quantity in a test-tube." He also admitted that he focused on Chicago because it had long fascinated him: "To all Englishmen, Chicago has more interest than any American city. It is the only city which has had anything romantic about its recent history."[51] By no means, Stead argued, did he thrust himself upon the people of Chicago against their will, and in fact he was repeatedly implored, in the face of his own resistance to get involved, to aid the cause. He stressed how much cooperation he received and asserted that the only Chicagoans who may have resented him were those who were the targets of his attacks.[52] In a letter to Shaw, Stead said that he could not accept the charge that he had taken advantage of gracious American hospitality and overstepped his bounds in Chicago, and as for his colleague's accusation that he had given into the temptation of the "devil," Stead, casting himself as the martyr, wrote, "I never yet did a good thing in the world which was not heralded by just such an expression of opinion."[53]

In his book Stead often moved beyond Chicago to draw general conclusions about American society, a liberty he defended when he wrote that a case study could be more illuminating than a broad survey. He offered this rationale in "My First Visit to America," an article in which he proceeded to comment further on the civilization he had observed. The initial impression Stead gained of America was that it bore a striking resemblance to Russia; New York was akin to St. Petersburg and Chicago to Moscow, and the uncultivated American countryside, dotted with wood-frame houses, looked like the Russian steppes. However, he contended that the analogy applied to more than simply the similarity in physical appearance; there were political parallels as well. "The fundamental characteristic of America, as it is of Russia," he wrote, "is the deep ingrained distrust of the popular sovereignty visible in the constitution of both countries." In both republican America and autocratic Russia there was no respect for the democratic expression of the people, the only difference being that in the United States the citizenry was asked to go through the motions of casting votes.[54]

The British, Stead maintained, adhered to the democratic process; at election time the people really could determine their nation's course. But elections meant little in the United States, because "America is not governed by the sovereign will of the sovereign people expressed at the ballot box; it is governed by the dead hand of those who framed its constitution." A majority could desire a certain path to be taken yet find the Constitution blocking the way. Besides the provisions of the document that explicitly restricted what government could undertake, Stead asserted—as had Bryce before him—that with fixed terms of office and divided powers, the constitutional structure ensured that the people's will could not easily be translated into action. A defender of the American system would argue "that it is necessary to have safeguards against sudden outbreaks of popular folly," but Stead pointed out that this was the Russian rationale as well.[55]

In late 1894 Stead published another book centering upon the city he had taken as his "specimen" of American life. This volume, called *Chicago To-day; or, The Labour War in America*, was intended as a sequel to *If Christ Came to Chicago*. He felt compelled to write this book to relate the dramatic events that had unfolded over the summer of 1894, when Chicago was gripped by a strike at the Pullman works that led to a violent nationwide action against the railroads and, ultimately, the intervention of federal troops. Because Stead prepared the book in his London office and did not actually witness these developments, he was forced to rely on secondhand accounts. He did not confine himself exclusively to Chicago, employing examples from beyond that city as well, in an attempt to analyze the meaning of the industrial unrest that was currently plaguing America. This book, which was to some extent mined from articles he had previously published and even from his first volume on Chicago, lacks the flourish and vigor of *If Christ Came to Chicago*, and it was not as great a public success.

The refusal of George Pullman to settle the conflict at his railroad car manufacturing plant through arbitration may have triggered the turmoil revolving around Chicago in the summer of 1894, but Stead argued that the true cause of the problem was more complex: "It is to be found in the rooted distrust which is the canker of American civilisation. In business, men have forgotten God, they have lost faith in man, and they are reaping the penalty." The commercial atmosphere of the United States had become one of "cut-throat competition" in "the headlong rush after the Almighty Dollar." It was possible, Stead asserted, that the outbreak of labor unrest was an omen of a new economic order that could one day take shape.[56]

Despite this environment of pervasive "distrust," Stead explained that the cataclysm that rocked Chicago would not have occurred had there not at that moment been so many unemployed, who weakened the position of those men still at work. He stated, "In England we have certainly no reason to indulge in any Pharisaic reflections upon the misfortunes of our American kinfolk." Yet he revealed for the first time how the year before, when Chicagoans had been doing so little to help the unemployed and homeless and he had tried to rectify the situation, initially "there was a disposition to resent the maudlin sentimentality of English philanthropy." Stead published here a speech he delivered the previous winter in Chicago in which he told the audience that while the city could be proud of many achievements, nevertheless, "you have allowed what we should call the pauper class, a poor, forlorn, dirty class, to grow up under conditions where they are without the appliances of civilization which an ordinary German or French or English city would think absolutely indispensable for the living of an ordinary human life."[57]

In that same speech Stead warned his audience that he believed it possible some Napoleon would rise to lead the unemployed in a sort of "industrial co-partnership or army." Though he conceded in *Chicago To-day* that Jacob Coxey was no Napoleon, Stead felt he had in his talk anticipated the industrial movement known as Coxeyism. He devoted a chapter of his book to the ragtag bunches of unemployed workers from the North and West who drew much attention when in the spring of 1894 they marched on Washington demanding, to no avail, that the government institute public works programs. While concluding that the movement's leaders were fanatics, Stead still maintained that the cause was legitimate. Again, he could not help but see a parallel to Russia: "Coxeyism in its methods of organising petitions in boots is an American adoption of a familiar Russian mode of airing grievances and of protesting against abuses."[58]

Not only did Coxeyism prompt Stead to raise once more the Russian analogy, but the phenomenon also led him to a discussion of the similarities between the America of the 1890s and the Britain of the 1840s described by Thomas Carlyle. Stead wrote, "It is like going back to the middle of the century to visit the American republic. In most matters pertaining to social evolution, in things industrial, and, indeed, in many other things, they are about fifty years behind us." That America had not made more progress, despite its free education and penny press, forced him to question the radicalism on which he was raised. Stead noted that the present industrial unrest in the United States came roughly thirty years after the Civil War, as a similar upheaval had broken out in Britain three decades following Waterloo. Coxeyism could be seen "as a kind of bastard Chartism of the New World." The American labor movement, he argued, maintained the same status as its British counterpart of a half century before, and thus it sometimes resorted to similarly physical tactics. Shocked by the violence that had recently erupted in America among striking miners, Stead commented, "when an Englishman returns from the United States to the worst strike region in the United Kingdom he is conscious of an immediate and unmistakable change for the better."[59]

Although sympathetic to the position of the union in its struggle with Pullman, Stead deplored the force to which the strikers resorted. The violent outbursts revealed how crude the American labor movement still was:

> The strike against the Railroads only brings into clearer relief the fact that Labour in America is not yet anything like prepared to enter the lists in serious earnest. Labour, in its present disorganised, undisciplined and irreligious condition, is doomed to writhe helpless for some time longer beneath the ironshod heel of Capital. It may from time to time flounder into a Jacquerie in which torch and dynamite will enable it to inflict hideous wounds upon its adversaries, but more than that lies beyond its reach.

Stead charged that American workers could not be unified into a cohesive force until they gained "religion," by which he meant faith in one another and in the cause. The Pullman strike might serve as the Bull Run of American labor, he suggested, as the calamity that would jolt the movement to reassess its position.[60]

Although he was harsh on the labor movement, Stead argued in *Chicago To-day*, as he had in his previous volume, that the source of the problem could be found in America's maldistribution of wealth. However, in offering solutions he departed here from what he had proposed in *If Christ Came to Chicago*. While socialism was a viable option in Britain, Stead asserted that the municipalization of services was impossible in America because of the corruption of city government, and without a genuine civil service system the national government was also unfit to assume a role in the economy. The only answer was for righteous Americans to band together to bring about a civic revival. Change would be difficult, he conceded, because of the intransigence of the constitutional system, but he implored reformers to persevere and suggested that they model themselves on the abolitionists who led the fight against slavery.[61]

A few years after visiting and writing about Chicago, Stead in 1897 made a trip to New York. The book that resulted from this journey—though dependent only minimally on firsthand observation—was provocatively titled, *Satan's Invisible World Displayed; or, Despairing Democracy*. Stead felt the term appropriate to describe the central subject matter of the work—the widespread corruption that, at least until a recent reform effort, had plagued the government of New York City. While detailing the abuses perpetrated by Tammany Hall, he argued in this volume that he disapproved of the long-term solution that had been arrived at to remedy the problem, a new charter for a Greater New York that would bestow on the mayor much more extensive powers. The basis of the book, which was released as the end-of-the-year "annual" of the *Review of Reviews*, was the massive report issued by the New York state senate's Lexow Committee revealing the corruption that had been so rampant in the city's police department. By relying so heavily on the Lexow report, Stead knew this book would not constitute the type of "personal study" that *If Christ Came to Chicago* was. But he felt the report was so extraordinary, yet unfamiliar beyond New York, that it would be beneficial to relate its findings, particularly to his British readers. He wrote, "What New York was, London, Glasgow, or Melbourne may—nay, will certainly become, if the citizens become indifferent to the good government of their city."[62]

On his visit to New York Stead was dazzled by the beauty of the harbor, which he found to be a fitting portal for the multitudes of immigrants who had come to America. New York had always been for those who longed to leave Europe for the United States like a "New Jerusalem," and when immigrants sailed into the harbor, they were like "the tribes of Israel" when they "first gazed upon the confines of the promised land." These immigrants all grew up revering America for its freedom and equality and for "a constitution that was at once the envy and despair of the world." Of his own fellow countrymen, Stead wrote, "To the great mass of English, Scottish, and Irish people—as distinguished from the traveled and more or less cultured minority—the United States has for a hundred years been the land of their ideal, often dearer to them than their own." At least, he explained, that had been the sentiment in Britain until the present generation, but now the enthusiasm had lessened. The fondness for America that such radicals as John Bright and Richard Cobden had shown in Stead's younger days could now be found primarily among the Irish.[63]

At the moment, Stead argued, it was impossible for most Europeans to look favorably upon New York, despite its outward sparkle. He asserted, "We have suffered a severe blow and a grievous discouragement in the betrayal of the cause of liberty in the very vestibule and entrance chamber of the republic." The chief culprit in that "betrayal" was Tammany Hall, the old and powerful New York Democratic machine that until very recently had held the reins of power in the city. Stead described the corruption in which Tammany had wallowed over the decades, particularly during the 1860s, when Boss William Marcy Tweed and his infamous ring stole millions of dollars from the city. But just as he could see the positive aspects of the Chicago machine, Stead showed some admiration—though less than in the case of Chicago—for Tammany Hall. He acknowledged that Tammany functioned effectively and believed the key to this success was that the organization was established on a "democratic" basis: "No one was too poor, too wicked, or too ignorant to be treated by Tammany as a man and a brother if he would stand in with the machine and join the brotherhood."[64]

During the first half of the 1890s, the tide turned against Tammany when its corruption of the New York City police force was exposed to the public. The Reverend Dr. Charles H. Parkhurst of the Madison Square Presbyterian Church, president of the Society for the Prevention of Crime, spearheaded the campaign that brought down the machine. He railed against the police for being accomplices in the crime and vice that plagued the city and single-handedly launched an investigation to obtain tangible evidence to support his accusations. When Parkhurst had built up a credible case and won over public opinion, the Republican-controlled state senate—without the cooperation of the Tammany Democratic governor—established a special committee to probe the charges of abuse swirling around the New York City Police Department. With freshman senator Clarence Lexow in the chair, this committee held extensive and sensational hearings throughout the year of 1894 and issued its thick report at the beginning of 1895. The hearings were so damaging to Tammany Hall that even before the report was released, the people of New York repudiated the machine and voted in a reform-minded administration.[65]

In *Satan's Invisible World Displayed* Stead related the findings of the Lexow Committee and then went on to tackle another, though not unrelated, issue—the new charter for a Greater New York. The connection was that many of the reformers who had railed against the abuses in the police department and against the stranglehold of Tammany Hall over the city also fought for the new charter. For example, it was Senator Lexow who chaired the legislative committee that in 1896 held hearings to discuss the prospects for a Greater New York, the idea of consolidating New York City with neighboring communities, particularly Brooklyn. The proponents of a Greater New York included not only reformers who believed such a fusion would lead to more honest and rational municipal administration, but also self-interested parties who felt they would benefit economically, and, most important of all, Republican boss Thomas Platt, who figured that the expanded city would benefit his party. The greatest resistance came from Brooklynites who feared they would lose their distinctive political and cultural identity. With Platt behind the measure, the Greater New York bill was passed in 1896, a charter adopted in May of 1897, and a new mayor elected in November, and on January 1, 1898, Greater New York, with its five boroughs, officially came into existence.[66]

Writing about the charter in late 1897, Stead did not object to the extension of New York City's boundaries but rather to the extension of the mayor's powers for which the document provided. He lamented the creation in New York City of a "czar-mayor." According to the blueprint for a Greater New York, the mayor was to have the exclusive authority to appoint virtually all of the principal members of the executive branch, which was to be vested with the bulk of the power to govern the city. The role of the popularly elected municipal assembly was, consequently, to be severely restricted.[67] In establishing this type of government, New York was part of a national trend in the late nineteenth century toward creating "strong" mayors, with the enlightened administrations of Seth Low in Brooklyn, Josiah Quincy in Boston, and Sam M. Jones in Toledo serving as the most prominent contemporary examples of what could be achieved. American reformers were seeking to take responsibilities, particularly fiscal responsibility, away from the traditionally corrupt city councils and hold one citywide elected figure accountable.[68] While American cities were placing greater power in the hands of the executive, the British were proudly adhering to the system of municipal government that had developed in their country over the course of the nineteenth century. In Britain virtually all of the authority in the cities was wielded by popularly elected councils, and executive duties were generally undertaken by appointed town clerks.[69]

Stead's preference for the British system of municipal government was clear. He charged that, like other American cities, New York was about to shift from a system in which the government was allowed little power and was thus subject to the whims of outside forces, namely Tammany Hall and the state legislature, to one in which a great deal of authority was to be vested in just one man, the mayor. Stead questioned why New York and other American cities could not establish strong, responsible municipal councils: "The idea of allowing citizens in their wards to elect representatives, who should wield all the powers vested in English, French or German town councils, was regarded by Americans as savoring of suicidal recklessness." To Stead it was baffling that Americans had resisted adopting the British model, since so many had acknowledged the validity of Joseph Chamberlain's claim that "Birmingham is the best governed city of the world."[70]

That New York had decided to institute a "czar-mayor" system, Stead believed, signified that, as he had found in Chicago, Americans were giving up on democracy. In making this charge, he said he meant by democracy the idea of representative government. Stead acknowledged, however, that democracy could be expressed in other forms. "I am no bigot of constitutionalism," he wrote, explaining that "for nearly twenty years I have been engaged in an attempt to compel hidebound devotees of parliamentary government to admit the virtue that is latent in the Russian autocracy." He asserted, "Russia, although governed autocratically, is nevertheless one of the purest democracies in the world." Yet in the English-speaking world democracy had always meant only one thing—government by a popularly elected assembly—and it was by that standard that the charter for New York had to be judged. In Stead's view the charter was based on the ideals of the Second Empire, and though Napoleon III may have considered himself a democratic leader, the New York plan had to be seen as a violation of the Anglo-American political tradition. Stead wrote, "It is this evolution of Bonapartism, of an elective dictatorship, based on universal suffrage, which is the most startling phenomenon of modern politics in the United States."[71]

Although Stead deplored the direction in which he saw American politics moving, he refused to be pessimistic. Feeling that the nation was passing through a temporary phase, he said, "I cannot believe that the American democracy is permanently forsaking what Jefferson proclaimed as the fundamental principle of democratic institutions." His advice to New York was to tear up its "czar-mayor" charter and institute a strong, popularly elected council system of government. But no matter what the form of administration, Stead said that New York, like Chicago, needed a phalanx of reform-minded citizens who would serve as the "Civic Church." As in his second work on Chicago, there was no suggestion here that socialism could be a panacea, but in this book he did place great stock in the notion of an empowered press, or "Government by Journalism." Stead concluded *Satan's Invisible World Displayed* on an ominous note by reporting that the November 1897 election for the first mayor of Greater New York had resulted in victory for the candidate put up by Tammany Hall.[72]

During the 1890s a number of Britons besides Stead traveled to the United States and found themselves horrified by what they witnessed in the cities. Like Bryce before them, and indeed like a great many Americans at the time, British visitors commonly found urban life to be one of the most unsatisfactory aspects of civilization in the United States. Over the course of the last decade of the nineteenth century, British observers often wrote scathingly about American cities, particularly about Stead's "specimen," Chicago. Perhaps the most prominent visitor of this era was Rudyard Kipling, who actually made his first trip to the United States in 1889 but whose controversial *American Notes* was not published until 1891. Among the many harsh observations Kipling made about America, observations reminiscent of Mrs. Trollope's acidulous writings, he was particularly vicious about the cities.

When he arrived in America, the young Anglo-Indian journalist was already in the process of establishing his fame as a master of verse and short stories. He was visiting America as he slowly made his way back to England, after having spent several years in India. Before landing in the United States, Kipling had traveled around Asia, and so he had the unique experience, for an Englishman, of starting his tour in San Francisco and seeing America from west to east. Kipling wrote about his New World experiences for an Indian newspaper, the *Pioneer,* but the commentaries were unknown in the United States until some of the pieces were published in American newspapers in 1891 and then collected in book form as *American Notes,* all without his permission. The sharpness of the writings provoked outrage among Americans, but that did not stop Kipling from actually planting roots in the United States in 1892. In that year he married the sister of his late American friend Charles Wolcott Balestier, the writer and publisher, and they settled down close by her family in Brattleboro, Vermont. Kipling spent over four years in this New England town, where he built a comfortable house, saw his first two children born, and produced his popular *Jungle Books,* before a feud with another brother of Mrs. Kipling's sent him and his family back to Britain. He made one more trip to America in 1899, which turned out tragically when he became desperately ill and his six-year-old daughter died, but on that journey he was finally able to put an end to publication of the pirated *American Notes.* Kipling gained copyright control over the *Pioneer* articles and then authorized the inclusion of his American writings in a two-volume work of travel commentaries called *From Sea to Sea.*[73]

Kipling may not have actually hated America. He forged friendships with several figures in the United States, and his years in Vermont were for the most part pleasant ones. Even on that first trip, which became the basis for his published writings on America, there were happy experiences—catching a salmon in the Columbia River, for example. Yet it is the nastiness of Kipling's commentary that offended Americans in the 1890s and still stands as the most prominent feature of his scattered anecdotes and impressions. He claimed a fondness for the Americans, but his writings are peppered with offensive statements. In a piece published in *From Sea to Sea,* one that did not appear in *American Notes,* the compliments he paid are overshadowed by the insults to which he inevitably resorted. He wrote:

> I love this People, and if any contemptuous criticism has to be done, I will do it myself. My heart has gone out to them beyond all other peoples; and for the life of me I cannot tell why. They are bleeding-raw at the edges, almost more conceited than the English, vulgar with a massive vulgarity which is as though the Pyramids were coated with Christmas-cake sugar-works.

Kipling said that their laws and government were flimsy and that their successes were attributable to their abundance of resources, not to their "brains," but that he loved the American people anyway. With friends like Kipling, Americans may well have thought, who needed enemies.[74]

There was a basic inconsistency to Kipling's writings on America. In one piece he argued, a few years before Frederick Jackson Turner enunciated his "frontier thesis," that the United States would face difficulties when its territory became filled and its resources depleted, that the much vaunted democratic principles would be severely tested. He said, "It will be a spectacle for all the world to watch, this big, slashing colt of a nation, that has got off with a flying start on a freshly littered course, being pulled back to the ruck by that very mutton-fisted jockey Necessity." But Kipling asserted in another article that America was a nation with a bright future. He wished he could see a century hence "the two Great Experiments," India and the United States: "At present the one is burned out and the other is only just stoking up." Furthermore, though irritated by Yankee flag-waving, he chided the British for not possessing the patriotic spirit of the Americans. The discrepancies can perhaps in part be attributed to the fact that Kipling's writings on America were purely impressionistic; he did not attempt to come to any general conclusions about American society. When he arrived in the United States, Kipling felt overwhelmed by the task of covering such a vast nation and determined he would not attempt to write, as Bryce did, the authoritative work. He said, "For me is the daily round of vagabondage, the recording of the incidents of the hour, and talk with the travelling companion of the day. I will not 'do' this country at all."[75]

In his travels around the nation, Kipling was more impressed by rural America than by urban. Some of his most positive comments were about the beauty of the landscape, and the man who would later find a great deal of pleasure living in the Vermont countryside waxed eloquent about the delights of a small Pennsylvania village. On the other hand, Kipling was at his most savage in describing the large American cities, namely the two he came to know, San Francisco and Chicago. While in San Francisco, Kipling, the reporter, soaked up the atmosphere in a diversity of settings, from the Bohemian Club and the sumptuous Palace Hotel to the neighborhood saloon to the seedy underworld of Chinatown. None of it suited him. Two aspects of life in San Francisco he found particularly objectionable were the pervasive violence and the political corruption. When he was in the Chinese quarter, Kipling actually witnessed a shooting. He was shocked by the prevalence of guns and by how quickly the citizens, from a variety of backgrounds, resorted to force. Furthermore, the press would detail every incident of brutality and at the same time ask "whether the world can parallel the progress of San Francisco." Kipling wrote about the boss system that prevailed in the city and how easy it was to buy votes, and he described the ward politicians whom he found gathered in a saloon: "They were not pretty persons. Some of them were bloated, and they all swore cheerfully till the heavy gold watch-chains on their fat stomachs rose and fell again; but they talked over their liquor as men who had power and unquestioned access to places of trust and profit." After hearing these politicians discuss so bluntly their rough tactics, Kipling said:

> Then I began to understand why my pleasant and well-educated hosts in San Francisco spoke with a bitter scorn of such duties of citizenship as voting and taking an interest in the distribution of offices. Scores of men have told me with no false pride that they would as soon concern themselves with the public affairs of the city or State as rake muck.[76]

The most striking comment that Kipling made about Chicago is, "Having seen it, I urgently desire never to see it again." He wrote, "It is inhabited by savages. Its water is the water of the Hugli, and its air is dirt."[77] Kipling was disturbed by the materialism he found in Chicago and by the boastful, self-satisfied attitude he sensed in its inhabitants. Just as he was repelled by San Francisco's Palace, he also looked unfavorably upon the crown jewel of Chicago hotels, the Palmer House, "a gilded and mirrored rabbit-warren" containing "a huge hall of tesselated marble, crammed with people talking about money and spitting about everywhere." Wandering around Chicago, by contrast, Kipling said he had never before seen "such a collection of miserables." He also found the city aesthetically lacking: "There was no colour in the street and no beauty—only a maze of wire-ropes overhead and dirty stone flagging underfoot." Whether emanating from the mouth of a cab driver or a Sunday preacher, the "progress" of Chicago was all Kipling kept hearing about, and it irritated him. Of the cab driver he said, "He conceived that all this turmoil and squash was a thing to be reverently admired; that it was good to huddle men together in fifteen layers one atop of the other and to dig holes in the ground for offices." Nor could Kipling subscribe to the idea that Chicago's boom economy represented "progress"; he found the competitive business climate of the city, the grasping after profits, to be unseemly.[78]

While Kipling, the Tory imperialist, and Stead, the imperialist radical, both expressed their disgust with the American city, they approached the issue from different angles. Suffice it to say that Stead was much more sympathetic to the United States than Kipling, who tended to attack the nation rather than offer constructive criticism. Closer to Stead on the political spectrum were Sidney and Beatrice Webb, who stood at the core of that formidable cadre of socialists organized in 1884 as the Fabians. It was the Fabians' goal to establish gradually, through the democratic process, the municipalization and nationalization of the means of production, so it was only natural that when the Webbs turned their attention to the United States in the 1890s, they would focus on city government. Like Stead, they were harsh in their reactions to urban America, and in fact, they could be as hostile in tone as Kipling.

Sidney Webb was a small, bespectacled man who had risen from his lower-middle-class background to take a place in the civil service and then devoted himself to the cause of Fabian socialism. Beatrice Webb was a handsome, imposing woman born to privilege, who fell under the influence of Herbert Spencer, was courted by Joseph Chamberlain, and ultimately established herself as a social scientist. The pair became not only husband and wife in 1892 but also intellectual partners, and after collaborating on two books on trade unionism, they decided to undertake the project that would result in the fifteen volumes of *English Local Government*. But before starting on the daunting task, the Webbs embarked on a trip to America.[79] The journey, which also took them to Australia and New Zealand, would, however, be a working vacation, for they were thinking about the next challenge and intent on looking at municipal institutions to compare them with the British model. The question they started with, Beatrice later said, was:

How had the political democracy which we knew in Great Britain succeeded or failed without any medieval background, under entirely different climatic conditions, with a strong admixture of races other than Anglo-Saxon, but with the same language, the same environment of capitalist enterprise, the same religion, and many of the same traditions?[80]

Most of what we know about the Webbs' trip, and about the impressions they formed on that trip, comes from Beatrice, who while in America recorded her thoughts in the remarkable diary that she kept for virtually her entire life. But based on his letters, insertions he made in Beatrice's diary, and comments she attributed to him, it is safe to say that Sidney shared the opinions expressed by his wife.[81] When, decades later, Beatrice went to work on the second volume of her memoirs, which consisted mainly of long excerpts from the diaries, she prepared a chapter on the 1898 trip called "Round the English-Speaking World." She explained in the chapter that, considering how casually she had made her observations, she was reluctant to include them in the book, but she did believe the commentary could be a valuable historical resource.[82] Nevertheless, she had her doubts about the material, as did Sidney. The entries from the trip read more like a study, with the various reports on city councils and state legislatures, than the other, more personal portions of the diary.[83] That Sidney kept delving into the diary himself in this period seems to have inhibited his wife from expressing her most internal feelings.[84] Beatrice did not live long enough to see the second volume of her memoirs to publication, but when Barbara Drake and Margaret Cole inherited the project, they made the decision to leave out of *Our Partnership* (1948) the chapter on "Round the English-Speaking World."[85]

In her diary Beatrice asked, "Who would recognise as distinctively American the essentially eccentric and ugly individuals portrayed by Dickens, Trollope and Martineau?" She found the Americans to be a well-mannered, friendly, and decent people who on the whole deported themselves more admirably than some of their counterparts in the British middle class. The fine American temperament, however, was the only national characteristic that she praised.[86] Although Webb tried to distance herself from the great earlier nineteenth-century observers, her sharp criticisms of the United States make her writings reminiscent of theirs. She made disparaging remarks about virtually everything and everyone she saw; the number of individuals she genuinely admired could be counted on one hand. It is true that Beatrice Webb was an ex-acting figure who as a rule judged others harshly, and that she was re-cording her impressions in a private journal, but it would still be difficult to read her diary for 1898 and not conclude that she found the United States abhorrent. Although the Webbs lived into the 1940s, neither of them ever set foot on American soil again.

As the Webbs traveled around the United States studying municipal government, they formed a dislike for the cities they visited. After seeing the nation's capital, Beatrice wrote that the city was charming and the sights delightful, but then immediately proceeded to say, "And yet Washington, with its purely mechanical arrangement of streets, with its per-fect finish in the centre of the city, and its ragged and untidy suburbs of wooden shanties and dust-bin spaces, is strangely unsatisfying." She stated that even the allure of the most impressive buildings wore off after further examination revealed how poorly designed and con-structed they actually were. At the end of the Webbs' journey across the continent, Beatrice, while in San Francisco, wrote, "Certainly our last impression of an American city will be like our first of New York: Noise, noise, nothing but noise. . . . In the city your senses are disturbed, your ears are deafened, your eyes are wearied by a constant rush."[87]

Although both of the Webbs were captivated by Jane Addams, she was the only positive feature of Chicago they could find. But as Beatrice herself admitted, attacks of the flu, hot summer weather, and the less-than-first-class accommodations they encountered while staying at Hull House colored their perceptions.[88] In a letter written from Hull House to his close friend and fellow Fabian George Bernard Shaw, Sidney called Chicago "an 'unspeakable' city, viler than tongue can tell, and as hopeless as the Inferno." He also explained that he and Beatrice had de-cided not to keep to their Midwestern itinerary, which included such destinations as Minneapolis and Omaha, but instead "to 'chuck' the rest of these overgrown, ugly cities, each more corrupt and misgoverned than the last, and to make a bee-line for Colorado."[89]

As Sidney said, they found American cities not only unappealing, but more important, considering their mission of studying municipal insti-tutions, "corrupt and misgoverned." When they were in New York, both Sidney and Beatrice sent letters back to England describing, in some of the same language, how shocking they found American municipal government. Sidney wrote to Shaw, "This people, in all that concerns the *machinery* of government, is infantile." A few days later Beatrice explained to her sister Catherine Courtney, "American municipal institutions, both in their rapidly changing constitutions and their infantile procedure make one think that we must be Alice in Wonderland witnessing a huge and somewhat grimy joke."[90] When Beatrice saw various city councils in session, she characterized the members—as she also did the congressmen she observed in the U.S. House of Representatives—in derogatory terms, with a focus on physical characteristics. For example, she wrote of the New York City aldermen: "Here again I noted a peculiar type that one sees in all American representative assemblies: heavy jaw, aquiline nose, eyes bulging, sandy hair, the main features of the face being embedded in unhealthy looking fat." She continued, "The type combined the characteristics of a loose liver, a stump orator and intriguer with the vacant stare of the habitual lounger."[91]

In New York City, as well as in Baltimore and Philadelphia, Webb was critical of both the men who filled the posts of city government and the manner in which these governments were operated. She found more to her liking when she moved up the coast to Boston. Some of the same problems existed there, but nevertheless she detected "a sweet flavour about Massachusetts government." In the tradition of Dickens, Webb was generally the most positive in commenting on New England and, for example, revealed her admiration for such Brahmins as President Charles Eliot of Harvard and Boston's mayor, Josiah Quincy.[92]

Like Stead, the Webbs were profoundly disturbed by the trend in American cities toward the concentration of power in the mayor's office. In New York they had lunch with the president of Columbia University, formerly the mayor of Brooklyn, Seth Low, who told them about the developments that had led up to the previous year's adoption of the charter of Greater New York, which he helped to frame. Beatrice wrote that the "one point" she took away from Low's explanation was "the constant and increasing distrust of the American—whether he be a superior person or the man in the street—of an assembly of representatives." She also said that "Seth Low, though he recognised that the American distrust of the representative body was itself proof that American democracy was less developed and efficient than that of England, accepted this distrust as inevitable." He believed strong measures were appropriate if the United States was going to solve the problems of the cities.[93]

When the Webbs were in Denver, they observed a convention drawing up a new strong-mayor charter for the city. Beatrice wrote, "The whole burden of the discussion was the evil of 'divided responsibility.' To-day the American has a perfect mania on this subject and it is extremely difficult for an Englishman to understand what he is aiming at." The general idea was "the necessity of making one man responsible," but "usually consists in endowing one man with *irresponsible power.*" The Americans, she argued, were in no way adhering to the principles of responsible government that underlay the British parliamentary system. Unlike with the prime minister, there was no mechanism to remove the American mayor; he served for a fixed term, and because it was generally nonrenewable, he was not even forced to account to his constituency in the next election.[94]

Beatrice wrote that Sidney did not accept the logic of the claim that if one-man rule was successful in business, then it would also work for municipal government. Thinking along alternative lines, she wondered "whether this childlike faith in the efficacy of one-man power is not a reaction from the theory of checks and balances introduced by the Federal Constitution." Such a system, she explained, was adopted at a time when there was a "fear of tyranny," but that fear no longer existed and what was needed now was strong, efficient government, not one always at odds with itself. It was ironic, she stated, that on the municipal level in America, a system was being created that fulfilled the worst nightmares of the Founding Fathers who instituted the principle of checks and balances—the vesting of power in one unaccountable individual. Webb argued that the happy medium between the poles of eighteenth-century checks and balances and the new urban autocracy was the sensible British system of placing all authority in a sovereign legislature and ensuring that the government was at all times responsible to the electorate.[95]

Aside from the structural defects of American municipal government, Webb asserted that the cities were bound to be misgoverned because of the influence of two fallacious American assumptions—the principle that no man was superior to any other and the belief that each individual's pursuit of personal gain would ultimately benefit the community. In this egalitarian, profit-obsessed society, it was little wonder, she felt, that genius and greatness were hard to find, and that government, particularly on the local level, would suffer. As long as the American people continued to maintain that the reins of power could be held by amateurs and tolerated personal profit in the public realm, nothing would change. Americans needed to realize the importance of bringing into government talented individuals whose overriding motive was "social service."[96]

Decades later, in "Round the English-Speaking World," Webb took a somewhat different line. She now wrote that there had been no shortage of honest, civic-minded men willing to serve in municipal administration; in fact, "Good Government" coalitions had sometimes been voted into office. The problem had been, as she thought back to the 1890s, that these well-meaning reformers had neither agreed upon a single program nor possessed the skills to hold the reins of government.[97] Furthermore, in this chapter intended for her memoirs, Webb wanted to soften the picture of America that she had painted in her diary. She wished "to apologise to American readers for what will appear to them an unfair vision of American life." According to her explanation, she and Sidney had not explored American private enterprise or American philanthropy, national strengths, but instead had focused above all on municipal government, the country's Achilles' heel. In retrospect, Webb acknowledged that their particular research interests had provided them with a distorted picture of the nation.[98]

Unlike the Webbs, Stead was not fortunate enough to live a long life, and in his remaining years he never found occasion to issue an apology to the Americans for what he had written following his visits to Chicago and New York. Yet during the second half of the 1890s, and particularly after 1900, he did reveal that there still burned within him an enthusiasm for America.

2

The Bonds of Blood

*W. T. Stead's Vision of Anglo-American Unity
at the Turn of the Century*

Despite Stead's experiences in the United States, which led him to form a critical view of American cities and to despair over the political course he thought the nation was following, he did not withdraw from his conviction that Britain and America should be united. Ironically, after he saw America for himself and wrote so harshly about the country, Stead's belief in tying the fortunes of the two nations together actually strengthened. He did not, as might have been expected, adopt an attitude that Britain would have been better off remaining disentangled from a corrupt, polarized, and cynical America. By the turn of the century, he was effusive in his praise for the United States and had taken the notion of Anglo-American unity to the extreme. Perhaps the explanation for Stead's contradictory thinking lies in the fact that the unity of the English-speaking peoples had for so long been a central tenet of his beliefs that he was not prepared simply to renounce it even if America did not turn out to be the place he had envisioned since boyhood. His affection for America was so deeply rooted that it could not be eradicated by the disappointment he experienced in the New World. Furthermore, by the end of the 1890s he apparently had got caught up in the spirit of the rapprochement between Britain and the United States.

The idea of uniting the English-speaking peoples was a concept to which Stead had subscribed from the beginning of his journalistic career. While editor of the Darlington *Northern Echo* in the 1870s and the *Pall Mall Gazette* in the 1880s, he wrote in his journal that linking together the English-speaking world was among his foremost political priorities.[1] In issuing his "Gospel According to the *Pall Mall Gazette*," he included among his major aims "Arbitration in all Anglo-American Disputes," which he felt could be the starting point leading to closer ties between Britain and the United States.[2]

When Stead launched the *Review of Reviews* in 1890, he took command of a journalistic vehicle that he could devote to the cause of uniting the English-speaking peoples. In the first issue, dated January 1890, he enunciated his hope, in a message "To All English-Speaking Folk," that the magazine would serve to tighten the bonds of the British Empire and to bring the empire and the United States into a closer relationship. Stead commenced this declaration by stating, "There exists at this moment no institution which even aspires to be to the English-speaking world what the Catholic Church in its prime was to the intelligence of Christendom." He was committing his journal to the fortification and unification of Anglo-American civilization because

> among all the agencies for the shaping of the future of the human race, none seem so potent now and still more hereafter as the English-speaking man. Already he begins to dominate the world. The Empire and the Republic comprise within their limits almost all the territory that remains empty for the overflow of the world. Their citizens, with all their faults, are leading the van of civilisation, and if any great improvements are to be made in the condition of mankind, they will necessarily be leading instruments in the work.[3]

Stead's commitment to strengthening the web of the British Empire was nothing extraordinary. By 1890 there was considerable imperialist sentiment among both Tories and Liberals, and the preceding years had seen the publication of such popular works as Charles Dilke's *Greater Britain* (1869), John Seeley's *The Expansion of England* (1883), and James Anthony Froude's *Oceana* (1886). Stead, however, stood somewhat out of the mainstream by throwing so much of his talent and prestige behind trying to tighten the bonds between Britain and America. By the 1890s, Anglo-American relations were more solid than they had been at the close of the Civil War, but they were still fragile. Americans were probably more hostile to Britain than vice-versa, but it was still unusual for an Englishman, at this date, to be so devoted to establishing an amicable relationship with the United States.

Nevertheless, there were precedents for Stead's enthusiasm for the English-speaking peoples. Throughout the nineteenth century many English thinkers subscribed to the idea of Anglo-Saxon superiority. What had begun in the sixteenth and seventeenth centuries as admiration for old Anglo-Saxon religious and political institutions had in the decades prior to 1850 become a racial doctrine. Thomas Carlyle was perhaps the first notable Englishman to enunciate a belief in Anglo-Saxon racial superiority, and, as he told Emerson, among the members of this select race he counted the Americans. By midcentury such other eminent figures as Thomas Arnold and Charles Kingsley were also exalting the Anglo-Saxon race.[4] An essential feature of Anglo-Saxonism was the recognition of the race's Teutonic origins, and this link back to the forests of Germany was described in the works of several prominent British and American historians in the latter half of the nineteenth century, including Bishop William Stubbs and Edward A. Freeman of Oxford. Freeman, when he came to the United States in 1881, stressed the bonds that existed between the British, the Germans, and the Americans, but he caused a stir when he went on to make disparaging remarks about one group of non-Anglo-Saxon Americans, the Irish.[5] Anglo-Saxonism reached the height of its influence in the 1890s, when it was embraced by many thinkers on both sides of the Atlantic.[6] The concept, however, also underwent a transformation, as it came to be used more and more to describe a civilization rather than a race. By 1900 "Anglo-Saxon" was often employed to designate Britons and Americans of both Teutonic and non-Teutonic stock, and now there was also less of a tendency to see any kinship with the Germans. To reflect this new reality, the designation "Anglo-Saxons" was being replaced by the more appropriate "English-speaking peoples."[7]

Stead virtually always employed the term "English-speaking peoples" or "English-speaking race." He was not prone to making biologically inspired racial distinctions or to denigrating groups outside of his cherished English-speaking community. Nevertheless, at times a harsh side did emerge—not uncommonly, in fact, in his discussions of America. In the pages of the *Review of Reviews,* in the journal's early years, he commented on the heavy influx into the United States of non-English-speaking immigrants in a way that was uncharacteristic of the

Christian Stead the world would come to know from his many books. In 1891 he wrote of the presence in the United States of a "mass of crude, undigested, and indigestible foreigners" and warned that Americans should "jealously guard the English-speaking character" of their nation. Whether America would remain "an integral part of the English-speaking world" might seem to his readers "as monstrously absurd as if it were to be asked whether the men of Kent were still speaking English. But, unfortunately, the question is not by any means nonsensical." Although Stead mainly framed his argument against immigration in terms of language, there is ample evidence that he was concerned with blood lines as well. He called the United States "one of the finest stud farms in the world for the production of human beings" and cautioned Americans not "to spoil their breed of pedigree stock."[8]

Stead need not have sent such a transatlantic warning; there was already plenty of apprehension within the United States. By the early 1890s the surge of poor immigrants from eastern and southern Europe had begun to alarm many Americans, particularly those of English descent living in the Northeast. Henry Cabot Lodge, the patrician senator from Massachusetts, believed in the superiority of the "Anglo-Saxon" sector of the population and feared that the new immigrants posed a threat to the survival of the republic. In an effort to curb the immigration, Lodge seized on the idea of instituting a literacy test to be administered to all foreigners who sought entrance into the United States. Immigrants would have to prove only that they could read and write in their native language, so Stead's concern that the United States was becoming a non-English-speaking country would not have been directly addressed. Yet there is no doubt that the purpose of the test was to cut down drastically on the number of foreigners settling in America. Some of Lodge's fellow Boston Brahmins joined forces with him when they established the Immigration Restriction League, which during the 1890s, and beyond, tapped into nativist sentiment as it campaigned for federal literacy-test legislation. Not until 1917, however, would such a test be passed into law.[9]

In the early 1890s Stead was still somewhat vague about what exactly he envisioned when he discussed Anglo-American unity. It was not always clear whether he was simply advocating more amicable relations, a formal alliance, or perhaps some sort of constitutionally mandated federation. Because the issue was potentially explosive in both the United States and Britain, Stead probably intended to play his cards close to his vest, but there are signs that he was willing to see the reunification of the two countries go as far as possible, to the point of breaking down traditional barriers of national sovereignty. When, in 1891, Congress finally granted Britons copyright protection in the United States, Stead hailed the legislation and frankly announced, "In the ideal English-speaking world for which we are working, all English speakers will be citizens of one great commonwealth, enjoying equally all rights, privileges, and protection without any question whether they are born in Melbourne, or Minnesota, or Manchester."[10] But generally he did not tip his hand and instead worked for reasonably attainable goals, which, however, he hoped would lead to more ambitious achievements. Above all he pressed for some permanent mechanism of arbitration between the two nations.

The Bering Sea sealing dispute between the United States and Canada, and by extension Britain, provided Stead with an opportunity to raise the arbitration issue. He opposed the eventually adopted idea of allowing the conflict to be settled by a third country: "This will never do. The two branches of the English family should never go outside the English-speaking world for the adjudication of disputes, which are, after all, legal rather than diplomatic." He therefore called for the establishment of an Anglo-American court.[11] Stead made it clear where he felt such an institution could lead when he wrote, "If the evil of George III. and his advisers is to be undone, and the two great branches of our common family are to be reunited—as they ought to be before the dawn of the twentieth century—it will be by the creation of some permanent judicial tribunal."[12]

By 1892 Stead had also fixed upon another instrument for promoting Anglo-American unity, the Chicago Columbian Exposition. The World's Fair's location, in the heart of the United States, prompted him to wonder if reunification would take place under American, rather than British, auspices. It was actually through a work of fiction, written a year before he would travel to Chicago himself, that Stead most fully conveyed his feelings about the potential of the World's Fair. For the 1892 Christmas extra of the *Review of Reviews*, he wrote a short novel called *From the Old World to the New*, which focuses on a group of English travelers who visit Chicago. The story, set in 1893, the year the exposition would open to the public, is a combination of sentimental Victorian romance, practical tour guide for prospective fairgoers, and propaganda. The propaganda consists of attempts by Stead to present the exposition, and America in general, in the best possible light and to convey the possibility of uniting the English-speaking peoples, even if that should mean under the aegis of America rather than Britain. In the preface he said that one of the purposes of the story was to reveal "the immense political possibilities that are latent in this World's Fair."[13]

The opening scene takes place on Christmas Eve, 1892, in an English country house. When an American woman, a poet and a professor at the University of Chicago, raises the question of visiting the World's Fair, she is met by condescension and derision. A Princess of Caprera answers, "No consideration in the world would ever induce me to go to America, that land of barbarians who have got the electric light, and therefore imagine they are civilized." She continues, "They are a clever people, ingenious mechanics, no doubt, with a remarkable talent for producing tinned meat and potted lobster. But I would as soon go to a candle-maker's as to Chicago." Sir Wilfrid Bruce, the host, chimes in that the Americans "are as a people industrious, ingenious, pacific; but their civilization like their mind is vulgarly materialist, and their mediocrity is monotonously uniform. They speak English after a fashion, but as they say nothing worth listening to, they might as well speak Choctaw."[14] Clearly, such sentiments were anathema to Stead, who was characterizing, and satirizing, the derogatory views of America typical of the European upper classes. Stead could never countenance such anti-Americanism; even as a young clerk in Newcastle, he recorded in his notebook his disapproval of Mrs. Trollope.[15]

One of the guests at the Christmas Eve festivities, Dr. Walter Wynne, decides he will go to the World's Fair, based upon the far-fetched hunch, which in the end proves to be valid, that he will find there his long-lost love. The story follows the steps of Dr. Wynne, and the other principals, as they cross the Atlantic, land in New York, make their way west, and then tour Chicago and the fair itself. Though occasionally a negative, or skeptical, note is sounded, the story's dominant chord is of an America that is a land of impressive sights and remarkable achievements. As Stead pulled the reader from the Statue of Liberty to the Brooklyn Bridge to Independence Hall and the Capitol, he promoted America enthusiastically. In paying homage to the United States, he even rebuked his own nation. While in Independence Hall, Dr. Wynne announces that the Founding Fathers were justified in breaking ties with the mother country in 1776: "The blame of that great schism lies at our door, not that of the men who drew up the Declaration of Independence."[16]

An old acquaintance of Dr. Wynne's, Jack Compton, turns up on the same ship also headed for the fair, and even more than Wynne, he serves as Stead's mouthpiece. On board Compton reveals that he would like to see the inception of a worldwide movement devoted to furthering progressive causes, one of the chief aims of which would be to reunite the English-speaking peoples. He feels that the shape that union would take could be determined at the World's Fair and tells Wynne:

> What is at stake at Chicago is the headship of the English-speaking world. The great problem of the immediate future in the sphere of high politics is this: Round what centre will the English-speaking communities group themselves? Will the great race alliance, which is the hope of the future, have its centre in Washington or in London? or will our race, permanently rent in two, continue to have two centres?[17]

While at the World's Fair, Compton and Wynne attend "the First Parliament of the English-speaking Race." After various eminent figures express their enthusiasm for the unification of the English-speaking peoples, Jack Compton steps forward and offers his views—that is, Stead's. He now seems to have answered for himself some of the questions he was posing on board the ship, for he tells the assemblage that the federation of the race will undoubtedly take place under American, not British, leadership. Compton makes the case that Britain's dependencies—its dominions and colonies—were already following the American example in establishing their social and political institutions: "The Australian is no more monarchical than the Kentuckian; the South African would as soon think of establishing a peerage as the New Yorker; and everywhere the principle of the Established Church is scouted, even by those who themselves belong to the Establishment in the old country." In words aimed at the Americans, Compton concludes:

> It seems inevitable that the hegemony of the English-speaking race will belong to you and not to us. You must increase; we must decrease. The Victorian age marks the culmination of the glory of Old England; the future belongs to the New England beyond the seas.[18]

When Stead finally visited the World's Fair in late 1893 and stayed on in Chicago through the winter of 1894, he clearly did not find an America as idyllic as he had portrayed in *From the Old World to the New*. However, despite the corruption and despair he observed in the United

States, he did not retreat from his commitment to Anglo-American unity. In fact, smack in the middle of his withering exposé of urban America, *If Christ Came to Chicago*, he published his message "To the English-Speaking Peoples," the plea for unity that originally appeared in the first issue of the *Review of Reviews.*[19] When he got back to Britain, he implicitly justified his contradictory viewpoint by stressing that each nation could assist the other in overcoming its problems. Britain, for example, could teach America about municipal government, while the federal system of the United States could serve as a useful model for the British Empire. Stead wrote, upon returning, "I have gained a deepened sense of the unity of the English-speaking race, and have re-enforced my conviction as to the help which each member of the race can render to the other."[20]

The next year, however, Stead's enthusiasm for Anglo-American unity would be tested to the limit when the Venezuela crisis broke out. He was clearly rankled by the assertive American behavior in this incident and staunchly defended Britain's position. In July 1895 the United States interjected itself into a border dispute between Venezuela and British Guiana when Secretary of State Richard Olney sent a note to Lord Salisbury, the prime minister and foreign secretary, invoking the Monroe Doctrine and insisting that Britain agree to arbitrate the matter. In December of that year, after receiving an unsatisfactory British response, President Grover Cleveland announced that an American commission would unilaterally fix the boundary and enforce its findings. The Cleveland administration's bellicose stance was largely motivated by domestic political concerns, while the British public hardly took any notice of the Venezuelan matter at all. But in 1896 the Salisbury government decided to back down and turn the dispute over to arbitration. Britain did not relish the prospect of being dragged into armed conflict with the United States, particularly as it was becoming increasingly wary of the menace imposed by Germany. When the award was made in 1899, the British claim was substantially upheld.

In September 1895, after Olney had sent his note but before Cleveland delivered his message, Stead wrote a piece for the *Contemporary Review* the title of which conveyed his feelings about the position of the United States on Venezuela—"Jingoism in America." He was incredulous that so many American leaders, including Senator Henry Cabot Lodge and Dr. Albert Shaw, were taking such a tough stance against Britain. Stead defended his country's claim in the boundary dispute but, even more important, Britain's right to have a presence in the New World. The Monroe Doctrine, he argued, could not apply to a British colony that predated the declaration, and his country could not be expected to arbitrate the matter until the legitimacy of British Guiana itself was clearly accepted. Stead was disturbed that Americans would choose to side with a Spanish nation against their British kin: "It certainly does not indicate a very keen appreciation of the doctrine that blood is thicker than water, or that the advantages of a union of the English-speaking peoples are much appreciated on the other side of the Atlantic."[21]

After Cleveland sent his message to Congress, Stead was irate. Concerning the administration's decision to name a commission to settle the Venezuelan matter, he wrote in the January 1896 *Review of Reviews:* "When this Commission has made its award, the President intimated he intended to thrust it down John Bull's throat, even if the operation necessitated the diversion to the purpose of fratricidal strife of the whole resources in men and money of the United States of America."[22] Stead blamed Washington's Venezuela policy on the inexperience of the United States in foreign affairs and used terms like "babes in the wood," "ingenuousness," and "childlike" in his description of American diplomacy. The United States, he argued, was following Britain's lead in attempting to impose its "will" beyond its borders but was doing so ineffectively. Of course, "it is only natural that the older Power should be much more tactful, much more astute, and much less like a bull in a china-shop, than the younger Power, which brings to the delicate problems of international diplomacy the bludgeon of the national will." Stead also recognized that Cleveland was playing politics with his message and that the president had to be tough to appeal to the American electorate. To anyone accustomed to the nuances of European diplomacy, it was "necessary to put cotton wool in your ears while you listen to American utterances on foreign affairs." The reality for American statesmen was that "if they do not shout in their own country, they are not listened to."[23]

In Stead's eyes the United States took the stand it did on the South American dispute in part because Venezuela called itself a republic while British Guiana was a colony of the crown, and "Americans still make a fetish of the word Republic." Stead again revealed his harsh side when he stated:

It is, of course, difficult to repress a smile when we hear white-skinned civilised English-speaking Christians writing and talking quite seriously as if any revolutionary junto of half-breeds who scramble to the top of seething anarchy by bribery and massacre in Spanish American states, had more in common with the great American Republic than such a self-governing community as the province of Ontario, merely because they label themselves a Republic.

A monarchy, Stead argued, no longer signified what it had in the late eighteenth century, and Great Britain was now actually like "a 'crowned Republic' in which there is much less of a one-man power than that which is wielded by any president of any republic in the world, the United States not excepted." Stead was so contemptuous of Venezuela that he felt it would actually be preferable if the nation came under either British or American rule.[24]

By February 1896, however, it seems that Stead had decided to cease his complaining about American policy on Venezuela and to work to defuse the crisis. Despite his earlier reservations, he now backed the idea of submitting the whole boundary dispute to arbitration, and he renewed his efforts to bring about a permanent Anglo-American court of arbitration.[25] When the United States and Britain came to an agreement on arbitrating the Venezuela dispute, he was pleased.[26] He was especially happy when in the waning days of the Cleveland administration a permanent Anglo-American arbitration treaty was worked out, but his hopes were only dashed later in 1897 after the Senate failed to ratify the accord.[27]

Although the Venezuela crisis threatened to aggravate the Anglo-American relationship to the point of open hostilities, the amicable settlement of the issue can actually be seen as the event responsible for ushering in the rapprochement between the two powers that developed in the latter half of the 1890s and laid the groundwork for the close ties that prevailed during the twentieth century. Although various cultural and social factors helped to make a reconciliation possible, the rapprochement came about mainly as a result of Britain's feeling uneasy about its position in the world as Germany loomed ever larger and deciding, based on its own geopolitical interests, to make a series of concessions to an increasingly powerful United States. As Britain grew more agreeable, America responded gratefully, and eventually a firm friendship between the two nations developed. Until World War I, the greatest efflorescence of warm feeling between Britain and the United States came during the year 1898, when Americans read the Salisbury government's neutrality in the Spanish-American War as tacit approval of the American course of action.[28]

In April of 1898, when war was imminent, Stead made it clear that he believed the United States was in the right. Although he did not think the blowing up of the *Maine* was cause for war, since the Spanish government had probably not been responsible, it was his contention that the miserable Spanish human rights record in Cuba justified American intervention. To Stead the United States was looking after long-suffering Cuba as, in the 1870s, Russia had taken responsibility for Bulgaria. He seemed convinced that America's chief motive in pressing Spain to free Cuba was humanitarian and that the United States would be entering into armed conflict only as a last resort.[29]

The greatest significance of the Spanish-American War, Stead repeatedly asserted, was that it marked the arrival of the United States as a global power. Despite the idealistic American goals, it was now possible to witness "the evolution of a self-contained home-keeping people into a second edition of John Bull, with ships and colonies and trade all over the world."[30] The new potency of the United States, Stead argued, made it all the more urgent for the English-speaking peoples to be unified as one, and he felt gratified that the war actually did appear to be bringing the Americans and British closer together.[31] The travails the Americans would face in liberating Cuba would force them to be more sympathetic to the British: "The experiences which they will gain in establishing free institutions in communities beyond the sea may perhaps make them regard with more charity the shortcomings of other fallible mortals who have preceded them in the same thankless task."[32] When, after the war, Spain ceded the Philippines to the United States, Stead wrote that the British understood it was never an American war goal to take over these islands, but simply a result of the conflict, and he added that he hoped Americans would now be better able to understand the position in which Britain was often placed.[33]

Stead's feelings were not atypical, for as the United States became an imperialist power and began to defend its policies, the British felt gratified that they were no longer isolated and that the Americans would now be hard put to be critical. In fact, fueled by an explosion of Anglo-Saxon sentiment in 1898 and the years following, the British heartily welcomed the United States into the great empire-building effort.[34] During this time, the Americans were justifying their new global conquests on the same racial grounds. Senator Albert Beveridge of Indiana, for example, championed the annexation of the Philippines by asserting that it was the destiny, and responsibility, of the United States to follow Britain's lead in colonization. For Americans to take on this task and to succeed was in "the blood."[35]

Stead saw much symbolism in the Spanish-American War, which he believed marked the downfall of Spain, Britain's predecessor as world leader, and the rise of its successor, the United States. He was struck by how America was mirroring Britain in its ascent as a global power:

> Uncle Sam is but John Bull magnified, democratised, with a whole continent to straddle over, instead of having no foothold but two islands of the Northern Sea. As the English have been, the Americans are; and as we English did, so will these stout sons of ours do. Our own history in the past is the prophecy of their future.

If the United States claimed that it had no interest in assembling an empire, neither had Britain, Stead said. America would simply find that imperial additions would be inevitable, as subject peoples all over the world would now be appealing not only to London, but to Washington as well.[36]

During the year 1898 there was talk of forming an Anglo-American alliance. Such powerful figures as the U.S. secretary of state, John Hay, and Joseph Chamberlain, the British colonial secretary, were sympathetic to the notion of an alliance, though for political reasons neither could promote such a concert enthusiastically.[37] Although Stead subscribed to grander schemes than a mere alliance between Britain and the United States, he nevertheless was one who advanced the idea. In May 1898, however, he took a cautious line in arguing that only a purely defensive alliance between the two nations would at that moment be tenable.[38]

Apart from discussion of a formal military alliance, there were calls as well in the exuberant atmosphere brought on by the rapprochement for closer cultural ties between Britain and America. Stead made the case for the observance of the Fourth of July throughout the English-speaking world by contending that the American Revolution had embodied traditional British political principles and that the cataclysm had taught the crown a valuable lesson about how to sustain a viable world empire. He also promoted the idea of establishing an organization composed of Britons and Americans to foster ties between the two peoples, a concept that came to fruition that year with the inception of the Anglo-American League, which was chaired by James Bryce and supported by several other notable individuals.[39]

The sentiment in Britain for establishing a political and military connection with the United States was by no means unanimous. The Fabian William Clarke, for one, lamented the prospect of America's following the same imperialist path as his own nation. Clarke had long been interested in the United States: he was an acolyte of Emerson and Whitman, and Henry Demarest Lloyd played a crucial role in shaping his socialist views.[40] After the Spanish-American War, he wrote Lloyd:

> I fear your people are going to take the Philippines, as all the Jingoes here who are gassing about an Anglo-American alliance hope will be the case. I need not tell you that Anglo-Americanism in reality means the robbery of the globe by capitalists under the guise of patriots & benefactors of mankind. This Anglo-Saxondom is the most hypocritical thing that has turned up in my time, but it is catching even with some who are well-meaning.[41]

Before the war, despite his criticism of American capitalism, Clarke had believed that the world needed to look for inspiration and leadership from the United States, and not Great Britain, which he viewed with mounting bitterness and alienation. However, by 1900 he was persuaded that America had become, like Britain, a corrupt, imperialist power and stated emphatically: "I hate the English-speaking countries."[42]

Though Clarke may not have been a lone voice in his country, it would seem that turn-of-the-century Britain was more in tune with Rudyard Kipling. While Clarke in 1898 lamented the possible American annexation of the Philippines, Kipling took the opposite position. He penned his famous poem "The White Man's Burden" for the direct purpose of influencing the debate over the Philippine question in the United States. Before the poem was published, Kipling sent a copy to Theodore Roosevelt, then governor of New York, who received it enthusiastically. Even more wholeheartedly than Stead, Kipling wanted to welcome the United States into the club of imperialist powers.[43]

Three years after the outpouring of goodwill between Britain and the United States in 1898, Stead published a book called *The Americanization of the World; or, The Trend of the Twentieth Century* (1901). In this work he was more explicit, and extreme, than ever before concerning his desires for Anglo-American union. Stead called for the consolidation of the United States, Britain, and Britain's colonies into one federation, with an elected chief executive and parliament located in Washington, D.C., which he considered the seat of the English-speaking race. He was not quite advocating the American annexation of Britain, but his scheme came close. Britain would still maintain its identity within his federal system, but its position would clearly be peripheral to that of the United States. In his previous writings, during the 1880s and 1890s, Stead had been vague in advancing his idea of Anglo-American union. At times he seemed to be referring merely to establishing closer cultural and social bonds; at other times he promoted such causes as Anglo-American arbitration or a military alliance. He broached the idea of political federation, but gingerly. Not until 1901 did he spell out his scheme and promote it vigorously. Furthermore, though he had often written of the center of power of the English-speaking race shifting westward—in his 1892 story, *From the Old World to the New*, for instance—in this book he for the first time contended that such an evolution was not merely inevitable, but in many respects desirable. He was so lavishly pro-American in this work that he went to the point of saying that only by tying its fortunes to the United States would Britain's future be bright. To what extent Stead may have long entertained such ideas and merely remained circumspect until the political climate allowed him to speak freely is not clear. Although there are indications that he had probably already resolved in his mind that political federation would be necessary, the rapprochement may have pushed his thinking one step further. There is also some evidence that Stead adopted an extreme position in the book at least in part to stimulate his British readership. As he told Henry Demarest Lloyd, "I want to wake up John Bull, and I think that it will give him fits to have it rubbed into him that Uncle Sam is beating him hands down."[44]

The title "Americanization of the World" was, and is, a provocative one, but Stead told his fellow Britons that they should accept this phrase as an accurate reflection of reality. He urged his countrymen not to begrudge the United States its success, explaining that "as the creation of the Americans is the greatest achievement of our race, there is no reason to resent the part the Americans are playing in fashioning the world in their image, which, after all, is substantially the image of ourselves." Britain should feel like the proud "parent" whose "son" has managed to go further in life. Stead also told the British that no matter how powerful and industrious America might become, they would always have the consolation of knowing that their land was a land of ancient history, a land that gave the world Shakespeare, Milton, and Scott.[45]

According to Stead, Britain could think of itself as Judaism and America as Christianity. It was the Christians who spread Judaic ideals around the globe as the Church became implanted in country after country. Likewise, Stead asserted, "The Americanization of the world is but the Anglicizing of the world at one remove." Another parallel that he drew served the purposes of this book even better. He said the English-speaking community of 1900 was like the German-speaking world of 1800, with Britain comparable to ancient, venerable Austria and America to the aggressive, burgeoning Prussia. The lesson for Britain, Stead suggested, was that by failing to come to terms with Prussia, Austria had been left out of the German nation that coalesced around the "upstart parvenus" to the north.[46]

Because the United States was now the supreme nation in the English-speaking community, Stead warned his fellow Britons, "The philosophy of common sense teaches us that, seeing we can never again be the first, standing alone, we should lose no time in uniting our fortunes with those who have passed us in the race." If Britain did not unite with America, he warned that it would be forever "doomed to play second fiddle." On the other hand, as a member of an English-speaking federation, Britain would be part of a political entity that would dominate the globe. Within the federation there could be healthy competition between America and Britain, as there was at present between American states, but the union would ensure that the two powers would not drift into war, which was a distinct possibility if they remained separate.[47]

The idea that the English-speaking peoples could be reunited by America's simply coming back into the British Empire was ridiculous, Stead asserted. It was too late for that possibility. The only feasible solution was for the two powers to join together in a federation, which would inevitably be based on American principles. In working out the terms, Britain would be compelled to make the greater concessions: "It is we who are going to be Americanized; the advance will have to be made on our side; it is idle to hope, and it is not at all to be desired, that the Americans will attempt to meet us half way." The federation, Stead maintained, would have to be a republic guided by an American-style written constitution; the leader of the federation would be elected, not a hereditary monarch, and there would be no aristocratic upper house or

established church. Such terms would actually not displease large seg-
ments of the British Empire, he argued. The colonies had been framing
their governments upon the American, not the British, model for years;
on the Celtic fringe of Britain there was discontent over such institutions as the Anglican Church; and many leading Britons, in both political parties, in contrast to the enthusiasm shown by Americans for the
U.S. Constitution, had come to doubt how well their political system
was working. Of course, Stead said, provision could be made under the
terms of the federation to permit the survival of the peerage and the established church within England only, as well as the monarchy within
the confines of the British Isles. He wrote, "The Crown might remain as
a picturesque historical symbol, as a distinctively British institution as
local as, although much more ornamental than, the London fog." While
Stead touted how the federation would be able to accommodate parochial traditions, he revealed a distinct bitterness that the typical Englishman would not be able to conform to republican customs:

> He must be allowed to retain his plush-breeched and powdered foot-
> men, his Lord Mayor's coach, and all the paraphernalia and trappings
> of monarchy and peerage, if only to enable him to feel at home in a
> cold, cold world, and cultivate that spirit of condescension towards
> America which is his sole remaining consolation.[48]

Although it was uncommon to advocate an actual political unification of Britain and America, two men in this period who, like Stead,
called for an English-speaking federation were his friends Andrew Carnegie and Cecil Rhodes. In *The Americanization of the World*, Stead pointed
to both of these giants as supporters of the federation concept, as well
as to Lord Derby, Gladstone's colonial minister, and Hiram Maxim, a
British arms producer who was born in Maine.[49] Carnegie and Maxim
were part of a growing group of "British-Americans in Britain and
American-Britons in America" who Stead felt could be at the forefront
of efforts to reconcile the two peoples.[50]

The Scottish-born Carnegie is best known as a steel magnate and a
philanthropist, but he also involved himself in an array of political, social, and economic issues in America and in Britain, where, starting in
the late 1880s, he would spend half of each year. Stead captured the paradox of Carnegie's pronouncements when he wrote that the industrial-
ist was "a bright and shining light of the Republicans in America and of
the Radicals in England."[51] Carnegie's major intellectual manifesto was

his best-selling *Triumphant Democracy* (1886), in which he praised his adopted land to the hilt with the idea of proving the superiority of American republicanism. Carnegie presented a dizzying array of statistics to show how successful the United States had become—politically, economically, and culturally.[52] Although Stead invoked this panegyric to American democracy in his studies of the cities to point out the discrepancy between Carnegie's lofty rhetoric and the urban reality, his own *Americanization of the World* bears a strong resemblance to *Triumphant Democracy*. In his attempt to show the "Americanization" process at work, Stead, like Carnegie, wrote lavishly about the United States and employed statistics to back up his claims.

It was Carnegie's addendum to *Triumphant Democracy*, a chapter called "A Look Ahead," first published in the *North American Review* and tacked on to the revised 1893 edition of the book, that most anticipated what Stead would later write. In this piece Carnegie, who had long advocated closer Anglo-American ties and been active in the movement to bring the United States and Canada into one union, called for the kind of English-speaking federation espoused by Stead.[53] When "A Look Ahead" was released, Stead stated, "Mr. Andrew Carnegie is not exactly the supreme type of the fairy match-maker who presides over the love affairs of nations," but nevertheless he "proclaims the banns between the Republic and the Empire."[54] Stead wrote to Carnegie personally to say:

> I am delighted to see how vigorously you are pushing forward the great idea of our race. I knew, of course, that you were sound upon this great question, but that which is so great a comfort to me is to find that you, who are so practical before all things, have convinced yourself that, so far from this being a Utopian scheme of the visionary, it is the root idea which must govern the future of the two most business-like nations on this planet.[55]

The arguments put forth by Carnegie in "A Look Ahead" and by Stead in *The Americanization of the World* are strikingly similar. Both maintained that it was in Britain's best interest to tie its fortunes to the surging United States, and they stressed that an English-speaking federation would dominate the world. Carnegie and Stead both wrote that the federation would have to be a republic, and they both envisioned its capital in Washington, D.C.[56] Whether Carnegie influenced Stead, or Stead Carnegie, or whether they were moving along parallel lines and simply reinforced one another, is not crystal clear. On the face of it, the federation scheme would appear to be Carnegie's; he published "A Look Ahead" well before Stead committed himself fully to a similar concept. Stead not only quoted Carnegie in *The Americanization of the World*—and introduced similar arguments—but he paid homage to his friend by titling a chapter "A Look Ahead." Furthermore, he later wrote to Carnegie, "I am taking the liberty of sending to you a copy of the German edition of my Americanisation of the World, of which you are one of the godfathers."[57] Yet it could have been Stead who inspired Carnegie, who once called the English journalist "one of the original geniuses to whom I am attracted."[58] Carnegie may have been first in print with the federation plan, but Stead had been coyly hinting at such a possibility for years, and he reacted enthusiastically to Carnegie's article when it appeared, though without, significantly, crediting the author with any originality. Furthermore, there is a suggestive bit of evidence in a letter Stead wrote to Albert Shaw in which he said, "Carnegie's article 'Look Ahead,' he told me, was written as the result of his conversation with me."[59]

In May of 1892 Stead wrote to Carnegie, in reply to a request by the steel magnate to be introduced to Cecil Rhodes, that Rhodes had just left England for Africa but that "he would have been very glad to have met you, because his ideas are almost entirely identical with your own."[60] Stead's comment, however, was not completely accurate. Although Rhodes was, like Stead and Carnegie, committed to the idea of bringing about a reunion of the English-speaking peoples, he did not envision an American-dominated republican federation. Rhodes dreamed that the United States would be reintegrated into the British Empire and that at last the folly of George III would be erased. He wished to see the English-speaking peoples eventually united again but was wary of America, which he saw, like Germany, as a rival.[61] Rhodes was a staunch patriot and imperialist, and in fact he and Stead parted ways at the turn of the century when Stead, though an imperialist of sorts himself, vigorously opposed British participation in the Boer War.[62] However, despite his intense loyalty to the crown, Rhodes, according to Stead, once said that he would relent to accepting a virtual American annexation of Britain if that was the only way to achieve a reunion of the race. But Stead possessed no illusions about what his friend really wanted: "Mr. Rhodes would undoubtedly much prefer to see the English-speaking race unified under the Union Jack, for his devotion to the old flag approaches to a passion."[63]

The Oxford University scholarships that Rhodes endowed with the fortune he gained from diamond mining in southern Africa resulted from his great interest in establishing the unity of the English-speaking peoples, and in the creation of the Rhodes Scholarships Stead was directly involved. After Rhodes and Stead met in 1889 and became close friends, Stead was designated one of the executors in Rhodes's ever-changing will and helped to shape its contents. From the time Rhodes was a student at Oxford in the late 1870s, he had planned simply to leave his money to some amorphous, secret Jesuit-style society to carry out his imperial ideas. Although Stead himself often used the Jesuit example to describe how English-speaking solidarity could be advanced, he apparently influenced Rhodes to be more practical and direct his legacy toward education. It was in Rhodes's 1893 will that the Oxford scholarships were established—but only for subjects from the British colonies, not for Americans. Not until his final will of 1899, which he worked out with Stead's counsel, did Rhodes provide for scholarships for Americans as well.[64] Stead's son John later insisted that his father had been the one responsible for persuading Rhodes to include the Americans in his scheme.[65] Following Rhodes's death in 1902, Stead himself took credit for the idea—in his book *The Last Will and Testament of Cecil John Rhodes* as well as in a letter to Carnegie, in which he said that as for the incorporation of American scholarships in the will, "I daresay you may discern in this provision some trace of a certain friend of yours, who has never lost the opportunity of preaching the doctrine of racial unity which you have often preached so eloquently."[66] Ironically, though, when Rhodes died, Stead was to play no part in the dispersal of the legacy. In 1901 Rhodes had added a codicil to his will that reads, "On account of the extraordinary eccentricity of Mr. Stead, though always having a great respect for him, but feeling the objects of my will would be embarrassed by his views, I hereby revoke his appointment as one of my executors."[67] Rhodes apparently was referring both to Stead's controversial opposition to the Boer War and to his increasing interest in spiritualism.[68]

In his letter to Carnegie, Stead not only took credit for the inclusion of the American scholarships but revealed that he wished Rhodes had done even more to make the United States central to his plan. In describing his consultations with Rhodes, Stead wrote:

> I raised the question as to whether he ought not to have established two
> centres, one in the United States, and one in the United Kingdom, for

it is just as important in his interweaving of the English-speaking world that the youth of Great Britain, Ireland and the Colonies should be introduced to the life of democratic America in an American university, as it is that the American and Colonial youth should have three years of residence at Oxford.

Rhodes, according to Stead, saw merit in this idea but asserted that an American millionaire should be responsible for providing such scholarships. So Stead asked Carnegie whether he would like to be the one to establish a "racial centre" in the New World by endowing scholarships for Britons at an American university, such as Harvard or Cornell. Without this American counterbalance, Stead argued, clearly appealing to Carnegie's anti-imperialism, detractors could portray "Mr. Rhodes's scheme as if it were a move on the part of British Imperialism to inoculate American youth with the virus of the Jingoism of the Old World." Carnegie never took up Stead's suggestion.[69]

In *The Americanization of the World*, Stead did not merely assert that the United States was now supreme and that Britain should therefore, for its own good, commit itself to joining an American-dominated federation. He strove, in the greater part of the book, to prove his case that America had gained world preeminence. One point he made was that the United States had become so influential within the English-speaking community that Britain, if it did not opt for union, could easily find its empire disintegrating and America picking up the pieces. Or, the metaphor that he repeatedly used was that Britain was no longer the "sun" around which the English-speaking peoples revolved, and that the force of "gravitation" would "pull" them into "orbit" around America.[70]

Stead, in this book, described the variety of forms the Americanization process had taken. By "Americanization," he did not mean the spread of American popular culture, as the term later came to be used, but rather more generally the impact and influence the United States was increasingly exerting around the world. One vehicle of Americanization to which Stead pointed, curiously enough, was the American woman. He noted how many prominent European men were choosing to marry Americans. For example, four well-known British cabinet members had taken American wives—Joseph Chamberlain, William Harcourt, James Bryce, and Randolph Churchill. There was also the phenomenon of English aristocrats' marrying American heiresses, the most conspicuous example being the Duke of Marlborough's betrothal to Consuelo Vanderbilt. When such marriages took place for purely financial reasons—simply to save the noble families from ruin—then Stead called the arrangements nothing more than "gilded prostitution." He wondered whether the infusion of American wealth could slow the decline of feudalism, because there was only so much the American heiress could do to prop up the aristocracy. After all, "her fathers and her brothers, from their farms on the prairie and their factories in Chicago, ceaselessly hurl across the Atlantic vast vessels which are like projectiles laden with food-stuffs, whose effect upon the old order in the Old World may be compared to so many dynamite shells." Stead's comment was justified, for in fact American food exports were partly responsible for the English agricultural depression of the late nineteenth century, which served to weaken the landed aristocracy.[71]

Stead addressed a weightier form of Americanization when he took up the issue of the so-called "American Invasion," the expanded economic presence of the United States in Britain at the turn of the century.[72] He said that Americans had now "secured the commercial primacy of the world," and in actuality by 1900 the United States was not only agriculturally supreme but it had surpassed Britain as the greatest industrial power.[73] Stead asserted, however, that the idea of there actually being an "American Invasion" in the sense of a hostile economic behemoth's forcing itself on Britain and causing terrible harm was absurd. He wrote, "The American invasion succeeds because the American invaders are able to give the British purchaser either better or cheaper goods, so that he gets more value for his money than he would get by trading with any one else." Britons chose to buy American out of their own self-interest. He continued, "The presence of the American invaders in our midst is resented as if it were an outrage on international amity, as if the Americans bearing gifts in their hands were bent upon doing us the greatest possible injury." It was hypocritical, Stead noted, for Britons to resent aggressive American trading practices when their own country had been employing similar methods for years. Also, while his fellow countrymen seemed to be so edgy about the influx of American manufactured goods, the true cause of the trade imbalance was the heavy importation of American foodstuffs and raw materials, which he claimed were responsible for sustaining the standard of living of the average Briton. Furthermore, many of the industrial goods that the Americans exported to Britain were new products that had never been manufactured in his country: "No one can say that in sending us the typewriter, the sewing-machine, the Linotype, the automobile, the phonograph, the telephone, the elevator, and the incandescent electric light, they invaded any British industry. These things were their inventions." Stead argued, as well, that although Carnegie envisioned Britain's losing all of its manufacturing and becoming "the garden and pleasure-ground of the race," imitation of American methods was already yielding results.[74]

In asking how the United States had attained its overall position of world preeminence, Stead concluded, "There is no one secret of American success. It is due to many causes co-operating to convert the modern American into a dynamo of energy, and make him the supreme type of a strenuous life."[75] American success was attributable to the nation's bountiful resources, its diverse population, and its freedom from encumbering Old World institutions. It was also possible to point to the nation's Puritan origins and its intense concentration on industry. But Stead chose to dwell on three features of American life that Britain could emulate—the belief in widespread access to education, the attention paid to innovations in production, and, surprisingly, considering his previous works, democracy. He argued that the British were trying to catch up with the United States in education, for only recently had they recognized that schooling was important for everyone, not simply the elite. Britain also needed to place greater emphasis on improvements in manufacturing, particularly when suggested by the workers themselves. And although Britain was ahead of the United States in municipal government, his country could not be fully democratic until it did away with its House of Lords.[76]

At the end of the work, after pressing once more for an English-speaking federation and asserting that even halfway measures would be welcome, Stead, in his final chapter, adopted a very different tone. Throughout the book he had written enthusiastically about the Americanization process, at times sounding like a chamber of commerce booster, and he had aggressively touted the blessings that would fall upon the British if they would only concede to reunification with America. But in the last few pages of the book, Stead appeared to have second thoughts. He did not pull back from his federation idea, but here he stressed how much Britain could offer to the United States, which he referred to in dark, foreboding terms. He drew a portrait of an America full of frazzled, harried people driven to the edge in their mad rush to compete. He quoted a British journalist who said, "In England, you work in order to live; in America, they live only in order to work." After printing a newspaper account of the frantic scene of morning commuters heading into New York City, Stead wrote, "This is an unlovely spectacle, which seems to those of us who are not without sympathy with the strenuous life, very much like a vision of hell." Within the federation he hoped Britain could exert a soothing, tempering effect on the younger nation.[77] In hitting this negative note about America at the end, Stead was perhaps suddenly overcome by a wave of British patriotism, or perhaps his old reservations about the United States once again rose to the surface. If the latter was true, however, his criticisms took a new form; there was no railing against American corruption or defeatism. Rather, Stead sounded more like, of all people, Matthew Arnold, who had found in America a distinct lack of "sweetness and light."

In the last decade or so of his life, Stead still touched upon American affairs in the pages of the *Review of Reviews,* but he wrote no more major works focused upon the United States. It seems that his journalistic influence was somewhat diminished in his final years. Not only were there no more great coups on a par with "Maiden Tribute" or *If Christ Came to Chicago,* but Stead's controversial position on the Boer War had cost the *Review of Reviews* readers and his income became increasingly dependent on the journal's American counterpart.[78] More than ever, Stead immersed himself in spiritualism,[79] and he also worked doggedly for world peace. His last trip to America, in 1907, was made for the purpose of participating in a New York Peace Congress presided over by Andrew Carnegie.[80]

If Stead was relatively less interested in America in his final years, perhaps it was because he apparently lost some of his enthusiasm for the English-speaking peoples as a whole. In December 1903, just two years after publication of *The Americanization of the World,* Stead compared his present principles with those he had adhered to nearly fourteen years before, when he established the *Review of Reviews:*

> I believed less in mankind as a whole, and more in that particular section of it which spoke my own language. Now, it seems to me, after wider opportunities of making the acquaintance of my fellow-men in many lands, that the English-speaking man, although a very fine fellow no doubt, has by no means such a monopoly of all the virtues as that with which in those days I was wont to credit him.

Perhaps chastened by the Boer War, a less parochial Stead wrote that English-speaking man was not immune from perpetrating evil.[81]

Stead embarked on yet another journey to the United States in 1912 to address a New York religious meeting but never reached his destination. The ship he took was the *Titanic,* and at age sixty-two, Stead found his final resting place in the Atlantic Ocean between Britain and America.[82]

3

The Promise of America

H. G. Wells and the Progressive Era

By the beginning of the twentieth century, H. G. Wells had established himself as one of the most innovative young writers in the English language. In the latter half of the 1890s, through publication of such popular tales as *The Time Machine, The Invisible Man,* and *The War of the Worlds,* he had become a pioneer of a new literary genre, science fiction. In the decade after 1900 Wells devoted himself to writing satirical novels, like *Kipps* and *Tono-Bungay,* and just as important, he turned to nonfiction and inaugurated his career as a social analyst and commentator. Over the course of his life, Wells, the journalist, theorist, educator, and propagandist, would advance a distinct and relatively consistent view of the world, and among the many subjects he touched on in his writings, few received as much attention as the United States of America. Although the nation played only a peripheral role in his fiction, he was ardently interested in the United States and became one of the foremost British interpreters of the American scene.

Wells first traveled to the United States in 1906, a journey that spawned his most famous and extensive treatment of the nation, *The Future in America.* He returned in the early 1920s to report on the Washington Disarmament Conference, and then in the 1930s he made several trips to the New World. But Wells's commentary on America was not always related to a particular voyage across the Atlantic, and that commentary must be considered in the context of the set of ideas he adhered to and doggedly advanced throughout his career, to the point that he eventually sacrificed his appeal as a literary artist. Wells's views can easily be encapsulated: he wished to see the creation of a world state, a socialist world state, which he believed could be ushered into existence through greater education of the masses and the concerted efforts of talented, enlightened elites around the globe. Contrary to a widespread impression, Wells did not believe in the inevitability of progress. Influenced by his teacher Thomas Huxley, the great Darwinian popularizer, he subscribed to the notion that the evolutionary process is neutral and unpredictable, and his fiction is distinguished by dystopian as well as utopian features. But he did feel that man was capable of taking charge of his destiny and carving out a bright future.

When Wells looked toward America, he saw much that displeased him; the nation was by no means a Wellsian utopia. Yet he believed that America would lead the way to the kind of future he envisioned. This optimistic view of the United States, which endured to varying degrees until his death in 1946, he conceived in the first decade of the century, when Theodore Roosevelt was in the White House and American society was caught up in the spirit of progressive reform. Upon visiting America in these years Graham Wallas was also impressed by that spirit, but George Bernard Shaw, who conspicuously stayed away, was not.

Herbert George Wells was born in 1866 in the Kentish town of Bromley, outside of London, to Joseph and Sarah Wells, who had met when they were in service together at Up Park, a stately home in Sussex. When H. G. was born, the couple ran a china shop on the high street, but Joseph was much more interested in playing cricket and the establishment was never lucrative. Sarah was a severe evangelical woman whose aspirations for H. G. were for him to learn a trade, but the bookish young Wells was bent on pursuing his education. Wells's teenage years were marked by a struggle between mother and son, with her trying to secure him a position—he did spend two years apprenticed to a draper—and his trying to get as much schooling as possible. H. G. eventually prevailed, for he was granted a scholarship to be trained as a teacher at the Normal School of Science in South Kensington, London. But after the excitement of taking Huxley's biology course in his first year, Wells lost interest in his studies and left the school with an undistinguished record. In the following years he taught, assisted in a university-level correspondence course, and increasingly immersed himself in journalism. Then, in 1895, when he was still shy of thirty, Wells was thrust into the public eye with the enthusiastic reception of *The Time Machine*.[1]

As a child Wells developed a dislike for the monarchy and aristocracy of his native land. His mother revered Queen Victoria, but he recalled in his autobiography, "I conceived a jealous hatred for the abundant clothing, the magnificent housing and all the freedoms of her children, and still more of my contemporaries, her grandchildren." He was forced to review the queen passing in procession so frequently that, he said, it "deepened my hostility and wove a stout, ineradicable thread of republicanism into my resentful nature." While contemptuous of the traditionalist sentiments of his mother, Wells must to some extent have inherited his rebelliousness from his father, who at least in his early years felt restrained by the hierarchical society of England. Sarah would eventually opt to leave her Bromley home and shop to return to Up Park in the responsible position of housekeeper, but Joseph, when he was still in service as a gardener, had been eager to escape the country-house world and considered the possibility of emigrating to America or Australia.[2]

Although Wells's parents worked as servants, they were upper servants and thus considered members of the middle class, albeit its lowest stratum. When this literate couple sent their son H. G. to school, they scraped together the money to enroll him in a middle-class "academy" rather than relegate him to the town's national school, where the students belonged to lower-class families. Distinctly aware of his middle-class status as a youth, Wells would carry that awareness for the rest of his life. Lenin would find him hopelessly bourgeois, and Wells, by his own admission, portrayed the ideal society as a sort of giant middle class. His refusal to champion the proletariat originated in his boyhood, when he felt as much disdain for those below him on the social ladder as he felt hostility toward those above him. He believed firmly in his inherent talents and wanted nothing to do with a class of people who he thought accepted their subservient position in life. In explaining this attitude, Wells enunciated a viewpoint that has an American ring. As a boy, he wrote, he "claimed at least an initial equality with every human being; but it was equality of opportunity I was after, and not equality of respect or reward."[3]

The radical, republican views that Wells adopted in his youth dictated that he would develop some affinity for America. As a child he also became familiar with the United States through reading, for example, about the frontier, the Civil War, and one of his heroes, George Washington. Ultimately, however, his perception of America would be shaped in large part by the socialism that he first embraced in his teenage years. And it was the American reformer Henry George who, along with Plato, was principally responsible for instilling in him the socialist spirit. As a schoolboy Wells read *The Republic* and a cheap edition of George's *Progress and Poverty*, and the two books influenced him enormously.[4] Henry George, whose diagnosis of society's ills was that land was being monopolized and whose prescription was that a confiscatory tax should be placed on rents, caused a stir when he visited Britain in the early 1880s. He played a crucial role in igniting the nation's incipient socialist movement, and many pillars of the British left in the decades to come would owe to George their initial inspiration. But George was a visionary whose ideas were crude and whose break with the capitalist past was only partial, and though he incited many young British intellectuals to rethink their socioeconomic assumptions, few followed him down his particular single-tax path.[5] Wells was exposed further to the socialist point of view when he and a few of his Normal School friends, wearing the obligatory red ties, attended meetings at William Morris's Hammersmith home, Kelmscott House. Here Wells heard an array of leftist voices—the nostalgic Morris, young Fabians like George Bernard Shaw, Sidney Webb, and Graham Wallas, and the foremost British Marxist, Henry M. Hyndman. At this stage in his life, Wells was resigned simply to listen.[6]

Although he was converted to socialism during his school years, it was not until after the turn of the century, with the popular scientific romances behind him, that Wells worked out his own unique sociopolitical philosophy. He first enunciated these views in a series of articles published in the *Fortnightly Review* in 1901 and then subsequently collected in the volume entitled *Anticipations of the Reaction of Mechanical and Scientific Progress upon Human Life and Thought*. Despite the forbidding title, the book sold briskly and established Wells as an important commentator. And although his line of thinking would undergo some changes over the years, it would not veer drastically from the direction set in this work. The task he carved out for himself in *Anticipations* was to predict the course history would take during the twentieth century. In this role of prophet, one he would retain throughout his life, he both described what he believed would happen and prescribed what he hoped would happen, though the distinction was not always clearly drawn.

Wells argued that the great improvements in transportation which had taken place in the past decades, and were sure to continue, would markedly alter the way people lived. He foresaw that the densely populated cities would spread out into vast urban regions, and though his projections were inflated, he did, in fact, anticipate the remarkable growth in suburbanization and the rise of the megalopolis in the twentieth century. Looking at the global picture, he maintained that the new developments in transportation would lessen distances and thus make national boundaries obsolete and a world state inevitable. Already, he said, it was clear that existing governments were not up to the task of ushering society into the modern world, and he was as contemptuous of the Western democracies as he was of the old-fashioned despotisms. As he would throughout his life, in *Anticipations* Wells expressed his disdain for democracy, which he said was based on the flawed assumption that the masses were capable of charting the course for the ship of state. From the growing scientifically trained sector of the middle class, he hoped, would arise a select group of men prepared to assume the helm of the world state, and he dubbed this global movement that would come to be the "new republic."

Over the next four decades, though he would rename the movement and change his mind about who should comprise its membership, Wells never departed from his notion of a cadre of elites leading the way to the world state. In *Anticipations* he stressed that these rational, enlightened figures would start to interact and discuss their progressive views of society—such as establishing a collectivist economy—but he felt their time to take control would most likely come when the existing national governments bumbled into a sophisticated modern war they would not be able to control. There would be no bloody revolution—simply a natural shift in power. Wells elaborated on the main points of *Anticipations* in his next series for the *Fortnightly*, which ran in 1902–1903 and was published as *Mankind in the Making*. In this sequel, which never pleased the author and failed to make the public splash that *Anticipations* did, Wells concentrated on the improvements that would, or should, come about in raising and educating children.

In *Anticipations*, and even more in *Mankind in the Making*, Wells revealed that although he had never been to America, he had developed some definite ideas about it. First of all, he believed that the United States was more technologically and economically advanced than Britain and would more rapidly become the kind of society he envisioned.

For example, he forecast that by 1910 America, as well as Germany, would already possess thousands of miles of the new roads necessary for the automotive age. He predicted that by the end of the century, greater London's population would surpass twenty million but that New York, Chicago, and Philadelphia would each top forty million. The United States, he also contended, was pointing the way for the rest of the world in lacking a servant class, a reality that was already benefiting the nation in spurring labor-saving technological innovations. As for the widely deplored American trust, he asserted it should in fact be welcomed as a progressive development that would be copied elsewhere.[7]

Although American society may have been moving with greater speed into a new, modern era, Wells argued that the United States was woefully unprepared for that era. American political institutions, like those of other countries, were inadequate to the challenges of the years ahead. In *Anticipations* he wrote:

> The United States, for example, the social mass which has perhaps advanced furthest along the new lines, struggles in the iron bonds of a constitution that is based primarily on a conception of a number of comparatively small, internally homogeneous, agricultural states, a bunch of pre-Johannesburg Transvaals, communicating little, and each constituting a separate, autonomous democracy of free farmers— slave-holding or slaveless.

Not only was American government, in Wells's eyes, based on an antiquated document, but he judged it to be the most thoroughly democratic government in the world, and because of his revulsion from democracy, such an assessment was an indictment. He believed that in a democracy, power tended to gravitate to one of two poles—the central party machine, controlled by the nation's wealth, or the ignorant voting mass. In America, he stated, there was already evidence that the political process was dominated by financiers and bosses.[8]

In *Mankind in the Making* Wells devoted several pages to a discussion of the contrast between the British and American political systems. While dissatisfied with the monarchical, aristocratic government of his own nation, he was not prepared to embrace American democracy as the alternative: "it does not follow that because one condemns the obvious shams of the British system that one must accept the shams of the United States." If the British model was marred by rigidity, the political structure in America was erected on a faulty foundation—the idea that all men are equal. In Wells's mind there was no need to choose between the British and American paths; there was a better way.[9]

Wells conceded one key advantage of the American system over the British: "equality of opportunity." He succinctly expressed his sentiments on this matter when he wrote, "In America 'presumption' is not a sin." But he maintained that this was the sole merit of which Americans could boast, because in other respects their political life was deficient. The American belief that all men should not only be afforded equality of opportunity but be viewed as equal in their capacities had permitted all sorts of "fools" to take center stage:

> One gets an impression that the sort of mind that is passively stupid in England is often actively silly in America, and, as a consequence, American newspapers, American discussions, American social affairs are pervaded by a din that in England we do not hear and do not want to hear.

According to Wells, the egalitarian ethos of the United States had led to a pervasive mediocrity, which was the source of religious fads and, even more significant, of rampant political corruption.[10]

Over the years, Wells contended, America's unique sociopolitical environment had shaped an American personality distinct from its British progenitor — "a type less deliberate and thorough in execution and more noisy and pushful in conduct, restless rather than indefatigable, and smart rather than wise." In Wells's eyes it was as difficult to succeed in the United States as in his own restrictive country: "The Englishman grows up into a world of barriers and locked doors, the American into an unorganized, struggling crowd." To get ahead, the American needed to be forceful, even rough, and it was also necessary for him to be conspicuous, to "advertise himself . . . as if he were a pill." Wells asserted that in the United States those who performed the most lucrative work were the most respected, but no one was singled out for special distinction. Actually, he felt that talent was accorded greater recognition in Britain, because even though the well-born garnered the bulk of the honors, and possessed the bulk of the power, this class at least felt responsible for making a place for the nation's brightest and most promising individuals. In America such worthy figures were forced to try to gain the attention of the crowd.[11]

Although a severe critic of America, Wells, like Stead, believed that the British Empire and the United States should be joined in an

English-speaking federation. His position, however, was not identical to Stead's. For Wells such a federation was not an end in itself but merely a halfway measure toward the ultimate goal of a world state; he saw similar federations arising on the continent of Europe and in Asia. Wells was not particularly chauvinistic about English-speaking civilization; in fact, in *Anticipations*, he pointed to the superior intellectual attainments of the French and Germans. Furthermore, whereas Stead envisioned an English-speaking federation as essentially an extended America, Wells was adamant that such a union would have to depart from both the British and American models.[12]

Nevertheless, to a large degree Wells's sympathies on this subject echoed Stead's. He felt that a natural bond existed between the British and American peoples and saw the irony in being a subject of an empire that compelled him to "hail as my fellow-subjects and collaborators in man-making a host of Tamil-speaking, Tamil-thinking Dravadians, while separating me from every English-speaking, English-thinking person who lives south of the Great Lakes." And although Wells did not envision an English-speaking federation constructed on American principles, the United States would be the dominant force in the arrangement:

> The head and centre of the new unity will be the great urban region that is developing between Chicago and the Atlantic and which will lie mainly, but not entirely, south of the St. Lawrence. Inevitably, I think, that region must become the intellectual, political, and industrial centre of any permanent unification of the English-speaking states.

Wells recognized that the United States had surpassed Britain economically and believed that military supremacy would follow. He was gratified by existing Anglo-American social and cultural contacts, even if mainly confined to the upper classes, because he viewed this interaction as a foundation for an English-speaking synthesis and the "new republic" that would usher in a world state.[13]

After *Anticipations* and *Mankind in the Making*, Wells rounded out what he considered a trilogy with his fictional *Modern Utopia* (1904). His outlook on future world prospects in this book was consistent with his previous works, though the elite "new republicans" were now called the "Samurai." The format of the novel, a dialogue between two mountain climbers who find themselves ascending into another place and time, was inspired by an alpine hiking trip that Wells had recently made with his friend Graham Wallas. It was through Wallas that Wells was introduced to the Webbs and Shaw, who were eager to take him up after he had made such a brilliant showing with *Anticipations*. The Fabian leadership was interested in harnessing Wells's talents for the cause, and he was flattered to be moving in the rarefied circle of the Webbs, who gathered around their dinner table Britain's most illustrious statesmen, including Herbert Asquith, Arthur Balfour, and Winston Churchill. Wells, however, turned out to be a Fabian gadfly, and in 1906 he challenged the Old Gang's hold over the movement. In his eyes the Fabians were too exclusive and too methodical; he wished to broaden the movement and make it more aggressive. The Fabians, he felt, had the potential to become the "Samurai" of which he dreamed.[14]

Although he drew considerable support, Wells lost the fight to transform the Fabian Society; he was no match, when it came to politics, for the crafty Shaw. Eventually, he renounced the Fabian movement, and his relations with the Webbs and Shaw would be rocky for decades to come.[15] It was in the midst of this 1906 Fabian struggle, with the outcome unresolved, that Wells made his first trip to America. Why he decided to travel to the United States at this time is not entirely clear. As a rising young literary star, he naturally would have wanted to follow in the footsteps of the great British writers of the past who had journeyed across the ocean and set down their impressions. It seems, also, that Wells was concerned with solidifying his American reputation. A perpetual self-promoter who hounded his publishers and agents, he admonished his agent, James Brand Pinker, in 1902, "You have got to make the American who doesn't know all about me feel like an ignorant ass."[16] The trip may have provided an escape valve for Wells, who was not only facing difficulties in getting his way with the Fabians, but was also being taken to task by his long-suffering wife, Jane, for neglecting her and their two boys.[17] Yet it seems likely that despite his troubles Wells sailed to America in a confident mood: he was at the height of his artistic powers; his pronouncements on society and politics were being taken seriously; and there was the scent of change and reform in the air. Just before he embarked on his voyage, years of Tory domination had officially come to an end with the Liberal landslide of 1906, an election that also saw a significant number of seats going to the inchoate Labour Party. And in the United States, to which Wells was destined, the political climate was also in flux.

Before Wells even embarked for the New World aboard the Cunard liner *Carmania* on March 27, 1906, he wrote the first of the series of articles on the United States that would be published in *Harper's Weekly* and the *London Tribune* and then collected in the volume entitled *The Future in America: A Search after Realities.* In this piece, which became chapter one of his book under the heading "The Prophetic Habit of Mind," Wells explained that he was visiting America to attempt to discern what the future held in store there. "I wouldn't for the world go to see the United States for what they are," he said, and "if I had sound reason for supposing that the entire western hemisphere was to be destroyed next Christmas, I should not, I think, be among the multitude that would rush for one last look at that great spectacle."[18]

In resolving to dwell on the future in his examination of America, Wells was adhering to the formula that he had exploited so successfully over the previous decade. From his scientific romances of the late 1890s to such speculative works as *Anticipations,* Wells's perspective was future-oriented.[19] In *The Future in America* he promised to place his prophesying onto an entirely new plateau. He discussed how his thinking about the future had evolved from the wild exaggerations incorporated in such stories as *The Time Machine* to the reasoned, scientific approach of *Anticipations* and how, with *The Future in America,* he had entered a final, mature phase. Now, Wells claimed, he was more cognizant of the force and unpredictability of man's will and had adopted an approach that was "critical, literary, even if you will—artistic." He wanted to explain this transformation in his assumptions to "disabuse" his reader of "the idea that in writing of the Future of America I'm going to write of houses a hundred stories high and flying-machines in warfare and things like that." In fact, he elaborated, "I am not going to America to work a pretentious horoscope, to discover a Destiny, but to find out what I can of what must needs make that Destiny,—a great nation's Will."[20]

Because of his reputation as a prophet, and because of the implications of the title *The Future in America,* Wells was wise to clarify his intentions. His book is no futuristic fantasy, nor even a compilation of predictions. Although concerned with where America was heading, he essentially addressed himself to where the nation stood as of 1906. He wished to discover "what, in short, there is in America, over and above the mere mechanical consequences of scattering multitudes of energetic Europeans athwart a vast healthy, productive and practically empty continent in the temperate zone."[21]

Anticipating the question of why he would focus on America rather than Britain, Wells stated that in the past he had found it difficult to be a detached observer of his own country. Besides, looking at America was a way of obtaining a perspective on Britain: "One comes to America at last, not only with the idea of seeing America, but with something more than an incidental hope of getting one's own England there in the distance and as a whole, for the first time in one's life." Wells also contended that it would be easier to get a fix on America than on Britain, because the United States was not a far-flung empire entangled in global politics. He believed it important for the British to be knowledgeable about the United States, for "our future is extraordinarily bound up in America's and in a sense dependent upon it." In a break from the position he had staked out in *Anticipations,* Wells suggested that a political reunion of the two nations would, for the foreseeable future, be unlikely; Britain's imperial difficulties were too great to expect the United States to share the burden. Nevertheless, he maintained that the British and the Americans would still form a common civilization, in which the Americans would increasingly be the dominant force. Wells said that he possessed a special feeling for the United States because if his father's plans to emigrate had not been dashed, he would have been born an American.[22]

In the chapter he wrote aboard the *Carmania* as the ship steamed toward New York, Wells argued that Americans felt assured of their nation's future success but had no conception of the kind of nation America should be. They possessed a sense of "national destiny," but not of "national purpose." In his reading on America, Wells said, "I haven't found anything like an idea." However, when Americans insisted on the greatness of the United States, although he found such assertions "a little undignified" and "a little overbearing," he could not disagree. He stated, "There are, one must admit, tremendous justifications for the belief in a sort of automatic ascent of American things to unprecedented magnificences, an ascent so automatic that indeed one needn't bother in the slightest to keep the whole thing going." But he warned that progress was not inevitable and that Americans were even more guilty than Europeans of deluding themselves that it was.[23]

When Wells arrived in the United States, he saw that the nation was indeed undergoing the kind of tremendous growth of which Americans boasted, though with mixed results. The towering skyscrapers and bustling activity of New York so overwhelmed him that on his first day in the city he experienced a kind of culture shock. He felt in New York a sense "of mechanical, of inhuman, growth." Although Wells found that Boston was planning its expansion, Chicago appeared to him to be growing chaotically, and he described the city as "undisciplined."[24]

Not only was Wells disturbed by the nature of the growth he observed in the United States, but he believed other problems loomed large
enough to call the nation's future into question. One of these was unrestricted immigration. His severe attitude toward the new immigrants
was first revealed when he wrote about the steerage-class passengers on
the *Carmania*, with their "hook-noses, shifty eyes, and indisputably dirty
habits." Like Stead he believed that the tide of immigration sweeping
into America posed a threat, that the nation could not possibly assimi-
late all of the newcomers, particularly since they now mainly hailed
from the alien peasant cultures of eastern and southern Europe. The
new immigrants were being lured to America merely to man the nation's
great industrial machine, as slaves were once brought over to work in the
fields, and he saw the prospect of the newcomers' coalescing into a distinct proletarian class.[25]

Another problem Wells saw in American society was the "fierce intolerance," the "quality of harshness" that would periodically rear its
ugly head. He was at a loss to explain this streak in the American character but was inclined to believe that it resulted from the nation's concentration on business. And related to this harshness was "a contempt for
abstract justice that one does not find in any European intelligence—not
even among the English." To illustrate his point, Wells described the
cases of two foreigners who he felt had been treated brutally in America.
One was William MacQueen, a radical who had recently immigrated
from Britain and played a minor leadership role in a 1902 Paterson, New
Jersey, silkworkers' strike that, despite his wishes, had turned violent.
MacQueen was arrested, and, according to Wells, the press inaccurately
portrayed him as a violent anarchist; he was subsequently tried and sen-
tenced to five years' imprisonment. Wells took up MacQueen's case—
he even visited the self-educated young workingman in his Trenton jail
cell—and was shocked that the Americans with whom he discussed the
matter felt no outrage over what he perceived to be a miscarriage of justice.[26] Wells's other example of a foreigner handed a raw deal in America
involved a great public figure, the Russian writer Maxim Gorky, who was
in New York at the same time as Wells to publicize the oppression in his
native land. Wells witnessed the tumultuous welcome that Gorky was
given, but the warm embrace would be short-lived. When it emerged that
Gorky's longtime companion was not legally his wife, the press mounted
a moral campaign against the couple, who soon could not even find a
hotel that would accommodate them. Wells was sickened that as Gorky

and his companion traveled about the country, they were ostracized and maligned, while the cause of Russian freedom was forgotten.[27]

MacQueen and Gorky were both outsiders in America, one a recent immigrant and the other a visitor, but Wells also pointed to the harshness that constantly confronted a native-born citizen, the black educator Booker T. Washington. Wells was sympathetic to the plight of blacks in the United States and likened the racism of white Americans to the narrow-mindedness often found in the British colonies. But in defending African Americans, Wells revealed that he himself subscribed to condescending racial stereotypes, as he referred to the black man's "indolence" and "slightly exaggerated vanity." Furthermore, he manifested that he too could resort to bigotry, as he argued that blacks, whatever their failings, certainly were preferable to the sharp, money-grasping Jews.[28]

Wells believed the problems of immigration and intolerance to be significant, but more central to his thesis was his conviction that the essential tenets that had guided the development of American civilization were faulty and that the society was as a consequence now confronting serious trouble. There existed, he maintained, something called "the American Idea," an idea that was distinctly the product of the middle class and of the eighteenth century. To understand the uniqueness of the United States, Wells asserted that it was crucial to comprehend that American society was, and always had been, essentially a middle-class society. There was no peasantry in America, with the possible exception of rural blacks tied to the soil, and no vast pool of servants, and on the other hand no aristocracy was evident, not even in the South:

> The American community, one cannot too clearly insist, does not correspond to an entire European community at all, but only to the middle masses of it, to the trading and manufacturing class between the dimensions of the magnate and the clerk and skilled artisan. It is the central part of the European organism without either the dreaming head or the subjugated feet.[29]

As important as the social composition of America, Wells maintained, was the era in which the nation was born. Though Britain was still tied to its medieval and Renaissance heritage, he asserted, "America is pure eighteenth century." The men who forged the new nation "took the economic conventions that were modern and progressive at the end of the 1700s and stamped them into the Constitution as if they meant to stamp them there for all time."[30]

In Wells's view, however, the assumptions underlying this liberal, individualistic economic philosophy were flawed. The idea of equal competition was a myth; inevitably wealth accumulated in the hands of a few, who then maintained an insuperable advantage. Such an evolution, he wrote, had already taken place in northern England, and now, "America is simply repeating the history of the Lancashire industrialism on a gigantic scale, and under an enormous variety of forms." At least, however, the process had been softened in the semi-feudal atmosphere of England, where, according to Wells, rising industrialists were eager to be accepted by the aristocracy and would adopt its paternalistic, duty-bound values. But in America there was no comparable class to set such standards, and the economic process was stark and unforgiving. There was a widening gap between a rich and civically irresponsible class and the mass of workers who knew they possessed no real chance to make a mark.[31]

The most conspicuous of the wealthy American class, Wells wrote, was that small group of men who had built up huge industrial enterprises. These successful figures "have found in America the perfectly favorable environment for their temperaments. In no other country and in no other age could they have risen to such eminence." These captains of industry had been attacked for their unscrupulous behavior, but Wells found that such criticisms rang hollow. He believed that these individuals had played the same competitive, cut-throat American game everyone else had; they had simply played it better and come out winners. They were not bad men, as any examination of John D. Rockefeller's upright Baptist upbringing would reveal; they were simply the quintessential products of a distorted American environment. Wells stated:

> It's the game that is criminal. It is ridiculous, I say, to write of these men as though they were unparalleled villains, intellectual overmen, conscienceless conquerors of the world. Mr. J. D. Rockefeller's mild, thin-lipped, pleasant face gives the lie to all such melodramatic nonsense.[32]

The liberal, individualistic philosophy that underpinned American society had led not only to a great disparity in wealth, but also, Wells asserted, to a disregard for the commonweal. As he put it, there was no "sense of the state."[33] Wells nevertheless was optimistic about the future of the nation. He saw signs that America had become aware of its problems and was beginning to confront them. The steady concentration of wealth, he wrote, "has become the cardinal type of thought and discussion in the American mind." And for Americans to acknowledge that their system was not working as originally conceived he believed signified nothing less than "a national change of attitude." He hailed the antitrust sentiment whipped up by Ida Tarbell through her revelations about Standard Oil and by Upton Sinclair through his exposé of the meat-packing industry in *The Jungle* (1906).[34]

Muckraking, left-leaning writers like Tarbell and Sinclair stood for Wells as a new breed of American hero because they were awakening the nation to stark reality and prompting a search for solutions. Wells believed, for example, that one of the most tragic consequences of the individualistic, laissez-faire American economy was the prevalence of child labor. In his own nation, he wrote, this scandalous practice had been confronted decades before. But when the sight of an eleven-year-old messenger boy on a New York subway at two in the morning incited Wells to explore the issue of child labor in the United States, he found that at least there existed a significant body of literature on this form of human exploitation. In *The Future in America* he quoted from John Spargo's *Bitter Cry of the Children* (1906) and stated that Robert Hunter's *Poverty* (1904) "should be compulsory reading for every prosperous adult in the United States."[35]

Another manifestation of what he believed to be the fertility of the American mind Wells found in the universities. While in the United States he visited Harvard, Columbia, and the University of Chicago, each "already larger, wealthier, and more hopeful than any contemporary British institution." But more than the magnificence of the facilities, Wells was impressed by many of the professors who taught at these universities and the direction in which they were taking their research: "In sociology, in pedagogics, in social psychology, these vital sciences for the modern state, America is producing an amount of work which, however trivial in proportion to the task before her, is at any rate immense in comparison with our own British output." He did not believe the American university to be flawless—as at Oxford, too much money was spent on lavish building and too much time spent on studying Greek—yet he was convinced that the state of higher education in the United States boded well for the nation.[36]

While gratified by the thoughtful, iconoclastic investigation he found underway at American universities, Wells was disappointed to discover that Washington, D.C., though the seat of government and a center for scientific inquiry, lacked "a teeming intellectual life." There was no ex-change of ideas in the capital—at least nothing beyond the genteel con-versation that filled the finely appointed homes of the city's northwest section.[37] The legions of scientists all confined themselves to their own narrow specialties, and the city could not boast of one important jour-nal or publishing house. But worst of all, when Wells set his sights on Capitol Hill, he observed a Congress that he deemed incoherent and ineffective.[38]

Yet Wells saw one ray of hope as he surveyed the capital—in the man who occupied the White House, Theodore Roosevelt. Like the muckrak-ers and the social scientists, President Roosevelt stood for Wells as the embodiment of a new American spirit. Wells gained the opportunity to talk with Roosevelt when he was invited to the White House for a private luncheon, apparently arranged by Lincoln Steffens.[39] He came away with an overwhelmingly favorable impression of the president, who had transcended the "Teddy Roosevelt" of myth and become a mature leader constantly "thinking and changing and growing." Roosevelt was a man with an "extraordinarily open" mind who read widely, but, Wells wrote, "he does not merely receive, he digests and reconstructs; he thinks." In Wells's opinion the Roosevelt presidency broke the mold, and of contemporary American politicians he believed that perhaps only William Jennings Bryan shared Roosevelt's insights. Roosevelt was an "extraordinarily representative" figure who could be seen as "Amer-ica for the first time vocal to itself." Wells believed that the president, like the nation he led, was groping for answers, and although Roosevelt would not have used the terminology, he was heading toward a socialis-tic solution:

> The trend is altogether away from the anarchistic individualism of the nineteenth century, that much is sure, and towards some constructive scheme which, if not exactly socialism, as socialism is defined, will be, at any rate, closely analogous to socialism. This is the immense change of thought and attitude in which President Roosevelt participates, and to which he gives a unique expression.

As Wells and Roosevelt walked about the White House grounds, they dis-cussed America's fate. The president said that he could not be sure what the future held for America but that he chose to think optimistically.[40]

In *The Future in America* Wells indicated that he too was sanguine about the nation's prospects. But in the final passages of the book, written after he had returned to England, Wells revealed that he was not as confident that America would overcome its problems as when he had been traveling around the country. He admitted that he had been caught up by the headiness of the national spirit. Yet, despite some second thoughts, he still believed that the intelligence and creativity he found in the United States would prevail. The problems facing America were not unique; nor was it the only nation showing signs that it could conquer such problems. But he asserted, "In spite of my patriotic inclinations, in spite, too, of the present high intelligence and efficiency of Germany, it seems to me that in America, by sheer virtue of its size, its free traditions, and the habit of initiative in its people, the leadership of progress must ultimately rest."[41]

Wells's enthusiasm for America was an enthusiasm for "progressive" America. The nation he encountered was in certain respects significantly different from the one Stead had seen in the 1890s. It is difficult to say when the progressive era actually began in the United States, although 1900 usually serves as a rough approximation, and defining progressivism can be problematical, since so-called progressives differed in their goals and objectives. Yet despite the fact that progressivism was not cohesive or monolithic, and that historians have diverged greatly in their interpretations of the movement, the term need not be cast aside. There was undeniably an upsurge of reform activity in the first two decades of the twentieth century, and it can be said, if nothing else, that progressives were figures who questioned the political, economic, and social assumptions that had prevailed in late-nineteenth-century America. Many wished to see a greater role for government and wider political participation. The trust caused virtually all of them great concern, and they advocated that these corporate entities be broken up or, alternatively, regulated more closely. They emphasized the need for creating a more efficient society or perhaps for establishing a greater sense of community. Each progressive set his or her own priorities and agenda, but each believed that reform was imperative.[42]

Although Wells tended to be more radical than the American progressives, he shared with them a dissatisfaction with the status quo and a yearning for positive, constructive change. There were parallels between the political developments sweeping Britain and the United States in these years, and reformers in each country were cognizant of their counterparts in the other. American progressives, especially, were influenced by British thought and experience.[43] That Wells came away impressed by what he saw as significant stirrings in the United States should be viewed in the context of this Anglo-American interaction. The comparison he implicitly drew between the two countries worked to the disadvantage of his own, for he apparently believed that the Americans were showing signs of surging ahead of the British in the task of reconstructing society. His difficulties in trying to prevail over Shaw and the Webbs had probably already dampened his enthusiasm for Fabianism, while his antiproletarian bent prevented him from extolling the rise of Labour. The New Liberals who came to power in 1906 bore a certain resemblance to the American progressives—they were, if anything, more advanced in their views—yet Wells would never display the fondness for them that he did for their kindred spirits across the ocean. His failure to pay homage to the Liberals was, it seems, at least partly attributable to class resentment and to contempt bred by familiarity.[44] In America Wells found what he could not—or perhaps would not—see in Britain.

In Theodore Roosevelt, Wells was embracing the nation's foremost exemplar, at least as of 1906, of progressivism. Roosevelt's brand, which emphasized a powerful state as regulator of the new corporate conglomerations, struck a responsive chord in Wells. In paying homage to the muckraking journalists and the social scientists, he was recognizing figures who played a prominent role in the progressive movement but often went even further and advocated socialism, though the line between progressivism and socialism could be a hazy one. This cast of characters— from the conservative progressive Roosevelt to the muckraking socialist Sinclair—contributed to shaping Wells's vision of America. Although he observed the nation with his own eyes, he had steeped himself before arrival in the utterances of these figures. Their frank revelations predisposed him to draw a more scathing portrait of America than he might otherwise have produced. Yet, it was the understanding that these people had shown of the nation's problems and of the measures needed to overcome them, as well as the receptivity of the general population to such thinking, that made him hopeful for America. To Wells, America was a far cry from a utopia, but it seems he found in the journalists and social scientists, and in the president of the United States, the elite "Samurai" that had eluded him in Britain. These Americans were the kind of bright, talented, forward-looking individuals whom Wells expected to take the lead in ushering in a new civilization.

Reaction to *The Future in America* was mixed—both in Britain and America. Responses ranged from hailing the book as a tour de force to condemning it as a colossal disappointment. There was no agreement as to whether Wells's view of America was positive or negative, or whether a tour of less than two months, which had taken him only as far west as Chicago and as far south as Washington, D.C., was sufficient for the drawing of general conclusions. Two prominent American weeklies published notices that were mainly favorable but pointed to the undue influence that leftist, sensationalist journalists had exerted on the author. The reviewer for *Harper's Weekly* wrote that Wells had "fallen under the spell of the muck-rake" but that his book was nevertheless "extraordinarily keen, searching, and suggestive." The *Nation*'s critic found the influence to be more deleterious. He argued that Wells, on his American visit, was not merely another traveler but an important social analyst and that in his book he had "struck some nails on the head that have, perhaps, never been struck before—at least with so emphatic a hammer." Yet the work was flawed, because Wells too often drew grand conclusions from insufficient evidence. He naively absorbed what others told him, and—in an apparent reference to the muckrakers—"it is obvious that the wrong men have sometimes got hold of his ear." The *Nation*'s critic concluded that although *The Future in America* was "one of the keenest and most brilliant works ever published about the United States," those who did not already possess a firm knowledge of the nation—namely foreigners—would be better off consulting the more balanced, judicious volumes of Bryce.[45]

Among the most enthusiastic letters that Wells received in response to *The Future in America* were those from the journalists and academics he had made the heroes of his book. Lincoln Steffens told Wells that in his diagnosis of "state-blindness," he had put his "finger on the spot" and that every American should read his work. In his generous letter, Steffens stated, "You have assembled and understood all I know and interpreted it for me." Robert Hunter, author of *Poverty*, was not so self-effacing. Though he called *The Future in America* "a rattling good book" and believed it "extraordinary" that Wells "could have got so comprehensive a view of the situation in so short a time," Hunter expressed some disappointment that he and his endeavors were not featured more prominently. However, he gave credit to Wells for capturing the "new spirit" pervading the country, which he called essentially socialistic.[46]

Two of America's foremost social scientists weighed in with highly laudatory comments. Franklin Giddings, who had shown Wells around Columbia, wrote of *The Future in America*, "As a general sociological description of the essentials of a big national society this study is immeasurably the best thing that has ever been done by anybody." In a letter written in the spring of 1908, Lester Ward complimented Wells for his reflections on America, and for his other nonfiction writings of the past decade, and stated, "Although you call yourself a socialist and not a sociologist, and I call myself a sociologist and not a socialist, the difference between us is certainly very small, and I find less to condemn and more to approve than I find in most self-styled sociologists."[47]

Norman Hapgood, the progressive editor of *Collier's*, wrote to Wells that he had enjoyed *The Future in America* but nevertheless commented that John Graham Brooks would have served as "a better-informed and less hysterical authority on poverty in the United States than Hunter." Although Wells may not have drawn on his work, Brooks, a Massachusetts-based reformer and social investigator, did endorse *The Future in America*. In a 1908 letter he told Wells, "It has been one of my vocations to make people read it who need it." That same year Brooks published *As Others See Us: A Study of Progress in the United States*, a pioneering work in the interpretation of foreign views of America. He devoted an entire chapter to Wells, whose socialist critique of America he believed useful because it was measured and insightful, rather than polemical or dogmatic. Brooks, who was a progressive but not a socialist, could appreciate Wells's particular brand of socialism and related with relish that when Wells had seen in the register of a Boston club, "Yours for the Revolution, Jack London," he in turn signed, "There ain't going to be no revolution, H. G. Wells."[48]

In his 1908 letter to Wells, Brooks stated that he was not alone in championing *The Future in America*: "My next door neighbor James has helped mightily in this propaganda." The James to whom Brooks referred was William James, whose ideas were so influential among the progressives. He was not in Cambridge when Wells visited in 1906, but Wells had already met him in England through his brother Henry and forged a strong friendship. William James was ecstatic about *The Future in America*. Even before the book was published, he wrote to Wells to praise him for the excerpt he had read in *Harper's Weekly*, the "Two Studies in Disappointment" dealing with Gorky and the radical MacQueen: "Exactly that callousness to abstract justice is *the* sinister feature and, to me as well as to you, the incomprehensible feature, of our U.S. civilization." He predicted, "You will have undoubtedly written *the* medicinal book about America." When the volume was released, James told Wells, "The 'America' will start up a lot of thinking in brains capable of it, which will eventually take effect, and on the whole, with its tact & brilliancy to boot, is as good a service as a foreigner has ever performed." In this same letter James dubbed Wells his philosophical kinsman when he exclaimed, "You're a *pragmatist!*" And in 1908 he suggested that Wells spend a year or two in America, perhaps in California, to gain further insights into the "future."[49]

While William James may have sung the praises of *The Future in America*, his brother sounded a few discordant notes. When Wells was a rising young writer in the 1890s, Henry had taken an interest in his career. In the first decade of the century, after Wells built Spade House on the southern coast at Sandgate, he lived close to James, whose Lamb House was in Rye, and they both belonged to a Sussex literary set that included Joseph Conrad, Stephen Crane, and Ford Madox Heuffer (Ford). Henry James, as senior member of this set, was in a sense also the master. Although James thought highly of Wells's satirical novels and their relations were ostensibly friendly, Wells resented James. In part, the resentment was social; Wells was a rebellious cockney upstart while James was a haughty, proper patrician. In part, the friction resulted from conflicting views about the purpose of literature. Unlike James, the quintessential artist, Wells considered himself primarily a journalist, not a novelist, and believed that the raison d'etre of his fiction, which he would produce in great volume, was to communicate certain social and political ideas. His interest was in propaganda—not art. Wells, nevertheless, was indisputably creative, and the artistic sensibilities he revealed in novels like *Kipps* (1905) impressed Henry James. But James could not forbear from lecturing Wells on what he considered the younger writer's literary sins, particularly after Wells started to publish such controversial works as *Ann Veronica* (1909) and *The New Machiavelli* (1911). Wells bristled at James's criticisms, and when they were compounded by what he perceived as a public slight to his reputation, he struck back with a vengeance. In his 1915 novel, *Boon*, he mercilessly mocked and parodied James, and so the wounded master called an end to their strained friendship.[50]

The correspondence between Wells and James over *The Future in America* and James's own *American Scene* constituted one contentious episode in the prickly relationship between these two very different men. *The American Scene* was released in 1907, a year after *The Future in America*, and by the same publishers—Chapman and Hall in Britain and Harpers in the United States. James, however, made the tour that inspired his volume in 1904–1905, and so when Wells wrote his book, he was aware of, and quoted from, certain impressions that James had already published. James's perspective on the United States was unique; he had been living in England for three decades, with the exception of a couple of years spent back in the States in the early 1880s, but he was still an American. Although he had made England his home, he toured the United States not as an Englishman visiting a foreign country but as an expatriate returning to the land where he was born and raised and first made his mark as a writer, a land to which he was connected by family ties, friendships, and associations with the past. Even if he chose to live in England, that the leitmotif of his fiction was the clash between American and European cultures revealed he had not forgotten his heritage.

The United States through which James traveled in 1904–1905 was a more opulent, urbanized, and heterogeneous country than he had remembered, and the tremendous changes left him feeling uneasy. The ephemeral quality of American civilization—the propensity, for example, to tear down old homes and churches to erect skyscrapers—offended him; he preferred the familiar, unchanging surroundings of the Old World. The resulting *American Scene* could hardly have been more different from *The Future in America*. Some of the authors' concerns were similar—the surge of immigration, the rampant commercialism—but their approaches were diametrically opposite. Whereas Wells tackled broad issues and laid out a clear, coherent argument, James recorded the impressions he gleaned as he observed and experienced America once again. James offered colorful descriptions of what he saw, as well as his personal responses and inner thoughts, and the text is marked by the same elaborate, opaque style as his later fiction.[51] James Fullarton Muirhead, a Scotsman who had toured the United States for Baedeker and published *The Land of Contrasts: A Briton's View of his American Kin* (1898), compared these two writers' treatments of America:

> Mr. Wells's direct and confident vision, focused solely on points of vivid interest to himself, is apt to appeal to us at once as either right or wrong; while Mr. James's greater subtlety and tremulous responsiveness to every evasive and nebulous suggestion often leave him and his readers alike in a dim region of surprise and uncertainty.[52]

James's analysis of *The Future in America* contained that combination of effusive praise and penetrating criticism that was characteristic of his treatment of Wells. After James had read the book, he wrote to Wells, "I have done nothing today but thrill and squirm with it and vibrate to it almost feverishly and weep over it almost profusely (this last, I mean, for intensity of mere emotion and interest)." He said that he was "wonder-stricken" by how Wells, based on such a brief association with America, could have written such a powerful and perceptive book. But subtly interlaced with the compliments were some undeniable put-downs. While James believed the book was a tour de force, he wrote, apparently with mixed feelings, that it revealed Wells's "sublime and heroic cheek." Furthermore, although James admitted that he himself was prone to "complicate" things, he felt Wells was guilty of the tendency to "simplify." And while he was fascinated with the ideas Wells presented, he said, "I think you, frankly,—or think the whole thing—too *loud,* as if the country shouted at you, hurrying past, every hint it had to give and you yelled back your comment on it." James did concede that yelling was often necessary in America and, in fact, anticipating the release of his own book, wrote that he feared his own "semitones" would not be heard. James also could not help pointing out—even if he did not mean it as blatant criticism—that while Wells concentrated on the future, he had found the present enough to tackle and was surprised to find nothing of the past in Wells's book.[53]

When *The American Scene* was published, Wells got his turn to be the critic, and he too adopted a bittersweet attitude. Wells told James he appreciated the vivid portraits of the American landscape: "The things are so completely done, the atmospheres return, elucidated." He noted that James approached the subject from the "opposite pole" from him, for *The American Scene* was "a criticism of life and manners," which had received only peripheral attention in *The Future in America*. Wells's main reservation about *The American Scene* was that, while he had found the critique illuminating, he realized he was not the typical reader. He implied that the book was too subtle and complicated for the general public when he left James with one final, trenchant question: "How much will they get out of what you have got in?"[54]

A year after Wells published *The Future in America*, his primary antagonist in the Fabian Society struggle, George Bernard Shaw, published his ideas on America in an article entitled "A Nation of Villagers." Whereas

Wells had viewed the United States as a black cloud with a silver lining, Shaw could see only the black cloud. His diagnosis of America's ills was not unlike Wells's, but he detected none of the positive stirrings that had encouraged Wells, and his tone was savage. Shaw could not have been mistaken for a friend of America, and in fact he would maintain a hostile and condescending posture toward the United States until the end of his long life.[55]

Actually, it was an American, Henry George, who inspired the Dublin-born Shaw to devote himself to social and economic reform. In 1882, when he was twenty-six, Shaw heard George deliver a speech in London on his theories concerning the monopolization of land, and the young man's life was set on a new course. At this point Shaw had yet to turn against America; though not many years had passed since he had departed Ireland for England, he had recently considered emigrating to the United States.[56] Looking back from a distance of over two decades on the impact that George had exerted on him, Shaw wrote of that era, "America, in spite of all its horrors of rampant Capitalism and industrial oppression, was nevertheless still a place where there was hope for the Individualist and the hustler." Britain, on the other hand, was a land where opportunity had been extinguished. According to Shaw, the contrast between the two nations compelled the British followers of George to transcend his single-tax ideas and embrace a more far-reaching socialist program. That George was an American, Shaw argued, was the source of both his originality and his limitations. Only an American who had been able to see in such a short span of time the transformation of his agrarian world into an industrialized, urbanized society would have been optimistic enough to assume that pressing problems were not permanent and could be quickly overcome. Yet, Shaw wrote, there was no doubt that George was about fifty years behind the English in his understanding of economics and sociology and that his emphasis on grand concepts like liberty and natural law stamped him as a relic of the eighteenth century.[57]

In these reflections on Henry George, contained in a 1904 letter to the writer Hamlin Garland to be read at a New York "Progress and Poverty" dinner, Shaw noted that he had never been to America but "my ambition is to repay my debt to Henry George by coming over some day and trying to do for your young men what Henry George did nearly a quarter of a century ago for me."[58] Shaw, however, was never to fulfill this promise. He would not visit America until the 1930s, when he was already in his late seventies, and only then for brief stops as he cruised around the world. His failure to come to the United States became the subject of discussion, and he was constantly called upon to explain his behavior. Actually, Shaw was untouched by wanderlust, and it was not until late in his life that he would travel anywhere beyond the familiar confines of Britain and the Continent.[59] Yet he still defended his staying away from America. By repeatedly insisting that he refused to visit the United States, he was in part merely adhering to his carefully cultivated cantankerous image; the excuses he offered were tinged by typical Shavian perversity. As he admitted on more than one occasion, he loved to taunt the Americans, and he knew they loved him to do so. Addressing the American people in his open letter to Hamlin Garland, he boasted, "I know ten times as much about your country as you do yourselves."[60] Fifteen years later, in 1920, he was still saying much the same thing: "We over here know more about America than Americans do." He explained that if he actually came to the United States, he would forfeit the unique perspective of the foreigner. Skyscrapers and natural wonders like Niagara Falls he had seen plenty of times in paintings, photographs, and movies, so there was no reason to observe them firsthand, and as for gaining the opportunity to meet Americans, Shaw stated, "Most of the interesting men and women sooner or later come over here. And they come to see me."[61]

By refusing to visit America, however, Shaw was not merely playing the bad boy having some mischievous fun tweaking Uncle Sam's nose. As he revealed in both public and private utterances, he genuinely disapproved of the United States. Like other British socialists who considered America at this time, he was put off by the rawness of the capitalist system and the inadequacies of the governmental process. In writing to a fellow Fabian at the turn of the century, Shaw minced no words in expressing his feelings about America. The British had to prevail in the Boer War or else South Africa would be transformed into an American-style republic, and he bluntly stated, "I prefer, on the whole, the history of New Zealand to the history of the United States. I prefer Downing Street, with all its faults, to American Freedom of Contract." A South African constitution would be framed that would meet the needs of Rhodes just as the American one had so well served Rockefeller, and the whole sorry history of capitalism in the United States would be repeated. Shaw argued that the American system was hardly to be emulated, that since the time of the Revolution the United States had fallen behind the mother country: "England is ahead—far ahead—miles nearer Socialism. America is suffering frightfully today because she has not an English Government and an English civil service."[62]

Shaw's quarrel with America was, just as important, personal. Like Dickens and Kipling before him, he bristled over what he perceived to be the rough handling of his works in the United States. Actually, American audiences received his plays with great enthusiasm, and their patronage gave him the financial independence to become a full-time dramatist. Shaw tasted his first box-office success when *The Devil's Disciple,* a melodrama set in Revolutionary America, became a hit on the New York stage in 1897–1898.[63] Furthermore, he accepted with surprising insouciance that American publishers pirated his early, non-copyrighted novels.[64] What did anger Shaw—and helped to sour his relations with America—was that his plays were deemed immoral in some quarters and actions were taken to suppress them. Though America, unlike Britain, did not have an official state censor who could deny licenses to works considered inappropriate, Anthony Comstock of the New York Society for the Suppression of Vice and other moralists in his mold stepped in to fill the void. Shaw became embittered by the attacks directed at him, attacks he was spared in Britain, if only because they were preempted by the censor's bans.

In September 1905 the American premiere of *Man and Superman* took place in New York, where the play would experience a long and successful run.[65] At the same time, however, the New York Public Library decided to restrict access to *Man and Superman* and certain other works of Shaw and pulled them off the shelves. When the *New York Times* solicited his response, he fired off a blistering letter that was published prominently on the paper's front page. He began, "Nobody outside of America is likely to be in the least surprised. Comstockery is the world's standing joke at the expense of the United States." This kind of action merely "confirms the deep-seated conviction of the Old World that America is a provincial place, a second-rate country-town civilization after all." Yet, Shaw argued, this was no laughing matter; he took the "public and official insult" seriously, for he took America seriously, "if only as a colossal social experiment." He knew that his criticisms of the institution of marriage in *Man and Superman* had prompted the Comstockers to anathematize his play and wrote that if he were an American citizen, "I should probably have my property confiscated by some postal official and be myself imprisoned as a writer of 'obscene' literature." He was glad that he lived in a "comparatively free country," the qualification constituting his only reference to his difficulties at home with the censor. While branded in New York as immoral, Shaw wrote that he actually considered himself a moralist and that if the nation could not withstand his strong message, then he had grave doubts about the "future for America."[66]

That same fall, in the year 1905, *Mrs. Warren's Profession*, a play dealing with prostitution Shaw had written over a decade before, was brought to the stage in New York. The royal censor had refused to license the play, and so it had never been publicly performed in Britain. The play's scandalous reputation preceded it, and on opening night in New York hundreds were turned away from the door and tickets were scalped at exorbitant prices. One newspaper polled the theatergoers as they left on whether they believed the play suitable to be presented in America—the audience turned out to be split—and the next morning the entire New York press joined in a chorus of condemnation. On the same day, the police, spurred on by Anthony Comstock himself, filed charges of "disorderly conduct" against the principals involved in the play's production, and *Mrs. Warren's Profession* closed after one performance. When a judge of the New York Court of Special Sessions read the play, he found nothing egregious—certainly nothing criminal—and acquitted the defendants.[67] After the decision was handed down and the *New York American* asked Shaw for his reaction, he was compelled to adopt a more conciliatory stand toward the United States and concede the shortcomings of the British system. While "every conceivable insult and outrage was heaped on me by the New York press," he now felt "publicly vindicated." Unfortunately, there was no such "remedy" in Britain, where the rulings of the censor, whose mind worked like that of the New York journalist, could not be overturned. Shaw was forced to admit, "I think America has the best of it this time."[68]

If the positive outcome of the trial over *Mrs. Warren's Profession* genuinely softened Shaw's views toward America—and it is not evident that it did—such sentiments must have been short-lived. In May of 1907, he was again railing against the United States, particularly Comstockery, in a letter to the English journalist and critic James Douglas. He began, "The reason I do not go to America is that I am afraid of being arrested by Mr. Anthony Comstock." The nation was "now infested by moral brigands, who have turned the Post Office into a most Unholy Inquisition, and are apparently in supreme command of the police." Shaw made reference to the arrest and incarceration of the eugenicist Moses Harman, the flap caused by the performance at the Metropolitan Opera House of Richard Strauss's *Salome,* and the ordeal, discussed by Wells, that Maxim Gorky experienced on his trip to America. Shaw was convinced that if he attempted to visit America, he would meet some untoward fate. The atmosphere was so poisonous in the United States that, he argued, "educated Americans crowd into Europe, whilst educated Europeans keep carefully away from America."[69]

In his 1907 article "A Nation of Villagers," Shaw for the first time discussed his ideas on America in a systematic fashion. He used the term "villagers" derogatorily, as he argued that the United States was a politically immature nation that ignored the pressing social issues of the day while it wallowed in the irrelevancies and stupidities of Comstockery. The most prominent evidence, however, of American "political imbecility" could be found in the people's insistence that the trusts be dismantled. Shaw conceded that President Roosevelt was an enlightened figure, but unlike Wells he saw Roosevelt not as the spokesman for a great progressive movement, but as a lone voice in the wilderness.[70]

"America has never been successful in politics," Shaw wrote. It never really believed in the much vaunted principles of 1776 and 1787, and today the American political system was actually inferior to the monarchies of central Europe. Government in the United States was failing to address the broad and serious human consequences of industrialization, but it was adept at delving into the personal beliefs and habits of individual citizens. Furthermore, government had conceded much of the maintenance of public order to lynch mobs and private security forces. American municipalities were so feeble that Shaw said he had long felt that their governance should be turned over to committees of trained, qualified Europeans. Here he went even further and asserted that Americans—African Americans excepted—should be disfranchised and proscribed from any sort of public service so that Europeans, or perhaps the Japanese, could assume the total task of governing the United States. The white American population, according to his scheme, would be consigned to Indian-style reservations.[71]

To Shaw the sudden outcry, at least as he saw it, for something to be done about the trusts confirmed the naiveté of Americans—"the childishness which enables them to remain simple New England villagers in the complicated hustle of New York and Chicago, never revising their ideas, never enlarging their consciousness, never losing their interest in the ideals of the Pilgrim Fathers." The typical American saw the trust as an evil monster stamping out the friendly village shopkeeper, but, Shaw asserted, morality was not the issue. The trust was an inevitable consequence of economic evolution and in many respects a positive development. If trusts had become abusive, Americans could blame only themselves for failing to come to terms with, and exert public control over, these corporate entities. Calling for their destruction merely constituted reactionary thinking.[72]

Theodore Roosevelt, by Shaw's estimation, did realize that the United States needed to move in a collectivist direction, but he believed the president would struggle in vain to make the nation budge. Americans loved Roosevelt not for his political perspicacity but for his reputation as the Rough Rider hero. Shaw pessimistically wrote, "President Roosevelt cannot realize his dream of making America a real national organism, sovereign over all anti-social powers within its own frontiers, and forcing all men to climb to prosperity instead of rooting for it as hogs root for truffles." Roosevelt would be better off, Shaw contended, leaving the United States and coming to Britain, where he could without any restraint tell his fellow Americans what they needed. As for a successor to Roosevelt, Shaw suggested that the presidency should be permanently turned over to that "Villager of Villagers," that "epitome of America," Anthony Comstock.[73]

Graham Wallas, friend of both Shaw and Wells, displayed a strong interest in America in the first decades of the twentieth century. The son of an evangelical Anglican minister and a product of Shrewsbury and Oxford, Wallas was one of the principal figures in the development of Fabianism, although by the mid-1890s he found himself increasingly at odds with the philosophy and methodology of the Webbs and began to drift away from the society. A teacher from the time he left Oxford, Wallas was elected to the London School Board in 1894 and in the next year became one of the original faculty members of the London School of Economics. He first visited America in 1896–1897—a trip that persuaded him to begin rethinking his assumptions about the rationality and effectiveness of the democratic process. He was appalled by much that he observed on his tour of the big East Coast cities and, like many of the Americans Stead encountered in these years, despaired that classical representative self-government could be made to work in the modern urban setting.[74] But after the turn of the century, he saw positive signs on the American scene and felt encouraged that the nation was making strides. Like Wells, Wallas placed much stock in the intellectual climate that prevailed on American university campuses.

Wallas's new-found optimism about the United States was evident by 1903 in his review of Moisei Ostrogorski's *Democracy and the Organization of Political Parties* (1902). In "The American Analogy," Wallas was guardedly critical of the Russian's massive comparative work on political parties in Britain and the United States and challenged his thesis that the ills of American democracy, the result of machine domination, would eventually afflict the British system as well. Wallas wrote that for years Americans had been telling him much the same thing—that as Britain became increasingly democratic, it would begin to experience the political problems that had beset the United States. But he suggested that the currents were actually running in the opposite direction, for "present tendencies make rather towards the Anglicisation of American democracy, than towards the Americanisation of English democracy." The United States was now a world power with an inchoate governmental bureaucracy. While these trends may not have wholly pleased Wallas, an anti-imperialist, he generally approved of the shape the American nation was assuming. Theodore Roosevelt, he suggested, was displaying much of the same forcefulness exhibited by Abraham Lincoln during the Civil War, and it was possible to perceive "something of the growing intellectual authority of the American universities, of the decay, perhaps, of the purely individualist forms of American Christianity, and of a slight but perceptible weakening in the dogma of the verbal inspiration of the Declaration of Independence." He argued that Americans would need to make a "conscious" effort to foster these developments because they ran so counter to the nation's political traditions.[75]

The greatest indictment Wallas leveled against Ostrogorski was that despite his genuine contribution to political science, he still had not been able to transcend the conventional conception of the role of reason in politics.[76] Wallas, in these years, was moving toward a new understanding of political behavior, a task that would culminate in his masterpiece, *Human Nature in Politics* of 1908. In this work he asserted that voters did not make clear, informed, rational decisions; more likely they were motivated by a variety of subconscious feelings and impulses. When *Human Nature in Politics* was published, Edward A. Ross, the University of Wisconsin sociologist, wrote to Wallas, "I fancy your book may be more keenly appreciated in this country than in England seeing that English political thinkers seem to be less psychological, more rooted in the intellectualist assumption than the younger political thinkers on this side of the water."[77] Ross's hunch was sound, for *Human Nature in Politics* was received much more warmly in America than in Britain. The American social scientists and theorists to whom Wells had paid homage and to whom Wallas would become increasingly drawn felt a greater enthusiasm for Wallas's work than the more traditional academics of Oxford and Cambridge.[78]

One American admirer expressed his regret that Wallas had treated the United States only briefly in the book.[79] If Wallas did give short shrift to America in *Human Nature in Politics*, it was not because he had lost interest in the nation. When Wells had traveled to the United States in 1906, Wallas wrote to say that he wished he could go along to see if "the American young men are getting anything in the nature of religion or philosophy to take the place of the eighteenth century corpse."[80] He would get his chance to size up these "American young men" for himself when in 1910 he came to the United States to teach a seminar at Harvard. This seminar has become legendary because of the bond that Wallas formed with his star student, Walter Lippmann, who was profoundly influenced by Wallas's notions about the role of psychology in politics. When Lippmann became an editor of the *New Republic* in 1914, he drew Wallas into the magazine's talented circle of progressives and through his popular books, from *A Preface to Politics* onward, made Wallas known to a wide American readership.[81]

In 1914 Wallas again sailed to America—to deliver the Lowell Lectures in Boston. By the time he got back to England he had moved far from the horrified attitude toward the United States that he had maintained in the late 1890s to a position of genuine affection and hope for America. The warm reception his work had received and the close contacts he had forged there, combined with the developments he could observe on the national scene, had turned him into a confirmed sympathizer of America.[82] Wallas revealed his enhanced respect for the United States in the article he wrote for the *Contemporary Review* upon returning from his 1914 trip. In "The Universities and the Nation in America and England," he explicitly asserted that the United States was now a very different place from what he had observed nearly two decades before.[83]

While conceding that his American experiences had always limited him to select circles in Eastern cities, Wallas still insisted that since his first visit he had perceived "an apparent growth in the United States of the authority of methodical and specially instructed thought on social and political questions, as against average unspecialized opinion." There was now greater respect in America for a college education and for "expert knowledge." Whereas in 1896 the Democratic presidential nominee, William Jennings Bryan, had threatened to push through a currency scheme of which financial experts thoroughly disapproved, in 1913 his fellow Democrat Woodrow Wilson signed into law the Federal Reserve Act, which was shaped by the counsel of these same authorities.[84]

The growing influence of science in America, Wallas argued, partly accounted for the nation's new receptivity to expert knowledge. He noted in particular the prominence of psychology, as represented by such leading lights as G. Stanley Hall, who had enticed Freud to cross the Atlantic to lecture at Clark University in 1909. But Wallas wrote that even more important than the sway of science to those who were endeavoring to make a concerted, informed effort to tackle America's problems was the magnitude of those problems. He likened his progressive friends in the United States to the post-Waterloo crop of British reformers that included Robert Owen, James Mill, and William Cobbett: both groups believed they were answering a "call" to treat dire national ills.[85]

Wallas found the trends in American higher education especially encouraging. He calculated that thirty times as many students and teachers at American universities were devoting themselves to such social sciences as economics and government as their British counterparts. Although American scholars tended not to turn out the seminal works in these fields, and academia in the United States suffered from other drawbacks, Wallas was optimistic: "The fact of the unprecedented volume of specialized social knowledge that is annually created in the United States still remains." It would take at least thirty years for the curricular innovations at the universities to be fully reflected in the nation at large, but already a new generation of American public servants college-trained in the social sciences, some of them even experts, were on the scene. Although Wallas's enthusiasm was dampened because these officials tended not to devote their careers to government, he believed that the British should pay close attention to American developments. He asked whether the typical British civil servant, an Oxford man steeped in the classics, was really as well prepared to meet the problems of modern life as the new American public official.[86]

In 1914, the year Wallas wrote "The Universities and the Nation in America and England," Wells published a volume of essays titled in Britain *An Englishman Looks at the World* and in the United States, *Social*

Forces in England and America. Since the appearance of *The Future in America* in 1906, he had not ignored the United States. New York, for example, provided a backdrop for his 1908 novel, *The War in the Air,* and when Roosevelt made his triumphal tour of Europe in 1910, Wells wrote glowingly about the ex-president in an article for *Collier's.*[87] Although references to America can be found scattered throughout his 1914 collection of essays, most of them previously published, the bulk of Wells's commentary on the subject was concentrated in one piece, the longest in the volume, called "The American Population."[88] It is essentially a recapitulation of *The Future in America,* but with some significant variations.

Although Wells believed that the progressive spirit he had identified in 1906 was still alive, he now introduced some new elements into his discussion of the nation. He apparently no longer felt that the journalists and academics could by themselves spearhead an intellectual revolution. If the United States was going to continue to move forward, constructive roles would have to be assumed by three key groups— plutocrats, socialists, and women.

While Wells had chosen to show understanding—rather than hostility—toward John D. Rockefeller in 1906, he now went a step further by asserting that the likes of Rockefeller, Morgan, and Carnegie should take a leading role in the revitalizing of America. Wells wrote that a whole class of aging titans had amassed their fortunes years before and "that these big industrial and financial organisers, whatever in their youth they proposed to do or be, must many of them come to realise that their organising power is up against no less a thing than a nation's future." Some of these men had probably already contemplated taking on such a task, he contended, and it was entirely conceivable they would turn to "statesmanship." Although Wells had been critical of Carnegie's philanthropy in *The Future in America,* he now wrote, "It seems to me that the educational zeal of Mr. Andrew Carnegie and the university and scientific endowments of Mr. Rockefeller are not merely showy benefactions; they express a definite feeling of the present need of constructive organisation in the social scheme." He pointed out that the universities, so crucial to the nation's future for the training they were providing in the social sciences, were beholden to the plutocrats and asserted that the best institutions in America were privately endowed, not state funded. In his vision plutocrats, both self-made men of the Rockefeller sort and old-moneyed gentry in the mold of Roosevelt, would form an American "aristocracy" that would take responsibility for guiding the nation.[89]

Wells believed the socialists, as well as the plutocrats, to hold the keys to the American future, though he was actually less sanguine about the former. He viewed American socialism, which was at its height in the early twentieth century, as a crude and vengeful movement. Socialism constituted the immigrants' sole contribution to American life, he claimed, the one instance in which they did not simply conform to the native mold. In language reminiscent of Stead's commentary on Western labor radicalism of the 1890s, Wells wrote of the socialism that had spread from Chicago into the rural hinterland:

> It is a fierce form of socialist teaching that speaks throughout these regions, far more closely akin to the revolutionary Socialism of the continent of Europe than to the constructive and evolutionary Socialism of Great Britain. . . . It is a Socialism reeking with class feeling and class hatred and altogether anarchistic in spirit; a new and highly indigestible contribution to the American moral and intellectual synthesis.

The American socialist movement should adhere to the British model, Wells argued, and strive to be a positive, rather than a destructive, force in the nation.[90]

If national progress was to be made, Wells furthermore believed that American women needed to gain a surer footing in society. It was imperative for women to end their "economic dependence" on men, which could be achieved only through what he called the "public Endowment of Maternity." The state would pay a mother for bearing and raising children so that she could be financially independent of her husband and free from the fear of his abandonment. Although Wells advocated such a measure not simply for American women, it was particularly relevant for the United States. He was worried about what Roosevelt termed "race-suicide," the idea that the birth rate was declining among old-stock Americans while at the same time the immigrant population surged. Wells again blamed economic individualism: families remained small to ensure their prosperity, despite the deleterious effects on the nation. While he knew it would be difficult to achieve, he wished to see the raising of children in the United States become a "collective effort."[91]

Although Wells was heartened that the United States was moving in a positive direction, he concluded, "There are many reasons for supposing the national government will always remain a little ineffectual and detached from the full flow of American life." The two chief reasons were the constraints of the Constitution and the inadequacies of

Washington as the nation's capital. Wells warned that these impediments could retard America's progress, so that by the year 2000 it could find itself being overtaken by nations all over the world. Despite these admonitions, however, he remained upbeat about America and the type of civilization it could become.[92]

The year that *Social Forces in England and America* was published, 1914, was, of course, a turning point in history. The year also marked a turning point in Wells's career, for when Europe plunged into war, he began to renew his commitment to reconstructing the world. And now when he looked toward America, he more and more saw the nation in terms of the role it could play in that global reconstruction.

4

The Global Stage

H. G. Wells on America's Emergence in the First World War

When the First World War broke out in August 1914, the global catastrophe that Wells had long held out as a possibility was becoming a reality. Convinced that Germany was the aggressor and that an Allied victory was imperative for the future of Western civilization, he enthusiastically lent his pen to promoting Britain's war effort. In fact, he was responsible for coining the phrase, "the war that will end war." Within a couple of years, however, he viewed the conflict more skeptically and came to regret his earlier zeal, which had generated bad feelings between him and many of his friends. Wells did not forsake his support of the Allied cause, but he became adamant that the objectives for fighting the war should be clearly defined and that a return to the status quo ante bellum would be unacceptable. He took an active part in the League of Nations movement, and by exploiting his appointed position in the British propaganda machine, he attempted to insinuate his idealistic aims into government policy. By the end of the war, Wells's mood was disconsolate, for his nation's leadership had shown little interest in his ideas, including the innovations he had suggested in military technology. When the Treaty of Versailles was worked out in 1919, he grew only more pessimistic about the world's prospects. During the late 1910s, as more and more men were slaughtered on the fields of France and as the war's purpose grew increasingly obscure, the atheistic Wells even turned—temporarily—to religion and embraced the notion of a strong, benevolent God.[1]

During this period in his life, from the heady days of 1914 through his post-Versailles years of despair, Wells was certain of one thing: national boundaries had to be erased to make way for a single, unified world state. He had long advocated such a union, but now, with the tragic failings of the nation-state system so starkly evident, he pressed for the idea with a new urgency. Working for international cooperation, and ultimate unification, became his top priority, while he placed less emphasis on his socialist beliefs and, for a time, his notion of bloodless revolution. From the First World War until the end of his life, Wells saw it as his mission to prepare people to think in global, rather than national, terms, and it is no coincidence that the war marked the end of his career as a lively, daring novelist lionized by young artists and radicals throughout the English-speaking world. His novels became painfully didactic—the functionalist tendency had actually been apparent even before the war—and though millions were now exposed to his popular educational texts and pervasive journalistic output, he forfeited his position as a leading writer of fiction.[2]

In the war and immediate postwar years, as he sought to bring a new sense of order to the world, Wells looked hopefully toward America—first in its role as the preeminent neutral power, then as an active participant in the struggle to defeat Germany, and ultimately as a major force in arranging the peace and determining the contours of the new international rapprochement. The optimism about American society that he had adopted in the first decade of the century now spilled over into global affairs, for he believed that the United States could play a unique and crucial role in reconstructing the world. Wells placed great faith in America, but he found it necessary to cajole the nation to assume the part he had carved out for it and often was left disappointed. Specifically, like many intellectuals throughout the West, he initially saw great promise in America's wartime leader, Woodrow Wilson, only to feel in the end that the president was a limited man who had betrayed his own stated principles. But when Wells made his second trip to America in 1921, to cover the Washington Conference, he was still prepared to cast the nation in a special role. During these years, while Wells was focused on the position of the United States in the world, some of his fellow Britons, namely George Bernard Shaw, Graham Wallas, and a young

Harold Laski, were concerned about what was happening to American freedoms at home.

For Wells the role of the United States was never to be that of a nation removed from the arena of world affairs, as many Americans had over the generations advocated. In a piece included in his 1916 book *What Is Coming?* he asserted that since the war had begun, America had fortunately broken free from its isolationist past: "No longer a political Thoreau in the woods, a sort of vegetarian recluse among nations, a being of negative virtues and unpremeditated superiorities, she girds herself for a manly part in the toilsome world of men."[3] When the war broke out, Wells saw American tourists who had fled the Continent packed into the Savoy Hotel, indignant that their summer vacations should be abruptly terminated: some seemed to feel that they should be able to continue their travels and that as Americans they would be immune from bombs and bullets. "Since those days the American nation has lived politically a hundred years," Wells wrote. The United States was now rapidly learning the lesson that Britain had learned in recent decades—that existing in isolation was not a viable option in the modern world. He stated, "From dreams of aloofness and ineffable superiority, America comes round very rapidly to a conception of an active participation in the difficult business of statescraft. She is thinking of alliances, of throwing her weight and influence upon the side of law and security."[4]

The British should, however, disabuse themselves of any notion that the Americans felt deeply affectionate toward them, Wells argued. The bond so many Britons, particularly those with radical, republican leanings, believed existed between them and the Americans was not recognized on the other side of the Atlantic. Although "the common language and literature" had kept the two peoples in the same orbit, Americans were still hostile toward the crown and furthermore, "they suspect every Englishman of being a bit of a gentleman and a bit of a flunkey."[5] The recent warm-up in Anglo-American relations did not so much signal a new-found fondness for Britain on the part of the Americans as it reflected the simple American conclusion that the British were in the right, and the Germans in the wrong, in their ongoing war. According to Wells, Americans felt closer to the French than to the British, for France had helped the United States gain its independence and now shared a republican form of government. Yet he believed that in the future America would perhaps develop its closest affinity with the third of the great Allies, Russia, which like the United States was a vast, developing nation. Wells had made his first trip to Russia in 1914, and he was struck, as Stead had been before him, by the physical similarity between the Russian and American landscapes. He felt that America and Russia were both assured of their destinies as nations: "France and Britain may perish in the next two centuries or they may persist, but there can be no doubt that two centuries ahead Russia and the United States will be two of the greatest masses of fairly homogeneous population on the globe."[6]

The great long-range task for both the Allies and America, Wells maintained, was to establish the principle of global cooperation so that wars between nations could be avoided in the future. Some sort of intellectual revolution had to be brought about, and he believed America could lead the way. Because it was not involved in fighting, Wells wrote, "There is an opportunity for guiding expression on the part of America such as may never occur again." He referred to the journalistic, literary, and educational strides that had impressed him on his journey to the United States in 1906 and speculated as to whether the vigorous, disciplined "American mind" was up to the task of leading the nations of the world to a new "intellectual synthesis." He would have been proud to see his own native Britain take the lead but believed that America would be more inclined, and more prepared in terms of its geographic position and physical resources, to assume that role.[7]

Much of Wells's commentary on America in *What Is Coming?* smacks of wishful thinking. There seems to have been little basis for him to conclude that the United States had come to side with the Allies. In the first half of 1916, the vast majority of Americans still wished to stay out of the war, and President Wilson was scrupulously adhering to a policy of neutrality. The American people were by no means overwhelmingly sympathetic to the British cause; significant portions of the populace, particularly among so-called hyphenated Americans, were actually pro-German. Wilson's top adviser, Edward M. House, and the secretary of state, Robert Lansing, tilted toward the British, and Wilson himself was an ardent admirer of British institutions, but the president believed neither side in the conflict possessed a moral monopoly and was determined to keep the United States outside the fray. Although Wells's assessment was unduly optimistic, he was on somewhat firmer ground in asserting that America was beginning to assume more international responsibility. Wilson was working behind the scenes to try to mediate between the belligerents, and in May 1916 he delivered a major speech in which he promised the United States would play a greater global role and called specifically for American entry into a postwar "association of nations."[8]

The British people, and their elected leaders, viewed Wilson at this stage of the war with disdain for his failure to rally the United States behind the Allied cause. What they desired was not necessarily military assistance, but at least full moral and material support. The only group of British subjects among whom Wilson was popular in 1916 was the radical left, who saw the president as the most likely candidate to arrange a peace.[9] George Bernard Shaw, who opposed Britain's role in the war, and the philosopher-mathematician Bertrand Russell, who became an outright pacifist, both wrote to Wilson asking for him to step in to effect a settlement.[10] Though Wells did not walk in lockstep with the left when it came to the war, he too singled out Wilson and America to perform a saving role. If there was little evidence that the United States was prepared to side with the Allies and ultimately take the lead in a postwar settlement, Wells may have hoped that his words would serve as a prod.

That Wells was perhaps more prescribing a future role for America than describing its present position is reinforced by his harsh treatment of the nation in his popular 1916 novel, *Mr. Britling Sees It Through.* In this work, one of his last great fictional successes, he struck a responsive chord among British and American readers by depicting how the war had affected the household of a prominent English writer named Britling, who bears a close resemblance to Wells himself. The subject of America arises only infrequently in the novel, but there is one telling episode in which Mr. Britling lectures his wealthy Yankee guest, Mr. Direck, on the position of the United States in the war. The monologue suggests that Wells harbored some deep resentments toward America that he felt safe to express only through his fiction.

Mr. Direck is staunchly pro-Ally and has taken part in Herbert Hoover's Belgian relief efforts, but he adamantly believes that the United States must not become involved in the war or even, as it was doing, allow its citizens to supply the Allies with armaments. He subscribes to "the idea of America as a polity aloof from the Old World system, as a fresh start for humanity, as something altogether too fine and precious to be dragged into even the noblest of European conflicts." In response Mr. Britling launches into a tirade against the United States. Although a critic of Britain and its antiquated institutions, he is rankled that "there in America was the old race, without Crown or Church or international embarrassment, and it was still falling short of splendid." When Mr. Direck asserts that America is something "exceptional," Mr. Britling objects and points out that the British were once captives to the same delusion.[11]

Mr. Britling attacks the American policy of neutrality by arguing that the United States cannot credibly pretend to have no stake in the war, for the freedom of the seas so dear to the Americans can be maintained only if the British prevail. He exclaims, "You are a nation of ungenerous onlookers—watching us throttle or be throttled." America stays out of the war, he asserts, to sustain its favorable business climate, and then the nation will reap further profits after an Allied victory is achieved. When Mr. Britling is through with his harangue, he knows he has been "preposterously unfair to America" but nevertheless feels content that he got the words off his chest.[12]

After Wilson, provoked by Germany's newly announced policy of unrestricted submarine warfare against both Allied and neutral shipping in the Atlantic, asked Congress to declare war in April 1917, it was obviously easier for Wells, and other disgruntled Britons, to feel more cordial toward America. The United States insisted that it was entering the war for its own reasons, and its troops remained officially separate from the Allied forces, but the doughboys would nevertheless be welcomed in Europe as crucial reinforcements. Before the American Expeditionary Force had arrived in France, Wells explicitly spelled out the political role he wished to see the United States assume in a letter intended for the eyes of President Wilson himself. The letter originated in a discussion that Wells held in November 1917 at the Reform Club in London with Bainbridge Colby, a Wilson administration official who in 1920 would be named secretary of state. Wells wrote the letter to Colby, who then sent it on to Joseph P. Tumulty, Wilson's secretary, with this explanation: "It follows pretty much the lines of a long and rather intimate conversation I had with Mr. Wells in London, and his conception of America's role at the present time, and his ardent admiration of the President led me to suggest that he set forth his views in writing."[13] In this letter, reprinted in its entirety in his autobiography, Wells stated that only the United States, or more specifically Wilson as its leader, was in a position to bring about the "Just Peace" that liberal-minded people around the world craved.[14]

Wells later wrote that even if the letter did reach the White House, he doubted the president ever read it.[15] But Wilson probably did inspect the letter, for in his acknowledgment to Colby, he stated, "I shall read it with the greatest interest."[16] Nevertheless, the notion, rejected by Wells himself, that the letter contributed to Wilson's construction of the Fourteen Points does seem flimsy. Wells and Wilson may have agreed on the best course to be pursued, but the ideas contained in Wells's letter were not unique and Wilson did not suddenly see the light just before declaring his Fourteen Points in January 1918. The president drew upon a vast body of liberal opinion, originating in both America and Europe, in formulating his war goals and officially charged an "Inquiry" with hammering out the specifics.[17] Although Wells concluded that his letter possessed "no grain of historical importance," he did believe that it had "considerable autobiographical significance."[18] And in fact, as a gauge of Wells's view of the world at the end of 1917, and more significantly America's place in it, the letter is an invaluable source.

In the letter, Wells contended that America was in a unique position to lead the way toward a "new order." Of the significant powers in the war, the United States was the only one that could be called "a dispassionate combatant." America was far removed from the battlefields and uninvolved in the territorial and colonial disputes that fueled the passions of the other belligerents. It was incumbent upon the United States to define the goals of the Allied side, set down the terms for peace, and officially propose a League of Nations. Wells wrote: "America alone can stand fearlessly and unembarrassed for that rational settlement all men desire."[19]

Wells placed the burden of leadership squarely on Wilson's shoulders. The United States, he claimed, was the only great power with "a real head, representative and expressive. Possessing that head, America can talk. Alone in our system America is capable of articulate speech." Russia was experiencing a leadership crisis, and Britain and France were internally divided, and the heads of the Allied nations were so weighted down by secret agreements that their latitude in enunciating priorities was severely restricted. Only Wilson, unencumbered by either claims or obligations and supported by the American people, possessed the clout to bring the warring parties to the peace table. According to Wells, "In all the world there is no outstanding figure to which the world will listen, there is no man audible in all the world, in Japan as well as Germany and Rome as well as Boston—except the President of the United States."[20]

This letter contained that note of encouragement characteristic of Wells's utterances on America and world affairs. Although the United

States was now one of the belligerents, and not a detached bystander, apparently he still felt the need to prod the Americans to assume their international obligations. He wrote, "America in the last three years has made great strides from its traditional isolation towards a responsible share in framing the common destinies of mankind." Yet he immediately added, "But America has to travel further on the same road." In attempting to coax the United States to accept the mantle of world leadership, Wells not only made a rational and compelling case for why only the Americans could lead the way, he also resorted to flattery. In discussing the unique position of the United States, Wells showed he was aware that Americans liked to think of themselves as a special people. More specifically, it seems that in carving out a nearly messianic role for Wilson, he was trying to ingratiate himself with the president. The fawning tone Wells at times adopted is nowhere more evident than in his closing sentences:

> You see the role I believe America could play under President Wilson's guidance, the role of the elucidator, the role of advocate of the new order. Clear speech and clear speech alone can save the world. Nothing else can. And President Wilson alone of all mankind can speak and compel the redeeming word.[21]

Four months before the war ended, Wells, in a letter to Sinclair Lewis, denounced Bolshevism and proclaimed, "I'm a Wilsonite. For the first time in my life there is a man in the world that I am content to follow."[22] But within a year's time Wells, like so many liberal-minded observers around the world, saw Wilson in an entirely new light; he believed that the president had failed at the Paris Peace Conference to uphold the progressive principles he had nobly championed as a wartime leader.

Wells drew a scathing portrait of Wilson in his massive work *The Outline of History*, which he had undertaken based on his conviction that at the end of the war, a general world history that could provide a coherent explanation of the past was sorely needed. When *The Outline* was published in 1920, it became a sensational best-seller, far outpacing the popularity of any of his novels. The book sold especially well in the United States, where there was a new curiosity about a world in which the Americans had assumed a more conspicuous role. Edition after edition was gobbled up by the American public, who in one particular year bought more copies of *The Outline* than any other book except the Bible. But if Americans had been expecting to see their national history treated extensively, they would have been disappointed, for the United States was accorded only a small fraction of space in a work that traces the history of the world from the origins of life through the Treaty of Versailles. Influenced by the "New Historians," Wells strove to present a total view of the past; he covered both East and West and stressed social and intellectual developments, at the expense of the "great men" who had dominated the traditional accounts of individual nations and empires. Just as important, Wells approached the work as a propagandist, and his agenda was none too subtle. He wished to show that the history of the world was a history of how disparate communities had been pulled closer and closer together, a process that would in the future lead to the establishment of the world state. While Wells may not have devoted much attention to the United States—the Civil War was relegated to three paragraphs—he did discuss in some detail the birth of the republic and the recent emergence of America in the First World War.[23]

In characterizing the American Revolution, Wells, ever the presentist, clearly made no effort to block contemporary realities from his mind. On the contrary, he attempted to trace links between the 1700s and 1910s. After describing the diversity of the colonies, he wrote, "The possibility of their ever becoming closely united would have struck an impartial observer in 1760 as being very slight." In view of Wells's dream of global unification, such a statement was fraught with meaning. And not only did the colonists unite and break their bonds with Britain, but, according to Wells, they established a nation that was definitely something new in the annals of world history. Though the Greek philosophers had theorized about it, never before had a nation simply been made from scratch. And furthermore, in the blueprint the Americans drew up for their republic, they rejected all of the fixtures of the European powers—monarchy, aristocracy, and a state religion. Wells wrote, "The new community had in fact gone right down to the bare and stripped fundamentals of human association, and it was building up a new sort of society and a new sort of state upon those foundations."[24]

Wells saw the American Revolution as the "repudiation" by the British people of the New World of the "Great Power view of life" that prevailed in the Old.[25] He picked up on that theme in the penultimate chapter of *The Outline*, titled "The Catastrophe of 1914." In sketching the background of World War I, he discussed how the United States, in contrast to the "European Great Powers," had never really turned into an imperialist nation. No grand, European-style foreign office had been established in Washington, D.C., and Wells argued that even when the United States won overseas territory in the late 1890s, the nation's motives and goals represented a departure from traditional imperialism.[26]

After providing an account of World War I, Wells proceeded to write about the Paris Peace Conference. "The story of the Conference," he said, "turns very largely upon the adventure of one particular man," Woodrow Wilson. Although Wells tended not to focus on individuals in *The Outline*, he did believe that certain figures in history, such as Alexander the Great and Napoleon, stood for the times in which they ruled. Wells stated, "The conclusion of the Great War can be seen most easily as the rise of the American President, President Wilson, to predominant importance in the world's hopes and attention, and his failure to justify that predominance." Wilson, Wells argued, was woefully unprepared for his day in the sun, because despite his academic background, he had never shown any interest in issues that ranged beyond the shores of America.[27]

In sketching the developments that brought Wilson to that postwar pinnacle of glory from which he would be toppled, Wells revealed that he believed the American tradition of remaining aloof from "Great Power" politics could cut two ways. The tradition yielded negative consequences when, in the early years of the war, America assumed an air of moral superiority and refused to take any actions that would imply a commitment to either side in the conflict. However, once Germany's submarine aggression had pulled the United States into the war, this same tradition translated into a positive good. The American denial of the "Great Power" system served as the basis for Wilson's adoption of a liberal, enlightened set of war goals, which he spelled out explicitly in the Fourteen Points. According to Wells, Wilson "unfolded a conception of international relationships that came like a gospel, like the hope of a better world, to the whole eastern hemisphere."[28]

Wells resented Wilson's failure to acknowledge his intellectual debts, as well as his assumption of the role of "Messiah," but he believed that if the Fourteen Points could have been translated into a peace settlement, world history would have been set upon a promising course. That the Treaty of Versailles failed to incorporate the liberal program was, in Wells's eyes, a tragedy for which Wilson himself was largely responsible. Here was a case where the traditional American isolation from "Great Power" affairs led to calamitous consequences, for that aloofness had created a generation of Americans, of which Wilson was one, marked by "a certain superficiality and lightness of mind." The Americans were not innately deficient, and the ideals they espoused were certainly exemplary, but they were unaccustomed to playing on the world stage. Wells depicted the peace conference as a clash of two cultures:

> One had on the one hand these new people of the new world, with their new ideas, their finer and better ideas, of peace and world righteousness, and on the other the old, bitter, deeply entangled peoples of the Great Power system and the former were crude and rather childish in their immense inexperience, and the latter were seasoned and bitter and intricate.[29]

When Wilson came out of the Conference "with his Fourteen Points pitifully torn and dishevelled" and "with a little puling infant of a League of Nations," it was little wonder, Wells contended, that Americans were disillusioned. In his own eyes the League, with no real sovereignty, was an "insufficient and unsatisfactory sketch" of the kind of world government for which he yearned. He did not blame the United States Senate for refusing to ratify the Treaty of Versailles, and its League Covenant, which "was virtually little more than a league of allied imperialisms for mutual insurance." The American people were right to reject the kind of "Great Power" politicking that had prevailed in Paris, though Wells was sorry that their revulsion was now going to pull the United States back into its prewar isolationist shell.[30]

In late 1920, the same year that the Senate voted against ratifying the Treaty of Versailles, Wells was scheduled to deliver lectures in America, but illness prevented him from making the trip. Nevertheless, the lectures he had prepared were published in 1921 as part of *The Salvaging of Civilization*. In this book Wells was more emphatic than he had ever been before about the need for a world state, and he elaborated on the role that education could play in laying the foundation. Influenced heavily by his visit to a devastated post-revolutionary St. Petersburg in the fall of 1920, Wells believed that the condition of the world's health was critical.[31] He wrote, "I want to say that this civilization in which we are living is tumbling down, and I think tumbling down very fast; that I think rapid enormous efforts will be needed to save it; and that I see no such efforts being made at the present time."[32] In *The Salvaging of Civilization*, particularly in the chapter entitled "The Project of a World State," intended originally for his American lecture tour, Wells wrote that the United States held a unique position in the world, but, in contrast to his exhortations of the war years, he now asserted that the nation could assume no active, immediate role to bring about global reconstruction. The major problems existed in the Old World, and the Old World would have to solve those problems before appealing to the New.

Wells argued that America constituted an exceptional case: "The government of the United States and the community of the United States are things different politically and mentally from those of the states of the old world." America was unique because of how it had been shaped by modern developments in transportation and communication, developments that, since his publication of *Anticipations* at the beginning of the century, Wells had stressed as the forces most responsible for necessitating the world state. This technological revolution in effect made the United States a possibility—a cohesive, homogeneous nation covering a vast continent. Without the steamboat, the railroad, and the telegraph, Americans would never have been able to push westward so rapidly and remain intact as a nation. According to Wells, "The growth of the United States is a process that has no precedent in the world's history; it is a new kind of occurrence." Although the world had seen "great empires," they were always amalgams of diverse societies: "There has never been one single people on this scale before." In fact, he felt it was absurd to call the United States a "country," for America and France or Holland "are as different as an automobile and a one-horse shay."[33]

In Wells's view the transportation revolution had affected Europe very differently from America. Rather than a boon, it was a source of conflict. As technological innovations encouraged European nations to expand, they found themselves constrained by boundaries fixed centuries before. States rubbed up against one another, and friction led to war. Wells argued that Europe could plunge into another great bloodbath if political unity was not established and that until the Europeans erased their borders and pulled together, they should not expect any cooperation from the Americans. He stated, "Before Europe can get on to a level and on to equal terms with the United States, the European communities have to go through a process that America went through—under much easier conditions—a century and a half ago."[34]

The historical precedent to which Wells referred was not the decision of the American colonies to declare their independence as the United States of America in 1776, but rather the decision in 1787 to abandon the Articles of Confederation and frame the Constitution.

Only at that point did Virginians and Pennsylvanians and citizens of other states commit themselves to being one people, Americans. He implied that the League of Nations was merely a "confederation" and argued that the French, the British, the Germans, and their neighbors would have to make a similar commitment and come to think of themselves as Europeans, and eventually citizens of the world state.[35]

The great contrast between the situation in the New World and the Old, Wells wrote, dictated that Americans and Europeans would view global requirements very differently, and he in effect endorsed the decision by the United States not to participate in the League of Nations. The American "can go on comfortably for a hundred years before he begins to feel tight in his political skin," and he is convinced "he has got peace organized for a good long time ahead." Wells apparently believed such confidence was justified, for he wrote, "I doubt if it would make any very serious difference for some time in the ordinary daily life of Kansas City, let us say, if all Europe were reduced to a desert in the next five years." Europeans, in contrast, needed to take some drastic steps to secure a peaceful future, steps that would carry them much farther down the path toward unification than dictated by the League of Nations. Therefore, Wells said, "I am convinced of the impossibility of any common political co-operation to organize a world peace between America and Europe at the present time." While individual Americans could contribute intellectually to the reconstruction that was needed in the Old World, there was no role for the U.S. government to play. Wells's view was that "the American type of state and the European type of state are different things, incapable of an effectual alliance; the steam tractor and the ox cannot plough this furrow together."[36]

Although Wells paid great attention to the international role the United States was assuming during the war and immediate postwar years, he was ostensibly oblivious to the American domestic scene. These years, however, were marked by government repression and public intolerance unprecedented in the nation's history. Even before they assailed the Treaty of Versailles, American progressives had lost faith in Wilson because of his record on civil liberties. To put a lid on antiwar dissent, he signed into law the Espionage and Sedition Acts of 1917–1918. Under these two laws, the postmaster general barred from the mails supposedly subversive publications and the Justice Department prosecuted individuals who actively opposed the war or even in certain cases simply denounced the government. Most vulnerable to prosecution were those—often hyphenated—Americans who belonged to such left-wing groups as the extremist Industrial Workers of the World (IWW) and the more mainstream Socialist Party. The Socialists' leader, Eugene Debs, was perhaps the most famous figure to be convicted and sent to prison. After the armistice of 1918, anti-German sentiment among the American people was transformed into anti-Bolshevism, and the Wilson administration continued to pursue tough policies. In 1919 Americans feared Communist advances abroad and were unsettled by a series of strikes and some well-publicized bombings at home. The Red Scare reached a peak in late 1919 and early 1920 when the attorney general, A. Mitchell Palmer, ordered a series of raids on suspected radical strongholds, which led to the deportation of hundreds of aliens.[37]

While Wells may have been blind to or perhaps purposely ignored the ominous domestic developments in America, they were not lost on George Bernard Shaw, Graham Wallas, or Harold Laski, who during the late 1910s was teaching history and government at Harvard. Shaw, of course, had never viewed American society as free and open, and the war only hardened his convictions. After his friend Frank Harris, the controversial Irish-born editor, left London to take over *Pearson's* in New York, Shaw wrote to him, in January 1918, that Harris's disappointment with America was predictable. Shaw chided him for embarking on his new venture imbued with the "wild notion that America is the land of freedom." He further stated that "I think it is impossible for anyone who knows American lynching, American Inquisition legislation, and American graft, to deny that America is illiberal, superstitious, crude, violent, anarchic and arbitrary."[38]

In a letter to Harris written a year later, in March 1919, Shaw was more explicit about the wartime abridgment of civil liberties in the United States: "You can tell the Americans from me that they have seriously compromised the credit of republicanism throughout the world by their outrageous repudiation, at the first shot, of all the liberties the Declaration of Independence proclaimed." Shaw wrote that the repression of individuals in America—he mentioned specifically the harsh prison sentence accorded to Debs—actually made the Kaiser's Germany look good by comparison. Even though Wilson had been firmly in favor of a strict policy on dissent and had failed to put a stop to his own appointees' excesses, Shaw chose to acquit the president. In fact, he charged that the American people had "disgraced Wilson" and called the president "a great man of whom his country is apparently utterly unworthy."[39]

Shaw took direct, public aim at American repression in the preface to his 1919 play, *Heartbreak House*. He asserted that the war had produced hysteria and led to a certain loss of liberty all over Europe but that these developments could to some extent be attributed to the constant presence of danger. According to Shaw, however, "it was in the United States of America, where nobody slept the worse for the war, that the war fever went beyond all sense and reason. In European Courts there was vindictive illegality: in American Courts there was raving lunacy." To point out the contrast, he wrote that Americans during the war were convicted for utterances no different from those made before large public rallies in Britain.[40] Because Shaw was one of those speaking out against British policy, he must have wondered what kind of treatment he would have received in America.

Whereas Shaw commented upon the poisoned atmosphere of America during the war, Wallas wrote principally about the extremism that endured after the armistice had been signed. He was in the United States in the fall of 1919, just as the Red Scare reached its climax, to teach at the New School for Social Research, which had just opened its doors, and to deliver the Dodge Lectures at Yale. When he left America after his previous visit of 1914, he left with a favorable impression of a nation that was intellectually and politically alive. Now, five years later, as progressivism had given way to repression, his view of America had grown darker. Upon his return to England, he published two articles expressing his distress over the Red Scare, one in the *New Statesman* and the other in the *Atlantic*.

Wallas's piece for the January 31, 1920, issue of the *New Statesman*, entitled "The 'New Virility' in the United States," was an answer to the call of Edward Price Bell, an American journalist, for progressive-minded Europeans to support the Red hunt. In the *Observer* of January 18, Bell had gladly announced that the anti-radical campaign signaled the arrival of "a new virility" in America. Wallas responded that he had just spent some months in the United States and could not accept Bell's sanguine view of the course of events there. Using clippings from American newspapers, he proceeded to relate to the *New Statesman*'s predominantly British readership, which may not have been fully informed about the Red Scare, some of the incidents that had troubled him. Teaching in New York had placed Wallas in the midst of some of the country's most concerted antiradical activity, and in his *New Statesman* article most of the examples he cited were drawn from the experiences of that city. He pointed, for instance, to the brutal November raid of the Russian People's House in New York, which was to be the first strike of Attorney General Palmer's nationwide campaign. Wallas also discussed the endeavors of the New York state legislature's Lusk Committee, which, even before the Justice Department got actively involved in the business of Red hunting, was doggedly investigating radicalism and initiating raids of its own. The work of the Lusk Committee led to one of the most notorious incidents of the Red Scare, referred to by Wallas here—the decision by the legislature in January 1920 to refuse to seat five elected Socialist representatives.[41]

While Wallas realized that it could be counterproductive for an Englishman to criticize American developments, he thought he could not leave Bell's appeal for foreign endorsement unchallenged. Furthermore, although he had been dismayed by the feeling of helplessness among his New York friends to combat the abuses, Wallas wrote that nevertheless there were voices in America bravely crying out against the "new virility" and he believed it important that they should know that they could count on some support from overseas. At the conclusion of the article, he also drew attention to those Americans who were still languishing in prison because of their convictions under wartime security laws and noted that no domestic campaign for their clemency was possible in the present climate. Foreign pressure should be exerted, Wallas reasoned, for

> if the American Government comes to feel that, now that America is the most powerful State in the world, the cause of toleration and human kindness in America is one that concerns the whole world, it may be that Eugene Debs and the rest will be released a few days or a few years earlier than they would be if their fate depended solely on the movements of internal American politics.[42]

The *Atlantic* article, published in January 1920, warned Americans of the consequences of their new restrictions upon open expression. In "The Price of Intolerance" Wallas wrote that he was disturbed by his recent stay in the United States, for while he had noticed on previous visits a certain tendency for the majority to ride roughshod over the minority, now "the whole tradition of political toleration has been broken." To Wallas it was an ominous sign that Judge Elbert H. Gary, the reactionary chairman of United States Steel responsible for crushing a 1919 industry-wide strike, was now a national hero. He also noted that Thorstein Veblen's *Imperial Germany*, a book he had once enthusiastically reviewed, had been inexplicably barred from the United States mails since 1918. The assault on free expression came at a particularly bad time, Wallas argued, because postwar America still needed to determine its future and a wise course could be chosen only through a bold exchange of ideas. The intellectual atmosphere in America was now stifling, and most of the output on political and social subjects was as a consequence weak and uninspiring. If a thinker with creative ideas to reform society were to arise in America today, a brilliant activist in the tradition of Jeremy Bentham, he would undoubtedly become the target of repression. To Wallas reestablishing freedom of speech in America was not only a moral and constitutional imperative; it was a matter of necessity.[43]

Harold Laski wrote to his friend Wallas that he appreciated the *Atlantic* article but remarked that when he himself had recently tried to place a piece in the same magazine, on the necessity for institutions to be criticized, the editor turned it down on the grounds that the readership would not be open to his views.[44] At that moment Laski was at the center of an academic and political firestorm. When he came to teach at Harvard in the fall of 1916, he was only twenty-three and had already established a reputation for brilliance. He was born in Manchester in 1893 into a wealthy Jewish family. His father, Nathan Laski, was the son of a Polish immigrant and had risen from office boy to the pinnacle of the British cotton trade, as well as to a position of leadership in both the Manchester Jewish community and the city's Liberal Party. While a student at the Manchester Grammar School, Harold exhibited great precocity and in 1910 won a scholarship to New College, Oxford. But before going up to Oxford, Laski, who at the age of seventeen had published an article on eugenics in the *Westminster Review*, spent time in London exploring the subject under Karl Pearson. Laski's interest in the scientific creed had been stimulated by his meeting Frida Kerry, a woman several years his senior who was devoted not only to eugenics but to the suffrage movement as well. She was also Gentile, so when Harold and Frida suddenly married in the summer of 1911, his staunchly religious parents were distraught and a family rift was opened. That fall Laski started at Oxford, but his parents insisted that his marriage remain secret. Despite the great personal pressures upon him, Laski, who switched his field of study from science to history, graduated in 1914 with a First Class degree. Because his father cut off all assistance at the close of his college career, finances were a dire problem, but in the summer of 1914, he was hired by George Lansbury to write leaders for the radical *Daily Herald*. When war broke out, Laski tried to enlist but was turned down for medical reasons. So instead, he accepted an offer of a lectureship in history at McGill University in Montreal.

In September 1914 Harold and Frida Laski sailed for Canada, where they would remain for nearly two years. While at McGill Laski met the young Harvard Law School professor Felix Frankfurter, who returned to Harvard singing Laski's praises. Frankfurter's recommendation led to the appointment of Laski as a Harvard instructor, and in the fall of 1916 he came to Cambridge to take up his new post. At Harvard Laski proved to be a popular teacher: his lectures on European history and political theory were well attended, and he became known for his practice of inviting students into his home for evenings of conversation. While he taught at the college, he also began to pursue a degree at the law school, and although forced to drop his formal legal studies, he remained close to the school and even served as book editor of the *Harvard Law Review*. Laski became a firm friend of such law school faculty as Dean Roscoe Pound, Zechariah Chafee, and, above all, Frankfurter, who also was responsible for introducing him to Justice Oliver Wendell Holmes Jr. Holmes and Laski, despite their vastly different backgrounds and philosophies and an age separation of over fifty years, developed an extraordinary personal and intellectual relationship, sustained over the years by faithful correspondence. Along with the rarefied Boston-Cambridge legal circles, Laski also gained entrance to the *New Republic* set that had previously opened itself to Wells and Wallas. He spent the summer before starting at Harvard in New York writing for the magazine and then became a regular contributor.[45]

In his years at Harvard, Laski began to make a name for himself as a political theorist, but the ideas he espoused were very different from the quasi-Marxism for which he later became known. During the late 1910s, and into the twenties, he was immersed in his "pluralist" phase. His orientation was radical, and his sympathy was extended to such groups as women and labor. But while he called himself a socialist, he believed in decentralized power and rejected the notions of collectivism and government control inherent in Marxism and even Fabianism. Directly challenging the traditional concept of sovereignty, he maintained that the state was only one legitimate locus of power in society and that individuals should feel compelled to obey only those acts of state they deemed morally justified. Too often, he would contend throughout his life, government merely served the interests of the dominant economic class. As an adherent of syndicalism, Laski advocated that unions play a crucial societal role, a position that would lead him to trouble at Harvard. Though at this point he disagreed with the aims and methods of Bolshevism, he would come to be labeled in postwar America as a Red.[46]

During his tenure at Harvard, even before he became submerged in controversy, Laski was not entirely happy. Although he forged close friendships on the faculty, was beloved by his students, and reveled in the bookstores of Cambridge, he found the university deficient, particularly when compared to Oxford. Only a few months after taking up his new teaching duties, he wrote to Holmes, "The great drawback about this place is its loneliness. There is nothing of the free intellectual intercourse I had at Oxford, the community of work, and the constant interchange of new ideas." A few weeks later he persisted in this vein when he wrote, "I miss in American life the tonic quality of Oxford where men sit down to examine great things greatly." The Harvard-educated Holmes responded that he was saddened to read of Laski's sentiments and wondered if the contrast drawn between the two universities was not exaggerated, but he conceded that what Laski had observed was a reflection "of the fact that England is a more educated and more civilized country than any part of the U.S. and that you could have found 100 men there to 10 or 1 here who knew the preliminaries for civilized talk." Holmes, however, was apparently trying to elicit from Laski greater understanding when he added, "It takes time to make an educated people or a turf." In his next letter to Holmes, Laski did retreat somewhat from the harsh assessment he had made:

> I don't want to overestimate the value of the atmosphere in Oxford. I am sure that here there is a real eagerness for scholarship and an enthusiasm for the play of the mind. But, if you know what I mean, it isn't *en plein air;* it has to be organised and nursed carefully; it has to be estimated in books and papers; and it doesn't interact with the college life. But I agree that age counts with colleges, just as with wine and I see in some men signs of the change I care passionately about.[47]

Laski's characterization of Harvard and of American higher education in general was in contrast with the praise heaped upon the nation's universities just a few years before by Wells and Wallas. To some extent, his misgivings about Harvard may have simply been the result of difficulties in adjusting to his new environment: he voiced his complaints mainly in his first year of teaching at the university. In 1920 he contributed to the *Manchester Guardian* an article in which he softened his criticism of the college system in the United States and lauded American graduate and professional training.[48] There is also no doubt that in drawing the Harvard-Oxford contrast, he idealized Oxford, which at other times he criticized for being parochial, detached, elitist, and even corrupted. In fact, one of his pet peeves was how ignorant Oxford was of America.[49]

In Laski's second term of teaching at Harvard, the United States entered the First World War. As he observed domestic developments, he grew concerned about the centralization of government power and the decline of progressive ideology, and it is clear that he was no admirer of President Wilson.[50] In the 1916 election neither Wilson nor his Republican opponent, Charles Evans Hughes, excited him, and a few months later he called the New Freedom "simply old dogmas wrapped up in new and greasy paper to keep the rain out."[51] In 1931, ten years after Wilson left office, Laski published an article assessing his presidency in which he praised Wilson for having been an articulate, principled statesman. But Laski, now a socialist, also wrote that the president had been a spokesman for classical liberalism at a time when global realities pointed toward collectivism. Laski's strongest indictment of Wilson, however, was that "in the war years, he permitted an undermining of democratic habits so profound that the period now reads like an essay in the habits of hysteria."[52] Actually, little evidence exists to indicate whether Laski opposed Wilson's civil liberties policy during the war, but as the Red Scare heated up, he vented his objections to the administration's course of action and also his general displeasure with the national mood.[53]

In the fall of 1919, Laski personally got caught up in the Red Scare when he spoke out publicly on the Boston police strike. The police called the strike in September when the commissioner, Edwin U. Curtis, refused to recognize their newly formed, AFL-affiliated union and threw the union's leaders off the force. With the city left virtually unprotected, looting, vandalism, and violence broke out in various sections, and it would be a couple of days before a volunteer force and the state guard brought an end to the lawlessness. Meanwhile, not only were the police receiving little sympathy for their action, but within Boston and around the country the strike was being characterized as a Bolshevik plot. Although Mayor Andrew J. Peters favored coming to terms with the police, Curtis took a hard line and was supported by Governor Calvin Coolidge, whose handling of the crisis brought him into the national spotlight. Curtis eventually dismissed all of the strikers and hired an entirely new force.[54]

Commenting on the police strike was a perilous action for Laski to take. He could not have assumed that he was safe behind the ivy walls of the university, because during the war and postwar years academic freedom in America was at a low point. Certain professors were fired for their alleged disloyalty to the war effort, the most infamous dismissals taking place at Columbia, where the imperious president, Nicholas Murray Butler, formally suspended academic freedom. After the war the groves of academe became a target for Red-hunters, and aspersions were cast on a number of prominent, liberal-leaning professors, including Laski's Harvard Law School friends Frankfurter, Chafee, and Pound. Actually, Harvard's president, A. Lawrence Lowell, had proved during the war to be a staunch defender of academic freedom, but as Laski was to find out, that did not mean that Harvard professors could utter unpopular views without consequence.[55]

On October 15, 1919, over a month after the police strike began, Laski took the fateful step of addressing remarks to a meeting of the officers' wives, in which he expressed his support for the strikers and criticized the actions of Commissioner Curtis. According to Laski the policemen were striking for a "principle," and he charged Curtis with both obstinacy and incompetence. He clearly was offering his encouragement to the beleaguered strikers when he uttered the words, "Labour will never surrender."[56] Needless to say, given the atmosphere both in Boston and throughout the nation in the fall of 1919, Laski was harshly attacked for taking this position. Recalling two decades later how he had become immersed in such controversy, he stated:

> It seemed to me that one ought to know why the police were striking before one accepted the view that the city was right. Accordingly, I took great pains to discover what had led to the strike, and found that it was the outcome of long-accumulated grievances met without sympathy or insight. I ventured to say so; and there broke about my head a storm of indignation in which I was described as almost everything from a villain who seduced youth to a Bolshevik who preached revolution.[57]

In 1919 Laski wrote to Wallas, who was then teaching in America, that it was necessary to realize that policemen could be just as "dissatisfied" as workers in other fields, and he told Holmes that the authorities, instead of trying to address the legitimate concerns of the policemen, had simply proscribed the union.[58] To Bertrand Russell he wrote, "I was charged with teaching sovietism when I said that men who get 1,100 dollars and work a seventy-three hours week are justified in striking after thirteen years' agitation."[59]

Laski's remarks created an uproar in Boston, but particularly within the Harvard community. Outraged alumni called for Laski to be fired, forcing the Board of Overseers to launch an investigation into the matter.[60] Even before commenting on the police strike, Laski had apparently already been criticized within the supreme governing body of the university, the Harvard Corporation, for being too left-leaning and too influential with the students. He had been satisfied that the indictment had been effectively answered within the corporation yet told Wallas, "It makes me long for the English climate."[61] When the Board of Overseers probed into Laski's conduct over the police strike, he was compelled to answer to a committee headed by a George Wigglesworth at a Boston club. By Laski's account, which was not always reliable, the overseers were unprepared to make any case against him and simply wanted him to respond to the charge lodged by a certain professor that he was an anarchist.[62] Based on one version of the story Laski told, perhaps apocryphal, Wigglesworth's inquisition took on a comic tone: "He looked at me and said: 'Mr. Laski, do you believe in bloody revolution?' I looked him straight in the eye and said: 'Mr. Wigglesworth, do I look as if I did?' We all laughed and had a good dinner."[63] Laski, however, did not simply shrug off the event as an amusing incident, for he wrote Wallas that he felt content about the decision he had by now made not to remain at Harvard: "One can't be useful where the directive force is timidity."[64]

Though Laski had resolved to leave Harvard, the decision was his own. He had not been forced to resign, to a great extent because President Lowell maintained his devotion to academic freedom and stood by the young teacher.[65] After Laski had left the university, Lowell wanted it understood that he had not been dismissed.[66] Laski did appreciate that the president defended his freedom of expression, and in the midst of the controversy he wrote to Holmes, "Lowell was magnificent and I felt that I had a president in him I would fight for."[67] Although Lowell supported Laski's right to speak out, he disapproved of the position that Laski had taken on the police strike—Lowell had encouraged Harvard students to enlist in the volunteer force—and of his radical activism in general.[68] The president wrote to his friend Wallas about Laski after the professor had departed Cambridge: "He certainly took great pains with his students; his real difficulty being that he loved to be in the limelight, which is not conducive to profound scholarship."[69] Lowell must have said essentially the same thing to Laski himself, for it seems that the president's displeasure was crucial in influencing his decision to return to England. As Laski told it a generation later:

> President Lowell explained to me with emphasis that a teacher limited his utility when he spoke on matters of current controversy. I was not, I inferred, to say my say on the living issues of the time if what I said was inconvenient to the rulers of Harvard. Mr. Lowell spoke with kindness, but his implication was clear.[70]

Although Lowell mixed his public defense of Laski with a private rebuke, unadulterated support did come from other quarters of the university. When at the end of 1919 the satirical *Harvard Lampoon* devoted an entire issue to a malicious attack on Laski, Dean Pound was outraged, as was the bulk of the student body.[71] The *Lampoon* branded Laski a Bolshevik and suggested that, like the Reds being rounded up by the Justice Department, he too should be deported. That Laski was not only a radical, but an English Jew to boot, had from the outset been an important factor in the campaign against him, but in the *Lampoon* he was now confronted with blatant, vicious anti-Semitism. Disturbing as the *Lampoon*'s assault was, Laski felt grateful that so many undergraduates rallied around him. The *Lampoon* was denounced in meetings and letters to the school paper, the *Crimson*, and students continued to pack his lectures. In fact, Laski assumed something of an heroic stature on campus.[72]

By the beginning of 1920, though Laski had resolved to leave Harvard, his future plans remained uncertain. He told Holmes, "It's been borne in on me these last months that I can't be useful in Harvard in the way I hoped when I first came over." According to Laski, the corporation viewed him as a foreigner with unacceptable political views, and the faculty resented him for believing that professors should be attentive to their students and saw the changes he advocated as constituting "Oxfordising." Laski related that he had asked Wallas to help find him a teaching position back in England.[73] While Wallas had been in the United States in the fall of 1919, he had endeavored to get a lectureship in American history established at Oxford and at one point even mentioned Laski as a possible candidate.[74] Laski, however, was not destined to return to Oxford. Instead, Wallas, aided by Lord Haldane, secured him a post at the London School of Economics, where he would remain as an institution for thirty years, until his death in 1950.[75]

In Laski's last term at Harvard, in the spring of 1920, not only did his personal troubles fade into the background, but he sensed, correctly as it turned out, that the repressive grip over the nation was also loosening. He was outraged by the massiveness of the January Palmer raids, but in February he detected "a lull in the anti-red hysteria." Then, in March, while he noted the continuing exploits of the Lusk Committee, he wrote, "Yet I think the deep bitterness has passed. Certainly here the atmosphere is clearer."[76] With national tensions easing and his own controversy receding into the distance, and with his position at the LSE set for the following fall, Laski's final months at Harvard appear to have been pleasant enough. Touched by the outpouring of affection shown him as his time wound down, he left Cambridge on a positive note. Two weeks before sailing back to England, Laski wrote to Wallas, "We've been so overwhelmed with dinners and books from faculty and students as to make the American adventure, in semi-retrospect, a very precious thing."[77]

When Laski was back in London teaching at the LSE, he wrote to Pound that he missed Cambridge and that "all the time I realise how vivid and vital has been that American experience. It has conferred a kind of detachment and perspective not otherwise obtainable and I can never be too grateful for it."[78] He elaborated on the notion that during his time in America he had gone through a crucial learning process when, decades later, he wrote, "There is, I think, a sense in which my years on the American continent were the most fundamental experience of my life." Not only did his stay in America confirm for him that he should be a teacher—an involved, activist teacher—but it shaped his sociopolitical views. He wrote of the United States, "I saw there, more nakedly than I had seen in Europe, the significance of the struggle between capital and labor. I learned how little meaning there can be in an abstract political liberty which is subdued by the control of an economic plutocracy." According to Laski, certain strikes, like those at Lowell and Ludlow, impressed upon him how brutal the state can be in upholding the economic elite, and an incident like the imprisonment of Debs showed how far societal intolerance can extend. The extreme American reaction to the Bolshevik Revolution provided evidence of how thought is molded by the prevalent economic arrangement. He stated, "I came back from America convinced that liberty has no meaning save in the context of equality, and I had begun to understand that equality, also, has no meaning unless the instruments of production are socially controlled."[79] In short, by Laski's own judgment, the American experience transformed him from a socialist-leaning radical into a confirmed socialist, and in the next decades he did travel a road that took him through Fabianism and eventually to Marxism. In those decades Laski would return to the United States frequently and develop a knowledge of America unparalleled by few others in Britain.

In late 1921, with his attention still focused on America's global role, Wells made his second trip to the United States. He journeyed across the Atlantic to report on the Washington Conference on the Limitation of Armaments, and his series of articles, published in a variety of newspapers in the New World and Old, was subsequently collected in a volume titled *Washington and the Hope of Peace* in Britain and *Washington and the Riddle of Peace* in America.[80] Although the Washington Conference has largely faded from historical memory, contemporaries viewed it as a momentous event, and joining Wells in covering the proceedings were such prominent journalists as H. W. Nevinson and H. Wickham Steed from Britain and Mark Sullivan and William Allen White of the United States. The conference represented the first major foreign policy initiative of the Republican administration of President Warren G. Harding, who had been elected in 1920 in a contest that revealed public disapproval of Wilsonian foreign policy and the League of Nations in particular. But if America was going to remain aloof from the League, some alternative short of total isolation was necessary, and so Harding enunciated the idea that the United States should participate in ad hoc "associations" to solve specific global problems. The Washington Conference was to be one such "association," and the issues to be addressed were the beginnings of an international arms race—Congress had urged Harding to press for disarmament—and the buildup of tensions in Asia and the Pacific. Leaders representing all of the major powers, except notably Germany and Russia, congregated in Washington, and the chairman of the conference, Secretary of State Charles Evans Hughes, guaranteed that the proceedings would be substantive when at the outset he offered some bold proposals. The conference resulted in three significant treaties, each ratified by the Senate. One agreement set limits on the size of battleship fleets; the Anglo-Japanese Alliance was junked and replaced by an accord between Britain, the United States, Japan, and France to submit disputes in the Pacific to negotiation; and nine powers signed an agreement to uphold the principle of an Open Door in China.[81]

While in Washington, Wells's role was not that of the reporter merely recording the proceedings of the conference. His articles were filled more with analysis than with observations, and even more commonly he simply used the conference as the starting point to launch into his views on global affairs. In fact, he stayed in Washington only for the first half of the nearly three-month meeting. As he had written a year before in the undelivered lectures that would become part of *The Salvaging of Civilization*, Wells in these articles enunciated his belief that the postwar world was rapidly deteriorating, and he still saw international federation as the only answer. Although he put little stock in disarmament and believed economic issues should have been accorded top priority at the conference, the idea that representatives from various nations were congregating in Washington to try to tackle some major global problems did appeal to him. One of the key themes of *Washington and the Riddle of Peace* is the world leadership role Wells hoped America would assume, and by playing host to this international conference the nation, he acknowledged, was already stepping into that role. Although in *The Salvaging of Civilization* Wells had been inclined to let America off the hook by arguing that the Europeans needed to get their own affairs in order before any appeals could be made to the United States, he now was calling, as he had during the war, for America to take the central position on the world stage. In *The Salvaging of Civilization* he had asserted that America could endure the disintegration of the Old World, but now he was not quite so confident.

In the first article that Wells wrote for his Washington Conference series, before the proceedings had even begun, he stated, "Coming as I do from Europe to America, I am amazed at the apparent buoyancy and abundance of New York. The place seems to possess an inexhaustible vitality." Nevertheless, he argued, New York was dependent on European trade, and if Europe were to sink under the weight of its economic troubles, as had already occurred in certain countries, the city would be placed in great jeopardy. New York might seem robust now, but

within a very few years the same chill wind of economic disaster that has wrecked Petersburg and brought death to Vienna and Warsaw may be rusting and tarnishing all this glistening, bristling vitality. In a little while, within my lifetime, New York City may stand even more gaunt, ruinous, empty and haunted than that stricken and terrible ruin, Petersburg.[82]

As he revealed in the course of the volume, Wells believed that America as a whole would fare better than New York, but he was not as sure as he had been in *The Salvaging of Civilization* that the New World would suffer little from calamity in the Old. His assessment was that although there would be "some very severe stresses," America would "pull through." American farmers and manufacturers dependent on exports would both suffer, and East Coast cities would be so adversely affected that the center of the nation would shift inland. Yet, despite the impact it would feel, America would "still be getting along in a fashion." The problem was that Americans knew they could muddle through catastrophe in Europe or Asia and so felt safe retreating into isolation.[83]

Although the United States could get by if the rest of the world fell into disarray, Wells argued that it would be "hoggish" for Americans to forsake playing a premier global role. He appealed to the nation to accept the moral responsibilities that accompanied its status as the world's strongest and wealthiest power:

> The cream of all the white races did not come to this continent to reap and sow and eat and waste, smoke in its shirt-sleeves in a rocking-chair, and let the great world from which its fathers came go hang. It did not come here for sluggish ease. It came here for liberty and to make the new beginning of a greater civilization upon our globe.

The time had come for America, its achievements secure, to turn its attention to the wider world. The United States was now so powerful, he contended, that it could virtually impose its will upon Europe.[84]

Wells acknowledged that America had already made great strides toward assuming its position of global leadership simply by convoking the Washington Conference and, earlier, initiating the League of Nations. He chose not to dwell here on the limitations and deficiencies of the League, but rather on its origins as the by-product of an idealistic American foreign policy unsullied by the traditions of European diplomacy. The conception of the League was "an adventure which threw a halo of greatness about the Nation that produced it and about that splendid and yet so humanly limited man who has been chiefly identified with its promise and its partial failure." Realizing that the League, as it turned out, fell short of expectations, "the American mind, with much freshness and boldness, has produced this second experiment, in a widely different direction, the First Washington Conference for the Limitation of Armaments."[85]

Warren Harding, who proposed the idea of international problem-solving associations and convened the Washington Conference, was treated by Wells with surprising deference. Wells was aware of the criticism heaped upon the president by his many detractors but found it to be unjustified. His first contact with Harding came when he heard the president speak at the funeral of the Unknown Soldier at Arlington on November 11, three years after the armistice was signed and one day before the Washington Conference opened.[86] Wells was impressed by Harding's mere physical presence: "He is a very big, fine-looking man and his voice is a wonderful instrument. . . . He is—how can I say it?—more statuesque than any of the American Presidents of recent times, but without a trace in his movements or appearance of posturing or vanity." Wells found the address Harding delivered at Arlington, though characterized by a typically American rhetorical style, to be exemplary, and he also praised the speech with which the president opened the Washington Conference. But above all, he felt a gratitude toward Harding for initiating the "association" concept into world politics. Wells hoped that the Washington Conference would lead to more conferences and eventually to a more permanent body: "Simply and naturally, step by step, the President of the United States will have become the official summoner of a rudimentary World Parliament."[87]

When Harding addressed a joint session of Congress, Wells was again favorably impressed. And he discovered that like Harding, the Congress also did not conform to negative advanced billing. He had heard nothing but disparaging remarks from both Europeans and Americans about Congress: "The Senate, by the unanimous testimony of the conversationalists of the United States, combines the ignoble with the diabolical in a peculiarly revolting mixture." Wells was worried, based on such assessments, that Congress would spoil "any dream of America taking her place as the leading power in the world, as the first embodiment of the New Thing in international affairs." But he found Congress to be an engaged, responsive body that was willing to consider new ideas, and as for its reputation for corruption, he stated, "I doubt if there is nearly as much business and financial intrigue in the lobbies of Washington as in the lobbies of Westminster."[88]

Wells was in one respect critical of the American government's organization of the Washington Conference: he lamented that Germany and, even more important, Russia were excluded. Although no admirer of the Bolshevik regime, Wells believed, as he had previously argued in *Russia in the Shadows* (1920), that America should be trying to help the Russians through their tough times. The Soviet Union needed to be assisted, not anathematized, and if such a policy were to be pursued, the nation could be transformed into "a democratic land of common people more like the free, poor, farming, prospecting and developing United States of 1840 than anything else in history." He wondered whether America would fulfill its destiny as leader of a new global order: "Are Germany and Russia to perish amid the incurable quarrels of the Old World or find their salvation in the New?"[89]

As a consequence of his trip to Washington, Wells at last made reference to the suppression of civil liberties that had plagued the nation in recent years. He sympathetically told of a protest held outside the entrance to the conference to draw attention to Debs's imprisonment. And Wells also made a point of shining a light on some of the disparities that existed within America. When he journeyed outside Washington into the countryside of Maryland and Virginia, he found that the grandeur of the capital did not extend beyond its borders. He was shocked by the terrible squalor he observed—by the "miserable wood houses," "hovels rather than houses," and by "the extreme illiteracy of many of the poorer folk, white as well as colored." He exclaimed, "I have to remind myself that I am in what is now the greatest, richest, most powerful country in the world."[90]

5

Main Street America

G. K. Chesterton and the Culture of the United States in the 1920s

G. K. Chesterton framed the decade of the 1920s by making two trips to the United States, both of which inspired books. Because Chesterton stood as Wells's ideological antagonist, it is not surprising that his view of America was substantially at odds with that of Wells. Though the 1920s marked a contrast to the progressive era that had shaped Wells's thinking on America, Chesterton's essential arguments about the United States would probably have been much the same no matter when he embarked on his transatlantic travels. Chesterton brought to bear on America his distinctive radical right-wing views and his penetrating powers of observation, and the result was commentary that is at once iconoclastic, subtle, and witty. The America that he cherished was the part that still conformed to the Jeffersonian ideal of small towns, farms, and a simple democratic citizenry. In contrast to both Stead and Wells, Chesterton emphasized that the two nations were not bound together in a common English-speaking culture but rather were distinct, separate societies. On this point he stood on common ground with his friend Hilaire Belloc and even a leftist like Rebecca West, while other Britons, such as John St. Loe Strachey, continued to champion Anglo-American solidarity.

When Chesterton first came to the United States, he was already an accomplished writer and well-known personality on both sides of the Atlantic. Born in 1874 in the Kensington section of London, Gilbert Keith Chesterton entered into a prosperous, cultured middle-class world.[1] His father headed the long-established family estate agency but showed more interest in literature, art, and his various hobbies. The household in which Gilbert and his younger brother, Cecil, grew up was Liberal in politics, Unitarian in religion, and properly Victorian in matters of conduct. Gilbert's childhood was happy and carefree, but he was never more than a lackluster student at St. Paul's School. Though his friends would eventually go up to Oxford, he remained in London and took courses at University College. The two years he spent at the university were tough ones for Chesterton: his foray into formal art training was apparently a failure, and as he tried to make the personal and intellectual transition to adulthood, he was left feeling depressed. He gained a sense of well-being once again when in 1895, after leaving the university, he found a niche in publishing, which provided him a living until 1901. Furthermore, in 1896 he met and fell in love with his future wife, Frances Blogg.

At the turn of the century Chesterton's literary career began to take off. In 1899 he was invited by the *Bookman* to review works about art, and in 1900 he published two volumes of verse and started to write for the radical *Speaker*. Chesterton gained a reputation for his tough pro-Boer stance, and by 1902 the Liberal *Daily News* had hired him to write a regular weekly column. Two collections of his journalism appeared in 1901 and 1902, the first of many such volumes to be published over the course of his career. So impressed, apparently, was John Morley with the sketches Chesterton had penned of various literary figures that he asked the young writer to undertake the life of Robert Browning for the prestigious "English Men of Letters" series. Chesterton's brilliant but unconventional study of Browning appeared in 1903, and he subsequently came out with original, engaging works on Dickens (1906), Shaw (1909), and Blake (1910). Chesterton, who by 1905 had added the "Our Notebook" column of the *Illustrated London News* to his duties, turned into a fixture on Fleet Street—a massive, disheveled figure donning a broad-brimmed hat and black cloak and carrying a sword-stick and revolver, who could generally be found in the pubs and taverns immersed in writing or conversation. Furthermore, he became one of the most versatile literary talents of Edwardian England: besides being a journalist, critic, essayist, and poet, he developed into a successful writer of fiction. Chesterton published three fantasies, *The Napoleon of Notting Hill* (1904), *The Man Who Was Thursday* (1908), and *The Ball and the Cross* (1909), and by 1911 a collection of his popular Father Brown detective stories had appeared. He would also soon venture into the writing of drama and history.

During the first decade of the century, Chesterton's social, political, and religious philosophy began to emerge. In formulating his ideas he was very much influenced by Hilaire Belloc, to the point that Shaw dubbed the pair "the Chesterbelloc." In 1900 Chesterton met and became close friends with the French-born, English-raised Belloc, who had made a brilliant showing at Oxford and was on the verge of inaugurating the same kind of diverse, successful literary career as Chesterton. The first splash that Chesterton made as a cultural commentator was with the 1905 publication of *Heretics,* a set of essays in which he skewered Wells, Shaw, and other noted British figures for what he saw as their godless devotion to progress. Although raised in a religiously indifferent family, Chesterton had become a devout High Church Anglican, and in *Orthodoxy* of 1908 he affirmed his adherence to Christianity. By the 1910s he was attracted to Catholicism, into which Belloc was born and to which his brother, Cecil, converted in 1913, but not until 1922 would he himself be received into the Church of Rome.

In enunciating his sociopolitical views, Chesterton defended the traditional values associated with family, home, and community, values he believed were under siege in the twentieth century. He also opposed imperialism while extolling patriotism: thus he was not inconsistent in denouncing the Boer War and then backing Britain's participation in the First World War. His sympathies lay with the common people, and as a young man he even considered himself something of a socialist. But he came to believe, as Belloc did, that the remedy of socialism could be as harmful as the disease it was supposed to cure, industrial capitalism. Not only did Chesterton voice his disapproval of Fabianism but he could not even countenance the more measured welfare schemes being implemented by 1910 under the aegis of the Liberal government. To Chesterton policies that placed greater wealth or power in the hands of the government deprived the people of their freedom. This view was encapsulated in Belloc's 1912 masterpiece, *The Servile State,* which also for the first time proposed what came to be called Distributism, a program that for the rest of his life Chesterton championed even more effectively than Belloc. The Distributist notion was that the best way to deal with the inequities of capitalism was not to turn all of the wealth over to the state, but rather to redistribute that wealth among the citizenry and maintain a small-scale, local-oriented economy. Chesterton and Belloc saw the Middle Ages as the golden era, and though they disdained utopias, they wished to usher in a new period of peasant farmers and craft guilds. By embracing such a scheme, Chesterton was being at the same time radical and reactionary. In the early 1910s he could maintain sympathies for the syndicalists and contribute to the socialist *Daily Herald*, while on the other hand during the 1920s he flirted with fascism and some of his most extreme Distributist followers disavowed the use of any modern technology. One scholar has suggested that the best term to describe Chesterton's ideology is "populist."[2]

Chesterton's views during the 1910s were also to a large extent affected by personal experience. In that decade his career became intertwined with that of his brother, Cecil, a journalist who, though originally a Fabian, had also come into Belloc's orbit. Cecil was five years younger than Gilbert, and his mind was sharper and his temperament fiercer than his older brother's. In 1911 Belloc and Cecil Chesterton co-authored *The Party System*, an exposé, informed by Belloc's own tenure as a Liberal MP, that charged that Parliament, though ostensibly divided along party lines, was actually controlled by a bipartisan clique of wealthy front-benchers. The two men in the same year also inaugurated the *Eye-Witness*, a hard-hitting, muckraking magazine that Belloc edited for one year before turning the helm over to Cecil, who subsequently relaunched the organ as the *New Witness*. In 1912 he played a leading role in unveiling the so-called Marconi Scandal, a complicated affair in which top members of the Liberal government bought, or were perhaps given, stock in the American Marconi Company while the British Marconi Company was on the verge of sealing a big contract with the government. Cecil Chesterton assailed these dubious dealings with a vehemence that at times led him to make reckless accusations, and he so wantonly attacked the reputation of Marconi director Godfrey Isaacs, the brother of the attorney general, Sir Rufus Isaacs, that he was sued for libel, found guilty, and fined one hundred pounds.

For G. K. Chesterton the Marconi Scandal and his brother's libel trial proved to be a turning point. The affair further soured him on Liberalism and forced him to follow Belloc and Cecil into disavowing parliamentary government altogether, and he became so embittered at the Isaacs brothers that a hostility to Jews that had been developing within him for years now became more blatant. While never as extreme as Belloc or especially his brother in his anti-Semitism, which had played a big factor in the assault on the "Marconi men" from the beginning, Chesterton would be openly critical of the Jews for the rest of his life. Although he defended himself against the charge of anti-Semitism by arguing that a few of his closest friends were Jewish and that he simply believed the Jews were a distinctive people who could not be assimilated into national cultures—and in the 1930s he did denounce Hitler's outrages—there can be no denying that Chesterton's feelings toward the Jews were antagonistic. After the Marconi Scandal he still maintained his sprightly, childlike qualities, as exhibited in the whimsical novel *The Flying Inn* (1914), but his outlook had hardened. Then when the First World War broke out, his life took another turn. Cecil enlisted in the army, and Gilbert agreed to serve as caretaker of the *New Witness*, to which he had frequently contributed. But when Cecil died while in the service, Gilbert felt obligated to become the permanent editor of the magazine, which he would reorganize in the 1920s as *G. K.'s Weekly*.

Chesterton's decision to journey to America in 1921 seems to have resulted from a variety of considerations. Since the last days of the war he had begun to travel, and two extensive trips had generated two successful books. In the fall of 1918 he visited Ireland—whose rural, Catholic character he loved and with whose nationalistic ambitions he sympathized—and recorded his thoughts in articles for the *New Witness* that were then published as *Irish Impressions*. Then, in 1920, he ventured much farther afield when he traveled to Palestine, which had just come under British protection, to write a series of articles for the *Daily Telegraph*. These articles became the basis for *The New Jerusalem*, in which Chesterton voiced his strong support for Zionism, though his motivation was clearly less a sympathy for Jewish yearnings than a desire to draw the Jews out of Europe. Having never crossed the Atlantic, Chesterton naturally chose America as his next destination. Like so many British observers before him, he planned to travel to the United States partly enticed by the prospect of profit. He had been sinking large sums of his own money into the financially precarious *New Witness* and needed to generate some income. As it turned out, the many lectures he would deliver in America, each at a fee of $1,000, permitted Chesterton and his wife to construct their own home in Beaconsfield, the town west of London to which they had moved in 1909, and the book that resulted from the American tour would also provide a windfall.[3] Furthermore, it is very likely that Chesterton was prompted to see America because Cecil had spent time there, and in fact the last book his brother wrote was the posthumously published *History of the United States* (1919), to which Gilbert contributed an introduction.

Cecil Chesterton visited America in early 1915 at the invitation of pro-Allied groups who arranged for him to lecture on the war. In New York he also debated the editor George Sylvester Viereck on the merits of the British position versus the German. As he traveled around the country, he was favorably impressed by what he observed, and upon returning from the trip he embarked on his *History of the United States*.[4] Chesterton explained in the preface to the book that what he "saw and heard of contemporary America so fascinated me that—believing as I do that the key to every people is in its past—I could not rest until I had mastered all that I could of the history of my delightful hosts."[5] The amount of research that he could undertake was limited because in 1916 he went on active duty, and the book was actually written in the time he spent on convalescent leave. In his introduction to the work, G. K. Chesterton stated that at his death Cecil felt gratified that "he had been able, often in the intervals of bitter warfare and by the aid of a brilliant memory, to put together these pages on the history, so necessary and so strangely neglected, of the great democracy which he never patronized, which he not only loved but honoured."[6]

D. W. Brogan, the British historian of America, published an annotated version of the work in 1940 and in his introduction wrote that he found the history seriously flawed yet compelling. According to Brogan, Chesterton's course of reading on America was often misguided and the book was rife with factual errors and faulty conclusions. But he thought Chesterton's style crisp and bold and the story of America's political development, the author's focus, magnificently told. Brogan wrote of Chesterton, "Because he had a point of view, heterodox, dogmatic, and very much his own, his narrative has a unity and a permanent interest that most professors and popularizers fail to attain."[7]

Cecil Chesterton's *History of the United States* reflects the perspective on society that he, his brother, and Belloc had come to share, and when G. K. wrote about America shortly after, he echoed some of the ideas contained in this book. Cecil traced the history of America from colonization through Reconstruction, with more recent decades receiving merely a cursory treatment in a brief final chapter. He depicted Puritan New England as an oppressive, fanatical society, and throughout the book sons of Massachusetts are cast in an unflattering light, from the Adamses to Charles Sumner, who is vilified for his extremist role in Reconstruction. Catholic Maryland, Chesterton stressed, was first in establishing the principle of religious toleration, and he also wrote glowingly of William Penn and his Quaker experiment. But he asserted that Virginia was the dominant colony and, later, state and displayed his admiration for the Founding Fathers who hailed from the Old Dominion, particularly Thomas Jefferson. To Chesterton, Jefferson played the key role in establishing the principles of American democracy and ensuring that Alexander Hamilton's more elitist, more traditionally English vision of politics and society would not prevail. If, however, Jefferson was a star in Chesterton's eyes, he nevertheless had to take second billing to the true hero of this *History of the United States,* Andrew Jackson. It is not difficult to see why Jackson would appeal so heartily to Chesterton, because the president, at least in the author's interpretation of events, was the representative of the common man who slew the money power, as embodied in Nicholas Biddle's Second Bank of the United States, and guaranteed that the oligarchy inherent in Whig dreams of congressional supremacy was defeated. To Chesterton, Jackson was like a benign, democratic king, and he saw the president as nothing less than "a second founder." A key, Chesterton believed, to understanding Jackson was his Western upbringing, and other Westerners, including Jackson's opponent Henry Clay, also fare relatively well in this history. But the product of the frontier Chesterton most revered, after Jackson, was Abraham Lincoln, whom he saw as the heir to the Jefferson-Jackson tradition and whose wisdom and political acumen could have averted what, in his eyes, became the tragedy of Reconstruction.[8]

When G. K. Chesterton visited America in 1921, two years after his brother's death, he spent three months touring the Northeast, the Midwest, and the South and crossed into Canada as well. At the outset of the trip he told reporters that he planned to go no further west than Chicago, for "having seen both Jerusalem and Chicago, I think I shall have touched on the extremes of civilization." But he ultimately did venture beyond Chicago to such destinations as Omaha, St. Louis, and Oklahoma City. As he made his way across America, Chesterton delivered talks on three topics, "The Ignorance of the Educated," "Shall We Abolish the Inevitable?" and "The Perils of Health." He found it more gratifying to lecture before American audiences than British because, as he told a reporter in the United States, "Here the good people are most appreciative of the individual's efforts, whether that individual be Charlie Chaplin, Mr. Dempsey or myself." Controversy, however, pursued Chesterton as he proceeded on his lecture tour, for he was denounced from the pulpits of synagogues for the anti-Semitism expressed in *The New Jerusalem*. In Omaha he exclaimed, "I have left a trail of wailing rabbis all across the continent."[9]

When Chesterton first arrived in the New World, he apparently had no intention of writing about America and scoffed at the idea that after such a short stay he could produce a book on the subject. He even poked fun at the superficial, hastily written books on America turned out by so many Englishmen. But after having been in the United States for only a month he was already recording his impressions for the *New Witness*, and these articles would become the basis for *What I Saw in America*. When the book came out, Chesterton was apologetic for having written it but defended himself by saying that he was adhering to tradition: "Everybody who goes to America for a short time is expected to write a book; and nearly everybody does." No one, he noted, expected a traveler to write a book upon returning from any other country.[10]

Despite its pedestrian title, *What I Saw in America* is an insightful study full of the famous Chestertonian sense of paradox. Chesterton did not write so much about what he saw in America as about what he believed to be the essential character of American civilization. The book, however, does contain the author's observations on, for example, American hotels, American weather, and American fashion, and he did devote significant space to conveying his impressions of the various cities he visited, particularly New York, which he concluded was unique.[11] What set it apart from other American cities of the same vintage was that it was so transient in quality; buildings were constantly being torn down to make way for new. In Philadelphia, Boston, and Baltimore, and even in younger inland cities like St. Louis and Nashville, he found a sense of tradition manifest in the prominence of historic monuments and the survival of old homes. He did not object on aesthetic grounds to New York's skyscrapers and massive illuminated signs; he disliked them for what they represented, the triumph of commerce. The illuminated signs along Broadway were not unattractive, but as advertisements their purpose was merely to enrich the few, and he contrasted them with the popularly inspired bonfires and fireworks of Guy Fawkes Day:

Mobs have risen in support of No Popery; no mobs are likely to rise in defence of the New Puffery. Many a poor, crazy Orangeman has died saying, "To Hell with the Pope"; it is doubtful whether any man will ever, with his last breath, frame the ecstatic words, "Try Hugby's Chewing Gum."[12]

While Chesterton's descriptions of various American cities reveal that he recognized the nation's diversity, even more important, as reflected in his contrast of New York's illuminated signs with Guy Fawkes displays, he stressed the differences that divided America from England. The social, cultural, and political gap between the two nations is one of the overriding themes of the book, making it much more like a comparative study than other works by Britons on the United States. By emphasizing the distinctions between America and England, Chesterton was not trying to sow the seeds of dissension. In fact, he felt that interaction between the two nations was amicable and hoped it would remain so. But he believed in the uniqueness of nations and peoples and contended that the Anglo-American relationship would be healthier if differences were not glossed over.[13]

At the very outset of the book, Chesterton wrote that a traveler in a foreign country can justifiably feel amused by what he encounters but should never be supercilious. The customs and mores of another society may, in the traveler's eye, be funny, but that does not mean they are inferior. The duty of the traveler is to try to understand the essence of a foreign culture's foreignness. Chesterton applied this principle to his own experience in coming to America. As Wells and Shaw had noted before him, the form to be filled out to obtain permission to enter the United States contained such questions as: "Are you an anarchist?" and "Are you a polygamist?" Chesterton found these inquiries to be amusing, but he came to realize, even before setting sail, that the questions were not as absurd as they seemed and actually revealed much about the uniqueness of the United States. According to Chesterton, "America is the only nation in the world that is founded on a creed. That creed is set forth with dogmatic and even theological lucidity in the Declaration of Independence." Furthermore, as immigrants from all over the world flowed into America, the notion of retaining some sort of ideological standard remained strong. America may have been a "melting-pot," but it was a pot of a "certain shape" "traced on the lines of Jeffersonian democracy." It was difficult, Chesterton wrote, for the English to understand the American litmus tests, because their own nation did not have a "creed," but merely a "character" built up over the centuries. An Englishman was an Englishman whether he was an anarchist or not.[14]

Chesterton argued that the English should appreciate America for its special American qualities and not for the vestiges of England that could be detected there. "We have never even begun to understand a people," he asserted, "until we have found something that we do not understand." To Chesterton the United States was more alien than either France or Ireland. Throughout his book, and particularly in two chapters titled "The Spirit of America" and "The Spirit of England," he attempted to draw the distinctions between the two peoples. He felt the Americans were more enthusiastic than the English, who prided themselves on being cool and restrained. America was intense, as manifest in a devotion to sports that were "not in the least sportive," as opposed to England, where the influence of the aristocracy had created a carefree, leisurely atmosphere. Furthermore, the American, in contrast to the Englishman, was unabashedly curious. And as Tocqueville had noted, Chesterton saw that the Americans were gregarious and given to joining all sorts of clubs and organizations, whereas the English, with a tendency toward moodiness, avoided such concentrated social activity.[15]

It was not Chesterton's intention to decide which nation's traits were superior, yet he was compelled to make some judgments. American "comradeship" had helped to bolster the nation's democratic spirit, but "on the other hand the Englishman has certainly more liberty, if less equality and fraternity." And the English, in their solitary existences, were blessed with a poetic spirit. He also believed, as Harriet Martineau and others had observed, that the democratic atmosphere of America bred conformity. According to Chesterton, it was ironic that the "individualism" so cherished by Americans actually led to a loss of "individuality," as competition fostered imitation. He took pride in the English embrace of eccentricity but conceded that the Americans put a higher premium on intelligence and paid greater attention to genius. The French, by his reasoning, had instilled in the Americans a veneration for the intellect that was lacking in England. He averred, "It is not so much that Englishmen are stupid as that they are afraid of being clever; and it is not so much that Americans are clever as that they do not try to be any stupider than they are."[16]

The tendency in America toward uniformity, Chesterton argued, took on an ugly manifestation in the prevalence of fads and the "petty tyranny" often exerted by public opinion. The most conspicuous contemporary example of this phenomenon of behavioral control was Prohibition, which Chesterton attacked in his book as he had in his interviews with the American press. It was inevitable that he would oppose Prohibition, because for years in his own country he had defended the right of the common man to have his glass of ale or cup of wine and protested any attempts by temperance reformers to open the way for government regulation of drinking. He charged that in "dry" America the Volstead Act, to the extent that it was enforced at all, was enforced among the poor, while the rich drank at will. The idea behind the legislation was to increase worker productivity to maximize profits. Chesterton asserted that Prohibition, even if it was more an ideal than a reality, violated the Declaration of Independence just as slavery had. One of the cardinal principles of Jeffersonian democracy was that government should allow individuals the greatest possible liberty in their personal lives.[17]

That prohibitive regulations could so easily take root in America Chesterton attributed to the nation's Puritan legacy.[18] He felt a disdain for Puritanism and deplored that the English, whom he charged with being lamentably ignorant of the history of the United States, seemed to believe that the Pilgrims were the first to settle America. Just as mistakenly, they thought of the Pilgrims as defenders of religious toleration.[19] In an article written around the time that he released his book, titled "The Myth of the 'Mayflower,'" Chesterton elaborated on the idea that the *Mayflower*'s meaning and significance had been distorted, in both Britain and America. He wrote that "the 'Mayflower' is not merely a fable, but is much more false than fables generally are."[20] As Cecil Chesterton had stressed in his *History of the United States*, G. K. in his book emphasized that Virginia was the first American colony and Maryland the first to establish religious liberty. Like his brother, he was an admirer of Virginia, and it had long rankled him that "a few crabbed Nonconformists should have the right to erase a record that begins with Raleigh and ends with Lee, and incidentally includes Washington."[21]

According to Chesterton, the English knew about Lincoln but not about Lee. Fighting for the Confederacy, he believed, had not been an ignoble cause, for there was more to commend about the antebellum agricultural South than the industrial North. Chattel slavery had been on the decline, while "wage slavery" was able to endure and prosper. The modern South remained attractive to Chesterton: "Old England can still be faintly traced in Old Dixie. It contains some of the best things that England herself has had, and therefore (of course) the things that England herself has lost, or is trying to lose."[22]

Despite his Southern sympathies, Chesterton revealed a respect for Lincoln, whom he felt the English really did not understand. They appeared to him unaware that Lincoln was a moderate on the slavery issue who felt no animosity toward the South. Chesterton was particularly upset that the English invoked Lincoln's name to justify the suppression of rebellion in Ireland and that they viewed the president as one of their own. First of all, Chesterton argued, Lincoln was "quite un-English" in character and, in fact, with his penchant for abstract thought, was closer to the French. Second, the English were making a great tactical blunder by using Lincoln's name, for they were in danger of alienating Southerners, who tended to be Anglophiles while the North tilted toward Ireland. And last, and perhaps most important, the English were guilty of making a false analogy. According to Chesterton, "If Lincoln was right, he was right in guessing that there was not really a Northern nation and a Southern nation, but only one American nation." Southerners soon became patriotic Americans again, but the Irish, after repeated conquests, had not come any closer to pledging themselves to the crown: "We have had not one Gettysburg, but twenty Gettysburgs; but we have had no Union."[23]

Jackson, Lincoln, and Roosevelt, Chesterton argued, were all "democratic despots." He did not intend this characterization to be derogatory, for to the thinking of Chesterton and Belloc, a strong leader who embodied the popular will was preferable to the oligarchy that inevitably emerged in modern elected legislative systems. The United States, Chesterton wrote, was actually "the last medieval monarchy," for ironically the president was like the powerful premodern king, while the present-day British constitutional monarch was a president in the sense that all he could really do was "preside."[24] Chesterton apparently did not idolize Old Hickory quite as much as his brother had—he more conventionally looked to Jefferson—but he was an admirer of Jackson as a foe of finance. Although Chesterton believed the distinction between the Democrats and Republicans had become blurred, he wrote that if he had lived in nineteenth-century America he would have belonged to the party of Jefferson and Jackson. And in the 1890s he would have been a committed Bryanite. As for the late-nineteenth-century epithet describing the Democrats as the party of "rum, Romanism, and rebellion," Chesterton stated that he, for one, approved of all three.[25]

In Chesterton's view, the Americans had developed a type of thriving "public life" missing in England. In contrast to Wells, who had accused Americans of lacking a "sense of the state," he charged that it was in England that "the very state itself has become a state secret." He wrote that the American republic was built on the foundation of eighteenth-century Deism, which had not exerted any impact on English society. At the heart of the American system was "the theory of equality":

> It is the pure classic conception that no man must aspire to be anything more than a citizen, and that no man should endure to be anything less. It is by no means especially intelligible to an Englishman, who tends at his best to the virtues of the gentleman and at his worst to the vices of the snob.

Citizenship was a concept vital in America but essentially unfamiliar to the English.[26]

Although Chesterton venerated American republicanism, he believed it was declining. He stood on common ground with Wells in arguing that capitalism fostered an "inequality" that counteracted the effects of republican ideology. Therefore, there was a gap between the "ideal" and the "realities" of American life. Republicanism was in decay around the world, but the problem was greatest in America, where the "democratic ideal" was running up against "industrial progress," which was distinctly "undemocratic." France espoused such democratic notions but was not industrial, while Britain and Germany were industrial but not essentially democratic.[27]

Chesterton may have believed that industrial capitalism was eroding the foundations of republicanism, but in this book he did not take an especially harsh view of American commerce. He did not subscribe to the notion that the American business climate was particularly loathsome. The idea of the "Almighty Dollar," he contended, was a "fable": the Americans were actually no more fond of money than the English. If money was often discussed in the United States, part of the explanation lay in the fact that Americans were inclined to taking all sorts of measurements. Furthermore, the Americans were not so much devoted to money as to the process of making money—that is, to work. The English, by contrast, all aspired to be gentry and to possess wealth without having to earn it: their "ideal is not labour but leisure."[28]

While Chesterton maintained that American business was not as uniquely evil as its detractors charged, he furthermore emphasized that the United States was not monolithically commercial and industrial. When he was on his tour, he told a reporter that the chief impression of the nation that he had lost since being able to observe it firsthand was "the idea that America was a great, clattering dynamo of continual industrial rush." In his book he wrote that in the United States there was "not only a great deal of agricultural society, but a great deal of agricultural equality." Although the South had declined, the vast farm belt of the Midwest was still thriving, and it was there, he asserted, that the flame of Jeffersonian democracy was still burning. One of the greatest differences between America and England was that England, to its disadvantage, could not claim the existence of a significant agricultural region, and furthermore the English were ignorant of this vital sector of the American nation:

> We in England hear a great deal, we hear far too much, about the economic energy of industrial America, about the money of Mr. Morgan, or the machinery of Mr. Edison. We never realise that while we in England suffer from the same sort of success in capitalism and clockwork, we have not got what the Americans have got; something at least to balance it in the way of free agriculture, a vast field of free farms dotted with small freeholders.[29]

If the English were unaware of rural society in the United States, even worse, Chesterton argued, certain Americans failed to appreciate it. The main object of his criticism was Sinclair Lewis, who would occupy his attention on his next visit to the United States as well. Chesterton strongly objected to *Main Street*, the 1920 novel in which Lewis scathingly depicted the provincialism and barrenness of small-town Midwestern life. For Chesterton it was difficult to comprehend why the heroine, Carol Kennicott, finds it so hard to adjust to her existence in Gopher Prairie, because what she confronts in her village "is merely the life of humanity, and even the life which all humanitarians have striven to give to humanity." In fact, "the march to Utopia, the march to the Earthly Paradise, the march to the New Jerusalem, has been very largely the march to Main Street. And the latest modern sensation is a book written to show how wretched it is to live there."[30]

The farmers of the Midwest, Chesterton wrote, formed "a true counterweight to the toppling injustice of the towns." They could not, however, qualify as a completely realized peasantry because "they do not produce their own spiritual food, in the same sense as their own material

food." Instead of generating a popular, grassroots regional culture, as
the peoples of medieval Europe had, they merely imported the culture
of the cities. The Midwest, Chesterton noted, lacked the Catholic
underpinning that had traditionally supported the cultural and spiritual
life of European agrarian societies:

> You would hardly find in Oklahoma what was found in Oberammer-
> gau. What goes to Oklahoma is not the peasant play, but the cinema.
> And the objection to the cinema is not so much that it goes to Okla-
> homa as that it does not come from Oklahoma.

Chesterton concluded that the people of the Midwest were "far in advance of the English of the twentieth century" yet "still some centuries
behind the English of the twelfth century."[31]

Despite the existence of a thriving Jeffersonian, agrarian society in
the center of the American continent, Chesterton by no means believed
that the future of democracy in the United States was assured. In fact,
he maintained that American democracy had been in decline since the
end of the eighteenth century and could conceivably be extinguished.
As a remedy, however, Chesterton did not explicitly propose a Distributist course for the United States—a nationwide return to a crafts and
farm-based society. Instead, he focused on the need to bring about a
fundamental transformation in philosophical values. Evolutionary theory, he argued, was inherently anti-democratic; it encouraged the control of the many by the few, whether in the form of chattel slavery or the
exploitation of industrial labor. If American democracy was to endure,
Chesterton believed that the citizenry must return to the faith in God
possessed by the Founding Fathers. The Declaration of Independence,
which was derived from Jefferson's Deist principles, "bases all rights on
the fact that God created all men equal; and it is right; for if they were
not created equal, they were certainly evolved unequal." In Chesterton's
view American democracy needed to stand on a Christian, and prefer-
ably Catholic, foundation.[32]

If for Chesterton the key to America's future lay in Christian democracy, the key to establishing a healthier Anglo-American relationship
depended upon the two nations' acknowledging and appreciating what
made them different. In a chapter entitled "Wells and the World State,"
he assailed the idea that advances in transportation would create
friendship between nations, particularly the notion that the advent of

transatlantic air travel would bridge the differences between the United States and Britain. He pointed out that Germany and Britain, though within a day's travel from one another, had just concluded a terrible war and that throughout history the worst conflicts had broken out between neighbors. Wells may have been too sophisticated a thinker to assert that improved transportation would automatically lead to amity between nations, but Chesterton resented the "necessitarianism" inherent in his argument for a world state that "men must abandon patriotism or they will be murdered by science."[33] Chesterton also believed that Wells was mistaken in pointing to the American experience to prove that it was feasible to conceive of a "United States of the World." Representative government, in Chesterton's view, could never work on a world scale, particularly since Wells's scheme dropped the most successful feature of the American constitutional system, the presidency, in favor of an "acephalous aristocracy." Furthermore, Wells was blind to the fact that American unification came at a price: the triumph of one type of state over another. Before the United States could be truly united, the industrial North prevailed over the agrarian South in a bloody war, and the resulting decline of Southern influence in America was by no means a positive development. Chesterton feared that in Wells's world state there would be an "Americanising" of England and the rest of the globe.[34]

Not only did Chesterton reject the idea that technological progress would bring about closer Anglo-American ties, he also vehemently opposed the arguments of those who maintained, as Stead and Wells had done, that the relationship between Americans and Britons should proceed on the basis that they were one people, bound together racially, culturally, and politically. "The aim of this book," Chesterton wrote, "is to suggest this thesis; that the very worst way of helping Anglo-American friendship is to be an Anglo-American." The most guilty offenders in this regard were those who were always speaking of the "Anglo-Saxon," an animal that in reality had never existed. Although such sentiments were certainly aired on both sides of the Atlantic, Chesterton directed his criticism at his own countrymen:

> We are perpetually boring the world and each other with talk about the bonds that bind us to America. We are perpetually crying aloud that England and America are very much alike. . . . We are always insisting that the two are identical in all the things in which they most obviously differ.[35]

In opposing the idea that there was a fundamental unity between the English and the Americans, Chesterton was not merely knocking down straw men. Although such sentiment may have peaked during the rapprochement at the turn of the century, when Stead was writing about the United States, the feeling that there was a special bond between the English-speaking peoples had never disappeared and had in fact been given a boost by America's participation in World War I. Wells, of course, continued to emphasize the ties between the two nations, but he had a larger agenda: the advent of a unified socialist world. One prominent Briton who during the 1920s expressed his unabashed affection for America and his belief in the kinship of the English-speaking peoples was the long-time editor of the Conservative-leaning *Spectator,* John St. Loe Strachey. A member of a prominent English family, he could claim that one of his ancestors was an officer of the Virginia Company and present at the settling of Jamestown. As an American historian told him, he was "founder's kin of the United States."[36]

When Strachey visited America in 1925, it was his second trip across the Atlantic. He had come once before during the Roosevelt administration and stayed at the White House. The result of Strachey's 1925 tour was his book *American Soundings,* in which he praised the United States lavishly and offered merely tempered criticism. The only feature of the work comparable to Chesterton's *What I Saw in America,* other than the typical condemnation of Prohibition, is Strachey's reverence for the small towns as the backbone of the republic, though he came to this conclusion not in the Midwest, which he never reached, but rather driving through upstate New York and Pennsylvania.[37]

Strachey's affection for America and his conviction that a bond existed between the British and American peoples cannot be missed in the many letters he wrote over the years to his correspondents in the United States. As he revealed in one letter of 1923, "My belief in the future greatness of America may be said to have been my first serious political impression. I was brought up, indeed, to be as proud of America as of my own country."[38]

After Strachey came back from his first transatlantic trip at the beginning of the century, he was convinced that Britain and the United States had more in common than he had ever imagined. In 1906 he wrote to Roosevelt that when upper-class Britons, particularly women, returned from traveling in the United States, they invariably remarked how "foreign" the nation seemed to them, to which "I always answer that what surprised me were not the contrasts but the agreements." He discovered that the assertions that America was so alien usually depended on such trivial matters as "the way in which people's tablecloths were laid or the manner in which dinner was announced, or the fact that it was not easy to get a railway porter to carry your hand luggage."[39]

When Strachey was critical of Wilson for his policy of uncompromising neutrality during the early years of the First World War, he was upbraided in the United States and at home. In a letter to Roosevelt he defended the appropriateness of his attacks on the president: "Personally as a man who speaks the English language and has nothing but British blood in his veins, English and Scotch, I refuse absolutely to treat the American people, kindred in race and language, and, what is far more important, in ideals, as I treat a purely foreign country."[40] After the United States had joined the war cause, Strachey was ecstatic: he was convinced that the action ensured that all differences between Britain and America would be patched up and that, furthermore, the Americans were now committed to the idea of being an undeniably English society, rather than a "polyglot" culture. In fact, the United States would be the dominant nation in the English-speaking world:

> As is inevitable with her size and population, America will assume the hegemony of the Anglo-Saxon race; but I for one, with I believe the majority of my countrymen will be quite content to see this happen, knowing that the Anglo-Saxon ideals—moral, religious, legal, literary, and social—will be safe in the hands of the English speakers beyond the sea.

As Strachey also put it, "Now that I am growing old, I am perfectly prepared to render up my business to my children."[41]

On his 1925 trip to the United States, Strachey delivered a talk in New York before the English-Speaking Union in which he expatiated on the importance of uniting the British and Americans and spoke of the two peoples as one: "We are going to save ourselves—the Anglo-Saxon race—by our own exertions, and then we have got to save the rest of the world by our example."[42] At the outset of *American Soundings*, Strachey justified his writing of the book by stating that he was as interested in the future of the United States as of his own country and asserting, as he had in New York, "that only through the joint action of the two English-speaking races can the World be saved."[43] By the 1920s not only was Strachey's rhetoric reminiscent of Stead's, but so were his journalistic ambitions, for he declared his wish to transform the *Spectator* into "a very valuable liaison officer" between Britain and the United States.[44]

Chesterton was not merely critical of the view of the Anglo-American relationship put forth by the likes of Strachey; he offered an alternative. Insight into placing the relationship between the two nations on a sounder basis, he wrote, could actually be gained through a reading of *Martin Chuzzlewit*. He had been well acquainted with the novel for many years, for he discussed it in his 1906 study of Dickens. In that book Chesterton defended his subject in his falling-out with the United States by arguing that Dickens had been prepared to like America, but the insufferable boasting of the people and their obstinacy on the copyright question turned him against the nation. The institution of slavery also offended Dickens, but, Chesterton conceded, he was even more repelled by the manners he observed: "His anti-Americanism would seem to be more founded on spitting than on slavery." Chesterton believed *American Notes,* despite the furor it caused, to be rather tepid and contended that Dickens failed to get at what made Americans uniquely American. In contrast, Chesterton praised the American passages of *Martin Chuzzlewit,* an otherwise "indifferent novel." The satirization of America he found splendid, not because Dickens had necessarily captured the essential reality of the United States but because he so skillfully punctured the chauvinist windbag, who could just as easily have been English as American.[45]

When Chesterton first visited America in 1921, he may well have thought of himself as following in the footsteps of Dickens, with whom he closely identified. If he did not make the connection, others did. A cartoon appeared in the American press contrasting the favorable sentiments Chesterton was expressing about the nation with the venom that had spewed forth from Dickens. Titled "Mopping up After Dickens," the cartoon shows a large, jolly Chesterton holding in one hand a bouquet of flowers and a sheet saying "Kind words for America," while in the other hand he holds a portrait of Dickens, who is wearing a fierce expression and carrying bricks labeled "American Notes."[46]

Chesterton's trip to the United States apparently made him more critical of Dickens's treatment of the nation. In *What I Saw in America* he dealt with *Martin Chuzzlewit* more harshly than in his biography of Dickens. Chesterton wrote that in the novel Dickens exaggerated in his depiction of America, though that sort of farcical portraiture is characteristically Dickensian and in this work England fares no better. Nevertheless,

Chesterton charged that *Martin Chuzzlewit* is a mean-spirited novel and that Dickens failed to show any sympathy toward, or even understanding of, the Americans he was lampooning. Dickens could not see that there could be worth in the American of the rough, tough backwoods Hannibal Chollop variety. The great sin of Dickens was "not in thinking his Americans funny, but in thinking them foolish because they were funny."[47]

If maliciousness taints *Martin Chuzzlewit*, Dickens did not fail in making the interaction between the two nations a great comedy. The English and American characters justifiably find one another amusing. Therefore, Chesterton argued, the novel could provide "the text for a true reconciliation" between the two peoples. The case he made was for "friendship founded on reciprocal ridicule, or rather on a comedy of comparisons." The "pompous impersonalities of internationalism," he asserted, would never succeed. An Anglo-American relationship based on humor, but also mutual respect, was what was needed. In Chesterton's view, the Americans and English could get along best if they could learn to laugh at, and appreciate, their vast differences.[48]

Hilaire Belloc technically deserves no place in a study of British observers of America because he was a citizen of France. However, when his French father died when Belloc was only a baby, his English mother moved the family to London, and though Belloc spent his boyhood summers in France and served in the French army, England would be his home for the rest of his life. With his dual allegiances, Belloc was very much the European, as opposed to Chesterton, who was thoroughly an Englishman. This distinction is reflected in their books on America that appeared at virtually the same time. A year after *What I Saw in America* was released, Belloc, in 1923, published *The Contrast*. As the title suggests, the work deals with how different America was, though, as Belloc stressed, different not merely from Britain but from the Old World as a whole. Although he decided not to limit his comparison only to Britain, his book is strikingly similar to Chesterton's. *The Contrast* lacks the grace, wit, and subtlety of *What I Saw in America*, and Belloc so single-mindedly drove home the thesis that the New World and Old were different that he was less successful than Chesterton at producing a fully developed picture of American society. But Belloc's central argument, though more stridently advanced, resembles Chesterton's to the extent that it would be possible to conclude that he simply copied his friend.

Who influenced whom, however, is not clear. Generally the ideas of the Chesterbelloc emanated from Belloc, but Chesterton often expressed them more eloquently. In regard to America, although Chesterton published his book first, Belloc may still have been the source of many of their views. Belloc's 1923 trip to the United States was not his first: in the 1890s, before establishing himself as a writer, he traveled to America several times. He first crossed the Atlantic in 1890, when he was only twenty, in pursuit of a young Irish Catholic Californian, Elodie Hogan, who had been introduced to the Belloc family in London by none other than W. T. Stead. Belloc made his way across the American continent by doing sketches to pay for his room and board, and as he plodded westward, he developed a disdain for the American landscape that he would never lose. Yet utopia greeted him at the end of his journey: he fell in love with California. He spent time in San Francisco with the Hogans but failed to gain permission to marry Elodie and so returned to England, and then in 1896, after he had been at Oxford, he again journeyed to America and the two were finally married. Belloc and his wife went back to England, but in the next few years he made two grueling lecture tours of America. Denied an Oxford fellowship, an embittered Belloc badly needed the modest income he could gain from lecturing in America on the French Revolution and other topics. The toll these trips took on him can be seen in what he wrote in 1898 from Harrisburg, Pennsylvania:

> This place is ugly. God made it the night after a debauch when His ideas were neither many nor interesting. . . . Here I lecture to horrible people, kindly, of the middle class (as I am) yet, oddly enough, not congenial to me. I am bored and lonely. Also the wine is dear and bad.

Despite the misery he experienced on these tours, Belloc by no means formed an entirely negative opinion of the United States. In fact, in the final years of the nineteenth century, he considered settling in California.[49]

When Belloc visited America in 1923, he had not crossed the Atlantic for twenty-five years, and in the interim his life had changed greatly. Elodie had died in 1914, and he was still morbidly mourning her passing. Although nothing could compensate for the loss of his wife and original link to America, Belloc returned to the United States as a distinguished man of letters. He was not, however, as famous in the States as Chesterton and hoped to enhance his reputation. He was known to complain that "there are 25,000,000 Catholics in the United States and none of them will buy my books."[50] But despite the passage of time, Belloc made it clear on his 1923 trip that he viewed America much as he had in the 1890s. In one letter he said of the United States, "It is, of course, in every way utterly unlike Europe: another world. I found it so when I first came here 32 years ago and I find it now after 25 years of absence. Nothing is much changed."[51] His dubious contention that the nation had not "much changed" since the 1890s is reflected in *The Contrast*, which failed to delineate what was distinctive about the America of the 1920s.

The purpose of Belloc's 1923 trip to the United States was to deliver lectures, and, like his American lecture tours of the late 1890s, this one seems to have been for him a disagreeable experience. Before he embarked on the journey, he had been apprehensive about the "interviewing and newspaper fuss" but knew that the best way to handle the Americans was "to praise them wholesale."[52] In the letters Belloc wrote back to England from America, he complained bitterly about what he had to endure on his trip, the dominant note being that he could not find a moment's peace and quiet. In one letter he said, "No one on this side of the Atlantic has the conception of concentration. They talk to each other incessantly and accompany anyone they choose anywhere."[53] To the same correspondent, he later stated, "The Americans never use privacy in any form and they fill the whole day and every day with slow and uninterrupted conversation."[54]

Although Belloc complained about America when he was on his lecture tour, he did not compare the nation unfavorably to Britain, or continental Europe, in *The Contrast*. His main contention was simply that America was very different. In laying out his case, he made many of the same points Chesterton had, but he pushed the argument further. On the other hand, Belloc was silent on possibly the most crucial assertion made by Chesterton—that America was different from England because it still maintained significant vestiges of an agrarian democracy. Because Belloc was as enthusiastic as Chesterton about the virtues of a self-governing peasantry, it can only be assumed that he did not concur with his friend.

At the outset of *The Contrast*, Belloc wrote that he had been surprised to find the chasm between the New World and the Old on his first journey to America. The "separateness of America," he discovered, was so complete as to be "almost incommunicable." His education had failed him, for it was responsible for providing him with a "false conception" of America. Old World observers of the United States were at least partly responsible for leading him astray: "Had I never read what Americans had written of themselves nor any description of what Europeans had reported upon their return, the shock of the real discovery would have been less overwhelming."[55]

Belloc's starting point for discussing the separateness of the New World and Old was to examine "The Physical Contrast." He argued that the landscape of America was something very foreign to the European, except for "the paradise of California," which was like "Europe glorified." The monotony of the vast American continent was overwhelming, and he posited that "the large similarity of the American soil has bred a similarity in man's act upon it." In America the towns all looked alike, and the houses in the towns all looked alike, and even the behavior of the people was very much alike. Belloc went so far as to assert that the unique circumstances of the New World had generated "a new race." American physical features were so unmistakable that merely by examining their portraits such figures as Harding, Bryan, and Pershing could never be identified as Europeans, and "an American face in the photograph of an English or French country-house party stands out at once."[56]

The "even topography" created "uniformity" in America, and so, Belloc argued, did the most conspicuous national social trait, the concentrated interaction among individuals. He was more emphatic on this point than Chesterton had been in his discussion of American gregariousness. Like Chesterton, he maintained that the emphasis on individual exertion in the United States actually led to conformity, and Belloc pointed to the standardization of American hotels, the prevalence of fads, and the "Best Seller" phenomenon as manifestations of this conformity. He also remarked that the idea that the majority should rule was deeply ingrained in the American system. The uniformity of American society was fostered by the penchant to adopt every new mechanical device and labor-saving system, whereas Europeans were inclined to stick to the old ways, no matter how inefficient. American life, Belloc felt, was more regimented and synthetic: "The American rhythm is more vibratory, the European more surging; there is in the one something more mechanical and less organic. I hear in one the sound of a hammer, in the other wind through trees."[57]

The gregariousness of the Americans, Belloc also argued, created a society in which there was much less privacy than in Europe. He noted how familiar Americans were with one another, how easily they struck up conversation with strangers. Whereas the wealthy European purchased isolation, his American counterpart built his suburban house adjacent to his neighbor's, with no barrier to divide the properties, and close by the noisy train tracks. On the matter of privacy, and in other respects, "wealth and opportunity in America connote the very opposites of what they do in Europe: extreme neatness, rarity of detail, an hospitable cleanliness of bath, drains, sinks; facile communication, plenty of noise and metal—and no seclusion."[58]

Americans used their wealth differently from Europeans, and furthermore, Belloc argued, unlike the Europeans they did not worship wealth. He agreed with Chesterton that the Old World notion of Americans' being devoted to money was a myth but went further than his friend in pressing the point that it was the Europeans themselves who were guilty of this "heresy" of "Mammon." In Britain, particularly before the war, the wealthy were revered merely for being wealthy, whereas Americans recognized wealth only as a sign of "success" and "achievement." According to Belloc, wealthy English and American hostesses both liked to bring literary "lions" to their tables, but in England the hostess was the center of attention and in America the "lion."[59]

Belloc not only defended the Americans against the charge of materialism, but he commended them for certain positive qualities that he felt characterized them as a people. He lauded the Americans, as Chesterton did, for the "universal courtesy" found in the United States. Furthermore, he believed "that the Americans were happier than any people of the Old World." Even those Europeans who were inclined to be critical of America, most notably the English upper class, were forced to concede this point. In Belloc's view, the happiness was a consequence of American "Candour." There was a "straightforwardness and unasking sincerity" that characterized American society and that was absent in Europe, which was tainted by "putrescent hypocrisies." Unfortunately, the honesty and frankness of America would probably evaporate as the civilization matured, but at least for the present the difference between the Old World and New was "the difference between foul air and fresh."[60]

In his assessment of the American political system, Belloc concurred with Chesterton that governance in the United States was, paradoxically, based to a great extent on "the principle of *Monarchy*." "The American Presidency," Belloc wrote, "is to-day far the strongest Monarchy on earth." That the American public grieved so much over

Harding's death showed that the people even identified with the president as if he were a king. Like Chesterton, Belloc believed the growth of monarchical authority was advantageous to America, while its decline on the other side of the ocean was detrimental to Europe. A strong leader, for example, could more easily check the power of "Big Business" than a legislature could.[61]

The American political system, according to Belloc, was functionally as well as structurally distinct from its European counterparts. In both the New World and the Old there was a yearning for freedom and democracy: the contrast lay in the fact that Americans were involved in securing their rights and determining their future on a "permanent" basis, whereas in Europe such involvement was "sporadic." In an analysis reminiscent of Bryce's discussion of public opinion in the United States, Belloc wrote how the people were perpetually generating and debating the ideas upon which government acted: "In a word, initiative, in America, is with the crowd. Initiative in Europe is not with the crowd, save in special moments when the crowd acts exceptionally and under some urgent necessity." Corruption was no worse in America than in Europe, Belloc asserted, simply more heavily scrutinized and discussed.[62]

In Belloc's view a nation's religious tradition, even more than its political or economic system, was crucial in determining its character. He was disturbed that a "false similarity" in religion between America and Britain concealed from most people how different the experiences of the two nations really were. Although a multiplicity of Protestant sects existed in both countries, these sects were on a firm footing in America but in Britain maintained the status of rebellious outcasts of the Established Church. Spiritually there was a contrast as well: the masses in Britain had turned away from religion, but in America the common people, at least of British descent, still clung to their Puritan faith. Regarding his own cherished creed, Catholicism, he predicted that, as in Europe, the Church in America would inevitably come into conflict with the state.[63]

The Jews of America Belloc dealt with in a separate chapter, entitled "The Contrast in the Jewish Problem." When he came to the United States in 1923, his anti-Semitism was well known, particularly because he had laid out his views in a 1922 book called *The Jews*. Like Chesterton he claimed not to feel any malice toward the Jewish people, only the conviction that they were different and should be treated differently; but though he was not an undiscriminating Jew-hater, his position was even more extreme, and more offensive to many, than Chesterton's. Undoubtedly aware of the problems that *The New Jerusalem* had caused Chesterton on his American tour, Belloc was apprehensive that his book would open him up to denunciation in the United States: "I am rather afraid the Jews may attack me, because apparently one thing they cannot bear is a work seriously dealing with their problem."[64] As he had anticipated, Belloc did in fact run into some resistance in America, with one prominent Jewish judge even calling for his deportation.[65]

In *The Contrast* Belloc discussed how the "Jewish problem" was different in America than in Europe. First of all, the Americans were much more honest and open about discussing this "problem" than the Europeans, who tended not to confront it directly. In fact, he found that the Americans were quite preoccupied with the Jews, who had not become a "problem" until they began pouring into the country in recent decades, and he praised Henry Ford for being so forthright on the issue. Despite the influx of Jews into the United States, Belloc wrote, they did not dominate vast areas, as in central and eastern Europe. Nor was their situation like that of their brethren in Britain, where, according to Belloc, Jews had joined the most exclusive clubs, married into the best families, and penetrated the corridors of power. He did not foresee, or desire, any violent persecution of the Jews in America but believed that the nation was taking necessary steps in limiting and isolating the Jewish population through such measures as immigration restriction, university quotas, and exclusion from clubs and hotels. The "Jewish problem," he felt, could be peacefully resolved through the passage of special legislation.[66]

Belloc was substantially correct in his assessment of the Jews' place in the nation of the 1920s. The decade saw a surge in anti-Semitism, and American Jews faced more impediments than they ever had before.[67] That Belloc would support the erection of such barriers comes as no surprise, but his uncritical endorsement of Henry Ford is somewhat perplexing. Beginning in 1920 Ford used his newspaper, the *Dearborn Independent*, to launch a campaign against "the international Jew," drawing heavily upon the notorious *Protocols of the Learned Elders of Zion*. Although he attracted a large following, Ford was an extremist—even close to paranoid—in his depiction of dark Jewish conspiracies. Besides, it quickly became known in informed circles that the *Protocols* were nothing more than a spurious set of documents concocted in Czarist Russia.[68] While Belloc may have seen in Ford a prominent ally in his efforts to draw attention to the dilemma he believed the Jews posed, it is baffling that he would wish to associate himself with such crude, and discredited, notions. Of course, Chesterton, who met with Ford on his trip to America, also lauded the auto magnate for shining a light on the "Jewish problem." Unlike Belloc, however, Chesterton did signal that he felt Ford was prone to dubious thinking, on this and other matters.[69]

Beyond outlining in his book the myriad differences between Britain and the United States, Belloc wrote that the great "contrast" had implications for the Anglo-American relationship. The idea that the two nations were naturally close because of some sort of "Anglo-Saxon" or "English-speaking" bond was ridiculous. These terms were often bandied about as part of a British propaganda effort to seal good relations with the United States, but they were meaningless. Belloc conceded that there were genuine ties of blood, language, and tradition between the two nations, but these were overshadowed by the immense differences. The two nations were compelled to be wary of one another, for, "of all states in the modern world the American community is by far the most egalitarian," whereas "the English is still by far the most aristocratic." Those Britons who stressed how English America was and how the United States would inevitably come to Britain's aid in a conflict were deluding themselves. Ever since America's emergence as a great power after the Civil War, British policy had been to coddle the United States and smooth over any transatlantic disputes. Like Chesterton, Belloc stressed that the Anglo-American relationship would be healthier if the differences between the two nations were candidly acknowledged.[70]

In early 1924 Belloc's antagonist H. G. Wells reviewed *The Contrast*. Whereas Chesterton was close to Shaw and on friendly terms with Wells, Belloc was another story. Shaw resented Belloc's influence over Chesterton, and the cool relations between Belloc and Wells became even chillier when Belloc emerged as the chief critic of *The Outline of History*. In 1926 their differences over history and religion would erupt into a nasty full-scale war of words. Even in *The Contrast*, Belloc took a shot at Wells by remarking that *The Outline*, while dismissed in Europe, was readily accepted by the less discerning, fad-prone Americans.[71] When Wells reviewed *The Contrast*, he, not surprisingly, was negative. At the very outset of the piece he revealed the caustic tone he would employ:

> Mr. Belloc has written a small imposing book about America and England, called *The Contrast*. Small it is in length and substance, but

imposing in its English edition at least by reason of large print, vast margins, thick paper, and all that makes a book physically impressive. It is the sort of book that has the first sentence of Chapter I on page nine.[72]

In Wells's view, *The Contrast* was an exercise in denial. Belloc understood that the world was becoming increasingly unified, particularly that the English-speaking peoples were drawing closer together and that "Rome will have a scarcely more important place in an English-knitted world than Babylon." According to Wells, Belloc saw this reality but refused to acknowledge it. In a quixotic effort to reassert the dominance of Europe, Belloc strove to drive a wedge between New World and Old and particularly between America and Britain, which, though not Catholic, in his eyes did hold a place on the fringe of European civilization. Wells maintained that Belloc, in trying to prove that America was something totally foreign, something wholly other, was attempting to preserve the sanctity of his beloved Latin Europe. In direct response to Belloc, Wells wrote, "Do the Americans present either a new race or even a new culture? I deny both these propositions." He asserted that the American people were racially an amalgamation, for the most part, of European peoples and that the unified transcontinental culture of the United States, far from being something bizarre, was the model that the rest of the world would inevitably follow. Better for Belloc to have spent his life chatting away in the café of some small French town, Wells suggested, than to have visited America and, despite what he must have observed, "come back to report a strange and terrible land where the mountains are not really mountains nor the rivers rivers, and where a strange race grows outside the pale."[73]

In the same year Wells attacked Belloc for his assessment of America, he also criticized Rebecca West, then emerging as an important critic and novelist, because he believed her published impressions of the United States placed her in the Belloc-Chesterton camp. When West embarked on her lecture tour of America in the fall of 1923, she did so in part to effect a clean break in her decade-long affair with Wells, which had yielded them a son, Anthony. In fact, advanced publicity about her American tour had been instrumental in leading her to the conclusion that her liaison had become untenable, for a Boston clubwoman had tried to have her denied entrance into the country on moral grounds. Wells attempted to persuade her not to scuttle their relationship because of "this Boston fuss": "Something of the sort happens about most people who go to America." But West did break with Wells, and when she journeyed to the United States, she was even considering establishing a new life there. Although she was to scrap that idea, West spent seven months in America, three in New York and four traveling and lecturing around the country.[74]

Upon returning to England, West recorded her impressions of America in a three-part series for the *Sunday Times*. She argued that the greatest problem in the United States was the widespread lawlessness and disorder. In contending that "crime is the chiefest curse of America," West noted that Britain experienced one hundred murders a year and the United States ten thousand. Although she thought Prohibition was silly and unfair and encouraged Americans to flout the law, she was sympathetic with the experiment to the extent that it abolished the saloon, which she believed had been a prime breeder of delinquency. But West knew that the violent, antisocial behavior that marked America had deeper roots—in a tradition of conflict between pioneer individualism and the strictures of modern industrialism. The nation, however, would not be plagued by a scourge of crime if there existed "a peasant class bred by centuries of feudal and military service to the idea of duty to the State." Not only were peasants necessary as the basis of a reliable police force—in America the police were too independent, powerful, and corrupt—but they formed the backbone of any healthy society. According to West, the peasant type could be found in the Midwest—that is, as the descendants of Lincoln—but there were not enough of them throughout the entire country.[75]

In critiquing West's impressions of America, Wells revealed that despite her having brought a halt to their relationship, he still respected her intellectually. At the outset of his piece he called her "that acute and brilliant observer" and praised her for concentrating on the big picture, not details. But he registered his firm disagreement with her conclusions, declaring that "she calls rather startlingly for peasants." By contending that a peasant population would bring order to American society, the reputedly "progressive" West, Wells wrote, was guilty of "turning back to the earthy romanticism of Belloc and Chesterton, and I think it shows the profoundest misapprehension of the fundamentals of the American situation." With its dependence on efficient agricultural machinery, "America is not developing a peasantry and probably never will." Wells furthermore argued that West's fundamental assumptions were faulty, since peasant Russia had long been plagued by disorder while peasant-less England was known for its great stability. His remedy for creating "a law-abiding social harmony" in America was not promoting a peas-antry, but rather promoting education.[76]

Aside from making the "peasant" argument, West stood with Ches-terton and Belloc in another respect. Like them, she believed that the United States and Britain were more different than similar. She began her series for the *Sunday Times* by remarking that nothing was more odd to the English eye than to visit an American drugstore at any hour of the day and see "men of all ages sit before a marble counter on very high swivel arm-chairs and eat fluffy chocolate layer-cake."[77] West elab-orated on the differences between the two nations in two articles she published in 1925 in *Harper's*. For example, she explained how much mis-understanding had resulted from the fact that an honored guest in En-gland would be invited to a small gathering while the American hostess showed her hospitality by throwing a large party. In passages very remi-niscent of Chesterton, she wrote of how American men traveling on a train liked to discuss business, the national preoccupation, while En-glishmen would chatter about gardening. The devotion to the garden in England, she argued, was also a manifestation of the English reverence for the public sphere, whereas Americans, who cared more about the private sphere, paid more attention to the interior of a house.[78]

In September 1930, almost a decade after his first trip to America, Chesterton set sail again for the New World with his wife, Frances, and indispensable secretary, Dorothy Collins. He had converted to Rome soon after his first journey and now returned to the United States as a hero among American Catholics. The main purpose of his trip, which would be the last great excursion before his death in 1936, was to de-liver two courses of lectures on Victorian history and literature to the students at the University of Notre Dame. The Chestertons enjoyed their six-week stay in South Bend, Indiana, where they found accom-modation with a local family. While at Notre Dame, which granted him an honorary degree, Chesterton soaked up the native culture by going to a football game and paying visits to the town's speakeasies. Because he needed to raise funds for *G. K.'s Weekly*, he also embarked on an am-bitious lecture tour that took him to a variety of cities in the United States and Canada. His lectures, often delivered at Catholic colleges or before Catholic organizations, addressed such topics as "The Curse of

Psychology," "The New Enslavement of Women," and "The Age of Unreason." Among the public debates in which he participated, perhaps the most notable was against the radical, atheistic lawyer Clarence Darrow, with Chesterton's taking the affirmative on the question, "Will the World Return to Religion?" The tour became so demanding that in January 1931, in Chattanooga, Tennessee, Frances took seriously ill, and while she recuperated, G. K. headed west with Dorothy Collins to meet his commitments on the Pacific coast. Frances soon joined them in California and rested in a hotel outside Los Angeles while Chesterton kept lecturing. They did not sail for England until April.[79]

While in the United States, Chesterton told one newspaper, "I don't detect many changes in your country since I was here before."[80] This attitude is reflected in his 1932 book, *Sidelights on New London and Newer York and Other Essays*, which is generally consistent with *What I Saw in America*, published ten years previously.[81] The nation had, of course, changed in at least one important sense: since the Stock Market crash of October 1929, it had been sliding into economic despair. Chesterton commented on the Depression while touring the United States: he offered the opinion that American "super-enthusiasm" was responsible for creating a level of "production" that "cannot be assimilated."[82] But in his book he barely mentioned the Depression, and the differences between *What I Saw in America* and *Sidelights* are not attributable to the transition in the United States from boom to bust. In his 1932 book Chesterton did treat America somewhat more harshly than he had a decade before. The point he stressed here, and had only touched on previously, was that a poisonous Puritan spirit suffused every aspect of American life.

At the very beginning of his section on the United States in *Sidelights*, Chesterton offered the American people a sort of backhanded compliment. "There is nothing the matter with Americans except their ideals," he wrote. Although the Americans were by nature a "candid" and "generous" people, "they have been deliberately and dogmatically taught to be conceited." Instinctively "a race of simple and warmhearted country people," the Americans had to learn how to be "boomsters" and "business bullies." The reason they became prone to "selfish, sensational self-advertisement" was that they had been made captives of the commercial idea of "Making Good." Chesterton despised American "bragging and go-getting," but he believed his "quarrel is not so much with the men as with the gods: the false gods they have been taught to worship and still only worship with half their hearts."[83]

The English, Chesterton contended, had been known to possess the same pomposity that now characterized the Americans. In fact, in lodging criticism,

> an Englishman, as a European, has a right to complain of the bumptious and purse-proud swagger of some Yankee globe-trotters in Europe. Only he ought to preface his protest by admitting that the same sort of complaint was made about Englishmen in Europe in the days when England had the same mercantile supremacy and the same materialistic mood.

The Americans, according to Chesterton, resented the hypocrisy of being chastised by the English for faults of which they, the accusers, had themselves been guilty. He wrote that the English should realize that the offensive American traits were not distinctively American but actually rooted in the nation's English past. These traits developed wherever an intensive commercial atmosphere prevailed, and well before the Americans, the English themselves had been the champions of business.[84]

While Chesterton pointed to the harmful consequences of commerce on the American spirit in *Sidelights*, as he had in his previous book on the United States, in this work he dwelled much more on the evils of Puritanism, as both a historical reality and a contemporary social ethic. Implicitly, however, he drew a link between Puritanism and commercialism. Even before making his second trip to the United States, Chesterton had praised the most notorious of the American anti-Puritans, the iconoclastic journalist H. L. Mencken. Although Mencken felt disdain for so much of what Chesterton cherished—that is, England and the American South and Midwest—Chesterton still endorsed his assault on Puritanism, in all its ferocity. He loved Mencken for being "the critic of Puritan pride and stupidity" and "the hammer of those false idealists who call themselves moral" based on all the wrong criteria. Yet Chesterton's support of Mencken was tempered, to say the least. Mencken, according to Chesterton, could be just as narrow-minded as the fundamentalists he targeted—as in his rejection of physics as a legitimate science. Even more important, Chesterton regretted that Mencken's anti-Puritanism emanated from a position of atheism and nihilism.[85]

In *Sidelights*, Chesterton again berated the Puritans of seventeenth-century New England and even suggested that his nation establish its own Thanksgiving "to celebrate the happy fact that the Pilgrim Fathers left England." The attention that the story of the Puritans managed to attract annoyed him, and when he was in Philadelphia and saw the statue of William Penn atop City Hall, he was prompted to wonder why people could not see "the immense superiority of that intellectual and spiritual leader to the clamorously advertised Calvinists of the *Mayflower*." The connection some made between Penn and the Pilgrims was absurd, for "an American Puritan in the seventeenth century would have regarded a Quaker very much as an American Puritan in the twentieth century would regard a Bolshevist."[86]

In his attempt to correct the Puritan view of American history, Chesterton again turned his attention to Abraham Lincoln. For his *Illustrated London News* column, he had written a piece in 1928 in which he praised Lincoln as a brilliant leader but tried to clear up some common misconceptions about him. The American "Puritans" revered Lincoln, yet as a young man he was "a rather crude sort of atheist," known to drink whiskey. These Americans, who put such a premium on success, did not realize that all of his life Lincoln was prone to failure and in the end succeeded only with luck. Most of them, if they had been able to encounter Lincoln during the better part of his lifetime, "would have avoided him as they avoid the drunkard, the lunatic, the impecunious poet, the habitual criminal, and the man who is always borrowing money."[87] A few months later Chesterton reported that an "American critic, apparently of the Baptist persuasion," had denounced him for his "slander" of Lincoln, though Chesterton said that he thought he had written a "eulogy." He stated that he and the American critic obviously disagreed as to what constituted admiration, for he believed it better to be "unworldly" than "worldly." Elaborating on his view of Lincoln, he wrote, "There was a great deal in him of the erratic genius who either succeeds as a genius or fails at everything." He put Lincoln in a class with "poets" and "martyrs," but the American critic wanted to distort him into "a Go-getter, a Booster, a Best-Seller, a Bright Salesman, and a Man Born to Succeed."[88]

When Chesterton took up the subject of Lincoln in *Sidelights*, he explained that his position was still that he was "a great admirer of Abraham Lincoln" but "not an admirer of his admirers." In the chapter entitled "Abraham Lincoln in London," Chesterton's emphasis was on how utterly different Lincoln was from the English. To Chesterton, Lincoln was "a great man, like Confucius, and a good man, like Uncle Remus," and he was as alien to the English as those two figures were.

Lincoln was the quintessential representative of America, particularly of the rural backcountry. "Whilst I was in America," Chesterton wrote, "I often lingered in small towns and wayside places; and in a curious and almost creepy fashion the great presence of Abraham Lincoln continually grew upon me."[89]

Chesterton blamed the same present-day Puritans who were prone to misunderstand Lincoln for the folly he believed Prohibition to be. In a 1927 piece "On American Morals," he had charged that Americans, despite their self-righteousness, really did not comprehend the meaning of ethics. They saw tobacco and alcohol as evils and smoking and drinking as sins, and they mistook this primitive anathematizing of inanimate substances for morality. The American penchant for taboos, he argued, was rooted in the New England heritage.[90] But when Chesterton traveled to America in 1930–1931, he was pleased to discover that, in contrast to his visit of a decade before, when it had seemed that almost everybody was for Prohibition, sentiment had now turned overwhelmingly against the ban. Among the only sincere and enthusiastic proponents of Prohibition left, he maintained, were extremist Protestant ministers. According to Chesterton, the primary reason Prohibition would soon come to an end was that it had become a rather vulgar national joke. The debate over whether the bootlegging gangster Al Capone could be charged for evasion of income tax on money he illegally made was so absurd as to be worthy of Gilbert and Sullivan.[91]

The Prohibition issue, Chesterton pointed out, was intertwined with the problem of American bigotry. In *Sidelights* he stated that President Hoover was constrained against doing anything to bring an end to Prohibition because he had made it into the White House in great part because his "wet" Democratic opponent, Governor Al Smith of New York, had been painted as a "drunken blackguard."[92] Right after the 1928 election, Chesterton had written a column in which he discussed the prejudice shown against Smith for being Irish Catholic. The outcome of the vote was predetermined by the fact that "for large sections of the electorate" there was "a general impression that American Catholics have horns." Chesterton argued that these elements in the American population actually knew nothing about Catholicism: in fact, their main problem was that they were profoundly ignorant of the greater world. Although he exonerated Hoover himself of partaking in the bigoted onslaught on Smith, Chesterton wrote that nevertheless the election came down to "a conflict between light and darkness."[93]

Many of the staunchest opponents of Smith, and proponents of Prohibition, surely hailed from those Midwestern villages that Chesterton had praised so heartily after his previous trip to America. In *Sidelights* he was not quite as enthusiastic about the small towns of the United States as he had been in *What I Saw in America*. He still considered them the best of what the nation had to offer but now believed they were tainted by urbanism, commercialism, and Puritanism. He even called the American village "ugly" in comparison to its English counterpart.[94] In *What I Saw in America*, Chesterton had been critical of the fact that the people of the heartland imported their culture from the cities. Now, in his second book on America, he went even further. The small towns, he argued, had become more and more like the cities, and it had become difficult to find the purely "rural note." The biggest factor was that the towns had become suffused with the commercial spirit, to the point that the people talked not of "Land," but of "Real Estate." In a way, it could be said that "Main Street is as urban as Wall Street." Chesterton could still see the existence of a democratic, agricultural society in America, but he believed that the character of that society had changed.[95]

Chesterton's altered posture toward "Main Street" America was reflected in his opinion of Sinclair Lewis. Since Chesterton's first trip to America, Lewis had built on the success of *Main Street* with the publication of *Babbitt, Arrowsmith,* and other popular novels that examined life in the heartland. When Chesterton was in the United States during the fall of 1930, Lewis became the first American to be awarded the Nobel Prize in Literature. As Chesterton made his tour, he responded to reporters' inevitable questions about Lewis by challenging his views and offering the opinion that he should not have received the Nobel. Chesterton told a Hartford paper, "I should have chosen someone more characteristic of the American people, someone who is not a satirist."[96]

In *Sidelights,* however, Chesterton acknowledged that up to a point he could now relate to Lewis's satire. In a certain respect, he wrote, "I have a pretty complete sympathy with Mr. Sinclair Lewis and the attack on Main Street." He could appreciate that Lewis had captured that the most respected individual in the United States, the one considered "a Regular Guy, or a Red-Blooded He-Man, or a hundred per cent American," was the businessman. And not only did Chesterton concede that the commercial mentality had reached "Main Street," he also regretfully accepted Lewis's characterization of the American small town as

Puritan. This concept was new to him, for in the Old World, Puritanism had always been an urban feature. But if Chesterton did acknowledge some of the flaws of the American small town spotlighted by writers like Lewis, he would not concur in their general condemnation:

> I am on the side of Main Street in the main. I mean by the statement, not that I prefer Main Street as it is to Main Street as it ought to be, but that I prefer even Main Street as it is to the views of those who think it ought not to be.

Put another way, he stated that he would rather be "a Methodist real estate agent in Gopher Prairie" than "an artist, anarchist and atheist in Greenwich Village."[97]

While Chesterton during the 1920s was generally critical of Sinclair Lewis, Wells and Shaw, on the other hand, were admirers of his work. Wells had exerted an important influence on Lewis and expressed his enthusiasm when Lewis's literary career began to flourish. In 1922 he wrote to Lewis, "*Babbitt* is one of the greatest novels I have read for a long time." Of Lewis's depiction of the American businessman, Wells stated, "You have got him. No one has been anywhere near getting him before."[98] Shaw, in contrast to Chesterton, believed that Lewis was a fine choice to receive the Nobel Prize. He felt that he and Lewis were kindred souls, for they both participated in abusing the American people. "Mr. Sinclair Lewis," he wrote, "has knocked Washington off his pedestal and substituted Babbitt."[99]

Shaw himself was the subject of a chapter in *Sidelights* titled "Bernard Shaw and America." Chesterton wrote that everyone in the United States asked him about Shaw, as though the two men were linked in the public mind. He felt that Shaw was to an extent right in contending that Americans were fascinated by him because he mocked them and refused to visit. It was actually "a good thing" for Shaw, Chesterton argued, that he had never traveled to the United States, because he had been spared from discovering "the awful truth of how large a part of America shares some of his Shavian notions; and how very common, not to say vulgar, these notions are when seen on so large a scale." Shaw's abstinence from alcohol and tobacco was merely eccentric in England, but such behavior, when fanatically adopted in America, became distinctly unattractive. In fact, if Shaw were to come to the United States, he would immediately start to drink and smoke. Chesterton also quarreled with Shaw's sneering characterization of America as a "nation of villagers." To be a "nation of villagers" would actually be good, Chesterton asserted, but unfortunately present-day America could not fit the bill.[100]

Though not to the same extent as in *What I Saw in America*, Chesterton in *Sidelights* did compare the United States with England. Ironically, considering how much he had stressed the differences between the two nations, he argued that in one important respect Americans were guilty of exaggerating the contrast. It was certainly true that there was more equality, if not democracy, in America than in England, but it would be wrong to think that the overriding note of English life was elitism. Actually, "the atmosphere of England is an extremely subtle blend of liberty and aristocracy and a universal belief in courtesy, with a sort of by-product of snobbishness; but a by-product which smells to heaven." He conceded that this "snobbishness" was absent in America, where true "social equality" prevailed. This reality struck him when after one of his lectures at an American college, a professor approached to offer his commentary, and then so did the professor's chauffeur.[101]

If the Americans tended to magnify the "snobbishness" of English life, Chesterton contended, the English seemed to be oblivious to "the real virtues of America." When England was on top of the world, the true worth of English life had been similarly overlooked. According to Chesterton, "While England is being . . . Americanised, while London is being made to look like a bad imitation of New York, nobody says anything at all about the simpler and saner elements of American life, which are almost as far from New York as from London." The English were copying the vices rather than the virtues of American society, though the Americans themselves tended not to tout the true greatness of the nation: "We are only called upon to admire the Americans for their hustle, their publicity, their commercial amalgamations. Nothing is ever said of the real republican virtues which still survive, in spite of the confused and corrupt politics of the Republic." The English would do well to imitate the qualities of small-town America and realize that the nation was great because, despite all of the changes, it still maintained its essential political creed.[102]

The Founding Fathers, Chesterton believed, needed to be accorded great credit for the political system they established in America. The equality that could be observed in the United States was as much a testament to Jefferson as Islam was to Mohammed. America's problem was not what the Founders created but what they inherited from England, namely Puritanism. Erected on a Puritan foundation, the nation was destined, despite the strength of its political principles, to a shaky existence. And Puritanism, Chesterton argued, was not the last dubious legacy left to the Americans by the English. The urbanization, commercialization, and industrialization that marked America had plagued England first, and long before there was any "Americanization of England" there had been an "Anglicizing of America." During the nineteenth century, the American republic of small farmers was spoiled by the adoption of the Victorian, Spencerian view of society. Tragically, Chesterton argued, "America, instead of being the open agricultural commonwealth for which its founders hoped, has become the dumping-ground of all the most dismal ideas of decaying epochs in Europe, from Calvinism to Industrialism."[103]

Because of all the forces that competed with the vision of the Founders, the American republic, Chesterton argued, was not truly republican. In a 180-degree turn from the stance he had taken in *What I Saw in America*, in *Sidelights* he asserted that there was no public life in America. Taking a position much closer to what Wells had always maintained, he wrote that the American people preoccupied themselves with purely private matters. There once was a concern among Americans for the commonweal, but "that pure and positive public spirit has faded from their life more than from that of any people in the world." The American had lost his sense of citizenry and now cared more about his job than his vote. Private loyalties were more important than public duties. The English had lost their public virtues too, but whereas they mourned the fact, the Americans were proud of their thriving private realm. At least, Chesterton argued, Americans did have their political creed to cling to, and as he had advocated after his first trip to the United States, he believed that creed could be strengthened by being made more truly Christian.[104]

6

The New Deals

Harold Laski, H. G. Wells, and Roosevelt's America
versus Stalin's Russia

After Franklin D. Roosevelt was elected president in 1932, H. G. Wells and Harold Laski each revealed a renewed interest in America. Since reporting on the Washington Conference, Wells had paid just one visit to the United States, in 1931, and commented only intermittently on American affairs. Laski, since settling in London in the summer of 1920 after two years at McGill and four at Harvard, had returned to the United States in 1926 and 1931 and published a mere handful of articles about America.[1] But after Roosevelt came into office, Wells made several trips across the Atlantic and Laski was frequently in the States in the role of lecturer and teacher, and they both wrote extensively about the American scene. What captivated their attention was the dynamic leadership of FDR and his implementation of the New Deal, which, though not the socialistic solution they advocated, nevertheless struck them as a positive and exciting development in American and world history. Throughout the 1930s, as they watched this American experiment, they also kept their eyes on a rival venture, the Communist program of the Soviet Union. In fact, these two Englishmen, as they looked both east and west, felt constantly compelled to make the comparison between Stalin's Russia and Roosevelt's America. During this decade others on the British left, like George Bernard Shaw, did the same.

That Wells would come to champion the New Deal, albeit with reservations, is not surprising. By the 1930s he was still fighting for the establishment of a world state and had resuscitated the notion that an elite group of individuals would lead the way. When he conceived of the "Open Conspiracy" in the late 1920s, he had in mind mainly businessmen and industrialists, but following the crash he once again shifted his hopes to the left.[2] It is not difficult to see why Franklin Roosevelt, like Theodore Roosevelt, would appeal to Wells, and why Wells would be drawn to the New Dealers as he had been earlier in the century to the progressives.

More problematic is that Laski would voice any approval for Roosevelt's program. By the beginning of FDR's first term, Laski had become a committed, though not doctrinaire, Marxist. When he returned to England from America in 1920, he was still espousing a pluralist political philosophy, but then in the mid-twenties he began to embrace Fabian socialism and the notion of the omnipotent, beneficent state. His new viewpoint, which had been shaped in part by his active involvement in the Labour Party, was evident in his massive 1925 work, *A Grammar of Politics*. But Laski's Fabian phase, like his pluralist phase, was short-lived, for by the early 1930s he had turned to Marxism. He did not abandon the Labour Party for the Communist, but his radicalization entailed a shift from Fabian gradualism to revolutionary socialism. Although he never advocated armed rebellion and especially the Leninist notion of an overthrow effected by a cadre of revolutionaries, he did believe in the 1930s that violent conflict was inevitable.[3]

The essence of Laski's ideology can be found in many sources, including his 1933 book, *Democracy in Crisis*, which was drawn from lectures he delivered in 1931 at the University of North Carolina. In this work he wrote that liberal democracy, based on the idea of a wide suffrage and minimal government, had over the years served the needs of the capitalist system. Property had been secure, and the people had been pacified by an ever-rising standard of living and periodic concessions from the government. But now, Laski argued, the masses had come to the point of desiring economic equality, that is, socialism, while at the same time capitalism was contracting. The result would be conflict, for the propertied class would never voluntarily surrender wealth and power. Instead, it would sabotage democracy in order to preserve capitalism. In Britain, Laski felt, an electoral mandate for Labour to come to power to implement a truly socialist program would never be honored by the governing establishment.[4]

Laski's new position was to a large extent influenced by the momentous British political events of 1931, when Labour prime minister Ramsay MacDonald accepted the king's invitation to lead a new government composed mainly of Conservatives and Liberals. The National Government was triumphant in the ensuing election, Laski argued, by convincing a fearful population that a victory by Labour, now in opposition, would jeopardize Britain's teetering economy. However, the motivation underlying the successful campaign was merely to defend the capitalist system against any socialist encroachment.[5]

Looking at the world through his radical prism, Laski might have dismissed the New Deal as merely a set of concessions to satisfy the masses while the capitalist structure was left intact. But he saw merit in the Roosevelt agenda. To adopt such a position may have contradicted his Marxist political philosophy—and Laski had a penchant for being inconsistent—but he always held out the hope that change could be effected peacefully. After all, he devoted most of his life to working for the Labour Party.

Although Laski and Wells would become supporters and personal friends of Roosevelt, their initial position was one of skepticism. They both wondered at first whether he would make the kind of president they desired. Laski welcomed FDR's election in 1932, but largely because he felt the new president would have to be an improvement on Herbert Hoover. To the extent that Laski had focused on the America of the 1920s, he was critical of it and of the Republican presidents who occupied the White House during those years. He conceded that the American economy, compared to the British, was healthy, a fact that he felt accounted for Holmes's continuing devotion to capitalism while he had tied his star to socialism.[6] He also objected to those Europeans, particularly certain Frenchmen, who patronized America and ignorantly disparaged the nation with glib commentary.[7] But even though Laski considered himself a friend of the United States, his assessment of the nation in the wake of his 1926 trip was nevertheless harsh. When he characterized "The American Scene" for the *New Republic* in January 1928, he depicted the United States as a thoroughly commercialized nation whose people were absorbed in material gain and oblivious to the political realm. Though he could detect some glimmers of hope, his appraisal of America as a selfish business civilization was bleak.[8] Over the next two decades of his life, Laski would alter his view of America, but to a large extent the essence of his 1928 indictment remained intact.

When Laski visited the United States in 1931, he came away with a more positive opinion of the nation. He believed that America "was a richer civilisation than in 1926," that there had been "a growth of intellectual stature." The country, he felt, was on the brink of a promising and exciting future.[9] While still in the United States, he had written to Holmes, "There is a spirit of critical enquiry abroad which is quite refreshing, even exciting to the witness."[10] In the fall of 1932, a year after he returned to England, Laski still subscribed to the notion that America was changing for the better and reported that Wells, who had also been in the States in '31, concurred with him. According to Laski, the two of them were together at a luncheon, and

> he and I maintained against the company that in the next generation there was going to be a great intellectual renascence in the United States—that the present coincidence of scepticism, material difficulty, absence of overmastering tradition, faith in experimentalism, made it probable that new views and new creativeness were far more likely there than in England or Western Europe.[11]

If Laski saw encouraging signs in the American people, his enthusiasm did not extend to the political leadership, namely President Hoover. Even before Hoover had moved into the White House, Laski could not abide him. Before the 1928 election he wrote to his close friend Felix Frankfurter that although he saw little to admire in Al Smith and the Democrats, "I hate what contemporary Republicanism means in American life, and a Hoover who has no word of criticism for its implications merely arouses in me contempt."[12] In 1931 he assailed the president for his total devotion to the principle of "private initiative" and his refusal to consider social legislation.[13] As the Depression became increasingly devastating, he told Frankfurter, "I follow your American tragedy with horror. It doesn't seem possible that a man could watch the spectacle so inertly as Hoover does."[14] After the 1932 election, he was much more elated that Hoover had lost than that Roosevelt had won.[15]

The prospect of a Roosevelt presidency did not excite Laski at all. In fact, before the election he wrote that the best that could be said about Roosevelt's campaign was that he had "recognised the existence of the common man." Laski expressed the hope that FDR would not win a mandate, that his victory would be narrow and that the Socialist candidate, Norman Thomas, would pick up two to three million votes.[16] The only benefit of a Roosevelt triumph, besides the ouster of Hoover, would be that Frankfurter, an adviser to FDR, might be appointed to an important post.[17] Essentially Laski was wary of Roosevelt, whose campaign utterances left American observers wondering what direction he would take as well.[18] After the election Laski challenged Frankfurter to "tell me which Roosevelt is going to enter the White House."[19] He expressed his lukewarm sentiments to Holmes when he wrote, "though I greatly like Frank Roosevelt, I am not able to feel enthusiasm at his victory." He explained:

> I thought he fought a second-rate campaign, evasive and timid; and I am no admirer of most of the people on whose advice he is going to depend. And I don't see how a Democrat, with Bryanism and Hearstism and such-like excrescences to consider, has got much of a chance of being decisive or courageous. I shall watch with enormous interest; but I suspect that this is in fact a pill to cure an earthquake.[20]

Between Roosevelt's triumph at the polls and his inauguration, Laski wrote an article for the Labourite *Daily Herald* of London in which he expressed an ambivalence about the president-elect. The doubts that he had aired in his letters to Frankfurter and Holmes once again surfaced, but he placed greater weight than before on Roosevelt's assets and on his potential to be a successful president. Laski's more balanced evaluation may have resulted from his not wanting to appear too negative before FDR had even taken office. Working to Roosevelt's advantage, he argued, would be his courage and engaging manner. The president-elect was certainly a more impressive personality than Hoover, and in fact, "he is the most hopeful figure who has entered the White House since Woodrow Wilson left it." Although Roosevelt had not so far enunciated a progressive agenda, he did display a Jeffersonian concern for the plight of the average man. Laski wrote, "I agree with those who think that, temperamentally, there is a real liberal somewhere in Mr. Roosevelt."[21]

What made Laski pessimistic about Roosevelt was, first of all, that he had run an evasive campaign in which he failed to grapple with key issues, including the overriding problem of unemployment. Furthermore, Roosevelt was too close, for Laski's liking, to such business titans as Owen D. Young and Bernard Baruch, and there was the drag that a backward-thinking Democratic Party would exert on his presidency. Laski also mentioned FDR's privileged upbringing and elite schooling as factors that would steer the president in a conservative direction.[22]

The question, according to Laski, was whether Roosevelt would be cautious or prepared to take bold steps. If he chose the latter, "he might make his presidency an epoch in American history." As Laski had written after his 1931 trip, he believed that there now existed in America a healthy questioning of traditional socioeconomic assumptions and a yearning for new solutions. The onus was on Roosevelt to transform that sentiment into a constructive force. If he would consult the likes of Frankfurter and call on the talents of a Frances Perkins, and if he would be willing to do battle with the vested interests, he could turn the nation around. Laski did not go so far as to suggest socialism but argued that Roosevelt had to see the need for economic reconstruction and equality promoted by a positive state. He concluded the article by saying, "Mr. Roosevelt stands at one of the great turning points of history. Let us hope he will have the strength to take the right road."[23]

In June 1933, a few months into the Roosevelt Presidency, Laski characterized European opinion of FDR for the *Yale Review*. When the article was published, Laski had recently returned from his first visit to the United States of the Roosevelt era—a trip he described as the most "stimulating" one he had yet made.[24] In his article he contended that in the Old World there was a cautious hopefulness about the president. Europeans felt a "sense of exhilaration" that America had "entered upon a period of positive policy after a long epoch of *laissez-faire*." They were uncertain about what direction Roosevelt planned to take, how far the nation would let him go, and whether he could ultimately succeed, but his inclination to action made them "feel the vague prospect of a possible dawn." Europeans were rooting for Roosevelt to prevail, Laski wrote, for they realized "his victory is the real guarantee of their own future." Because so many looked to Roosevelt, it was incumbent upon him to follow the example of Wilson after America entered the war and "assume the leadership of the progressive public opinion of the world."[25]

Wells first made his feelings about Roosevelt widely known in his popular 1933 novel, *The Shape of Things to Come*, which unfolds in the form of a history recorded in the twenty-second century. Wells presciently described a long, terrible war breaking out in Europe in 1940, but from the ashes of that war the elite "airmen" establish the utopian world state. President Roosevelt, referred to as "Roosevelt II," is discussed in connection with the World Economic Conference held in London in the summer of 1933, the last event in the "history" that had actually occurred at the time Wells completed the novel. The conference, which broke up in failure to a large extent because FDR would not tie the United States to a currency stabilization agreement, is presented as an early but insufficient attempt at global unification.

The narrator, serving, of course, as Wells's mouthpiece, is critical of Roosevelt, whom he depicts as another Wilson in the sense of being an American leader to whom the world turned in hope but who failed to deliver. After FDR was elected in 1932 and as the conference approached, there was a desire for him to "speak plainly to all mankind and liberate the world from the dire obsessions and ineptitudes under which it suffered and to which it seemed magically enslaved. But the one thing he failed to do was to speak plainly." Europeans read his book *Looking Forward* and found it "vague and wanting in intellectual grip." Nevertheless, everyone knew that only Roosevelt could make the London Conference a success, and there was a sense of satisfaction that he was receiving expert advice from a "Brain Trust." The problem was that Roosevelt, while aware of some of the actions necessary to combat the Depression, was never committed to international cooperation. But Wells was also pessimistic that FDR could achieve much domestically, for, according to the "history," the president introduced ambitious schemes, though with no satisfactory civil service in place to carry them out. By 1937, it is told, "America, in spite of, or perhaps because of, the bold experimenting of Roosevelt II, was in a state of deepening economic and political disorder."[26]

At the end of 1933, Wells was asked by *Liberty* magazine to speculate on "Roosevelt's Place in History," and again he criticized the president for failing to take a global approach. By late 1933 the National Recovery Administration (NRA), the Tennessee Valley Authority (TVA), the Public Works Administration (PWA), and the Civilian Conservation Corps (CCC) were all in place; the Agricultural Adjustment Act (AAA) had been passed; and monetary, banking, and security reforms had been implemented. Although the efficacy of the early New Deal program was still much in question in December 1933, Wells refrained from any specific discussion of this unprecedented tide of legislation. He did question whether Roosevelt possessed "a philosophy" or was "merely meeting each emergency as it arises." But above all, Wells dwelled on the fact that Roosevelt was pursuing a national course rather than assuming the mantle of global leader, and he argued that consequently the president would not be credited by a history of the year 2033 with having played a role in shaping the new world order.[27]

Though he was skeptical of the prospects for the New Deal and lamented Roosevelt's failure to look for international solutions, Wells was by no means dismissive of the president. FDR, he believed, was "the most conspicuous, exciting, and interesting individual in the world just now, Stalin, Mussolini, and Hitler notwithstanding." Like Wilson, Roosevelt would be counted, if not as one of the figures responsible for laying the foundation for a world state, at least as one of the "Great Men" who people the chapters of history. Wells conceded that the task of building a new global future was beyond the scope of any one leader, and he wondered, as well, if perhaps the president possessed an international plan he simply had not revealed. But he was inclined to feel that "history may have to tell of Franklin Roosevelt as a significant gesture and a failure," though "that will detract nothing from the real heroism and the real pathos of his lonely and manifestly quite honest attempt to face the needs and menace of his time."[28]

Wells did admit that the British were not undertaking anything as significant as the Americans or the Russians and that the New Deal, even if its fate was dubious and even if it did not extend beyond the borders of the United States, was worthy of being closely watched. The Europeans were destined to copy the New Deal, which was more relevant to their situation than Stalin's efforts in his less developed nation: "The American Experiment, for all its intensifying isolation, will probably remain more edifying and influential to Europe, the British Empire, and South America than the Russian Experiment, because it is being made on a much more kindred social and economic structure."[29]

By 1934 Laski had come to look much more favorably upon Roosevelt, and during that year Wells was to come around also. They were not now certain that the president could succeed but were solidly supportive of his program. Only two months after Wells's *Liberty* article appeared, Laski published a piece, titled "The Roosevelt Experiment," in the *Atlantic* of February 1934 in which he hailed the New Deal legislation that had been pushed through Congress in the previous year.[30] Wells reassessed his position on the New Deal after he visited the United States in the spring of 1934 and met with FDR at the White House. He dropped his accusation that Roosevelt's program was inadequate because it was not international and enthusiastically praised the president's efforts.

At the outset of his *Atlantic* article, Laski signaled how much he had come to embrace the New Deal when he wrote, "Russia apart, no modern state has undertaken an experiment which even approaches in magnitude or significance the adventure upon which President Roosevelt has embarked." In his view Roosevelt was the first leader of a capitalist nation ever to call for a reappraisal of laissez faire and to place the authority of the government behind important economic and social reconstruction. "Success or failure," the New Deal "bears upon its face the hallmarks of great leadership." Roosevelt's program, he wrote, was particularly impressive when compared to the cautious approach of the present British government.[31]

While he believed the New Deal represented a significant departure from the past, Laski defended Roosevelt against the charge of "radicalism." Despite the hysterical conclusions drawn by the administration's opponents, he asserted that a "sober conservatism" underlay the legislation that had been enacted over the past year. Such laws as the National Industrial Recovery Act, which would serve to place American workers in a much better position, were eminently sensible and embodied reforms that should have been undertaken years before. While the New Deal legislation was passed in response to the present crisis, its origins could be seen in the progressive efforts waged earlier in the century. Only in his experiments in currency manipulation, Laski asserted, could Roosevelt be judged radical, and in fact misguided. On the whole the president had acted reasonably and in direct response to the disillusioned electorate that had voted him into office in 1932 with a mandate to effect change. Roosevelt was answering the call of the American people to rein in the capitalist system so that it would be the "servant" and not the "master" of the public. The president "is not a revolutionist pursuing some private Utopia by the light of an inner wisdom. He is the logical expression of social forces and could hardly have acted otherwise if he wished to retain the characteristic contours of American life." Had FDR merely followed in the footsteps of his Republican predecessors, America would surely have entered into a "revolutionary" stage.[32]

Whether the New Deal would actually succeed in the long run Laski believed to be an open question. Although the general public was supportive of the president's endeavors, businessmen were not: "Wall Street is confident that traditional America is being handed over to wild professors with no regard for the practical limits to government action." Laski contended that a propertied class never surrendered its wealth and authority voluntarily, and although Roosevelt was not actually calling for socialism, he was endeavoring to curtail the power of the financial and industrial captains. Already the reaction of these men to the New Deal had been negative, and though they had not yet waged a counterattack, they had muttered their complaints and refused cooperation. There were signs that they meant to "sabotage" Roosevelt's program. What the president was facing, Laski wrote, was what the Liberals had to confront when they swept into power in Britain in 1906 and began to undertake social reform. In both cases the propertied interests tried to stand in the way; Wall Street had now assumed the role of the House of Lords.[33]

Despite the massive obstruction that the business class placed in Roosevelt's path, as well as such other significant problems as the lack of an experienced, nonpartisan civil service, Laski did not rule out the possibility of the New Deal's prevailing. After all, the nation was in a crisis, the people were behind the president, and the businessmen who opposed him had been discredited in the forum of public opinion. Laski felt that the stakes were high: "The failure of Mr. Roosevelt means the end of political democracy in America, for the simple reason that it will prove itself thereby incapable of adapting to its purposes the institutions of its economic life." If Roosevelt failed, he warned, violent class conflict would erupt in the United States. The masses would attempt to achieve through force what the president was trying to obtain for them constitutionally. Though Laski consistently wrote of the inevitability of violent revolution, and in 1934 he saw that as a real prospect for America, he preferred peaceful change. Employing a term he would use frequently during World War II, he wrote that Roosevelt was trying to spearhead a "revolution by consent." Laski did not use the word "socialism" in the *Atlantic,* but at the end of the article he implied that Roosevelt could serve as the link to a socialist America. The president, he said, was endeavoring "to find those intermediate terms between traditional America and that new American society the ultimate emergence of which is written in the inescapable facts of her economic and social life."[34]

In 1934 Wells, like Laski, became a champion of the New Deal. After his assessment of Roosevelt was published in *Liberty,* the president wrote him a gracious letter, saying, "It is because I have read, with pleasure and profit, almost everything that you have written, that I send you this note to tell you that I like and appreciate your article in Liberty Magazine." Roosevelt acknowledged neither the criticisms nor the compliments that Wells had directed at him. Instead, he stated that he agreed with Wells's point that no one man could single-handedly solve the world crisis but that he felt there was a growing recognition that a concerted effort was necessary. He concluded by saying that he hoped he could see Wells on his next visit to America.[35] In April 1934 Wells replied to Roosevelt, "You wrote me a very pleasant note some months ago. These indiscretions carry their penalties. I am profoundly interested in the world situation and I want very much to have half an hour's conversation with you." He told the president that he would be in the United States in May, and "if I could talk to you *and to Mrs Roosevelt* all sorts of things that are vague in my mind will become definite. I am more and more persuaded that you are in a key position in the world's affairs and extraordinarily right-minded and right-spirited."[36]

Wells's request for a meeting was granted, and in his *Experiment in Autobiography*, published later in 1934, he discussed his visit to the White House and other experiences in America and drew some new conclusions about the president and the New Deal. He noted that the trip to the White House was his fourth, whereas he had never been invited to Buckingham Palace. The White House had regained the "country house" atmosphere he remembered from his 1906 visit with Theodore Roosevelt; in the Harding years it had seemed like a "popular club," and in Hoover's time it had become "a queer ramshackle place like a nest of waiting-rooms with hat-stands everywhere, and unexpected doors, never perceptible before or since, through which hurrying distraught officials appeared and vanished."[37] Wells related that in 1934 he was a guest at a small White House dinner, and then he sat and talked with the president, Mrs. Roosevelt, and the president's secretary Missy LeHand until almost midnight.[38]

Franklin Roosevelt clearly won Wells over, just as Theodore Roosevelt had done almost three decades before. Physically FDR reminded him of the legendary English poet and editor William Ernest Henley— "the same big torso linked to almost useless legs." Roosevelt's mind he compared to Arthur Balfour's, but whereas the president was as intelligent as the late prime minister, he was furthermore a man of action. Wells was also much taken with Eleanor Roosevelt, who did not strike him at all as the severe "school marm" that others had painted. Of both Franklin and Eleanor he said, "There was no pose about either of them.

They were not concerned about being what was expected of them, or with the sort of impression they were making; they were just interested in a curious keen detached way about the state of the world."[39]

In Franklin Roosevelt, Wells had found a kindred spirit. He was well aware that FDR did not go so far as to endorse any notions about a socialist world state: "I do not say that the President has these revolutionary ideas in so elaborated and comprehensive a form as they have come to me." But Wells believed that "these ideas are sitting all around him now, and unless I misjudge him, they will presently possess him altogether." Roosevelt was not yet "consciously" an "Open Conspirator," but he was destined to become one. The creation of a world state was the only clear answer to the problems besetting modern society: "Franklin Roosevelt does not embody and represent that goal, but he represents the way thither." Because the president was such a "bold" and "flexible" leader, because he could be "revolutionary" without precipitating revolution, and because he could comprehend sophisticated ideas while remaining attuned to popular sentiment, he stood as "the most effective transmitting instrument possible for the coming of the new world order."[40]

While Wells was enthusiastic about Roosevelt, he understood that there would be no smooth sailing for the New Deal. As he had argued before, he wrote that the "inadequacy" of the American civil service posed a great threat to Roosevelt's program. And not only was the civil service deficient, but Wells was even somewhat disappointed by the Brain Trust. He had no criticism for the particular individuals who advised Roosevelt. In fact, on one occasion he found himself seated next to Adolf Berle, who, according to Wells, "began to unfold a view of the world to me which seemed to contain all I had ever learnt and thought, but better arranged and closer to reality." Wells's problem with the Brain Trust was that although its members were a bright group of men committed to solving the nation's problems in an informed, systematic manner, they did not make up a cohesive group. As Raymond Moley himself explained to Wells, the president's advisers could be broken down into different factions pursuing different goals, united only by a common devotion to FDR. Wells was compelled to conclude: "I have seen enough of this Brains movement to realize that it is no sort of conspiracy; that it is not a body of men formally associated by a concerted statement of ideas." The Brain Trust, he found, was not as unified as either the Bolshevik revolutionaries of 1917 or the spearheads of the republic in Spain.[41]

Resistance to the New Deal among the American public, Wells contended, was significant. "Franklin Roosevelt is one of the greatest shocks that has ever happened to the prevalent mental assumptions of the United States," and opposition to his program was widespread. Three decades before, Wells had maintained that Americans needed a "sense of the state": "Now they are getting a sense of the state put over them rather rapidly, and they are taking it very ungraciously." On his trip to America he found that the corporate executive and the Marxist radical could be equally vociferous in their denunciations of the Roosevelt administration. While in Washington he also encountered Clarence Darrow, who, to Wells's disappointment, was then taking a leading role in opposing the New Deal.[42] In March 1934 Darrow had been named chairman of a National Recovery Review Board charged by the administration with evaluating the NRA codes that had been hammered out in various industries and become the object of significant criticism. In May, while Wells was in the capital, the Darrow Board issued its first report, which concluded that the codes fostered monopoly and benefited large corporations at the expense of small businesses.[43] Despite a certain affinity he felt with Darrow, Wells characterized him as an old-fashioned American radical who championed the "little man" against the corporation and the government. His ardent individualism made him a kind of "sentimental anarchist." In Wells's view the Darrow Board was wrongheaded: "It is not the New Deal and the N.R.A. which are sacrificing the small man to large-scale operation. The stars in their courses are doing that."[44]

Like Laski, Wells maintained that if the New Deal did not succeed, the consequences would be cataclysmic. "If Roosevelt and his New Deal fail altogether," he wrote, "there will be further financial and business collapse, grave sectional social disorder, political gangsterism and an extensive decivilization of wide regions." But he was inclined to believe that despite all of the obstacles it faced, the New Deal could prevail. Wells admitted that he had thought otherwise before making his trip to Washington and that meeting Roosevelt made him change his mind. He even repudiated the negative *Liberty* article he had written a few months before.[45]

While it is not difficult to see that Wells could have been charmed by Roosevelt and gotten caught up in the headiness of the early New Deal atmosphere, it is baffling that he said no more about the major charge he had leveled against the administration in *The Shape of Things to Come* and the *Liberty* article—that the president's efforts were strictly national rather than global in scope. Did he come to feel that the domestic program was so important that it was better for him to acquit Roosevelt, at least for the time being, of any failure to take an international approach? Did the president perhaps tell Wells he would broaden his horizons in the future? In any event, the inconsistency is glaring.

When Wells traveled to the United States in May of 1934, his purpose was not merely to assess the New Deal on its own terms but to make a comparison between the programs of Roosevelt and Stalin. As he wrote in his autobiography, he was interested in the question, "What is the relation of the New Plan in America to the New Plan in Russia and how are both related to the ultimate World-State?" Therefore, in late July, less than two months after returning from the United States, he headed off to Moscow.[46] Wells had not been in the Soviet Union since he made the 1920 trip that was the inspiration for his book *Russia in the Shadows.* In that work he argued that it was not so much that the Bolsheviks had overthrown the Czarist regime as that the old order had simply disintegrated and the Communists were the only group who could pick up the pieces. He thought the Bolsheviks crude and strictly tied to Marxist ideology, though he conceded that Lenin and a few of his associates were talented. Lenin was apparently not enamored of Wells, for after they met, he allegedly dismissed him as "a narrow petty bourgeois." Despite Wells's criticisms of the Bolsheviks, he did feel that it would be better for the West to work with rather than try to destroy the Soviet Union.[47]

When Wells visited Moscow in the summer of 1934, he met with Stalin as he had only weeks before in Washington with Roosevelt. While the substance of Wells's talk with the Roosevelts was never revealed, the *New Statesman* published a transcript of his dialogue with Stalin. Wells told Stalin that he had been "excited" by his trip to America: "It seems to me that what is taking place in the United States is a profound reorganisation, the creation of planned, that is, socialist economy." Although he realized that Roosevelt and Stalin "begin from two different starting-points," he asked, "is there not a relation in ideas, a kinship of ideas and needs, between Washington and Moscow?" He wanted Stalin to see that the New Deal was built on "socialist ideas" and that America and Russia were not really worlds apart. But Stalin would accept none of Wells's points. The New Deal, he argued, was not a socialistic program but rather an attempt to save capitalism from the crisis it was facing. While conceding that Roosevelt was an impressive figure, he asserted that the United States was dominated by the capitalist class and that even if the president wished to champion the cause of the proletariat, he could never be successful. No meaningful change could ever take place in America as long as the idea of private property prevailed.[48]

Though Wells appreciated Stalin's directness, he found that he had "little of the quick uptake of President Roosevelt." More important, he was irritated that Stalin would not agree that there was any connection between the experiments being simultaneously undertaken in Washington and Moscow. Instead, Stalin could only utter the strict Marxist-Leninist line. Wells hoped that the capitalist West and Communist East could converge in a socialist center but discovered that the Russians thought they had nothing to learn from the world beyond their borders. He was also upset to find that Gorky, whom he had defended in America in 1906 and whom he had visited in Russia in 1920, had become a staunch Stalinist who did not believe in literary freedom. It seemed, as well, that the material progress the Russians had made was meager; everything was promised for the future. Wells left the Soviet Union disappointed with Stalin and disillusioned with the Communist experiment.[49] He would never give up on Russia, but the impressions he formed on this 1934 trip were decidedly negative. In Wells's comparison, FDR, the New Deal, and America had come out the winner.

While Wells was critical of Communist Russia, during the 1930s the tendency among British intellectuals on the left was to extol Marxism and embrace the Soviet Union. In a decade beset by depression and fascism, the Stalinist regime seemed to many in Britain and throughout the West to offer a hopeful alternative. Not only did young English radicals like Laski and John Strachey, son of John St. Loe Strachey, pay homage to the Soviet system, but Wells's old friends Sidney and Beatrice Webb and George Bernard Shaw, the apostles of Fabian gradualism, now found their spiritual home in Moscow. The Webbs journeyed to Russia in 1932, but unlike Wells they came away with overwhelmingly positive feelings. Their *Soviet Communism: A New Civilization* (1935), written with the assistance of Russian authorities, was so much a panegyric that even Laski felt they could have shone a brighter light on the harsh aspects of the regime.[50] When Wells sent the Webbs a copy of his autobiography in 1934, Beatrice, in her note of thanks, took issue with his assessment of the American and Russian experiments: "As for a planned society, I doubt your preference for Roosevelt's controlled capitalism over the planned production for communal consumption inaugurated by the U.S.S.R. However, time will show which project is successful."[51]

Shaw defended Stalin's performance in his 1934 interview with Wells by arguing that Wells had not been at all interested in any of the leader's responses.[52] That Shaw became a proponent of the Soviet system is not as surprising as that the Webbs did. He was attracted to Marx from the time he first read *Das Kapital* in the early 1880s, and though he would come to see Fabianism as an improvement on Marxism and believe that each nation had to follow its own distinctive path to socialism, he never disavowed the kernel of the Marxist creed he had assimilated as a young man. He endorsed the Bolshevik Revolution and, despite the contradictions, considered himself both a Fabian and a Communist. In 1931 he accompanied Lord and Lady Astor to the Soviet Union and, like Wells a few years later, was afforded a meeting with Stalin. On his brief trip, Shaw was generally impressed by what he observed.[53]

After returning from Russia, he addressed the American people over radio. His tendency to needle them had not been lost, as evidenced by his opening words: "Hello, all of my friends in America! How are all you dear old boobs who have been telling one another for a month that I have gone dotty about Russia?" Although the Soviet Union was no "paradise," he argued that the nation was certainly in better shape than Depression-ravaged America. President Hoover, who had led the effort to save Europeans from starvation during the war, was now unable to keep even his own people fed. Shaw compared the Bolshevik revolutionaries to the Founding Fathers and asserted that there was a clear parallel between the present anathematization of Russia in the West and the treatment accorded the newly established American republic in the late eighteenth century. Just as a statue of Washington now stood in London, one day a statue of Lenin would be erected in New York. According to Shaw, the American tourist was welcome in the Soviet Union but should be prepared for the Russians to feel "a mixture of pity for you as a refugee from the horrors of American capitalism, with a colossal intellectual contempt for your political imbecility in not having established communism in your own unhappy country."[54]

In 1933, as the Roosevelt administration was just taking form, Shaw at age seventy-seven finally came to the United States. He had not, however, suddenly made the decision to take the grand tour of America. In late 1932 the Shaws embarked on a round-the-world cruise, and San

Francisco and New York were merely brief stops on the crowded itinerary. When the *Empress of Britain* arrived in San Francisco in March of 1933, the press was poised to pounce upon Shaw.[55] He had made good copy less than a fortnight before when Helen Keller revealed that he had been rude to her in England. According to Keller, after Shaw had taken an irritable tone with her, he was asked by Lady Astor, at whose home the incident occurred, whether he was aware that Keller was deaf and blind. His alleged response was: "Why, of course! All Americans are deaf and blind—and dumb."[56] In the news conference he granted aboard ship in San Francisco harbor, Shaw touched upon various subjects, including fascism, of which he approved: "You Americans are so fearful of dictators. Dictatorship is the only way in which government can accomplish anything. See what a mess democracy has led to." When asked about Hitler, who had just come to power, he answered:

> I don't know anything about him. The whole of Germany is in suspense and chaos—just like the United States. They've decided to try Hitler just as America has decided to try Franklin Roosevelt. I shall tell you what I think of both of them in four or five years—when I see what they've done.[57]

The Shaws did no sightseeing in San Francisco. Instead, they immediately flew off to the San Simeon ranch of William Randolph Hearst. After four days at the Hearst estate, they traveled south to Los Angeles, where they spent an afternoon touring the MGM studio and meeting with such Hollywood stars as Charlie Chaplin, Clark Gable, and John Barrymore. They then rejoined their ship to steam, via the Panama Canal, toward New York.[58]

The *Empress of Britain* docked in New York for only a day. While the Shaws managed to slip off of the ship, past the horde of reporters and photographers, to tour the city, the highlight of their New York stay was the address that GBS delivered that evening before the Academy of Political Science at the Metropolitan Opera House, which was also broadcast to a national radio audience.[59] He had written to his former American publisher, "My brief appearance in New York will be to say some unpopular but necessary things to your people before I die."[60] The address that Shaw delivered, titled "The Future of Political Science in America," was long and uncharacteristically serious. His main argument was simply that the future of the United States depended upon the elimination of the Constitution.[61]

Echoing the themes he had enunciated over a quarter century before in his article "A Nation of Villagers," Shaw called the Constitution "a Charter of Anarchism." The idea behind the Constitution was to establish a system in which government would be nonexistent. He told his audience, "to symbolize this state of things, this defeat of all government, you have set up in New York Harbor a monstrous idol which you call Liberty." The British, he conceded, had been as guilty as the Americans in their devotion to laissez faire, but now the United States, through Hollywood, was spreading anarchism throughout the world. The hero in every American film was "an unhesitating and violent anarchist": "His one answer to everything that annoys him or disparages his country or his parents or his young lady or his personal code of manly conduct, is to give the offender a 'sock' in the jaw." Shaw wanted to see a Hollywood movie in which the hero, instead of punching someone in the face, would resolve his dispute by summoning a policeman.[62]

However, a new kind of American—and specifically American statesman—was emerging who understood the need for positive government. When Shaw was a boy, the typical American was "Uncle Jonathan," an unsophisticated "provincial" whose lack of confidence made him acutely sensitive to foreign criticism.[63] "Uncle Jonathan" was succeeded by the "Hundredpercent American," an imposing figure whose greatest asset was his tendency to be gregarious and hospitable rather than, like the Englishman, to crave privacy, and whose greatest fault was his superficiality. But Shaw saw change in the wind:

> The Hundredpercent American is being succeeded by a more highly developed American. He is more muscular and less adipose than the Hundredpercent American. He has the same imposing presence, the same eloquence, the same vitality, the same dignity, the same enthusiasm. But his dignity is not pompous; and his enthusiasm is attached to definite measures and not to selections from the poetry and rhetoric of the day before yesterday.[64]

Franklin D. Roosevelt was an example of this new type of American. Shaw told his audience: "President Roosevelt is appealing to you at the present time to get rid of your confounded Constitution, and give him power to govern the country." If the people did not comply, the president would fail. Hoover had been unable to succeed because of the restrictions on his ability to take action. The American people now expected much from Roosevelt, but "you will get nothing from him if he has to act constitutionally through the usual routine of Congress. His four years will inevitably end in as great a disappointment as Mr. Hoover's."[65]

Despite Shaw's enthusiasm for the Soviet Union, he did not attempt to win his American audience over to Communism. He did make the argument that Americans should be glad the Russians were not capitalistic and competitors for world markets and should hope that the Chinese go Communist too: "Think of the United States with not only Japan capitalist, but Russia and China capitalist! You may well shudder." Furthermore, Shaw contended that in drawing up their new constitution, the Americans should pay no heed to Marx. Just as Fabianism was thoroughly English and Stalinism uniquely Russian, the Americans needed to construct their own distinctive political creed "from the American facts, with American thought, on American lines." But Shaw did feel that the revamping of the American governmental system could have global implications: the Americans could "yet take the lead in political thought and action, and help to save the soul of the world."[66]

Shaw's address was to an extent a disappointment. Although the audience was receptive to the talk, which he delivered in one hour and forty minutes with only an occasional glance at his notes, the New York press was critical of, among other things, how long-winded he had been.[67] The next day Shaw himself said of the address, "Some of it was very bad; I'm afraid I bungled a very great deal of it."[68] The *Times* commented that after he had avoided America for decades, it was inevitable that his appearance would be an "anti-climax."[69] But the paper also pinpointed what might have been the specific problem with his address. For years Shaw had been saying, apparently with accuracy, that Americans loved him to abuse them. But when he finally arrived in the United States, he delivered a solemn speech in which he even boasted, "I came here firmly resolved that not a single word should pass my lips which could give the slightest offense to any American."[70] The *Times* wrote of his Metropolitan Opera House audience, "They went expecting to enjoy a series of sparkling epigrams, mixed up with insults, but instead got a long and tedious political harangue, worthy of a dryasdust professor."[71]

In 1936 Shaw returned to the United States for the last time. Again, he and his wife were on a cruise, and again they stayed only a few days in America. They spent two nights in Miami, and when the ship stopped on the West Coast, they took a train inland to see the Grand Canyon.[72] On his previous trip to America, Shaw had said he would be able to comment on Roosevelt after four or five years' time. Now, three years later, he seemed pleased with FDR but again attacked his favorite target. As he told the press in Miami, "You have a good President and a bad Constitution."[73] When Shaw's ship arrived in Havana, he announced approvingly that Roosevelt was a Communist. The president did not know he was one, but he was slowly coming to that realization.[74] Although Shaw never fell for Roosevelt as Wells and Laski had done, over the years he apparently sustained an admiration for the president. In 1941 he summed up his feelings when he wrote, "I still rank Stalin first, Roosevelt second, and the rest nowhere."[75]

In February 1935 Roosevelt wrote to Wells, "Your experiment in autobiography was for me an experiment in staying awake instead of putting the light out." He asked, "How do you manage to retain such vivid pictures of events and such extraordinarily clear impressions and judgments?" Although the president did not refer directly to Wells's passages praising his leadership and the aims of the New Deal, he stated, "We are still moving forward, not only as a Government but very distinctly as a people." Roosevelt felt that his greatest achievement so far had been in stimulating the thought process of the citizenry: "They may not think straight but they are thinking in the right direction—and your direction and mine are not so far apart; at least we both seek peaceable conveyances in our travels." The president furthermore said to Wells, "I do hope you will come over again this year."[76]

Wells was to fulfill Roosevelt's wish; by March he was back in the United States to take another look at the progress the New Deal was making. As he revealed in a series of articles he wrote for *Collier's* that spring, then published as the slender volume *The New America: The New World*, Wells had lost none of his admiration for Roosevelt but was now much more pessimistic about the New Deal. That Wells left the United States less hopeful in 1935 than in 1934 largely reflected a change in the Washington atmosphere. By the spring of 1935, the New Deal had entered a period of stagnation. Between the Democratic successes in the 1934 midterm election and the inauguration of the "Second Hundred Days" in the summer of 1935, Roosevelt was unsure about what direction to take and the only significant legislation passed by Congress was the bill establishing the Works Progress Administration (WPA).[77] The NRA, the centerpiece of the New Deal effort to bring about industrial recovery, had turned out to be largely ineffective and widely unpopular, so when the Supreme Court declared it unconstitutional in May, even within the administration there was some sense of relief.[78] Meanwhile, as the Roosevelt Presidency had ground to a halt, a formidable challenge for the public's attention was being waged by such charismatic radicals as Senator Huey Long of Louisiana and the radio priest, Father Charles Coughlin. As Wells arrived in America in March 1935, Walter Lippmann assessed the political situation by saying, "We have come to a period of discouragement after a few months of buoyant hope. Pollyanna is silenced and Cassandra is doing all the talking."[79]

In *The New America: The New World*, Wells harked back to his previous trip to the United States in the spring of 1934. On that visit, he wrote, "I was enormously impressed by the personality and fine mental quality of the President, and by the implication conveyed by such a phrase as the Brain Trust. The available intelligence of America, I assumed, was to be drawn together into a synthesis of understanding." He felt that in 1934 he had been optimistic but not unrealistic. Now, a year later, Wells was sorry to find that his enthusiasm had been misplaced, for no unified effort to bring about a transformation of American society had really materialized. The Brain Trust had failed to congeal into a solid force.[80]

After Wells examined the New Deal in 1935, he concluded that the United States was devoid "of any vital social and economic philosophy at all." Or, as he put it another way, "there is as yet no clear idea of what America is up to." He came to this harsh assessment as a consequence of his discussions with various administration officials who possessed no coherent notion of where the New Deal was heading. On the most basic philosophical level, there was no agreement, Wells discovered, as to whether the New Deal was supposed to establish a small-scale, Jeffersonian-style economy or a highly complex, centralized structure, or merely recreate the system of the 1920s, with perhaps some of the hard edges smoothed out. The diversity of the New Deal programs, with their contradictory goals, revealed that there was no plan, merely a "sort of discursive experimenting."[81]

With the New Dealers in disarray, Wells argued, the political void was being filled by the "raucous voices," Long, Coughlin, and Francis Townsend, the California doctor who was championing a radical old-age pension plan. In the spring of 1934, President Roosevelt had been master of the radio, but now the "raucous voices" were filling the airwaves. Wells listened to Father Coughlin's broadcast and lamented that the priest was telling his listeners that their woes could be attributed to the banks and to foreign interests: "The empty poverty of his method, considered in relation to his undeniably immense popularity, was a disconcerting symptom to a visitor who still hoped to find in America a practical and moral constructive lead for the rest of the world."[82]

When Wells arrived in the United States in 1935, Long was immersed in a very public fight with Hugh Johnson, the former director of the NRA. Wells visited Long in his Capitol Hill office, and though he found his ideas about redistributing wealth even more primitive than Coughlin's economic notions, he viewed the senator as an engaging figure. Wells wrote, "He is like a Winston Churchill who has never been at Harrow." Because of Long's youth and political talent, Wells predicted that he would be a force on the American scene for years to come. Though Long and Hitler shared a "certain mental crudity," Wells stressed that the link that some drew between them was weak: both were demagogues, but "the German brand of popular poison is profoundly different from the American."[83]

The "raucous voices" held little appeal for Wells. Aside from questioning their economic assumptions, as a prophet of the world state he found them "ignorantly anti-cosmopolitan." Nevertheless, he took these figures seriously: "I do not think it possible to minimize the significance of their voices as an intimation of a wide-spread discontent and discomfort, and of an impatient preparedness for sweeping changes in the great masses of the American population." The pace of the New Deal had been too slow and its measures too modest for the American people, who were now expressing their frustration. Wells adopted an ominous tone when he wrote, "In a little while they may be demanding not a New Deal, but a new sort of game." He did believe that if nothing was done to check the "raucous voices," then America could well be plagued not by Communism or fascism but by "an intellectually cruder and more instinctive sort of revolutionism."[84]

The blame for the present listlessness of the New Deal and consequent publicity gained by the likes of Long and Coughlin did not, Wells believed, lie with Roosevelt. He had lunch with FDR at the White House and was once again overwhelmed. In Wells's eyes Roosevelt had so much transcended the office of president as traditionally carried out that there was about him virtually "the effect of a divinity floating in a cloud a little off the earth." If Roosevelt was at the moment silent, if his policies were in "a state of suspense," there was good reason. Wells asserted that the role of the president—any president—was to serve as a "sounding board" and then "to sublimate, clarify and express the advancing thought of the community." Roosevelt was "listening," but he was hearing little that was "constructive" and as a consequence was resigned to "waiting." The task of reconstruction was no "one-man job" reserved only for the president, and, according to Wells, "if the New Deal is still inchoate, it is because there are no strong, clear leads to support him."[85]

Wells's assessment of Roosevelt's predicament in the spring of 1935 might suggest that he believed the Brain Trust was at fault. Though such a condemnation of the president's advisers was implicit in his analysis, and he did criticize them for their philosophical disunity, Wells directed his accusations elsewhere. The individuals he openly held accountable for the paralysis of the New Deal were not administration insiders but the financial and business leaders who denounced Roosevelt while failing to articulate alternative policies. Wells dubbed these figures the "inconsistent inexplicit men." They were contemptuous of Roosevelt's reliance on theoretically inclined intellectuals, but their own unwillingness to lend assistance was "why the President went to the Professors." Not only did they withhold their expertise from the president, but they refused to do battle with the "raucous voices" in the court of public opinion. For example, bankers, instead of merely grumbling about Father Coughlin, should have been explaining to the people why his financial theories were flimsy. Wells held out the prospect that if the "inexplicit men" would not cooperate with the president, they could still make an important contribution by forming a set of coherent, detailed policies that they could champion as partisans opposed to the president. In fact, he wrote:

> The thing most conspicuously absent from the contemporary American scheme and the thing most urgently needed in American political affairs, is a clear-speaking, well-led opposition of honorable men, a Radical Republican opposition, as resolutely creative as the President himself, neither obstructive nor malignant, but critically helpful and ready to take over the constructive task if by any reason he presently falters and fails.

The worst scenario would simply be for the "inexplicit men" to remain "inexplicit."[86]

While Wells believed the future of the New Deal was alarmingly unclear, he was also critical of much of the program already in place. He favored the "expansive" side of the New Deal but opposed its "restrictive" aspects, those measures designed to curb production that had already led to "devitalization." The AAA policy of paying farmers not to grow crops or raise livestock he found objectionable, and he asserted that in practice other nations were filling the gap anyway. Nor could he support the NRA codes, which he called "restrictive and slackening, on the worst lines of European trade unionism." Wells now accepted Darrow's conclusion that the codes put small businesses in jeopardy, and he maintained, with much justification, that the strategy of fixing prices was failing to bring about a recovery: "As a piece of constructive policy, it is hardly better than boiling the thermometer to warm the house."[87]

Wells offered qualified praise for the "expansive" side of the New Deal, by which he meant the relief programs that put the unemployed back to work, but he wished to see much more in the way of "social consumption."[88] In a sense, he was advocating the Keynesian approach that the Roosevelt administration was already trying and would pursue more explicitly and extensively in the late thirties. But while Keynes advocated government spending to jump-start the capitalist system, Wells was clearly interested in more than temporary economic stimulation. His goal was still to see America, and the world, turn to socialism. Although he knew Roosevelt was committed to capitalism, he felt that the president, who revealed during their White House lunch his disgust with financial speculation, "may presently be reflecting and considering a much more socialistic America than any of us imagined possible ten years ago."[89]

Despite his disappointment in the New Deal, Wells still believed that America, along with Britain, held the keys to the future. Although he had for decades singled out the United States for the role of world leader, in this book he generally placed his hopes in a joint Anglo-American partnership. As he had since the beginning of the century, he called for a unification of the English-speaking community as the first step toward a world state, but there was now little emphasis on Britain's taking a subordinate position to America. Wells's inclination to place Britain and the United States on a par seems to have resulted less from any new-found enthusiasm for his native country than from disappointment with the America of 1935. Counter to what he had believed before, he now wrote that the United States was not doing much more than Britain to overcome the economic crisis. But in contrast to the other great powers, America and Britain seemed to him the most promising nations. Germany and Italy had become reactionary; France was simply standing still; and Russia was now captive to rigid Marxist dogma. Yet Americans and Britons remained "progressive," largely as a result of a history in which they had been able to expand, into the West and into the Empire. Only the Russians had over the years been equally as fortunate. The man searching for clues to a new social order, Wells stated, "turns" away from the overcrowded continent of Europe "to the great sprawls of the English-thinking and Russian-thinking populations, and then, realizing the temporary mental exhaustion of the latter, comes back to Westminster and Washington." Furthermore, according to Wells, only in the English-speaking world was there the civil peace and, particularly in America, the freedom of discussion for real strides to be made. He believed that "America is still in what, in the school geographies of my childhood, used to be called so hopefully the New World."[90]

Laski's course of travel duplicated Wells's to the extent that he also was in America in the spring of 1935 after having visited Russia the previous summer. When Laski lectured in Moscow, he criticized the Soviet system but was still attacked in the British press and in the House of Commons for expounding his radical views in hostile territory. After pressure was applied to the London School of Economics, a public debate on academic freedom ensued.[91] Though no doctrinaire Communist, Laski certainly viewed the Soviet Union in a much more favorable light than the anti-Marxist Wells did. Yet at the same time, Laski in the mid-1930s remained as enthusiastic about Roosevelt as Wells was and actually tended to perceive the New Deal less harshly. On his 1935 trip to America, Laski met with Roosevelt at the White House for the first time, which established him as a solid friend of the president as well as a useful source of information on British politics.[92] In an October 1935 letter to Frankfurter, Laski said of Roosevelt, "I feel that he is, with all his sins, one of the two or three beams of light in this bloody world."[93]

In 1936 Laski was once again in the United States. With such landmark measures as the Social Security Act and the Wagner Act, which established the National Labor Relations Board, now passed into law, Roosevelt was riding high and destined for a landslide reelection victory in November. Writing for the *Daily Herald* prior to the election, Laski was decidedly enthusiastic about what he had found in the United States. "America remains," he said, "after Soviet Russia, the most exhilarating country in the world. It is a whirlpool of ideas. It has a receptivity to experiment, a passion for discussion, the intensity of which is literally bewildering." The intellectual ferment in America was comparable to the atmosphere in France in the years leading up to 1789. On university campuses "radical" students held the initiative; "protest" was the dominant note in American literature; labor had become politicized; and even in the churches there was a new spirit of questioning. Furthermore, government service was back in style.[94]

However, Laski by no means believed that the progressive forces in America would inevitably prevail. Elaborating on his comparison to pre-Revolutionary France, he wrote that there were the "Bourbons" to contend with—that is, the businessmen. As he had maintained before, he was persuaded that the capitalist class would do everything in its power to block positive change. American businessmen, according to Laski, were "terrified even by the mild liberalism of the President" and saw the New Deal as akin to the *Communist Manifesto*. Business was going to try to regain its complete dominance, and, suffused with a "latent fascist temper," it would resort to corruption and exploit xenophobia and anti-Semitism to attain its goals. Wells's "raucous voices," Laski wrote, were tied to big business just as Hitler and Mussolini were. The left, faced with such stiff competition, was going to have to fight hard to win over the American public. The outcome of the battle had still to be decided, but, he stated, "If liberal America triumphs, it will make a new and fundamental contribution to our common civilization."[95]

The need for the American left to be strong had been a continual concern of Laski's when he wrote these words. He wanted the left to see the president as a sympathetic ally and strive not to alienate him. In August 1934, after having read the latest issue of the *New Republic*, Laski warned Frankfurter "that the Liberals *must* understand that their job is to develop their criticism not by shrill announcements that FDR has betrayed them but by insistence on a minimum programme."[96] A year later, in the *Daily Herald*, Laski was still adamant that the left needed to learn how to handle Roosevelt more wisely. "It is no use blaming the President for not sharing the ideals of Norman Thomas or W. Z. Foster," Laski wrote in reference to the Socialist and Communist leaders in America, because "if he shared them, he would not be President of the United States." The task for the radicals was to put aside their differences and develop a definitive, coherent ideology. The more unified and effective the left could be, the more likely the president was to embrace its program, though no one should ever expect him to adopt it completely.[97]

While Laski coached the American left, he also offered his advice to the right. Though he constantly wrote that the capitalist class in America would never consent to change, he was nevertheless ambivalent enough to chart out a course for the Republicans. Just as Wells challenged the "inexplicit men" to speak up and stressed the need for a responsible Republican opposition, Laski too believed that a constructive conservative alternative to Roosevelt had to coalesce. In October 1935 he published an article in *Harper's* titled "A Word to the Republicans: The Duty of an Opposition Party." The bulk of the piece was devoted to the idea that if representative democracy was not based on an effective two-party system, it would disintegrate into a dictatorship. The two parties, Laski contended, needed to accept one another's legitimacy while offering distinct philosophies and programs. The opposition party had to be credible in the eyes of the electorate and prepared to assume power.[98]

When Laski applied these general principles to the American political scene, he found that the Republicans did not comprise a viable opposition. According to his reading of American history, prior to 1932 the Republicans and Democrats were so philosophically identical that the electorate was presented with no true choice. Then in 1932 Roosevelt offered "an intelligible alternative," but since that time no such alternative to the president and his program had formed. The Republicans had been unable to develop any "organic criticism" of the New Deal partly because they were still in "panic" from the defeat of '32 and partly because the "crisis" of the Depression made formulating opposition policies difficult. But furthermore, the Republican Party "has nothing to say that is either positive or profound, because the principles for which it stood as a party have largely lost their meaning in the new economic orientation." The Republicans, Laski argued, could no longer simply attack the president, particularly from an outdated right-wing vantage. The burden on the party now was to "reconstruct the philosophy of conservatism for the new environment which has emerged."[99]

Two years later, in another article for *Harper's*, Laski was more explicit about what the new conservatism should entail. In "A Formula for Conservatives," he charged the American right, both Republicans and anti-Roosevelt Democrats, with being devoid of any ideology at all. The Liberty League's call for a return to the status quo before Roosevelt was simply not a credible program. Laski advocated that a flexible, pragmatic conservatism sensitive to the needs of the public should replace the reactionary thinking that characterized the right. Conservatives were going to have to retreat from laissez faire and embrace the notion of the positive state, and more specifically they were going to have to accept the legitimacy of unions and see the need for reform in taxation, trade policy, public utilities, and general business practices. If the right remained on its current path, Laski argued, its destination could well be fascism. Therefore, the very future of American constitutional government depended on a rejuvenation of conservatism.[100]

The bastion of the kind of conservative thinking Laski deemed obsolete was, in the mid-1930s, the Supreme Court. When the Court virtually gutted the New Deal by declaring the NRA unconstitutional in the unanimous Schechter decision of May 1935 and then in January 1936 striking down the AAA in the Butler case, Laski was enraged. While commenting on Schechter, as well as other New Deal rulings by the "Nine Old Men," Laski consistently dredged up the infamous Dred Scott case of 1857.[101] In the aftermath of Schechter, Laski tried to see a ray of hope shining through the clouds. Although he understood the ominous implications of the decision, he also believed that it presented the administration with an "opportunity." The president could seize the moment to make a renewed commitment to organized labor.[102] When Roosevelt signed the Wagner Act into law in the summer of 1935, he in fact took just such a step.

After the Supreme Court knocked down the AAA at the beginning of 1936, Laski commented in the *Manchester Guardian* on the course the Court was pursuing.[103] Central to the Butler decision, as to the Schechter decision, was the justices' contention that the federal government could not assert its authority in areas constitutionally reserved for the states. This reasoning prompted Laski to remark, "Some fifty million farmers and their dependents are to suffer because the founders of the American Constitution could not foresee the kind of world in which we are now living." In Laski's eyes, such other federal programs as the Tennessee Valley Authority and the Reconstruction Finance Corporation were now also in jeopardy. The Court's actions, he explained to his English readers, were tantamount to a declaration by the House of Lords that all of the British social legislation passed since 1906 was unconstitutional. He argued that the Court had abused the power of judicial review by destroying democratically enacted, constitutionally legitimate measures in order to force upon the nation the justices' own reactionary personal views. The United States government was ready to take positive steps on behalf of the general citizenry, but standing in the way was a Supreme Court devoted to "an obsolete social philosophy in which the rights of property are placed before the claims of the common welfare." The only solution Laski could see was to overhaul the Constitution.[104]

When FDR soundly won reelection the following November, Laski wrote to an American friend, "I did not doubt that F.D.R. would romp home; but such a victory was beyond my wildest dreams. The people it disappointed were the measure of his achievement. Now I want to see him show courage and energy and a sense of the central objective."[105] Roosevelt did move boldly at the beginning of his second term when he addressed the obstacle the Supreme Court posed for his program. Although he considered trying to solve the problem through constitutional amendment, as Laski had suggested, the president ultimately decided on a statutory scheme that would have allowed him to add new members to the Court. Writing in support of the "Court-packing" plan in the *New Republic*, Laski stated that Roosevelt had shown his "characteristic courage" in attempting to battle the Supreme Court's "judicial usurpation" of the legislative function. He implied that FDR had gained the mandate to carry out his proposal: "Since 1932 it has been difficult to distinguish the philosophy of the Supreme Court from that of Wall Street. It was not to maintain that identity that President Roosevelt was returned triumphantly to the White House." Changing the composition of the Court, Laski now asserted, was actually preferable to going through the long process of obtaining a constitutional amendment that would then be subject to judicial interpretation.[106] When the packing plan died in Congress, he stated that there was clearly an insufficient understanding of the Court's new role as "the true veto-power."[107]

By heartily endorsing Roosevelt's Supreme Court scheme, Laski did not quite stand alone, but he certainly stood in opposition to prevailing opinion in the United States, even liberal opinion. Although the president was able to muster the support of enough Democrats in Congress to make passage of some variation of his plan a viable possibility through the first half of 1937, that support was weak and ultimately insufficient. In the Senate FDR failed to win over such progressive Republicans as Hiram Johnson of California and, even more important, drew the opposition of Burton K. Wheeler, the liberal Montana Democrat, and other reliable New Dealers. During Senate hearings Raymond Moley, former member of the Brain Trust, testified against the legislation, as did Professor Erwin Griswold of the Harvard Law School.

While the outcry that emanated from conservative editorial pages was to be expected, the Court-packing scheme did not even receive the endorsement of papers traditionally friendly to the administration, and Oswald Garrison Villard, the venerable erstwhile editor of the *Nation*, spoke out publicly against Roosevelt. Perhaps most significant, there is evidence that Frankfurter, though a key adviser to the president, had reservations about the plan. That Laski turned out to be such a full-throated supporter of the Supreme Court scheme revealed the extent of his radicalism and, perhaps just as important, the extent of his devotion to FDR[108]

In the fall of 1937, after the storm over Roosevelt's Court proposal had passed, Wells traveled to America to lecture on his latest idea for establishing global unity, a massive world encyclopedia that would include all of the knowledge essential to civilization. The trip was actually his second to the United States since he had come in the spring of 1935 to reevaluate the New Deal. At the end of 1935, suffused with a new interest in movie-making, he had journeyed to Hollywood, where he stayed with Charlie Chaplin and toured the studios. When he returned to America in October of 1937, the nation was experiencing a sharp recession that was wiping out the economic gains made in recent years. This descent back into deep depression would exert an impact on Wells's assessment of the nation. Again he lunched with Roosevelt at the White House, and afterward he told the press that there was no "danger" of the president turning into a "dictator." But while he praised Roosevelt, he argued that the New Deal was not working. The problem lay not in the White House, but in a Constitution that was "too rigid" and an inadequate civil service.[109]

After returning to England, Wells published an article in *Collier's* in February 1938 in which he discussed what he had found in America. Although he saw some cause for optimism, the tone of the piece was generally negative. He wrote about the New Deal, in the past tense, as if it were a noble experiment that had failed: "The New Deal was a magnificent promise, and it evoked a mighty volume of hope. Now that hope has been dissipated." The Brain Trust, he said, had proved to be a great disappointment. Furthermore, in contrast to his previous adulation of Roosevelt, he was now mildly critical of the president. Comparing FDR to Balfour and Grey, he portrayed him as a genteel, detached statesman. After his 1934 trip, he had written that while Roosevelt's mind was similar to Balfour's, his temperament was very different. Now he stated that because the president was of the "Olympian type," he had never bothered to get rid of the spoils system and introduce a genuine civil service. Wells was surprisingly blunt in describing "cultural development" projects in the Hudson River Valley in which Roosevelt had expressed an interest as being "about as adequate to the urgencies of our contemporary situation as polishing a brass button would be in a naval battle." The president acknowledged the need for a new social order but was not actually committed to the goal. According to Wells, the American people had grown more cynical about Roosevelt, an attitude he apparently shared. Whereas earlier in his presidency, Americans either worshipped or hated Roosevelt, "the mood has changed. They like him now. They like him more than ever they did, and they believe in his magic no more."[110]

Though Roosevelt and the New Dealers had lost their luster in Wells's eyes, he was not prepared to put any faith in John L. Lewis and the increasingly active labor movement either. Ever the anti-proletarian, he was much less impressed in his meeting with Lewis than in his encounters with the two young presidents of Harvard and Yale. Even more important, he saw much to admire in the students of Harvard and Yale and other members of their generation. He was heartened that Marxism had lost its grip on the college campuses since Stalin's abuses had been exposed and that the students seemed clear-eyed and prepared to tackle the problems of the time. Wells wrote, "After this harsh winter a new spring may break upon the world from America. Through its renascent young people."[111]

Despite the hope Wells placed in the younger generation—he always managed to find a silver lining—there can be no denying that in the wake of his 1937 trip his assessment of Roosevelt, the New Deal, and America was tough. In fact, Wells was actually more critical and pessimistic than is suggested by the *Collier's* article, which had been substantially edited. In an appendix to the 1938 edition of his *World Brain*, a volume containing the lectures he had delivered in America, he published the piece in the form in which he had presumably submitted it to *Collier's*. The editors excised Wells's references to "the new depression," to the sharp economic downturn that he wrote "has been like the unaccountable failure of an engine." Omitted from the article that ran in *Collier's* was Wells's bleak pronouncement that an increasing number of Americans "will be short of food and shelter this winter—with no end in sight and nothing of the trustfulness that staved off disaster, perhaps only temporarily, in 1934."[112]

The year 1938 in a certain sense marked the end of the New Deal. By summer the nation began to climb out of the recession, and Congress was interested in no more reforms. The 1938 wages and hours act was the last piece of New Deal legislation to be passed, and by 1939 there was even some chipping away at existing New Deal programs.[113] In the years 1933 to 1938, Wells's admiration for Roosevelt and the New Deal rose and fell. Initially he was a skeptic, but after visiting Washington and meeting the president in 1934, he became a convert. Then, however, his enthusiasm declined: his 1935 trip caused him to be concerned about the vitality of the New Deal, and after his visit of 1937 he characterized Roosevelt more soberly and viewed the New Deal as having been a failure. Laski, also wary of Roosevelt at first, had by 1934 gained a deep appreciation for the president, even though the New Deal did not go nearly as far as he would have liked and he wondered whether it could succeed in the face of business opposition. In contrast to Wells, he remained consistently supportive of the Roosevelt administration through the 1930s. While Wells, however, clearly preferred FDR's program to Stalin's, Laski tilted more toward Moscow than Washington.

Laski returned to America for visits in 1937 and early 1938 and then in September 1938 began a stay of several months in the United States.[114] Writing in the *University of Chicago Law Review* in December 1938, he summed up his feelings about Roosevelt and the New Deal. The article was prompted by the publication of the first five volumes of *The Public Papers and Addresses of Franklin D. Roosevelt,* and although Laski was ostensibly commenting on the contents of these volumes, he must also have been drawing upon his years of observing the administration in action.[115] His appraisal of Roosevelt as a political leader was overwhelmingly positive. "The outstanding qualities of the President that these papers reveal," he wrote, "are first, courage, and, second, the experimental temper." Although the president could take a circuitous and at times seemingly illogical path, he was always aware of his ultimate goal. Roosevelt's control of the scene, according to Laski, was masterful: "He commands, he persuades, he cajoles, he warns, he threatens; the variety of his artifice corresponds to the complexities of his situation." Furthermore, the president was gifted with a sense of humor, a facility with words, and an ability to relate well to others. With certain exceptions, such as his dubious understanding of the monetary question,

Roosevelt had over the years displayed an impressive grasp of the issues. And, Laski asserted, the president's political instincts were superb. He was, to use Bagehot's phrase, "an uncommon man of common opinions." Only in his Court-packing scheme did Roosevelt miscalculate public sentiment.[116]

Laski attempted to pinpoint where Roosevelt stood ideologically. Although he believed that the president did not possess "any considered and systematic philosophy," he labeled him as a "liberal." Roosevelt was by no means a "socialist" or a "revolutionary," but he was a liberal in the sense that he was inclined to use the power of the state to meet pressing needs. Laski's quarrel with Roosevelt's viewpoint was that the president accepted the validity of the American economic system and saw his task as being to make that system function better. According to Laski,

> A large part of Mr. Roosevelt's approach to his problems is conditioned by the belief that the pathology of American economic life is occasioned by the malpractices of evil men; and from this he draws the general inference that it is in the power of legislation, wisely administered, to correct these malpractices.

In Laski's opinion, the ills besetting America could not simply be attributed to bad individuals; the capitalist structure underpinning the nation was rotten and needed to be overhauled.[117]

Although Laski, in spite of his various utterances over the years, did not consider it appropriate "for an outsider to pass judgment upon the policies of Mr. Roosevelt," he felt free to discuss the general impact of the New Deal. He pointed to certain positive "psychological results" as the legacy of the Roosevelt presidency. First of all, borrowing Wells's phrase, he argued that the American people had gained a "sense of the state." Washington was now a force in the lives of everyday citizens, who, more than ever, were politically aware. Furthermore, according to Laski, the 1930s had witnessed the rise of the intellectual to a prominent place in American life. Last, he contended, the United States had shown the world over the past dark decade that democracy was not dead. While other nations were gripped by fascism, the American people retained their faith in a government that at least attempted to respond to their needs and aspirations. Laski wrote, "If our age emerges successfully from this period of blood and iron, I believe that the Roosevelt experiment in America, with all its blunders and follies, will be regarded by the historian as having made a supreme contribution to the service of freedom."[118]

The eclipse of the New Deal did not signify the end of Laski's interest in America. Over the course of the next decade, until his death in 1950, he continued to travel across the Atlantic and comment on American affairs. Furthermore, during the 1940s he published two major works on the United States, *The American Presidency* and *The American Democracy.*

7

The Businessman's America

Harold Laski's View of the United States in the 1940s

Although Laski felt a genuine affection for America, during the 1940s his commentary on the nation became increasingly negative. As the experimentation of the New Deal faded into history, he found less cause for optimism. Laski did welcome American participation in World War II—and he was not nearly as critical of the United States as the aged Wells was during the war years—but when the nation became fiercely antagonistic to Communist Russia in the second half of the decade, he voiced his disapproval. In his opinion, the Truman era marked a sharp and unfortunate contrast to the age of Roosevelt. Beginning in the late 1930s, however, Laski made an attempt to do more than simply react to contemporary developments. He stepped back to try to capture a complete picture of American civilization. Yet in *The American Presidency* of 1940 and his massive, all-encompassing 1948 work, *The American Democracy*, Laski still dealt with the United States harshly. When he viewed America from his Marxist perspective, he saw a society completely dominated by business and a political system inadequate to address the needs of the modern world. These two books represented Laski's bid to stand as the twentieth-century successor to Tocqueville and Bryce, but it is difficult to place him on that pedestal, for while *The American Presidency* is a thoughtful study, *The American Democracy* suffers from being polemical and unwieldy.

When Laski got back to England after his long sojourn in the United States in 1938–1939, he wrote an article for a London-based publication in which he lamented the widespread British ignorance of America. Although the two books on the United States that he would publish in the 1940s were apparently intended for consumption in the New World as much as in the Old, Laski was to some extent assuming the role of interpreter of America for the British people. In this 1939 article he stated that whereas Americans were interested in the British scene, the British virtually ignored what was happening on the other side of the Atlantic. According to Laski, "An occasional dinner at the Pilgrims, or a reception at the English Speaking Union does not compensate for the remarkable absence of any well-informed public opinion about America."[1] The British actually did a disservice to themselves by remaining in the dark about innovative programs instituted under the New Deal or curriculum changes at the leading American law schools. There was a variety of ways in which the British could learn from the Americans, and in a general sense, Laski wrote, "I think there is a quality of democracy in their social relationships we have not yet begun even to understand." The recent visit by the king and queen to the United States, the first ever by British monarchs, he hoped would be the starting point on a road to "a far wider grasp of American civilization than any we have now." But he knew that the real key to establishing a greater comprehension of American society was for the British educational system to place a greater emphasis on the study of the United States.[2]

After returning to England in 1939, Laski was decidedly upbeat about America. The flickering flame of the New Deal still cast a glow over the nation, while at the same time Europe was drawing steadily closer to war. According to Laski, he had felt a "sense of exhilaration" in America. It was true that the United States was no paradise: most important, a business community that had not significantly changed its viewpoint since the 1920s posed a serious threat to the nation's progress. But the intellectual vigor of America, whether exhibited by the new breed in Washington typified by such key administration figures as Thomas Corcoran and Ben Cohen or by writers like John Dos Passos, Archibald MacLeish, and Edmund Wilson, made Laski feel optimistic about the future of the nation. If the progressive elements could achieve unity, America would be able to add to the liberal gains made in recent years.[3]

One feature of the American scene that Laski did criticize, following his stay in the United States, was the universities, which he thought lacked vitality and independence.[4] After two decades the sting of his Harvard experience must have been revived as he lectured at the University of Washington for ten weeks in 1939. Strong community opposition arose to the appointment of a Marxist, and even the Washington state legislature got into the fray. As had been the case at Harvard in the 1910s, the university president stood by Laski and students packed his lectures. No doubt he enjoyed the adoration, and in the wake of his time at Washington he was sufficiently unperturbed to take a jocular tone in writing to Roosevelt that "I have ceased to be Public Enemy No. 1" and "your sins are back in their place as the proper topic of righteous indignation." However, it seems that Laski was not as insouciant as he projected in his letter and that the experience was responsible for further souring him on American higher education.[5]

While Laski was generally impressed by the spirit he found in the United States in 1938–1939, at the same time he examined the permanent structure of the American system and determined that it was seriously flawed. The political arrangement worked out by the framers of the Constitution in the 1780s, he believed, was no longer viable as the mid-twentieth century approached. In May 1939 he published an article in the *New Republic* titled "The Obsolescence of Federalism," in which he criticized the division of responsibilities between the national and state governments that stood at the heart of the constitutional system. Federalism may have made sense in an evolving, developing nation, but in the America of 1939, with its mature economy, an unencumbered centralized government was a necessity if the rights and welfare of the public were to be guaranteed. There was no way, he asserted, for "forty-eight separate units to seek to compete with the integrated power of giant capitalism." Big business, such as DuPont in Delaware, was able to dictate to state government. Only the federal government in Washington, if the constitutional restraints that had hampered its effectiveness were removed, could confront the corporations and fulfill the democratic aspirations of the American people.[6]

An even more significant product of the assessment Laski was making of the political system of the United States was the lectures he delivered at Indiana University in the spring of 1939. These lectures, which became the basis for *The American Presidency*, were conceived as an elaboration on the piece he had published in December 1938 in the *University of Chicago Law Review* on Roosevelt's papers and speeches.[7] In that article he discussed not only Roosevelt in particular but the presidency in general.[8] *The American Presidency,* in a broader sense, seems to have been inspired by Laski's overall interest in Roosevelt's leadership, and he received permission to dedicate the volume to FDR.[9] In fact, he foresaw his work as serving the interests of the Roosevelt administration. He wrote to FDR, "I have written a book on the Presidency which, maintaining all the proper spirit of what the professors call 'objectivity' will, I hope, make your enemies furiously angry."[10]

The American Presidency did lend support to Roosevelt in the sense that Laski argued that only a president could provide the kind of positive, activist leadership that was required in the modern United States. To a certain extent, he implied, the Roosevelt presidency met the standard he set down. But because of constitutional restraints, there was no possibility for FDR to have been as effective a president as his talents might have allowed. Central to Laski's thesis in this book is that though the presidency should be strong, the Constitution prohibited the executive from being a forceful instrument of government. He refrained from rendering a blatant judgment but made it clear that he preferred Britain's parliamentary system to the presidential system as defined by the Constitution.

Although Laski pointed to the *University of Chicago Law Review* article as the genesis of *The American Presidency,* there were other precedents as well. As he wrote in the preface to his book, he had been interested in the presidency since his time at Harvard during the late 1910s.[11] In 1928 he published a substantial article in *Harper's* called "The American Political System" that anticipated many of the points that he would make a decade later in *The American Presidency.* The *Harper's* piece was a more negative assessment of the American political process, as reflected in Laski's comment that "if we assume that democratic government is desirable, there is hardly a canon of institutional adequacy against which the American system does not offend." As of 1928, Laski had not yet observed Roosevelt in the White House and come to see at least the potential effectiveness of the presidency.[12]

In 1938, the year before he delivered his lectures on the presidency at Indiana University, Laski published *Parliamentary Government in England,* in which he treated the political system of his own country favorably. Although he again enunciated his pessimistic view that parliamentary government would break down when the Conservative opposition refused to accept the legitimacy of a newly elected, truly socialist Labour government, he did believe that through the years the British political system had generally functioned well. In the passages in which he directly compared the British and American forms of government, the United States consistently came out the loser, for reasons that he would expand on in *The American Presidency*.[13]

At the outset of *The American Presidency*, Laski stressed that an Englishman studying the political system of the United States needed to set aside the assumptions he had internalized in his native land. He had to realize that the presidency "is an *American* institution, that it functions in an American environment, that it must be judged by American criteria of its response to American needs." To view the president, for example, as a cross between a king and a prime minister was to fail to understand the office in its full complexity. Even Americans like Woodrow Wilson had measured American institutions against a British standard. Although Bryce had brought a great knowledge of the United States to bear on *The American Commonwealth*, Laski argued that the book needed to be seen as the product of a "Gladstonian Liberal." Weighted down by his cultural and ideological baggage, Bryce not only failed to understand the realities of American labor, but even in his political analysis he assessed the United States in the context of the British world he knew.[14]

Laski's primary criticism of Bryce's treatment of the United States governmental system was his disagreement with the chapter of *The American Commonwealth* titled "Why Great Men Are Not Chosen Presidents." Laski maintained that the quality of the presidents had been as high as the quality of the prime ministers and that America had witnessed as many years with "extraordinary men" in the top office as Britain. He was by no means an apologist for the presidential selection process: the party conventions that had assumed the task of picking the candidates had become unseemly affairs, and the tendency was to fix upon men who seemed the most electable. Nevertheless, Laski argued, the American system of choosing a president worked at least as effectively as the British system of choosing a prime minister did. Although party compromises had been common and superb men frequently passed over, the same had been true in Britain. Before assuming office, a prime minister could point to years of national legislative experience that an incoming president generally lacked, but virtually every president had been in politics for a long time, though perhaps on the state level. The greatest testament to the presidential selection process was that whenever a crisis had erupted in American history, a strong president always emerged.[15]

Although Laski differed with Bryce on the question of whether "great men" reached the White House, *The American Presidency* in a larger sense is not at odds with *The American Commonwealth*. Laski and Bryce stood on common ground in their preference for the government of Britain over the American political system. Despite Laski's contention that American government should not be judged according to British criteria, he clearly, and it seems inevitably, used the parliamentary system as his model. While charitable toward the much maligned presidential selection process, he criticized the system in which a president then had to function. Like Bryce he believed that the separation of powers created a weak, fractured government with no clear center of accountability. Furthermore, he echoed Bryce in asserting that the president's cabinet lacked the stature and authority to be an effective body.

The American system of checks and balances, Laski argued, not only worked to "paralyze" the president but created "the far more evil effect of completely destroying any idea of responsibility in government." A president could not control Congress in the way a prime minister dominated the House of Commons, even when a president's party held a majority. Congress was inherently "anti-presidential" and strove for supremacy over the executive branch. Committee chairmen in the House and Senate were like "little Presidents," and the best known members of Congress tended to be those who tried to thwart the administration. Congress deferred to the president in crises, but normally to be successful on Capitol Hill he had to rely on the loyalty legislators owed him as party leader and dispenser of patronage and even more so on the clout he could build up among the general public. Certain presidents had managed to win the cooperation of Congress, but generally the system of divided powers generated "incoherency and irresponsibility."[16]

Not only was the president's effectiveness frustrated by the separation of powers, but, according to Laski, the executive branch itself was deficient. The president's job was made more difficult by virtue of the fact that the cabinet shared none of his burdens. Unlike in Britain, the members of the cabinet tended not to be the nation's leading statesmen but rather figures appointed by the president for a variety of personal and political reasons. In the American system the president possessed all executive authority, and the cabinet secretaries merely carried out his policies as heads of the various government departments. There was no adherence to the British concept of collective responsibility. A president was more likely to consult unofficial advisers on crucial issues than his cabinet officers, who were not as powerful and visible as key members of Congress.[17]

The weak presidency, Laski well understood, was created intentionally. The Founding Fathers believed in the "negative state" and when framing the Constitution were careful to make sure that no branch of government, particularly the executive, would be able to wield too much power. During the period of American development and expansion, little public sentiment existed to bolster the federal government's authority. The influential business community had over the years taken the lead in opposing any growth in Washington's role. Until the late nineteenth century, Laski argued, minimal government had been appropriate in view of the nature and needs of American society. But ever since frontier conditions had faded and the capitalist economy had matured, there existed the necessity for a greater governmental presence. America in recent decades had developed along European lines, as wealth grew concentrated and a proletarian class emerged, and the New World was experiencing many of the problems that had plagued the Old. The only answer was for Americans to embrace the concept of the positive state.[18]

If American government was going to be strong, Laski believed, the powers of the presidency had to be redefined. The president needed to be in control, for Congress, the only alternative, was too disjointed and unwieldy a body to govern effectively. Not only was Congress institutionally inadequate to address the nation's problems but it would have to move out of the president's way: "No democracy in the modern world can afford a scheme of government the basis of which is the inherent right of the legislature to paralyze the executive power." Although there had been strong presidents in the course of American history, the executive had to be made powerful on a permanent basis.[19]

Laski contended that constitutional revision, while desirable, was unlikely. An expansion of presidential authority would instead result when social and economic developments forced changes in practice. Furthermore, he wrote that the president's job would be made easier by a party realignment along clearer "conservative" and "progressive" lines. The chief executive would become the leader of his party in the way a prime minister was. Presidents in the future, to be effective, would also have to follow the British precedent of assembling cabinets of superior men and delegating to them real responsibility. Laski made it clear that the activist, reform-minded government he envisioned for the United States, led by a forceful president, would move beyond what the nation had experienced even during the Roosevelt years: "The state will be forced into an attitude far more emphatically positive than anything for which, so far, the 'New Deal' has been responsible." If the president was given the power he needed, Laski argued, then America would be in a position to provide leadership for the entire world.[20]

After Britain declared war on Germany in September 1939, Laski wished to see his nation prevail, but in his eyes a military victory would be insufficient. The war, he believed, provided the ideal circumstances to bring about a peaceful transformation to socialism in Britain, a "revolution by consent." When the war was over, there could not simply be a return, in terms of the British social and economic arrangement, to the status quo ante bellum. In his quest to reshape Britain, and to an extent all Western society, Laski saw an ally in Roosevelt. Although no socialist, Roosevelt was, in Laski's opinion, still a great innovator and much more sympathetic than Churchill to the changes that needed to take place. Roosevelt loomed especially large in Laski's thinking in the early years of the war, for Stalin had disappointed him by signing a pact with Hitler. Laski did not wish for the United States to enter the war, but rather to act as a force to help bring about peace and set the terms for the postwar world. Once America had been dragged into the war after the attack on Pearl Harbor, he viewed Roosevelt as being in a unique position to shape the goals of the Allied cause.[21] His conception of the global role Roosevelt could play in the Second World War was strikingly similar to what Wells and others had hoped for Wilson during the First World War.

Before Roosevelt's election to an unprecedented third term as president in 1940, Laski wrote to him, "It just does not matter to me one tinker's damn that I am a left wing socialist and you a liberal; the purposes I care for more than life itself cannot be fulfilled unless you sit in that room for the next four years." The "privates" who were fighting the ongoing "battle" for a more progressive world looked to Roosevelt as their "general."[22] When Roosevelt defeated Wendell Willkie in the November race, Laski wrote to Frankfurter that there was a feeling of great relief in London that there would be no change in the White House.[23]

In the first year of Roosevelt's third term, Laski encouraged the president to use his immense influence to set the agenda for the postwar world. In February 1941 he wrote to Roosevelt that he had been traveling all over Britain and that people everywhere were eager for him to talk about the president: "Ordinary folk here see in your presence at the White House their right to believe that victory when it comes means a new deal in these maimed and stunted lives." He urged Roosevelt to exert an impact on British policy: "If liberal America makes England speak the right words and *do the right acts* even this agony may in the end be worth the blood and tears that will have been shed."[24] In August 1941 he wrote to Frankfurter that a revolutionary spirit had risen in the world and that Roosevelt was the leader best able to understand that spirit and channel it into peaceful, constructive change.[25]

At the same time Laski was urging Roosevelt to take a commanding global role, he also felt the need to prod the American people—specifically the student population—to understand the importance of the war. In *The Strategy of Freedom: An Open Letter to American Youth,* a slim volume published in 1941, Laski tried to counteract the isolationism and neutralism he understood to be prevalent on American college campuses. Though he did not advocate that the United States join in battling the Nazis, particularly now that the Soviet Union had been pulled into the war, he did want the Americans to support—both morally and economically—the British war effort. Not only did Laski appeal to the Americans' sense of principle in arguing that they should wish to see Hitler defeated, but he also appealed to their self-interest by making the case that a triumphant Germany would be catastrophic for the United States. "It cannot be a matter of indifference to America," he wrote, "that half the civilised world stands on the brink of an enforced subordination. Were it to go down to the abyss, what safety would remain for the American way of life?"[26]

A year later, with the United States now in the war, Laski warned that Roosevelt had to avoid making the mistakes of Wilson: the "reformation" had to be initiated immediately or else the "counter-Reformation" would be ushered in by "the new Jesuits of privilege."[27] To Laski the enemy was not merely Hitler, Mussolini, and Hirohito, but also the reactionary forces within the Allied nations, those elements that had during the 1930s advocated appeasement in Britain and opposed the New Deal in America. The burden on Roosevelt was to make sure the stage would be set for a progressive postwar world. As Laski told Frankfurter in September 1942, "I want, in a word, the deliberate reorganisation of the mood of those first 100 days of the New Deal."[28]

While Laski remained enthusiastic about Roosevelt and hoped to see the New Deal internationalized, he was critical of his own prime minister. Laski had known Churchill since his Manchester childhood, when his father, Nathan, extended the then-Liberal MP his patronage. Though Laski believed Churchill to be a great war leader, he thought the prime minister failed to see the immense task of reform that needed to be undertaken domestically. Laski was also tough on the Labour leader, Clement Attlee, who was a member of Churchill's coalition government but refused to press a socialist agenda on the prime minister. Both Churchill and Attlee were irritated by Laski, who they felt could not understand that winning the war was what mattered at the moment and that changes at home could come only after that goal had been achieved and after the electorate had spoken. Laski became such a thorn in Churchill's side that when he asked the prime minister for his approval to visit Washington in 1942, after Eleanor Roosevelt had invited him to speak to an international students' conference and stay at the White House, Churchill refused.[29]

Central to the task of leading the way into the postwar world with which Laski charged Roosevelt was for the president to win Churchill over to the progressive point of view. Laski lauded Churchill for being an inspirational orator and dogged fighter but compared him unfavorably with Roosevelt: "The President, I think, differs from the Prime Minister in his deeper sense of the immense impersonal forces by which they are both surrounded."[30] In August 1942 Laski wrote to Frankfurter, "My fear remains that the P.M. is fighting the war with a backward look instead of a forward one. The great difference, I think, between him and F.D.R. is that he is battling to preserve a tradition while F.D. is battling to create one." According to Laski, only Roosevelt possessed the clout to influence Churchill to see that winning the war had to be connected to certain ideals. He told Frankfurter, "F.D. is that rare thing, an aristocrat who understands democratic aspirations. Such a lot of the future turns on his power to communicate that understanding to Winston."[31] Laski also took his message straight to Roosevelt. In a letter to the president written at the end of 1942, he stressed that the war was precipitating great social change and said, "I hope you will teach our Prime Minister that it is the hopes of the future and not the achievements of the past from which he must draw his inspiration."[32]

In the following year, however, Laski also lost faith in Roosevelt, whom he now lumped together with Churchill. In fact, this harsher assessment of the president strained Laski's relationship with Frankfurter, which in turn contributed to a nervous breakdown Laski suffered.[33] In an "Open Letter to President Roosevelt" published in April 1943 in the *New Statesman,* Laski questioned the administration's commitment to liberalism at home and abroad.[34] He told Frankfurter in December 1943, "I am not able to see that either Winston or F.D.R. understands the nature of the war, or still more, of the peace we have to try to make." According to Laski, Roosevelt had "lost that passion" for championing "the little man" and become super-sensitive to criticism. He did not cut the same figure that he had in 1939.[35] Why, exactly, Laski soured on Roosevelt in 1943 is not clear. He may simply have come to the realization that the president was moving no faster than Churchill to the kind of socialist society he desired.

Whatever the cause of Laski's disillusionment, by the time FDR had been elected to a fourth term in November 1944, he seems to have embraced the president once more, though perhaps not quite as enthusiastically. He wrote to Roosevelt, "If you are on a different road from mine, and if, sometimes, I do not easily understand your decisions, believe me I have never doubted that we march to the same goal." Laski's letter to the president was supportive, but it nevertheless contained the implication that FDR had not yet fulfilled his promise:

> I beg you to make this term the Lincoln-term of your four terms, in which the spirit of the Gettysburg speech comes to be a living thing, and the Four Freedoms are not great rhetoric in a great speech but hopes fulfilled in the lives of little people everywhere.

Churchill had descended into being simply a partisan leader, so the onus more than ever was on Roosevelt "to lay the foundations of peace."[36] Just before FDR died in April 1945, Laski wrote that he felt the president still stood above all other American politicians, and upon hearing of Roosevelt's death, he told Frankfurter, "This is a blow beyond words. If you knew how much I had counted on him for the first years of the peace."[37] Several weeks later, he added that Roosevelt "was certainly the greatest person I have ever known or hope to know in supreme office."[38]

Just as Laski was determined the war should bring about positive social change, Wells too became preoccupied with influencing the Allies not merely to secure a military victory but to establish certain global ideals. During World War I he had got off to a late start in taking part in the enunciation of war aims, but in 1939 he became involved immediately. Wells was the driving force behind the committee, chaired by Lord

Sankey, that by 1940 had framed the Declaration of Human Rights. This declaration was essentially Wells's creation, and he spent the rest of the war spreading its message.[39] Whereas during World War I he had been mainly interested in establishing guidelines for the conduct of nations, as ultimately expressed in Wilson's Fourteen Points, the Declaration of Human Rights concentrated on the freedoms and guarantees that individuals should be able to enjoy. Like Laski, Wells saw the dire need for social revolution, and he predicted that the war would result in collectivism. The Sankey Declaration, in his view, was the framework necessary for the new civilization already in the making.[40] Along with such traditional liberties as the "Freedom of Thought and Worship," the declaration enunciated such principles as the "Right to Work" and the "Protection of Minors."[41] According to Wells, the Sankey Declaration could trace its origins to various English instruments, beginning with Magna Carta, as well as the French Declaration of the Rights of Man and the American Declaration of Independence and Bill of Rights.[42] But in addressing both political freedom and social justice, the declaration was also forward-looking and anticipated Roosevelt's Four Freedoms.[43]

Wells's wartime efforts on behalf of the Sankey Declaration did not come at the expense of his ongoing campaign to establish a world state. In the fall of 1940, he made his last trip to America to deliver the lecture "Two Hemispheres or One World." The seventy-four-year-old Wells wore himself out as he traveled from coast to coast speaking to audiences who in that presidential election season were indifferent to his message.[44] He turned out to be as much of an embarrassment to His Majesty's government as Laski could conceivably have been if Churchill had given him the blessing to go to America. In comments to the press, Wells said there were "appeasers" in the British government who were not enthusiastically pressing the war effort, and he singled out the foreign secretary, Lord Halifax.[45] A resolution was introduced into the House of Representatives condemning Wells for his remarks, which were said to "constitute an abuse of the hospitality of the United States."[46] Even more significant, in the House of Commons a Conservative backbencher sparked a heated debate by questioning why the government had allowed Wells an exit permit. The MP said that Wells "has for years past suggested the throne is a medieval and useless institution, that the Christian religion is a senseless superstition, and the whole structure of society rotten. I think it is dangerous to allow a man of that type to go to America."[47]

If some thought Wells should not have been permitted to cross the Atlantic, he was critical of the practice of sending aristocrats and royals to the United States to drum up support for the British war effort. In 1941 he wrote to an American that he should cry out, "We want the common British. Take the Windsors away."[48] When Wells was in America in the fall of 1940, he had judged the British propaganda effort there to be misguided largely because Britain lacked a clear conception of the war's purpose. He thought it foolish that pictures of the king and queen in their coronation robes were being sold at the New York World's Fair, for they only highlighted the gap that separated Britain and the United States. Furthermore, he felt the Tory upper class was playing upon American sympathies for the courage shown by the RAF and the beleaguered British citizenry merely to preserve its own privileged status. Even the prime minister, that master of persuasion, was taken to task by Wells: "Mr Winston Churchill has now repeated his grave heroic warning speech four times to the world. The Americans have liked it so far, but I think with diminishing effect."[49]

Wells did not advocate that the United States join Britain in fighting Germany. He believed that the British could achieve victory without American assistance and was afraid of a repetition of the World War I scenario in which the United States would enter the war politically divided and then sacrifice the peace process on the altar of party rivalries. America, he hoped, would be supportive of Britain yet stand "as a clear-thinking community" outside of the fray. He furthermore wished that the United States would work in concert with the Soviet Union, but his suggestion was poorly received by his American audiences in 1940, for as he put it later, "America at that time was stupidly and ignorantly anti-Bolshevik and sentimentally but still rather ineffectively pro-British."[50]

The role Wells carved out for America, however, was more than that of a sympathetic, cooperative noncombatant. He viewed the United States as potentially the moral and intellectual center for the establishment of the new world order. According to Wells, "America has made herself the 'Arsenal of Democracy.' She has also to make herself the Democratic Forum. Her role is not simply to 'lease and lend' but also to listen, read and think." He believed that President Roosevelt, in particular, could be a central force in the coming world reconstruction.[51] Although Wells's enthusiasm for Roosevelt had faded in the wake of his 1937 trip to America, the president was now back in his good graces. Wells did not meet with Roosevelt in 1940, but he nevertheless realized, as he later wrote, in that year the president was standing for the New Deal and against Wall Street more than ever: "He had sacrificed all that genial popularity with the theatre-going classes by a return to radical realism."[52] In international affairs, according to Wells, Roosevelt was making encouraging comments about the future and could "be heard even more plainly than President Wilson was heard in 1917–1918." Wells was being complimentary, if not actually effusive, when he wrote, "It may be true that President Roosevelt is first and foremost a skilful politician. But nobody denies his quick response to any constructive thought about him."[53] Later in the war, after the United States had become involved, Wells echoed Laski when he said that Roosevelt was "more alive to constructive ideas than our very Anglicized Anglo-American Winston."[54]

While Wells looked to leadership from Roosevelt during the war, he eventually also saw great possibilities in another American politician, Wendell Willkie. During his 1940 trip to the United States, Wells had viewed presidential candidate Willkie as simply another Republican exponent of business who was waging an unusually mean campaign against Roosevelt. Furthermore, the idea that Willkie could take the reins of foreign policy out of Roosevelt's hands in the midst of the world crisis he considered unthinkable.[55] But by October 1943, Wells was writing to Willkie to proclaim, "I am now a confirmed Willkie-ite."[56] What had caused Wells to change his mind was the publication in 1943 of Willkie's best-selling book, *One World,* an account of the global tour he had been sent on by his erstwhile opponent, President Roosevelt. Willkie, who, as Wells conceded, had not been an isolationist even in the 1940 presidential race, took a strong stand in this work on the need for international unity.[57] In fact, Willkie as of 1943 was on this issue in advance of Roosevelt, who had not yet fully committed himself to the "United Nations" approach espoused in *One World.*[58] Willkie was apparently not directly influenced by Wells, and his proposals for international cooperation fell far short of Wells's vision of a world state.[59] Nevertheless, Wells had often embraced figures, such as the two Roosevelts, who seemed at least to be heading in his direction, and so in 1943 it was not anomalous that he latched on to Willkie. Writing after the publication of *One World,* Wells announced, "The possibility of Willkie playing a prominent constructive role in the conflicts ahead of mankind grows stronger as the human crisis develops steadily."[60] In early 1944 Wells encapsulated his thoughts about Willkie, and indicated his hopes for the future, when he stated: "I didn't like the Willkie of the last election—it was a bad-spirited election—but I doubt if anyone has learnt more or faster than he has done. F.D.R. as President and Willkie as Secretary of State would be an admirable combination."[61]

Although Wells doggedly pressed for human rights and the world state through the war, during these final years of his life he became increasingly frustrated and negative. The tragedy of the war, of course, affected him, but his failing health and the realization that he had lost much of his influence also took a toll. His bitterness was displayed most clearly in an anti-Catholicism that became extreme and obsessive. By the time he wrote his last work, *Mind at the End of Its Tether* (1945), Wells, who had always found cause for optimism, now could see only a faint stream of light penetrating the darkness.[62] His increasingly bleak view of the world influenced how he perceived America during the war. He had always been capable of directing stinging criticism at the United States, but in his wartime writings on the nation, despite the hope he placed in America's leadership potential, he was uncharacteristically vicious. With each succeeding work he released in the early forties, his remarks about the United States became more and more extreme. The words were not those of the Wells who had been observing America for four decades but of a tired and despondent old man.

Despite his profession of socialism, over the years Wells had tended not to see business, with its vast corporate institutions, as the enemy. He had exhibited a certain admiration for such American industrial moguls as Rockefeller and Ford. But by the 1940s he had become so disgusted with the American business community that his denunciations matched, and even exceeded, Laski's Marxist rhetoric in intensity. In the *Guide to the New World* (1941), Wells wrote that on his trip to the United States in the fall of 1940, he came to realize that there was a harshness to American life he had not really thought about since his first visit in 1906. The propensity of Americans to play hard and try to win at all cost was manifested most clearly in the lengths to which the vested interests had gone to attempt to keep Roosevelt from winning a third term. Like Laski, Wells believed that America was experiencing European-style class conflict and that the business community was fighting savagely to sabotage any liberal effort that threatened its supremacy. The future in the United States looked dismal to Wells because without any American tradition of compromise, business would press its war to the bloody end.[63] In his book *Phoenix*, published in 1942, Wells was even more extreme in his description of a corporate dominated America:

The Constitution, considered as a going concern and not as a rhetorical document, works out as an open conspiracy of big business executives, corporation lawyers and political bosses, operating in close cooperation with an advertisement-sustained press and the mercenary religious organisations of the country. It is a government, savage when attacked and suffocating when ascendant. The essential meanness of its spirit is ill-concealed by a large vulgarity of personal stunting and display.[64]

Another dominant theme in Wells's writings about the United States in the 1940s was that the American people were narrow-minded and intellectually shallow. On his 1940 trip to America he found that "obscurantism" was rampant. In Tuscaloosa the University of Alabama students stayed away from his lecture after an influential history teacher had branded him as a disseminator of "pro-British propaganda," and everywhere in the States he was struck by the refusal to read *Mein Kampf* or *The Communist Manifesto:*

> "We do not want to hear these strange ideas," they say. "The American Way of Life is good enough for me." And when you ask what that way of life is, they quote you the Gettysburg oration, and if you ask more questions after that, they lose their tempers.[65]

In *Phoenix* Wells characterized the Americans as a people who packed lectures without really absorbing their content, read best-sellers but actually preferred books in digest form, and scanned the headlines of the daily newspaper while skipping the articles. The nation, he wrote, suffered from "mental anaemia."[66] In his 1944 book, *'42 to '44*, Wells charged the entire Anglo-American community, in which he had always placed his hopes, with intellectual inadequacy. In both America and Britain, there was a tradition of "self-satisfied mental boorishness." But the problem was less severe in his own country than in the United States, which he called a "vast illiterate thoughtless instability."[67]

In August 1946, one year after the atomic bomb brought the Second World War to a close, Wells died just shy of his eightieth birthday. He did not live long enough to witness the shaping of the postwar world, but Laski, though his own death would not be many years away, was at the height of his career. When Labour swept into power in the 1945 election and Churchill had to vacate Number Ten Downing Street to make room for Attlee, Laski was chairman of the party. Although the position was not as powerful as the title might suggest, he found himself in a conspicuous role. The Conservatives had tried to make Laski an election issue and tar the entire Labour Party with his radical, left-wing views, and a newspaper accusation that he advocated violent revolution had prompted him to initiate a libel suit, which would be unsuccessful. During the postwar period Laski was gratified that the Labour government was enacting a socialistic program, though the ease with which the measures were adopted and implemented belied his long-standing prediction that the opposition would force a crisis rather than submit to an erosion of traditional property rights. However, he believed the government was not going far enough in the direction of collectivism and vehemently criticized its foreign policy, particularly the strong line taken against the Soviet Union.[68]

After the war Laski was once again able to travel to the United States and took as active an interest in American affairs as ever. Furthermore, he became a well-known—and often vilified—figure in America. When Labour came to power, with Laski as party chairman, he personified to many Americans the new socialist-leaning British government. In continuation of a trend begun during the war, Laski received prominent attention in the leading American magazines and played the role of whipping boy for right-wing columnists and congressmen. The *Saturday Evening Post* referred to him as the "Red Prof. Laski, a London hot-house brain." In 1945, when he made his first trip to the United States since before the war, Laski managed to alienate many Americans by attacking business, criticizing Washington's monopoly on the atomic bomb, and assailing the Vatican for its support of Franco. The Labour government saw him as such a liability that it feared he could jeopardize the massive loan Britain was trying to secure from the United States. It is difficult to believe that at the end of the war, Laski, with dreams of following in Bryce's path, had asked Attlee to post him to Washington as the British ambasssador.[69]

The America Laski saw in the years after the war he did not much like. He believed that the nation had turned to the right and that Truman was not providing the kind of inspired, progressive leadership that had been characteristic of FDR. Laski's disenchantment with Truman and the direction in which the United States was moving paralleled the sentiments felt by the American left, who viewed the administration harshly, at least up until the 1948 election. Laski's opinions were very much in harmony with the editorial positions of the liberal journals in which he placed his commentaries on America, the *Nation* and the *New*

Republic. American liberals saw Truman as a mediocre machine politician who could not possibly fill the shoes of FDR and who had usurped the position that should have gone to Henry Wallace, the vice president during Roosevelt's third term and the progressives' darling. When Truman brought a more conservative cast into the White House, the stalwarts of the American left voiced their disapproval and complained about the administration's domestic and foreign policies.[70]

Laski was not timid about making direct comparisons between Roosevelt and Truman, which, of course, always worked to the detriment of the latter. A year after FDR's death, in April 1946, Laski wrote an article for the *Nation* titled "If Roosevelt Had Lived." In this piece he not only mourned the loss of Roosevelt's great leadership qualities but indulged in the dubious exercise of predicting that if Roosevelt had not died, he would have been pursuing a different path than his successor. For example, Laski wrote of FDR, "Had he lived, I am confident that the distrust between the Anglo-Saxon powers and Soviet Russia would never have been permitted to assume its present and unnecessary proportions."[71] After returning from a 1946 trip to the United States, Laski characterized Truman as a "weak President." "To the foreign observer of the American scene," he stated, "the outstanding characteristic of the landscape is the absence of effective leadership." From the perspective of Laski, who had championed vigorous executive government, the Truman administration was a disappointment: "Little seems left of the deep national interest in the activities of Washington which, in the era of Franklin Roosevelt, made the White House the inescapable center round which the effort of the nation was built."[72] In a 1947 letter to Frankfurter in which he complained about Truman and the rightward drift of American politics, he mentioned that what the nation really needed was a Roosevelt fireside chat.[73]

In Laski's view, postwar America was experiencing a kind of counterrevolution. "Conservatism is firmly in power in the United States at a time when the rest of the world is overwhelmingly moving leftward," he wrote. According to Laski, the New Deal era was now definitely over. Truman was not at all interested in central planning, and business had regained total control over the economy. But Laski directed his blame at more than one branch of government and more than one party: "With the Republicans dominating both houses of Congress, and with a President who now, on economic matters, has no effective difference with the Republicans, the business man is, in fact, reinvested with the authority that he lost in 1932." Since the war, Laski argued, there had also been a tendency toward intolerance in American social relations: the South had witnessed a resurgence in racism, and nationally the ground had been softened for anti-Semitism to take root. One explanation Laski offered for the conservative political and social thinking of the American people was the immense influence exerted by the Catholic Church.[74]

In the years after the war, Laski well understood, no nation could parallel the United States in wealth and power. With a huge industrial capacity, cities spared from destruction, and a monopoly on the atomic bomb, the United States was unrivaled. Laski wrote, "America bestrides the world like a colossus; neither Rome at the height of its power nor Great Britain in the period of its economic supremacy enjoyed an influence so direct, so profound, or so pervasive." The actions taken in Washington reverberated around the world.[75] Unfortunately, as he told Frankfurter, America was failing to provide the world with enlightened leadership:

> The Truman Government has more power behind it than any country has ever had before in history, and the psychological background in which it operates seems to me to show more political immaturity than I should have deemed possible in a people which, after all, has produced Franklin, Jefferson, J. Q. Adams, Lincoln, and F.D.R.[76]

The greatest mistake that America was making on the world stage, Laski felt, was its pursuit of a hostile policy toward the Soviet Union. During the second half of the 1940s, he continued to be a qualified supporter of Communist Russia, and in 1946 he was part of a Labour Party delegation that traveled to Moscow and met with Stalin. Although Laski would have liked to see the Russians enjoy the kind of civil liberties integral to Anglo-American society, he also was sympathetic to the idea that the necessities of revolution, coupled with the nation's unique history, accounted for the restrictions on freedom. Despite his misgivings about Soviet actions in Eastern Europe, Laski was more inclined to blame the Cold War on the behavior of the United States.[77] While not an outright apologist for Moscow, he sincerely wished to see the Soviet experiment succeed. In defending Russia, Laski even turned the tables on the United States. Civil liberties may have been a problem in the Soviet Union, he conceded, but the American record was not unblemished either. He asked whether blacks were free in the South and if a press owned and run by moguls like Hearst was so superior to the government-controlled organs of the Soviet Union.[78]

According to Laski, instead of trying to understand Russian fears and needs, the Truman administration viewed every action taken by the Soviets in the worst possible light and considered making friendly overtures to Stalin tantamount to the prewar appeasement of Hitler. Furthermore, the government had whipped the people into an anti-Russian frenzy.[79] In his private correspondence Laski was more candid than in his published writings concerning his reservations about the Soviets but argued that American foreign policy did not have to be tied to Russian faults. In May 1947 he told Frankfurter, "Why Communist blindness should necessitate American folly I do not even hope to understand."[80]

When the Truman Doctrine and the Marshall Plan were both enunciated in the spring of 1947, Laski's reaction was negative. Before the war had even ended, he was warning that after the peace the United States would have to bolster the economies of other nations or its own economy would once again sink into depression.[81] But he could not accept the thrust of the Truman program, which he felt could well lead countries accepting the American aid into "political subordination to the United States."[82] He argued that the Truman administration was above all interested in preventing socialism from taking root in Europe and that "gravely as we need American help, the United States needs the renovation of European prosperity no less urgently. We ought not to accept that renovation upon conditions which would make Western Europe the outer defense zone of American capitalism."[83] Laski wrote to Frankfurter that the American government was attempting to impose on Europe and the rest of the world the kind of conservative social order that prevailed in the United States.[84]

The primary answer Laski offered to counteract the drift to the right in the United States was for liberals to regroup. Since Roosevelt's death there had been a "disintegration" and "atomization" of American liberalism. There were as many liberals in America as before but no one around whom they could coalesce. Furthermore, during the Roosevelt years liberals could flock to the Democratic Party, but now, as before 1932, no real distinction existed between the Democrats and Republicans. In fact, neither party was much interested in ideas, only in winning elections. Liberals had to realize, according to Laski, that they no longer had a place in the Democratic Party. It was incumbent upon them to form a new progressive party with organized labor as its base. This would stand as one of the nation's two major parties, with conservatives grouped in the opposition, after the badly needed realignment and rejuvenation of American politics.[85]

In 1948 Laski published *The American Democracy: A Commentary and an Inter-pretation*, a massive work in which he drew upon his three decades of observing and studying the United States. Over the course of the book's 750-plus pages, he examined American government, culture, and society and in discussing the nation of the present delved into its past. *The American Democracy* was an immense achievement, and it is doubtful that in the 1940s more than a handful of Britons, or many Americans, for that matter, possessed as extensive and sophisticated a knowledge of the United States as Laski. Yet as impressive and insightful as it is in many aspects, the book is also deeply flawed. First, the prose is lacking in clarity and precision. Though Laski was never a great stylist, as George Orwell, for one, pointed out, by the late 1940s his writing had grown worse.[86] The book contains its share of well-turned phrases and passages of sharp wit, but the overall text is marked by a loose, hazy quality. Furthermore, the work is repetitive, haphazardly organized, and often contradictory.

Some of the structural problems of *The American Democracy* undoubtedly resulted from the fact that the book to a certain extent was a cut-and-paste job. Several critics have noted that the work was already dated when it appeared, that it reflected a prewar America rather than the nation as of 1948. In the preface Laski remarked that he conceived of writing the book when he was visiting America in 1937 and began work in 1940 but that in a larger sense, it had "been a generation in the making."[87] His statement can be taken more literally than he undoubtedly intended, for a sizable portion of the book actually consists of recycled material. Much of what Laski said in *The American Democracy* he had already said before in previously published writings. Anyone in 1948 familiar with his magazine articles from the 1930s and forties would have recognized the essence of his comments on FDR, the New Deal, Truman, and the American party system. Although his discussion of the federal government expands on *The American Presidency*, the core of his argument can be found in the earlier work. Laski was not even beyond taking an old piece and weaving it virtually word for word into the book. His discussion of the shortcomings of the governmental system of American colleges was lifted almost verbatim from a 1932 article he wrote for *Harper's* titled "The American College President."[88]

In the preface to *The American Democracy*, Laski announced "that this book is written out of deep love of America."[89] His sincerity should not be questioned, for he did feel a visceral affection for the United States, particularly because of the close friendships he had forged there over the years. Furthermore, there was much, as he revealed in this book, that he objectively admired about America. Nevertheless, it would be difficult to deny that Laski, both in the hostile tone he often employed in these pages and, more important, in the implications of his argument, took a stand distinctly unflattering to the United States. His indictment of American society was, if not distorted, certainly heavy-handed. In places it smacks of Marxist propaganda.

To an extent, Laski's conclusions about America echoed those of Wells. He believed that in the early history of the United States there developed an individualistic ethos that fitted the conditions of the vast, emerging nation. But by the late nineteenth century America was evolving along European lines, with wealth increasingly concentrated in the hands of the few. Americans, however, never gave up the creed adopted in that earlier and very different time. Like Wells, Laski stressed that Americans never gained a "sense of the state." But he also took his argument down a path Wells did not pursue. The point he stressed more than any other in *The American Democracy* was not only that business was in command of the economy but that businessmen dominated every facet of society in the United States. The only solution to this great American dilemma, he believed, was for labor to form a socialist party and win over the reins of state control. Laski had once been skeptical that real change could be effected through the electoral process, which he had contended would be circumvented by the vested interests as soon as they were threatened. But Labour was now in power in Westminster, and therefore he must have felt that America could emulate Britain's social democratic model.

The individualistic spirit of the United States, Laski argued, could be traced to the nation's religious origins and to the influence of the American environment. The seventeenth-century settlers fled Europe to escape religious establishments, and in the eventual separation of church and state in the New World, the individual's spiritual quest became the focus. Although not as disapproving as Chesterton, Laski too stressed the crucial role of Puritanism in shaping the national character: "It is not wholly fanciful to argue that American individualism is the secularized form of American puritanism, that it leaves the individual face to face with his fate, as the chief forms of puritanism left the individual face to face with his God." Furthermore, the sheer physical struggle for existence that confronted the early settlers fostered an ethic of individualism.[90]

Over the years, according to Laski, the immensity of the American continent continued to promote the individualistic "pioneer" spirit. This spirit was always tinged, as the nation grew in size, wealth, and population, with an edge of "seriousness": "It is as though Americans realized that the challenge of Nature over that vast continent could not be taken with gaiety or light-heartedness. The American lives hard, works hard, even plays hard; he seems to feel that only intense living will make him the master." Yet the "pioneer" spirit was also a hopeful spirit, for it led Americans to believe they could overcome any obstacles. There were no bounds to what Jefferson would undertake, and even great industrialists like Rockefeller saw themselves as conquering new territory. "From the very outset," Laski wrote, "the psychological roots of the American idea have been built upon the foundations of expansionism."[91]

The vastness of the continent, Laski felt, had made the American "a restless person, anxious rather to do than to be." In the United States pragmatism was preferred to abstract principle, and the "practical man" was more respected than the "theorist." "Contemplation" was viewed as a "luxury" that could be indulged in only in old age; to devote a life to reflection, as Thoreau had done, was considered suspect. The "supreme symbol of the American spirit" was not Washington, who was too aloof, or Lincoln, who tended to be sullen, but rather Benjamin Franklin, who "made a success of all that he attempted." The American people had several times tapped generals to serve as president, and there was a common belief that Wilson's failures could in part be attributed to his having been a professor. While Jefferson and Lincoln possessed fine minds, they were also skillful politicians. Until the emergence of the great New England writers of the mid-nineteenth century, the most notable American creative achievements were all of a practical nature, in the fields of law, politics, and architecture. And Edison and Ford were heroes not because they had ever advanced scientific knowledge but because they could successfully apply science in inventing useful technologies.[92]

The "individualistic tradition" in America, Laski believed, was also a democratic, egalitarian tradition. The Americans broke with the pattern of aristocratic supremacy that characterized the Old World and established a society in which merit would play a larger role in determining a person's fate. The United States, according to Laski, had afforded "opportunities for individual advancement which, save for Russia since 1917, have been unparalleled in their scale in modern times." In recent decades, Laski wrote, it had become increasingly difficult for the common man in America to attain his goals, but the dream of advancement was still prevalent. Recognizing the "difference in expectation" between the average citizen in the New World and the Old was "vital to the understanding of the difference between the American tradition and that of Europe." Even when the American worker conceded that an economic gap existed between him and his employer, he would not show any social deference. Laski noted that butlers and valets trained in the English tradition of service could scarcely be found in the United States and that the distance between an American military officer and his men was never as great as in Europe.[93]

"Political democracy," as well as "social equality," was a reality in America, Laski felt. The Constitution established a democratic form of government, and the victories of Jefferson in 1800 and Jackson in 1828 ensured that there would be no backsliding toward elite rule. The American political system, Laski believed, was notable for the accessibility it had always provided for citizens from various social backgrounds, at least if they were white and Christian. Although the ascent from the log cabin to the White House was a great American myth, "the political career has been more fully open to ordinary people in the United States than in any other country in the world right down to our own day." The "poor and the humble" made it into Congress and the state legislatures, and since the demise of the Virginia dynasty, seekers of the presidency were actually better off if they had not been born into a prominent family or attended a prestigious university. "New men" like Wendell Willkie, who would have had slim prospects in European politics, were constantly being brought into the American corridors of power. Henry Adams's great mistake was in thinking that because he was an Adams, he would not have to fight for a political position, that he would simply be called upon to serve.[94]

Despite the positive aspects of American civilization, Laski argued that in the late nineteenth and early twentieth century, the nation underwent changes that were inevitable, but for the worse. The decentralized, largely agricultural economy of the United States was transformed into an industrialized, corporate-dominated system. Wealth was increasingly concentrated in the hands of a few, and an "invisible government" came to hold the reins of power. According to Laski's analysis, the two most important turning points in this evolution were the Civil War, which marked the beginning of the economic transformation, and the advent of the Depression in 1929, which forced Americans to realize just how far that transformation had gone. Well into the twentieth century, most Americans continued to cling to the individualistic, egalitarian ethos that had for so long guided the nation, but the widening gap between the ideal and reality led to low morale and cynicism.[95]

With the emergence of an oligarchy, Laski argued, America had come to resemble Europe. Such an eventuality had seemed so improbable in the nation's early years: "That the history of the United States would, despite everything, follow the general pattern of capitalist democracy in Europe occurred only to a few men of special insight like John Taylor of Caroline." The evolution of the United States along European lines, Laski contended, proved that the nation was not unique or exceptional. He dismissed as mere mythology the idea "that America was different, that her destiny was special, that her hopes were on a higher plane than that of any other country in the world."[96]

Not only did developments of the late nineteenth and early twentieth century lead to corporate domination of the American economy, but central to Laski's thesis is the notion that businessmen came to dominate every aspect of American society and culture. In fact, vast stretches of his book are devoted to how business held an iron grip on politics, education, the churches, the media, and the professions. Laski contended "that in no previous civilization has the business man enjoyed either the power or the prestige that he possesses in the United States." Not only had business become "the religion of America," but as nowhere else in the world, it is "simply assumed that the opinions of a successful business man are important." Despite Laski's criticism of the negative nineteenth-century British commentators on the United States, his own depiction of the American business community, and the central place it held in the nation, was just as corrosive. According to his view, the American businessman was above all interested in gaining wealth, status, and power. He tended to be intellectually limited, culturally narrow-minded, and indifferent to the needs of the general community. His philosophy was to extol free enterprise, condemn organized labor, oppose any extension of governmental power, and stand clear of anything that smacked of radicalism. Laski wrote, "He seeks to live by a creed so long outmoded that its recitation belongs less to the realm of thought than of ritual."[97]

According to Laski, the domination of business over American society had over the past decades been challenged, though never overcome.

Certain voices had drawn attention to the disparity between traditional individualistic values and the reality of oligarchical control in the United States, but not until the Depression and the arrival of Franklin D. Roosevelt, Laski argued, did the business community face a formidable threat. Yet he also asserted, as he had in the previous decade, that Roosevelt essentially believed in the soundness of the American economic system and that the purpose of the New Deal was not to upset that system. In Laski's view, "what occurred was in no sense a revolution. The Great Depression transformed America into a social service state such as Great Britain had become under the Liberal government of 1906–1914."[98]

Laski's concern was that as mild as the New Deal had been, in post-war America there was no sentiment to continue along the path trod by Roosevelt. The only hope he held out that the grip of business over American society could be broken was for labor to form a socialist party. The Republicans and Democrats, he argued, both supported the status quo, and labor would never be accorded justice as long as the two of them held a monopoly on power. Laski was aware that what he was proposing ran counter to precedent, for labor in America had traditionally played a modest role in politics and instead concentrated on the bread-and-butter issues of direct concern to workers. To a large extent, labor had actually reflected the business ethos by championing the free enterprise system and holding the idea of a positive state in contempt. Furthermore, labor had always worked within the two major parties and during the Roosevelt years even made some real gains. But Laski argued that labor could not expect to see another New Deal, as the nation was moving to the right. The idea that a socialist workers' party may have been appropriate for Europe, but not for America, he rejected, because the United States was clearly developing along European lines and "proletarianization" was a reality. If the labor movement, allied with farmers and like-minded progressives, formed a political party, the conservatives would all coalesce in opposition, and America would be able to boast of a party system based on true ideological distinctions. The socialist labor party, Laski believed, could become the majority party, assume the reins of power, and fulfill the aspirations of the American people that for so long had been thwarted by the business oligarchy.[99]

When *The American Democracy* was published in 1948, considerable attention was accorded to the work, which was inevitably compared to the analyses of the United States by Tocqueville and Bryce. Several leading scholars of American civilization wrote reviews, and the general consensus was that *The American Democracy* was an ambitious work of commentary, but one fraught with problems. These academics differed in their assessments as to whether the problems were fatal.[100] Three of the most probing and critical reviews of *The American Democracy* were written by the Columbia historian Henry Steele Commager and two young luminaries on the Harvard history faculty, Oscar Handlin and Arthur M. Schlesinger Jr. All three believed that Laski's devotion to socialist dogma skewed his perception of America.

According to Commager, *The American Democracy* was more like Tocqueville's *Democracy in America* than like Bryce's *American Commonwealth*, for not only was it "analytical rather than expository, interpretive rather than descriptive," but one of Laski's purposes was that Europe should learn from the lessons of America. If Tocqueville's "formula" for interpreting American society was "equality," Laski's was "inequality." Commager believed *The American Democracy* reflected great scholarship and insight as well as an unabashed subjectivity. The problem with the book was that "Mr. Laski's partisanship carries him too far. It is a very useful thing to have a point of view; it is a very dangerous thing to fit facts to that point of view." The book was filled with distortions—at least some deliberate—that served the thesis Laski so relentlessly tried to drive home.[101]

Schlesinger was even more harsh than Commager. Writing in the *New York Times Book Review,* he stated, "In no recent work of Laski's have his remarkable talents for disinterested analysis been brought so fully into play as in 'The American Democracy,' yet at crucial moments the analysis is almost invariably stopped dead in its tracks by the iron abstractions of the pamphleteer." According to Schlesinger, Laski wore two different hats while writing this book: at times he was the social scientist making a genuine scholarly attempt to represent the nation faithfully while at other times he was the socialist propagandist hammering away at his thesis that America was a society in the grasp of business. Laski's "Marxist boilerplate about America as the citadel of monopoly recedes when he gets down to the detail of American life," and in places he revealed a sympathy for the United States that made Schlesinger wonder how much Laski actually subscribed to his own argument. The overall effect was one of "profound intellectual confusion," even "schizophrenia." Furthermore, Schlesinger found Laski's political ideology to be a relic of British socialist thinking of a quarter century earlier. By fixing upon a collectivist, state-controlled economy as the answer for the United States, he revealed he had grappled with none of the problems that the realities of socialism had presented over the past years.[102]

Oscar Handlin, in his *Atlantic* review-essay, concurred with Schlesinger that Laski was a product of British socialism and that his ideological rigidity doomed his effort to make a credible assessment of American society. According to Handlin, "That Laski fails in this earnest attempt to understand the culture and people of the United States is not due to want of ability but to the distorted perspective of his intellectual position." The case that Laski made in *The American Democracy* rested on the faulty premise that the most powerful group in a society, the group that invariably controls the reins of government, can mold the national culture to its specifications. This assumption led him to present "an unreal estimate of the businessman's place in American life." Of course, Handlin charged, by defining "businessmen" so fuzzily as to include virtually everyone who believed in private property, Laski could more easily get away with his exaggerated claims. Handlin did admit that the values of business were pervasive in American society but asked how such a reality could have developed. Could businessmen, in a democracy, simply have shoved these ideals down the throats of the American people? In his view, "the spread of business values cannot be accounted for without conceding that the Americans were, in advance, not hostile but receptive." Laski was misguided in applying the single, simplistic argument of business domination to explain the complexities of American culture, and he failed to see that the different socioeconomic groups in the United States, rather than being locked in struggle, actually shared certain basic assumptions.[103]

In the December 1948 issue of the *Harvard Law Review*, Mark DeWolfe Howe, the Harvard Law School professor who would edit the Holmes-Laski correspondence, answered the reviewers of Laski's book who had made "efforts to write off his volume as the doctrinaire application of outmoded standards of Fabian socialism to American life."[104] Far from "the argument of a stuffy English socialist" that his detractors depicted, the case made by Laski was provocative and penetrating, and *The American Democracy* should "prove to be far and away the most important book on the civilization of America which has been produced in the first half of the twentieth century." However, although Howe came to Laski's defense at the outset of his review, he himself then proceeded to dissect the work. Like other critics, he charged that Laski was guilty of "repetitious exaggeration" and of casting "the business man in a role of decisive villainy in every phase of American life."[105]

During the first years of the Truman presidency, when Laski felt such disappointment in the White House, he apparently looked to General Dwight David Eisenhower as his great hope for 1948. Surely, the two made strange bedfellows, but Laski had come to revere Eisenhower during the war.[106] The general, however, was not yet ready to plunge into electoral politics, and furthermore, when Truman did win the Democratic nomination and the '48 election, Laski was not displeased. In an article for the *New Republic* in which he spoke for European "progressive opinion," Laski revealed a new respect for Truman that paralleled the president's improved standing among American liberals as well:

> Everyone I know thinks that Truman fought a remarkable campaign, single-handed. We all think it was a very great victory. We are not convinced that Truman will be a great President, even though he owes no political debts and can stand on his own feet. But we do think he may have acquired a new self-confidence.

Laski characterized Truman's surprise defeat of Thomas E. Dewey as a progressive triumph, particularly because it was clear that the electorate had voted on the issues and not because a sparkling figure like FDR topped the ticket. He compared the election to Labour's defeat of Churchill and the Conservatives a few years earlier. What Europeans above all desired, according to Laski, was for Truman now to take the initiative and ease tensions with the Soviet Union. Laski was much more openly critical of the Soviets than he had been before and less willing to blame the United States for the Cold War: "Russia, no doubt, is obstinate, brutal, foolish, secretive. Russian political leaders act with an irresponsibility that is often somewhere between the criminal and the contemptible." But he stressed that Truman and Stalin had to come to terms and that the president should ignore conservative opinion in the United States that would characterize any overture he might make to the Russians as "appeasement."[107]

Having crossed the Atlantic in the spring of 1948 to lecture at Chicago's predominantly black Roosevelt College, Laski, a year later, made his last trip to the United States. Under the auspices of the Sidney Hillman Foundation, he visited several university campuses in the spring of 1949 to deliver a series of talks that would become the basis for *Trade*

Unions in the New Society (1949).[108] Upon returning to England he contributed five articles to the *Nation,* three discussing the American scene and two addressing the specific issue of academic freedom in the United States. His assessment of the country's political situation in these 1949 articles was distinctly negative. Although he had welcomed Truman's electoral victory in late 1948, he was already once again questioning the president's commitment to liberalism. In general Laski believed that "the forces of reaction" in the United States were "far better organized than the forces of progress." He was disturbed to see how much influence was wielded by a conservative press and by the Catholic Church. To his regret, he was also compelled to admit that the American labor movement was no closer to abandoning the free enterprise system or adopting an independent political identity than ever. Furthermore, he was worried that "militarism" was for the first time becoming a permanent feature of American civilization and that the Pentagon was turning into a powerful force in the nation.[109]

Laski was concerned about the implications of the chilly relationship between Washington and Moscow for the preservation of world peace, but he also saw that the Cold War was exerting a profound impact on American society:

> J. Edgar Hoover and the FBI are still allowed to run amok all over the United States; and though there are brave voices raised in protest, witch-hunting and intolerance are as widespread, though not, I think, as profound, as they were in the evil days of 1919–1920, under Attorney General A. Mitchell Palmer.

Laski, of course, wrote these words before the rise of Senator Joseph McCarthy, which he did not live long enough to witness. But even by 1949, the situation had deteriorated so badly in America that, Laski stated, "it is possible to be marked down as dangerous if your wife buys her spring costume from a shop where the salesgirl has a Communist cousin." Reflecting his new toughness toward the Soviet Union, he actually placed some of the blame for the hysterical atmosphere in the United States on the Russians themselves, who he charged had engaged in unwarranted spying and propaganda. He did not, however, exonerate the Americans.[110]

In his two articles on academic freedom in the United States, Laski discussed how the witch-hunting atmosphere had penetrated college campuses. Although for years he had been outspoken in his criticism of the restrictive atmosphere of American higher education, his experiences in 1949 only hardened his convictions. First of all, the Justice Department asked that he register as "a foreign agent," a request he was successful in denying. When he arrived in the United States, the University of Washington was in the process of dismissing faculty members for their left-wing views, and the tension on various campuses, under the close scrutiny of state authorities, was great. Laski was seen as such a disturbing influence by both the University of Washington and the University of California at Los Angeles that his lectures there were canceled, and when the Harvard Law School Forum asked him to speak, the city of Cambridge refused the group permission to use a public school auditorium on the grounds that he was a Communist and an enemy of the Catholic Church.[111]

Actually, Laski did not complain much about his reception in America. He felt that overall he had been treated well and was used to those elements in the United States who attacked anyone for "the dual handicap of being a Socialist and, in spite of deep affection for America and Americans, of not being prepared to transform himself temporarily into a belated imitation of Dr. Pangloss on all things American." Laski's concern was for the American professor, particularly the young professor, who felt restrained from teaching and speaking out as he saw fit for fear of jeopardizing his career. According to Laski, an academic in the United States could not possibly be a Communist, and in fact showing any sympathy for Russia or uttering criticism of America's basic institutions was risky. The tendency of American professors, therefore, was to be cautious in every step they took.[112] Only a few weeks before he died in March of 1950 at age fifty-six, Laski told a former student, "I could not bear to teach at an American college today if I did not know that there was always a ship at New York on which I could come home."[113]

Exactly three decades earlier, Laski had, in fact, felt compelled to abandon his Harvard teaching post and sail back to England. After more than a dozen years, however, he became reacquainted with the United States and even transformed himself into an authority on the nation's history and institutions. But while he embraced America during the 1930s, when Roosevelt was in the White House, during the 1940s—and particularly after FDR's death—he adopted a very different attitude. In the last years of his life, Laski still maintained close ties to America, but the nation now embodied for him the most deplorable excesses of capitalism.

Conclusion

Lost Republic, Lost Tradition

The British observers of America who followed in the footsteps of Bryce were a diverse lot. These commentators, writing about the United States in the years between 1890 and 1950, by no means marched in step in their assessments of American civilization. Nevertheless, certain general themes are common to their works, and the conclusions that they drew, while not identical, are similar in a few fundamental respects. Among Stead, Wells, Chesterton, and Laski, Chesterton tended to be the odd man out; his views on America often contradicted those of the other three. But while he did not share their socialist, internationalist perspective, his own unique brand of radicalism drove him to agree with their diagnosis of, if not prescription for, the ills that plagued America.

Unlike so many of their predecessors, the notable British commentators on America between 1890 and the mid-twentieth century generally liked the United States. The hostile, condescending attitude epitomized by Mrs. Trollope became a rarity. Kipling and Beatrice Webb were her legitimate heirs, but Kipling never intended to publish his derisive articles in the United States and Webb confined her scathing opinions to her private diary. It is also significant that both recorded their impressions prior to the turn of the century. Shaw, of course, could be abusive of America, but to a large extent he was simply being Shaw. On the other hand, a panegyric like Strachey's *American Soundings* was as atypical of this period as it would have been in Trollope's day. Essentially, the tone Bryce adopted in *The American Commonwealth* set the precedent for those who followed him. Like Bryce, these commentators were friends of the United States and admirers of many of the nation's traits and institutions while at the same time fierce critics.

There were various aspects of American civilization upon which the post-Bryce observers looked favorably. First of all, they seem to have been fond of the American people. The nineteenth-century complaint that Americans were crude and boorish disappeared; even Beatrice Webb found kind words for their manners. There was a certain amount of grumbling about American boastfulness, but it was tolerated, and the characteristic gregariousness was viewed as problematic yet endearing. Virtually all of the observers found the nation's egalitarian spirit, the feature that had horrified nineteenth-century Tories, to be a positive good. From their perspective it was refreshing to see a people free from the rigid hierarchies and customs of deference that marked the Old World. In general, the commentators were proponents of the republican ideals that had underlain the establishment and development of the American nation, and they saw nineteenth century democratic leaders like Jefferson and Lincoln as true heroes.

The primary criticism upon which the British observers between 1890 and 1950 agreed was that noble as the history of the nation had been in its first century, America was no longer the simple, virtuous republic of its youth. According to these writers, economic forces were transforming the United States into a society in which wealth was concentrated in the hands of the few and the people were divided along class lines. Capitalism was forcing America to repeat the scenario already played out in Europe. Alongside the political and social equality of America, there was now economic inequality. In fact, these commentators believed that the consequences of capitalism were proving to be even harsher in the United States than in Europe, for in no other nation had business ever taken such a supreme place. The observers argued, in contrast to their predecessors, that Americans were no more greedy and materialistic than Europeans; they were simply driven to work hard by an individualistic ethos rooted in the nation's Puritan past. Nevertheless, the success of business in America, while impressive, was taking a heavy toll. Though the European aristocracy could be easily criticized, at least this governing class had been able to mitigate the effects of capitalism, which was ceaselessly eating away at the fabric of American society.

To Chesterton, the answer was for America to preserve whatever vestiges of Jeffersonianism survived and to bolster that republican spirit with a renewed commitment to Christianity. Stead too saw Christianity—more precisely, Christian humanitarianism—as central to a solution. Yet he also agreed with Wells, Laski, and the other socialist observers of the United States that the nation needed to move toward collectivism. These observers discovered, however, that America was reluctant to veer from the principles that had informed the thinking of the Founding Fathers. Despite the reality of monopoly capitalism, Americans still paid homage to the ideal of minimal government and laissez-faire economics. As Wells put it, Americans lacked a "sense of the state," and Shaw dubbed them a "nation of villagers." There was, however, encouraging evidence—in Theodore Roosevelt and Franklin Roosevelt, in the progressive movement and the New Deal—that the nation was finally breaking with tradition and entering into the era of the positive state. But the advances were modest, and no mainstream American politician would explicitly call for socialism. Furthermore, American labor seemed decades behind its British counterpart in political consciousness: workers tended either to accept the existing economic system or to vent their anger in crude, often violent, protest.

In modern capitalist America, the British observers believed, republican government as conceived of by the Founders was simply a lost dream. The nation was now in the hands of a plutocracy that had debased the governmental process. The commentators maintained that though there was more equality in America than in their own country, this did not mean that there was more democracy. Like Bryce before them, many revealed a deep appreciation for the British political system when they compared it to the American. Stead and the Fabians were shocked by American municipal government in the 1890s, and only Chesterton and Belloc, with their preference for one-man rule over legislative bodies, believed the presidential system superior to the parliamentary. Virtually all of the observers were critical of the Constitution, which they felt was responsible for tying America to a rigid, ineffective framework of government and ensuring that the process of reform would be glacial. A blueprint that may have been appropriate for an agrarian nation of the 1780s was held to be obsolete in the urbanized, industrialized America of the twentieth century.

Despite the deep flaws in American civilization, the British observers between 1890 and 1950 were well aware that the United States was quickly becoming the wealthiest and most powerful nation in the world.

They saw that America was assuming the role of global leadership long held by Britain and that Americanization was replacing Anglicization as the dominant force in the world. But there was hardly more than a trace of resentment in their writings; they accepted the shift in fortunes with apparently little difficulty. Instead of bemoaning the changes, they attempted to adjust to the new reality. They understood that in the twentieth century, decisions made in Washington had the potential to exert a profound impact on their lives, and they came to scrutinize the ideals and actions of each president as though he were their own elected leader. During the World Wars, especially, they looked to Wilson and FDR to use America's new clout to influence the course of events. Yet, on a deeper level, the ascendancy of America forced them to assess what it now meant to be British. At one extreme was Stead, who liked to think of America as Britain's successful son and went so far as to suggest that the British should cheerfully submit to being absorbed into an American-dominated English-speaking federation. Wells too was an exponent of Anglo-American kinship and an advocate of the unification of Britain and the United States. At the other end of the spectrum stood Chesterton and Belloc, who believed that the British and the Americans constituted two very different peoples and that it was to the advantage of both societies to remain as distinct and separate as possible. What placed Chesterton and Belloc on common ground with Stead and Wells was the need they all felt to define the British identity in a world in which America was looming ever larger.

When Harold Laski died in 1950, a year that also saw the demise of George Bernard Shaw at ninety-four, the great British observers of America were a vanishing breed. The tradition of visiting the United States and venturing to make an overarching statement about American civilization was then fading into history. When Laski's *American Democracy* was published in 1948, the work was in more ways than one a relic of another era.

The Second World War put an end to the age of the grand tour and precipitated the decline of the travel book as a literary genre. In the decades after the war, as the jet airplane forced transatlantic liners into mothballs, travel gave way to tourism.[1] As more and more Britons were able to fly to the United States on business or holiday, and as images of America became a common feature on British television, the notion of some literary lion taking on the responsibility of describing America to his fellow Britons became an anachronism. The United States was no longer a distant and exotic land that could be viewed only after a lengthy and expensive ocean voyage; it was now a familiar, accessible reality. Furthermore, the British and Americans became so culturally and politically intertwined in the postwar era that the two peoples gained a much more sophisticated knowledge of each other than ever before. Any British writer who attempted to explain or interpret American civilization in its entirety would probably have been dismissed as a pretentious fool.

While technology, as Wells had always predicted, bridged the distance between Britain and America, the postwar years also witnessed the passing of the titanic British man of letters. Writers like Wells and Chesterton were polymaths who tackled a broad range of topics in a variety of literary forms for a wide readership. They were financially dependent on producing a steady output of material for the scores of newspapers and magazines that throve in the first decades of the twentieth century, and naturally they turned to the profitable, time-tested practice of visiting and commenting on America. After the war the writer as creative artist, political and social analyst, educator, and public figure all rolled into one, in the mold of a Wells or Chesterton, virtually disappeared. Furthermore, the sources, both British and American, that had sustained such literary giants began to dry up. The outlets in which Wells, Chesterton, and Laski too, had placed their commentaries grew scarce, and certainly the ability to command an important journal the way Stead once did became an anomaly.

It would be a mistake, however, to think that after mid-century the British essentially gave up on writing about America. On the contrary, they simply abandoned the practice of undertaking a broadly conceived travel book like Wells's *Future in America* or a massive project along the lines of Laski's *American Democracy*. Their writings on America became more specialized, more narrowly defined. American political developments and social trends were actually scrutinized more closely than ever before by British journalists and authors, including by some in the thriving expatriate community in the United States, such as Jessica Mitford and Alistair Cooke.[2] The novelist Martin Amis is an example of a noted literary figure who in the latter half of the twentieth century focused his attention on America, though the volume he published consisted of scattered pieces, mainly biographical sketches, that had previously appeared under his byline.[3] British writers, like Jonathan Raban, continued to turn out travel books, but the tendency was to concentrate on personal impressions gathered in particular places in America rather than to draw generalizations.[4] Perhaps most important, in the postwar decades a significant number of British scholars finally began to devote themselves to examining American history and institutions.[5]

Although the gap left by the British observers of America was filled after 1950 by a variety of talented individuals who dealt with the United States intelligently, there was nevertheless a loss attached to the end of an intellectual tradition that had endured for well over a century and encompassed the likes of Dickens and Martineau, Arnold and Bryce, and Wells and Chesterton. Never again would the great British writer embark on the grand tour of the States and take on the burden of explaining to the world the meaning of American civilization. These missions, though always presumptuous, also proved at their best to be eminently worthwhile, as the rich legacy can testify.

Acknowledgments

I would like to express my appreciation for the assistance offered me as I examined manuscripts in the following repositories: the University of Illinois Library at Champaign-Urbana, the British Library of Political and Economic Science, the House of Lords Record Office, the New York Public Library, the Library of Congress, and the Harvard Law School Library. I am particularly grateful to the late Dorothy Collins for allowing me into her Beaconsfield, England home, Top Meadow Cottage, to see the Chesterton papers, and to Judith Lea for the hospitality she extended me there. (These papers have since been moved to the British Library.) I thank Joseph O. Baylen for pointing me to Stead letters in America. Grants awarded by the Charles Warren Center for Studies in American History at Harvard University, I would like to acknowledge, helped to meet the cost of research trips to London and Champaign-Urbana.

This work originated as a doctoral dissertation in history at Harvard, and I am indebted to Donald Fleming for providing me with his advice, for giving the thesis a close reading, and for setting a high standard that I at least tried to obtain. I also would like to express my gratitude to Michael Kammen for reading the work at different stages and offering his insightful comments, and for all of his efforts on my behalf over the years. Others who have provided assistance—in various ways—are Lee Davison, Peter Mancall, Maeva Marcus, Gerald McFarland, Jack Rakove, Stephen Tull, and Natalie Wexler. The editor of this series, Paul Boyer, was enormously helpful in guiding me as I shaped my manuscript into a book, and I thank him for being so generous with his time and energy. Everyone I have dealt with at the University of Wisconsin Press has been attentive and accommodating—namely, Gwen Walker, David Herzberg, Matthew Levin, Carla Aspelmeier, and Susanne Breckenridge. I appreciate, as well, the improvements to the work effected by Erin Holman, the copyeditor. Last, for their support over the years it has taken to complete this project, I thank my brothers, Richard and Donald Frankel, and particularly my parents, Robert and Doris Frankel, to whom the book is dedicated.

Notes

Preface

1. To consult a study of a wide range of such travel books, see Richard Rapson, *Britons View America: Travel Commentary, 1860–1935* (Seattle, 1971). For an anthology of British travel writing about the United States, see Allan Nevins, ed., *America through British Eyes* (New York, 1948).

2. For scholarly examinations of travel writing, see Christopher Mulvey, *Anglo-American Landscapes: A Study of Nineteenth-Century Anglo-American Travel Literature* (Cambridge, England, 1983); Christopher Mulvey, *Transatlantic Manners: Social Patterns in Nineteenth-Century Anglo-American Travel Literature* (Cambridge, England, 1990); Paul Fussell, *Abroad: British Literary Traveling between the Wars* (New York, 1980); Paul Fussell, ed., *The Norton Book of Travel* (New York, 1987); and Peter Hulme and Tim Youngs, eds., *The Cambridge Companion to Travel Writing* (Cambridge, England, 2002).

3. Comparative histories involving the United States include Robert Kelley, *The Transatlantic Persuasion: The Liberal-Democratic Mind in the Age of Gladstone* (New York, 1969); George M. Fredrickson, *White Supremacy: A Comparative Study in American and South African History* (New York, 1981); Patrice Higgonet, *Sister Republics: The Origins of French and American Republicanism* (Cambridge, Mass., 1988); and Peter Kolchin, *Unfree Labor: American Slavery and Russian Serfdom* (Cambridge, Mass., 1987). The value of viewing American history in an international context is stressed in Thomas Bender, ed., *Rethinking American History in a Global Age* (Berkeley, Calif., 2002).

4. A prime example of a scholar's embracing the theory of American exceptionalism is Seymour Martin Lipset, *American Exceptionalism: A Double-Edged Sword* (New York, 1996). Michael Kammen discusses the mixed view of the concept among academics in an essay, "The Problem of American Exceptionalism: A Reconsideration," in his book *In The Past Lane: Historical Perspectives on American Culture* (New York, 1997), 169–98.

5. See James T. Kloppenberg, *Uncertain Victory: Social Democracy and Progressivism in European and American Thought, 1870–1920* (New York, 1986); and Daniel T.

Rodgers, *Atlantic Crossings: Social Politics in a Progressive Age* (Cambridge, Mass., 1998). For scholarship specifically on Anglo-American reform connections during the early twentieth century, see chapter 3 of this volume.

Introduction

1. Nevins, *America through British Eyes*, 79–102.

2. See Henry Pelling, *America and the British Left: From Bright to Bevan* (London, 1956).

3. Two notable contemporaries of Trollope who viewed the United States in a similar vein were the retired naval officers Captain Basil Hall, author of *Travels in North America* (1829), and Captain Frederick Marryat, who wrote *A Diary in America, with Remarks on Its Institutions* (1839).

4. The edition used here is Frances Trollope, *Domestic Manners of the Americans*, ed. Donald Smalley (New York, 1949).

5. For an account of Trollope's life and her stay in America, see Donald Smalley's introduction to *Domestic Manners*, vii–lxxvi.

6. The edition used here is Harriet Martineau, *Society in America*, ed. and abr. Seymour Martin Lipset (New Brunswick, 1981 [1962]). In 1838 Martineau also came out with *Retrospect of Western Travel*, a more accessible and conventional, but less important, account of her journey.

7. Martineau did not follow in the footsteps of the Scottish-born radical Frances Wright, who, after her first trip across the Atlantic, published an effusively laudatory book about the United States, *Views of Society and Manners in America* (1821).

8. For an account of Martineau's life and American trip, see Seymour Martin Lipset's introduction to Martineau, *Society in America*, 5–41; also, R. K. Webb, *Harriet Martineau: A Radical Victorian* (New York, 1960), particularly 134–74.

9. Kemble was a member of a celebrated theatrical family and in 1832 traveled to America to perform on stage. Her journal of that highly successful tour was published in 1835. While in America, she met and married Pierce Butler, and they eventually went to live on the large Georgia plantation he had inherited. Repelled by the institution of slavery, she recorded her observations in the well-known *Journal of a Residence on a Georgian Plantation in 1838–1839*, which did not appear until 1863.

10. Webb, *Martineau*, 157.

11. For an account of Dickens's American experiences, see Edgar Johnson, *Charles Dickens: His Tragedy and Triumph*, rev. and abr. ed. (New York, 1977), 197–246; Fred Kaplan, *Dickens: A Biography* (New York, 1988), 122–44.

12. The edition used here is Charles Dickens, *American Notes and Pictures from Italy* (Oxford, England, 1978 [1957]).

13. Dickens's friend and biographer, John Forster, makes this point, as does Edgar Johnson. See John Forster, *The Life of Charles Dickens*, ed. B. W. Matz, 2 vols. (New York, 1911), 1:233–34; Johnson, *Charles Dickens*, 245. These letters may be consulted in *The Letters of Charles Dickens*, vol. 3, *1842–1843*, ed. Madeline House, Graham Storey, and Kathleen Tillotson (Oxford, England, 1974).

14. Johnson, *Charles Dickens*, 239–40; Forster, *Life of Charles Dickens*, 1:279–81.

15. The edition used here is Charles Dickens, *Martin Chuzzlewit* (Oxford, England, 1984).

16. Works of note from this era include Sir Charles Lyell's *Travels in North America* (1845) and *A Second Visit to the United States of North America* (1849), Alexander Mackay's *Western World* (1849), and Anthony Trollope's *North America* (1862). Also, during the Civil War two eminent British journalists who went to America as war correspondents published in book form some of their findings: in 1863 William Howard Russell's *My Diary North and South* and Edward Dicey's *Six Months in the Federal States* were issued.

17. For an account of Arnold's American tour, see Matthew Arnold, *The Complete Prose Works of Matthew Arnold*, vol. 10, *Philistinism in England and America*, ed. R. H. Super (Ann Arbor, Mich., 1974), 53–73, 143–86, 462–66, 498–500, 504–8. Also see Park Honan, *Matthew Arnold: A Life* (New York, 1981), 393–408; and Howard Mumford Jones, "Arnold, Aristocracy, and America," *American Historical Review* 49 (April 1944): 393–409. For a discussion of Arnold's contemporary and enduring intellectual impact on America, particularly in the area of literary criticism, see John Henry Raleigh, *Matthew Arnold and American Culture* (Berkeley, Calif., 1961), especially, in regard to the American tour, pp. 57–76.

18. R. H. Super notes that this volume, published in Boston by Cupples and Hurd, was "presumably unauthorized." See Matthew Arnold, *The Complete Prose Works of Matthew Arnold*, vol. 11, *The Last Word*, ed. R. H. Super (Ann Arbor, Mich., 1977), 487.

19. Arnold, *Complete Works*, 10:1–23, 449–57. See pp. 19–20 for quotations.

20. Ibid., 194–217, 518–29. See pp. 202–3, 217 for quotations.

21. Griffin made this comment in "A Visit to Philistia," *Fortnightly Review*, January 1884; see Arnold, *Complete Works*, 11:487–88. Griffin's *The Great Republic* (1884) is one of the most harshly negative books about America ever written by a Briton.

22. Arnold, *Complete Works*, 11:350–69, 485–95. See pp. 357–58 for quotations.

23. The edition used here is James Bryce, *The American Commonwealth*, 3 vols. (1888; repr., New York, 1973).

24. For an account of Bryce's life, with particular focus on his American experiences, see Edmund Ions, *James Bryce and American Democracy, 1870–1922* (London, 1968). A work centered on Bryce's magnum opus, and its intellectual

underpinnings, is Hugh Tulloch, *James Bryce's* American Commonwealth: *The Anglo-American Background* (Woodbridge, England, 1988).

25. Bryce, *American Commonwealth*, 1:4–6.

1. The Plight of the Cities

1. The only full-scale biography of Stead that exists is Frederic Whyte, *The Life of W. T. Stead*, 2 vols. (London, 1925). A study of Stead that focuses on his journalistic career during the 1880s is Raymond L. Schults, *Crusader in Babylon: W. T. Stead and the* Pall Mall Gazette (Lincoln, Nebr., 1972). A lengthy portrait of Stead written by one of his *Pall Mall Gazette* protégés can be found in J. W. Robertson Scott, *The Life and Death of a Newspaper* (London, 1952). For a negative assessment of Stead's life, see the chapter on him in Hugh Kingsmill, *After Puritanism, 1850–1900* (London, 1929).

2. W. T. Stead, *The Americanization of the World; or, the Trend of the Twentieth Century* (New York, 1902 [1901]), 264–67.

3. Whyte, *Life of Stead*, 1:15.

4. [W. T. Stead], "James Russell Lowell: His Message, and How It Helped Me," *Review of Reviews* (London), September 1891, 235–38, 240. See p. 238 for quotation.

5. According to the leading student of the "agitation," Stead did more at first to mobilize public opinion against the Turks, and against the pro-Turk policy of Benjamin Disraeli's Tory government, than any other figure in Britain, including William Gladstone, who lent his name to the movement only after it was in full swing. R. T. Shannon, *Gladstone and the Bulgarian Agitation 1876*, 2nd ed. (Hassocks, England, 1975), 49–50, 69–81, 251.

6. Schults, *Crusader*, 32–33, 61–62.

7. The anonymous author of *The Bitter Cry of Outcast London* was Rev. W. C. Preston, who used data about impoverished East London that had been collected by the secretary of the London Congregational Union, Rev. Andrew Mearns. The pamphlet's enormous success, among Congregationalists and the general population, was largely attributable to Stead's decision to publicize the work in the *Pall Mall Gazette*. See Peter d'A. Jones, *The Christian Socialist Revival, 1877–1914: Religion, Class, and Social Conscience in Late-Victorian England* (Princeton, N.J., 1968), 414–17.

8. Sudanese rebels had been threatening British-led Egyptian troops based at Khartoum. As a result of an interview Stead conducted with Gordon early in 1884, and subsequent prodding in the pages of the *Pall Mall Gazette* and other papers, the Gladstone government reluctantly opted to send the general. But in January 1885, after a ten-month siege, the Sudanese rebels overtook Khartoum and inflicted massive casualties.

9. An Australian edition was soon started as well.

10. Lloyd J. Graybar, *Albert Shaw of the* Review of Reviews: *An Intellectual Biography* (Lexington, Ky., 1974), 47–57.

11. Joseph O. Baylen, "A Victorian's 'Crusade' in Chicago, 1893–1894," *Journal of American History* 51 (December 1964): 420–22. For Stead's visit to Chicago, see also Dennis B. Downey, "William Stead and Chicago: A Victorian Jeremiah in the Windy City," *Mid-America* 68 (October 1986): 153–66.

12. For a history of Chicago in the years leading up to 1893, see Bessie Louise Pierce, *A History of Chicago*, vol. 3, *The Rise of a Modern City, 1871–1893* (New York, 1957); Ray Ginger, *Altgeld's America: The Lincoln Ideal versus Changing Realities* (New York, 1958); and Donald L. Miller, *City of the Century: The Epic of Chicago and the Making of America* (New York, 1996). For a discussion of how Chicago developed into an economic center, focusing on the interplay between the city and the hinterland, see William Cronon, *Nature's Metropolis: Chicago and the Great West* (New York, 1991). The culture and society of Chicago in the early 1890s are examined in James Gilbert, *Perfect Cities: Chicago's Utopias of 1893* (Chicago, 1991). The European critique of the architecture and other physical characteristics of late-nineteenth-century Chicago forms the focus of Arnold Lewis, *An Early Encounter with Tomorrow: Europeans, Chicago's Loop, and the World's Columbian Exposition* (Urbana, Ill., 1997).

13. [W. T. Stead], "My First Visit to America. An Open Letter to My Readers," *Review of Reviews*, April 1894, 410.

14. Ibid., 414–15.

15. Pierce, *History of Chicago*, 3:503–12; Ginger, *Altgeld's America*, 15–18, 22; Gilbert, *Perfect Cities*, 80, 84–85; Lewis, *Early Encounter*, 167–94.

16. [Stead], "My First Visit," 415–16.

17. Ginger, *Altgeld's America*, 20–21, 91–92; Pierce, *History of Chicago*, 3:197–99, 509; Miller, *City of the Century*, 534–35.

18. Baylen, "A Victorian's 'Crusade,'" 422.

19. [W. T. Stead], "If Christ Came to Chicago! My Book and Why It Was Written," *Review of Reviews*, May 1894, 509–10.

20. Baylen, "A Victorian's 'Crusade,'" 423–25; Whyte, *Life of Stead*, 2:42–49.

21. Whyte, *Life of Stead*, 2:42–45.

22. Baylen, "A Victorian's 'Crusade,'" 425–27; Whyte, *Life of Stead*, 2:48–49, 51–52.

23. Baylen, "A Victorian's 'Crusade,'" 433; Ginger, *Altgeld's America*, 249–53.

24. Baylen, "A Victorian's 'Crusade,'" 425–29; Whyte, *Life of Stead*, 2:49–52.

25. In this same letter, Stead was more blunt than he had been in public when he stated, "My thesis is that the really disreputable in Chicago are not those who are supposed to be disreputable but those who are clothed in purple and fine linen and occupy the high places in the synagoge [*sic*] and the Board of Trade. etc. etc." W. T. Stead to Henry Demarest Lloyd, January 12, 1894, Henry Demarest Lloyd Papers, Library of Congress, Washington, D.C.

26. W. T. Stead, *If Christ Came to Chicago! A Plea for the Union of All Who Love in the Service of All Who Suffer* (Chicago, 1894), 140–53; Whyte, *Life of Stead*, 2:51–52; Baylen, "A Victorian's 'Crusade,'" 427, 430.

27. Jane Addams, *Twenty Years at Hull-House* (New York, 1910), 122.

28. Ray Stannard Baker, who covered Stead for the *Chicago Record*, attributed the quote to one of his paper's editorial writers. Ray Stannard Baker, *American Chronicle* (New York, 1945), 31.

29. W. T. Stead to Henry Demarest Lloyd, February 20, 1894, Lloyd Papers.

30. Stead, *If Christ Came*, 17–32, 123–33. See p. 124 for quotation.

31. Ibid., 33–48, 243–60, 378–85, 446–53. See pp. 244–45 for quotations.

32. See [W. T. Stead], "Miss Frances E. Willard," *Review of Reviews*, October 1892, 333–47.

33. Whyte, *Life of Stead*, 2:44–45.

34. Stead, *If Christ Came*, 139–40, 368–74. See p. 139 for quotation.

35. Ibid., 49–68, 171–86, 207–42, 303–17, 378–79. See p. 306 for quotation.

36. Ibid., 49–68. See p. 67 for quotation.

37. Ibid., 319–26. See p. 319 for quotation.

38. Ibid., 283–302. See pp. 283, 292 for quotations.

39. Ginger, *Altgeld's America*, 172, 250, 279; Blake McKelvey, *The Urbanization of America, 1860–1915* (New Brunswick, N.J., 1963), 82, 103.

40. Stead, *If Christ Came*, 361.

41. Ibid., 69–97. See p. 91 for quotation.

42. Ibid., 99–121 (see pp. 103, 113 for quotations); Baker, *American Chronicle*, 29–30.

43. Stead, *If Christ Came*, 187–206. See p. 189 for quotations.

44. Ibid., 339–47. See pp. 339–40 for quotations.

45. Ibid., 187–206, 363–67, 421–42. See p. 422 for quotation.

46. Baylen, "A Victorian's 'Crusade,'" 431–33; [Stead], "If Christ Came," 508.

47. Graybar, *Albert Shaw*, 75.

48. Albert Shaw to W. T. Stead, December 30, 1893, Albert Shaw Papers, New York Public Library.

49. W. T. Stead to Albert Shaw, March 31, 1894, Shaw Papers.

50. Goldwin Smith, "If Christ Came to Chicago," *Contemporary Review*, September 1894, 380–89. See pp. 380, 387–89 for quotations.

51. [Stead], "My First Visit," 416–17.

52. [Stead], "If Christ Came," 510.

53. Stead to Shaw, March 31, 1894, Shaw Papers.

54. [Stead], "My First Visit," 412–13.

55. Ibid., 413.

56. W. T. Stead, *Chicago To-day; or, The Labour War in America* (1894; repr., New York, 1969), 5–6.

57. Ibid., 7–17. See pp. 8–9, 14 for quotations.

58. Ibid., 16, 18, 21–70. See pp. 16, 25 for quotations.

59. Ibid., 21–24, 71–86. See pp. 22–23, 72 for quotations.

60. Ibid., 248, 261–62.

61. Ibid., 263–73.

62. W. T. Stead, *Satan's Invisible World Displayed; or, Despairing Democracy* (New York, 1897), iii–ix, 33–34. See pp. iii, viii for quotations.

63. Ibid., 14–20. See pp. 14–15 for quotations.

64. Ibid., 20, 33–55, 255–300. See pp. 20, 41 for quotations.

65. Ibid., 58–68; Isabelle K. Savell, *Politics in the Gilded Age in New York State and Rockland County: A Biography of Senator Charles Lexow* (New City, N. Y., 1984), 9–20, 49–50, 53–54.

66. Stead, *Satan's Invisible World*, 26–27; Savell, *Politics in the Gilded Age*, 52–57; Richard L. McCormick, *From Realignment to Reform: Political Change in New York State, 1893–1910* (Ithaca, N.Y., 1981), 90–94; David C. Hammack, *Power and Society: Greater New York at the Turn of the Century* (New York, 1982), 185–229.

67. Stead, *Satan's Invisible World*, 218–26.

68. Ibid., 210–15; McKelvey, *Urbanization*, 102–3.

69. P. J. Waller, *Town, City, and Nation: England, 1850–1914* (Oxford, England, 1983), 240–53, 281–88.

70. Stead, *Satan's Invisible World*, 210–11.

71. Ibid., 204–7.

72. Ibid., 227–51.

73. Charles Carrington, *Rudyard Kipling: His Life and Work*, rev. ed. (London, 1978), 167–76, 221–94, 345–54; Howard C. Rice, *Rudyard Kipling in New England* (Brattleboro, Vt., 1951); James McG. Stewart, *Rudyard Kipling: A Bibliographical Catalogue* (Toronto, 1959) , 96–99, 172–78; Rudyard Kipling, *American Notes* (1899; repr., New York, 1974), 5–8.

74. Rudyard Kipling, *From Sea to Sea: Letters of Travel*, 2 vols. (New York, 1899), 2:120.

75. Ibid., 1:449; 2:13–15, 121–22, 154–57. See 1:449, and 2:122, 155, for quotations.

76. Ibid., 1:436–60; 2:3–17. See 2:3–4, 10, for quotations.

77. The Hooghly is a branch of the Ganges.

78. Kipling, *From Sea to Sea*, 2: 139–53. See 2:139–40 for quotations.

79. For the circumstances surrounding the Webbs' trip, and biographical background on the two figures, see the introduction to *Beatrice Webb's American Diary, 1898*, ed. David Shannon (Madison, Wis., 1963), vii–xv. More extensive information on the Webbs can be found in, among other sources, Kitty Muggeridge and Ruth Adam, *Beatrice Webb: A Life, 1858–1943* (London, 1967).

80. Beatrice Webb, "Round the English-Speaking World," unpublished

manuscript [prospective chapter for *Our Partnership*], 1, Passfield Papers, British Library of Political and Economic Science, London.

81. In 1899, on returning from their journey, Sidney apparently delivered a course of lectures at the London School of Economics, titled "The Actual Working of the American Constitution," but efforts to find a text, or even any account, of these lectures have been fruitless. For a reference to the lectures, see Richard Heathcote Heindel, *The American Impact on Great Britain, 1898–1914* (Philadelphia, 1940), 242.

82. Webb, "Round the English-Speaking World," 1–2.

83. This sentiment was expressed by Felix Frankfurter, to whom Beatrice had sent a manuscript of the chapter. See Felix Frankfurter to Beatrice Webb, August 6, 1936, Passfield Papers.

84. *The Diary of Beatrice Webb*, vol. 2, *1892–1905: All the Good Things of Life*, ed. Norman MacKenzie and Jeanne MacKenzie (Cambridge, Mass., 1983), 137.

85. Beatrice Webb, *Our Partnership*, ed. Barbara Drake and Margaret I. Cole (London, 1948), v.

86. *Beatrice Webb's American Diary*, 73, 142–43.

87. Ibid., 40–41, 136–37.

88. Ibid., 99–102, 107–9; Webb, "Round the English-Speaking World," 104.

89. Sidney Webb to George Bernard Shaw, June 5, 1898, in *The Letters of Sidney and Beatrice Webb*, vol. 2, *Partnership, 1892–1912*, ed. Norman MacKenzie (Cambridge, England, 1978), 69–70.; *Beatrice Webb's American Diary*, 109.

90. Sidney Webb to George Bernard Shaw, April 26, 1898, and Beatrice Webb to Catherine Courtney, April 29, 1898, in *Letters of Sidney and Beatrice Webb*, 2:61, 64.

91. *Beatrice Webb's American Diary*, 33–34, 44–45, 63. See p. 63 for quotation.

92. Ibid., 74–87. See p. 79 for quotation. Webb was also impressed by Theodore Roosevelt and Woodrow Wilson. However, Roosevelt was then assistant secretary of the navy in the McKinley administration, and when Webb met him on the brink of the Spanish-American War, she was disturbed by his jingoism. She found Wilson, then a professor at Princeton, to be an "attractive-minded man—somewhat like a young John Morley—literary in language, but with a peculiarly un-American insight into the actual working of institutions as distinguished from their normal constitution." Nevertheless, she said that in his *Congressional Government*, Wilson revealed less understanding of the subject than Bryce. See Webb, "Round the English-Speaking World," 52; *Beatrice Webb's American Diary*, 14–16, 23, 48–49 (pp. 48–49 for quotation).

93. *Beatrice Webb's American Diary*, 8–9.

94. Ibid., 114–15.

95. Ibid., 115–17. Beatrice wrote that she and Sidney concluded that checks and balances was a failed principle on the national level as well. The Constitution assured that there was no one responsible locus of authority in the government,

and they believed that at present the greatest power was wielded, informally, by a group that included Speaker of the House Thomas B. Reed, top party bosses like Republicans Marcus A. Hanna and Thomas Platt, and a few congressional committee chairmen. The Webbs also attacked that other pillar of American constitutional theory, federalism, which again, they felt, simply fragmented responsibility. See pp. 35–37, 117–18.

96. Ibid., 146–52. See p. 152 for quotation.

97. Webb, "Round the English-Speaking World," 31–32. This was the position Sidney adopted in his April 26, 1898, letter to Shaw, written from New York, in which he said, "All good men bemoan the evil state of their government machinery, but we have found hardly any glimmering of an idea as to how to get it any better. The 'Reform' party are feeble folk as a rule, with no more knowledge than an S.D.F. [Social Democratic Federation] branch, and no more energy than a mothers' meeting." See Sidney Webb to George Bernard Shaw, April 26, 1898, in *Letters of Sidney and Beatrice Webb*, 2:61.

98. Webb, "Round the English-Speaking World," 3–4.

2. The Bonds of Blood

1. Scott, *Life and Death*, 109, 117.

2. Whyte, *Life of Stead*, 2: 323.

3. [W. T. Stead], "To All English-Speaking Folk," *Review of Reviews*, January 1890, 15.

4. Reginald Horsman, *Race and Manifest Destiny: The Origins of American Racial Anglo-Saxonism* (Cambridge, Mass., 1981), 62–77.

5. Thomas F. Gossett, *Race: The History of an Idea in America* (Dallas, 1963), 98–101, 108–10.

6. Stuart Anderson, *Race and Rapprochement: Anglo-Saxonism and Anglo-American Relations, 1895–1904* (Rutherford, N.J., 1981), 17–61.

7. Bradford Perkins, *The Great Rapprochement: England and the United States, 1895–1914* (New York, 1968), 79–82.

8. [W. T. Stead], *Review of Reviews*, February 1891, 110–11; [W. T. Stead], *Review of Reviews*, April 1891, 324–26; [W. T. Stead], *Review of Reviews*, May 1891, 421.

9. John Higham, *Strangers in the Land: Patterns of American Nativism, 1860–1925* (New York, 1981 [1955]), 97–105, 106, 108, 112, 141–42, 162–63, 202–4; Barbara Miller Solomon, *Ancestors and Immigrants: A Changing New England Tradition* (Chicago, 1972 [1956]), 110–19, 202; Matthew Frye Jacobson, *Barbarian Virtues: The United States Encounters Foreign Peoples at Home and Abroad, 1876–1917* (New York, 2000), 196–200.

10. [Stead], *Review of Reviews*, April 1891, 319.

11. [Stead], *Review of Reviews*, March 1890, 181.

12. [Stead], *Review of Reviews*, February 1891, 107.

13. [W. T. Stead], *From the Old World to the New; or, A Christmas Story of the World's Fair, 1893* (London, 1892), preface.

14. Ibid., 2.

15. Whyte, *Life of Stead*, 1:64.

16. [Stead], *Old World to New*, 68.

17. Ibid., 37–38.

18. Ibid., 87–92. See pp. 91–92 for quotations.

19. Stead, *If Christ Came*, 341–45.

20. Stead, "My First Visit," 411.

21. W. T. Stead, "Jingoism in America," *Contemporary Review*, September 1895, 334–47. See p. 346 for quotation.

22. [W. T. Stead], *Review of Reviews*, January 1896, 8.

23. [W. T. Stead], "President Cleveland," *Review of Reviews*, January 1896, 22–24.

24. Ibid., 25, 31.

25. W. T. Stead, "To All English-Speaking Folk," *Review of Reviews*, February 1896, 99–101; Whyte, *Life of Stead*, 2:84–86. In February 1896 Stead published the pamphlet *Always Arbitrate before You Fight*.

26. [W. T. Stead], *Review of Reviews*, December 1896, 481.

27. [W. T. Stead], *Review of Reviews*, June 1897, 521.

28. Perkins, *Great Rapprochement*, 7–11, 13–20, 31–49, 62–63, 156–57, 312. Perkins argues that the rapprochement occurred between the two governments and the two cultures but points out that the new sentiments did not necessarily take hold below the elite classes in each society. See p. 6.

29. [W. T. Stead], *Review of Reviews*, April 1898, 316–19.

30. Ibid., 316. See also [W. T. Stead], *Review of Reviews*, May 1898, 425–26; [W. T. Stead], "Uncle Sam, Lord Chief Justice of America," *Review of Reviews*, May 1898, 433; [W. T. Stead], "The Anglo-American Alliance," *Review of Reviews*, May 1898, 453–54.

31. [Stead], *Review of Reviews*, April 1898, 316, 319; [Stead], *Review of Reviews*, May 1898, 426.

32. [Stead], *Review of Reviews*, May 1898, 426.

33. [W. T. Stead], *Review of Reviews*, December 1898, 538.

34. Perkins, *Great Rapprochement*, 64–88; Anderson, *Race and Rapprochement*, 112–29.

35. Paul A. Kramer, "Empires, Exceptions, and Anglo-Saxons: Race and Rule between the British and United States Empires, 1880–1910," *Journal of American History* 88 (March 2002): 1331–35.

36. [Stead], "Anglo-American Alliance," 453–54.

37. Perkins, *Great Rapprochement*, 52, 55–62.

38. [Stead], "Anglo-American Alliance," 454–58.

39. [W. T. Stead], "Why Not a British Celebration of the Fourth of July?" *Review of Reviews,* June 1898, 599–613; Perkins, *Great Rapprochement,* 54; Anderson, *Race and Rapprochement,* 119–20. See also W. T. Stead to Albert Shaw, April 10, 1898, May 18, 1898, Shaw Papers.

40. For information on Clarke, see *William Clarke: A Collection of His Writings,* ed. Herbert Burrows and John A. Hobson (London, 1908), xi–xxix; *Dictionary of Labour Biography,* ed. Joyce M. Bellamy and John Saville, vol. 2 (London, 1974), 94–98; Peter Weiler, "William Clarke: The Making and Unmaking of a Fabian Socialist," *Journal of British Studies* 14 (November 1974): 77–108; and George Bernard Shaw, ed., *Fabian Essays in Socialism* (London, 1889), 62–101. Clarke's views are dealt with intermittently in Peter Clarke, *Liberals and Social Democrats* (Cambridge, England, 1981 [1978]).

41. William Clarke to Henry Demarest Lloyd, [before October 28, 1898], Lloyd Papers. See also William Clarke to Henry Demarest Lloyd, October 28, 1898, December 5, [1898], Lloyd Papers.

42. William Clarke to Henry Demarest Lloyd, July 28, 1899, November 21, 1900, Lloyd Papers. For Clarke's views on the United States and Britain before the war, see William Clarke to Henry Demarest Lloyd, May 7, 1897, August 26, 1897, November 18, 1897, January 25, 1898, Lloyd Papers.

43. Christopher Hitchens, *Blood, Class, and Nostalgia: Anglo-American Ironies* (New York, 1990), 63–68.

44. W. T. Stead to Henry Demarest Lloyd, October 12, 1901, Lloyd Papers.

45. Stead, *Americanization,* 1–3.

46. Ibid., 3–4, 13–15. Stead also wrote of Britain as Athens and America as Persia, though the comparison does not make sense. He should logically have designated America as Rome, as Harold Macmillan later would. See p. 3.

47. Ibid., 4–13, 15. See pp. 5–6 for quotations.

48. Ibid., 15–26, 414. See pp. 19, 23, 414 for quotations.

49. Ibid., 403–12. He also focused on Rhodes, Carnegie, and Maxim in W. T. Stead, "The Future of the English-Speaking World," *Cosmopolitan,* January 1902, 341–46.

50. [W. T. Stead], *Review of Reviews,* July 1893, 4. William Waldorf Astor, the heir to the great New York fortune who settled in England, was one of these hybrids. Stead wanted to see Astor take a leading role in the Anglo-American unity movement, but at the same time he questioned the millionaire's capability and commitment. See [Stead] *Review of Reviews,* July 1893, 4; W. T. Stead to Andrew Carnegie, June 16, 1893, Shaw Papers; W. T. Stead to Albert Shaw, July 10, 1893, Shaw Papers; W. T. Stead to Albert Shaw, August 1, 1894, Shaw Papers; W. T. Stead to Andrew Carnegie, April 2, 1902, Andrew Carnegie Papers, Library of Congress, Washington, D.C.

51. Joseph Frazier Wall, *Andrew Carnegie* (New York, 1970), 421–70; [W. T. Stead], *Review of Reviews,* August 1892, 109.

52. Edition used is Andrew Carnegie, *Triumphant Democracy: Sixty Years' March of the Republic,* rev. ed. (New York, 1893). See Wall, *Andrew Carnegie,* 442–47.

53. Carnegie, *Triumphant Democracy,* 512–49; Wall, *Andrew Carnegie,* 674–80.

54. [Stead], *Review of Reviews,* July 1893, 3–4.

55. Stead to Carnegie, June 16, 1893, Shaw Papers.

56. In "A Look Ahead" Carnegie, despite his excessive praise of America in the bulk of *Triumphant Democracy,* refrained—in contrast to Stead—from touting the United States as the leader of the federation. In fact, he wrote that the premier place would belong to England, though this seemed to be held out as an enticement to the English, whom he saw as the most difficult group to bring into a federation. Carnegie, however, did not originally—it appears he subsequently changed his mind—make any provision in his federation scheme for allowing the English to maintain their monarchy, peerage, and established church. And later in the 1890s he expressed thoughts that would hardly have been attractive to the British; he spoke of the federation as an expanded United States of America, with the British gaining entry as approximately eight new states. See Carnegie, *Triumphant Democracy,* 512–49; Stead, *Americanization,* 405–12.

57. W. T. Stead to Andrew Carnegie, April 2, 1902, Carnegie Papers.

58. Scott, *Life and Death,* 196.

59. W. T. Stead to Albert Shaw, June 17, 1893, Shaw Papers.

60. Andrew Carnegie to W. T. Stead, May 16, 1892; and W. T. Stead to Andrew Carnegie, May 17, 1892; in Carnegie Papers.

61. Stead, *Americanization,* 403–4; Stead, "English-Speaking World," 342–43; Whyte, *Life of Stead,* 2:206; Perkins, *Rapprochement,* 80; Robert I. Rotberg, *The Founder: Cecil Rhodes and the Pursuit of Power* (New York, 1988), 100, 102, 281–82, 316, 416; J. G. Lockhart and C. M. Woodhouse, *Cecil Rhodes: The Colossus of Southern Africa* (New York, 1963), 421.

62. In his pro-Boer stance, Stead put himself at odds not only with Rhodes but with his two former protégés from the *Pall Mall Gazette,* Alfred Milner and Edmund Garrett. Rhodes chided Stead, in 1900, for not accepting the course of action in South Africa advocated by himself, Milner, and Garrett. He said, "Take, for instance, America. I read your book on Chicago. That tells me what America is. I would not set myself against you, because you have been there. Now in Africa *we* have been there. Why should you set yourself against us?" See Whyte, *Life of Stead,* 2:211–12.

63. W. T. Stead, ed., *The Last Will and Testament of Cecil John Rhodes* (London, 1902), 102; Stead, *Americanization,* 403–4; Stead, "English-Speaking World," 342–43; Whyte, *Life of Stead,* 2:207. See Stead, *Americanization,* 403, for quotation.

64. Rotberg, *Founder*, 101–2, 316, 416, 662–68; Lockhart and Woodridge, *Cecil Rhodes*, 421–24; Whyte, *Life of Stead*, 2:208–11. Rhodes set up scholarships for Germans, too, in 1901, but Parliament abolished these during the First World War.

65. Scott, *Life and Death*, 175, 178.

66. Stead, *Last Will and Testament*, 108; Stead to Carnegie, April 2, 1902, Carnegie Papers.

67. Scott, *Life and Death*, 174.

68. Whyte, *Life of Stead*, 2:210; Rotberg, *The Founder*, 678.

69. Stead to Carnegie, April 2, 1902, Carnegie Papers.

70. Stead, *Americanization*, 27–144. See pp. 27–28 for quotations.

71. Ibid., 318–29. See p. 323 for quotation.

72. Stead, in discussing the "American Invasion," dealt mainly with American exports to Britain, but Bradford Perkins, in *The Great Rapprochement*, defines the term as "the establishment of English subsidiaries or the control of English firms by American companies" (p. 124).

73. Stead, *Americanization*, 342; Philip S. Bagwell and G. E. Mingay, *Britain and America, 1850–1939: A Study of Economic Change* (London, 1970), 158; Graeme M. Holmes, *Britain and America: A Comparative Economic History, 1850–1939* (Newton Abbot, England, 1976), 71.

74. Stead, *Americanization*, 342–59. See pp. 346, 356 for quotations. Also, see Perkins, *Great Rapprochement*, 122. If Stead focused on the economic muscle of the United States, most of his fellow Britons at this time were actually more concerned about Germany, because while the bulk of American manufactures was designated for home consumption, Germany competed heavily with Britain in world markets. See Perkins, *Great Rapproachment*, 121.

75. Stead, *Americanization*, 381. President Theodore Roosevelt, as Stead surely knew, was well known for exalting the "strenuous life."

76. Stead, *Americanization*, 381–95.

77. Ibid., 439–44. See pp. 441, 443 for quotations.

78. Graybar, *Albert Shaw*, 56–57.

79. Whyte, *Life of Stead*, 2:271. There was a connection between Stead's spiritualism and his interest in America. The late Julia Ames, who Stead, believing himself to be her amanuensis, featured in his well-known *Letters from Julia* (1897), was an American. See Whyte, *Life of Stead*, 1:327.

80. [W. T. Stead], "Notes on My American Tour, Humorous and Otherwise," *Review of Reviews*, June 1907, 595–600.

81. [W. T. Stead], "The Daily Paper. By Its Founder, Editor, and Proprietor," *Review of Reviews*, December 1903, 571–83. See p. 571 for quotation. Also see Whyte, *Life of Stead*, 2:226.

82. Whyte, *Life of Stead*, 2:311–15.

3. The Promise of America

1. There is a substantial literature on H. G. Wells. The mandatory starting point for any exploration of his life is his own remarkable *Experiment in Autobiography: Discourses and Conclusions of a Very Ordinary Brain (Since 1866)* (New York, 1934). The two most recent full-scale scholarly biographies are Norman MacKenzie and Jeanne MacKenzie, *H. G. Wells* (New York, 1973) (published in Britain under the title *The Time Traveller*), and David C. Smith, *H. G. Wells: Desperately Mortal* (New Haven, Conn., 1986). The most helpful study of Wells in preparing this work was W. Warren Wagar, *H. G. Wells and the World State* (New Haven, Conn., 1961).

2. Wells, *Experiment*, 27–28, 35–38. See p. 28 for quotations.

3. Ibid., 68–69.

4. Ibid., 55, 74, 132, 140–42.

5. Pelling, *America and the British Left*, 55–59; John L. Thomas, *Alternative America: Henry George, Edward Bellamy, Henry Demarest Lloyd, and the Adversary Tradition* (Cambridge, Mass., 1983), 181–82, 195–99; A. M. McBriar, *Fabian Socialism and English Politics, 1884–1918* (Cambridge, England, 1962), 29–30.

6. Wells, *Experiment*, 192–93, 198, 216; MacKenzie and MacKenzie, *H. G. Wells*, 62.

7. H. G. Wells, *Anticipations of the Reaction of Mechanical and Scientific Progress upon Human Life and Thought* (New York, 1902 [1901]), 20, 54, 123, 261, 296–97.

8. Ibid., 111, 166, 169–70. See p. 111 for quotation.

9. H. G. Wells, *Mankind in the Making* (New York, 1904), 240–41, 248.

10. Ibid., 241–43.

11. Ibid., 242–46. See pp. 242, 245–46 for quotations.

12. Wells, *Anticipations*, 252–62, 282–87.

13. Wells, *Mankind*, 25; Wells, *Anticipations*, 282, 285–87.

14. MacKenzie and MacKenzie, *H. G. Wells*, 168–74, 184–86, 194–200, 205–20.

15. Wells further alienated the Old Gang by his conspicuous sexual exploits—particularly his affair with Amber Reeves, the daughter of a prominent Fabian, who bore him a child—and his frank sexual writings. Then Wells portrayed the Webbs unkindly in his novel *The New Machiavelli* (1911).

16. Mackenzie and MacKenzie, *H. G. Wells*, 177–78, 187, 201. In a 1904 letter to the English critic Edmund Gosse, Wells complained about his lack of literary standing in the United States and said, "I think even of going to America." See H. G. Wells to Edmund Gosse, November 26, 1904, *The Correspondence of H. G. Wells*, ed. David C. Smith, 4 vols. (London, 1998), 2:57–58.

17. MacKenzie and MacKenzie, *H. G. Wells*, 201.

18. H. G. Wells, *The Future in America: A Search After Realities* (New York, 1906), 1–3.

19. Wells defended his speculative approach in a 1902 lecture to the Royal Institution called "The Discovery of the Future."

20. Wells, *Future*, 6–13. See pp. 12–13 for quotations.

21. Ibid., 16.

22. Ibid., 16–19.

23. Ibid., 21–34. See pp. 21–22, 24 for quotations.

24. Ibid., 35–67. See pp. 36, 58, 60 for quotations.

25. Ibid., 32–33, 43–47, 133–51. See p. 33 for quotation.

26. In October 1906 MacQueen wrote Wells from the state prison in Trenton to thank him for becoming his "champion" and to say, "Your article in 'Harper's' has stirred things up." (See William MacQueen to H. G. Wells, October 24, 1906, H. G. Wells Papers, University of Illinois Library at Champaign-Urbana.) MacQueen was paroled in the spring of 1907. (See *New York Times*, May 2, 1907; M. G. Hope to H. G. Wells, May 3, 1907, Wells Papers.) The paucity of press coverage of MacQueen, however, reveals that Wells could not make the case a cause celebre.

27. Wells, *Future*, 167–84. See p. 168 for quotations.

28. Ibid., 185–202. See p. 191 for quotations. Wells's chapter on "The Tragedy of Color" is full of disparaging remarks about Jews. His anti-Semitism was not atypical in Britain at the turn of the century, particularly among socialists, who viewed Jews as prime offenders in the capitalist system. Wells sounded an anti-Semitic note in much of his writing, and he was also vocally anti-Zionist, but as the years went on, his anti-Catholicism was even more pronounced.

29. Wells, *Future*, 71–73. Wells's analysis is similar to Matthew Arnold's assertion that whereas European society was comprised of the Barbarians, Philistines, and Populace, only one component, the Philistines, could be found in America.

30. Wells, *Future*, 74–76.

31. Ibid., 79–82. Although Wells was ardently anti–Marxist, his economic analysis in many respects resembles Marx's. To a large extent the explanation lies in the fact that while Wells abhorred Marx's revolutionary enthusiasm—his advocacy of a class struggle and a dictatorship of the proletariat—he respected Marx in his role as economic historian. See H. G. Wells, *New Worlds for Old* (New York, 1908).

32. Wells, *Future*, 98–103. See pp. 99–101 for quotations.

33. Ibid., 152–66. See p. 153 for quotation.

34. Ibid., 82–84. Wells's attitude toward the trusts in this work represented a 180-degree turn from the position he had taken in *Anticipations*, in which he hailed the corporate structures as modern, efficient innovations. In *The Future in America*, he characterized the trusts as massive concentrations of property that had stifled competition and outmuscled state governments. It seems that the trust in the abstract appealed to him, but when he explored the trust in reality he found something completely different.

35. Wells, *Future,* 104–15. See p. 111 for quotation.

36. Ibid., 210–18. See pp. 210, 217 for quotations.

37. Wells wrote to his wife about his Washington socializing. See H. G. Wells to Amy Catherine Wells, May 12, 1906, Wells Papers.

38. Wells, *Future,* 236–45. See p. 236 for quotation.

39. J. Lincoln Steffens to H. G. Wells, [n.d.], Wells Papers.

40. Wells, *Future,* 245–53. See pp. 247–51 for quotations. In a supplement to his autobiography, published decades later, Wells revealed that upon leaving the White House, he took a cab to a house of prostitution and procured the services of a cultivated mulatto woman for whom he claimed he developed a lasting affection. See H. G. Wells, *H. G. Wells in Love: Postscript to an Experiment in Autobiography,* ed. G. P. Wells (Boston, 1984), 65–66.

41. Wells, *Future,* 152–53, 205–6, 254–59. See p. 257 for quotation.

42. For a discussion of the problem the term "progressivism" has posed for historians, see Daniel T. Rodgers, "In Search of Progressivism," *Reviews in American History* 10 (December 1982): 113–32.

43. See Kenneth O. Morgan, "The Future at Work: Anglo-American Progressivism 1890–1917," in *Contrast and Connection: Bicentennial Essays in Anglo-American History,* ed. H. C. Allen and Roger Thompson (London, 1976), 245–71; Morton Keller, "Anglo-American Politics, 1900–1930, in Anglo-American Perspective: A Case Study in Comparative History," *Comparative Studies in Society and History* 22 (July 1980): 458–77; Arthur Mann, "British Social Thought and American Reformers of the Progressive Era," *Mississippi Valley Historical Review* 42 (March 1956): 672–92; Kenneth McNaught, "American Progressives and the Great Society," *Journal of American History* 53 (December 1966): 504–20. See also Kloppenberg, *Uncertain Victory,* and Rodgers, *Atlantic Crossings,* which cover the ties between American and, more broadly, European reformers.

44. Wells knew Richard Haldane and Sir Edward Grey from their mutual participation in the group known as the "Coefficients," and in his autobiography he dismissed them both as rigid, uncreative minds. Grey, he wrote, had been a superficial country gentleman, and Haldane, despite his reputation as a scholar and philosopher, a second-rate thinker. Wells believed that Haldane had lacked the insight into the problems facing the modern world displayed by Roosevelt. None of Edwardian Britain's political figures, he felt, stood on the same pedestal as Roosevelt, whom he described as "the most vigorous brain in a conspicuously responsible position in all the world in 1906—when I was turning forty." See Wells, *Experiment,* 649, 651–52, 655–59 (p. 649 for quotation).

45. James Wellman, "A Nation's Will—The Future of America," *Harper's Weekly,* December 29, 1906, 1898; "Two Views of America," *Nation,* December 20, 1906, 537–38.

46. J. Lincoln Steffens to H. G. Wells, [n.d.]; Robert Hunter to H. G. Wells, January 8, 1907; in Wells Papers.

47. Franklin H. Giddings to H. G. Wells, February 6, 1907; Lester Ward to H. G. Wells, April 17, 1908; in Wells Papers.

48. Norman Hapgood to H. G. Wells, December 11, 1906, Wells Papers; John Graham Brooks to H. G. Wells, [1908], Wells Papers; John Graham Brooks, *As Others See Us: A Study of Progress in the United States* (New York, 1908), 274–93 (p. 276 for quotation).

49. Brooks to Wells, [1908]; William James to H. G. Wells, September 11, 1906; William James to H. G. Wells, December 4, 1906; William James to H. G. Wells, July 25, 1908; in Wells Papers.

50. Accounts of the famous Wells-James conflict can be found in all of the biographies of Wells, as well as in his autobiography. This summary, however, is particularly dependent upon the introduction to Leon Edel and Gordon N. Ray, eds., *Henry James and H. G. Wells: A Record of Their Friendship, Their Debate on the Art of Fiction, and Their Quarrel* (Urbana, Ill., 1958), 15–41.

51. The edition used here is Henry James, *The American Scene*, ed. Leon Edel (Bloomington, Ind., 1968). Edel's introduction provided information about James's trip as well as crucial insights into the text itself (see pp. vii–xxiv).

52. James Fullarton Muirhead, "Some Recent Books on the United States," *Atlantic*, October 1907, 566.

53. Henry James to H. G. Wells, November 8, 1906, in Edel and Ray, *Wells and James*, 113–15.

54. H. G. Wells to Henry James, March 20, 1907, in Edel and Ray, *Wells and James*, 116.

55. George Bernard Shaw, "A Nation of Villagers," *Everybody's Magazine*, December 1907, 861–65.

56. Dan H. Laurence, "'That Awful Country': Shaw in America," in *Shaw Abroad*, ed. Rodelle Weintraub (University Park, Pa., 1985), 279.

57. G. Bernard Shaw to Hamlin Garland, December 29, 1904, in *Bernard Shaw: Collected Letters*, vol. 2, *1898–1910*, ed. Dan H. Laurence (London, 1972), 476–78.

58. Ibid., 478.

59. Hesketh Pearson, *G.B.S.: A Full Length Portrait* (New York, 1942), 358.

60. Shaw to Garland, December 29, 1904, in *Shaw Letters*, 2:478.

61. *Observer* (London), February 15, *1920*.

62. G. Bernard Shaw to George Samuel, ca. December 23–24, 1899; G. Bernard Shaw to George Samuel, ca. December 26–30, 1899; in *Shaw Letters*, 2:121–26. See pp. 123, 125 for quotations.

63. Pearson, *G.B.S.*, 177; Frank Harris, *Bernard Shaw* (New York, 1931),

383–84; Michael Holroyd, *Bernard Shaw*, vol. 1, *1856–1898: The Search for Love* (London, 1988), 453, 462–63.

64. G. Bernard Shaw to Herbert S. Stone & Co., October 4, 1899, in *Shaw Letters*, 2:108–9; Pearson, *G.B.S.*, 44; Harris, *Shaw*, 383.

65. Pearson, *G.B.S.*, 211–12.

66. G. Bernard Shaw to Robert W. Welch (London correspondent of the *New York Times*), ca. September 22–23, 1905, in *Shaw Letters*, 2:559–62; *New York Times*, September 26, 1905.

67. Pearson, *G.B.S.*, 164–66; *Shaw Letters*, 2:573–74, 631–32.

68. G. Bernard Shaw to Editor of the *New York American*, [July 6, 1906], in *Shaw Letters*, 2:633.

69. G. Bernard Shaw to James Douglas, May 9, 1907, in *Shaw Letters*, 2: 683–84.

70. Shaw, "Nation of Villagers," 861–65. See p. 861 for quotation.

71. Ibid., 861–63. See p. 861 for quotation.

72. Ibid., 862–65. See p. 863 for quotation.

73. Ibid., 862, 865. See p. 865 for quotation.

74. Martin J. Wiener, *Between Two Worlds: The Political Thought of Graham Wallas* (Oxford, England, 1971), 43–47, 62–64; [newspaper unidentifiable], February 13, 1897, Clippings Scrapbook, Graham Wallas Papers, British Library of Political and Economic Science, London.

75. Graham Wallas, "The American Analogy," *Independent Review*, November 1903, 505–16. See p. 511 for quotations.

76. Ibid., 505–16; Wiener, *Two Worlds*, 81–85.

77. Edward A. Ross to Graham Wallas, April 9, 1909, Wallas Papers.

78. Wiener, *Two Worlds*, 166–69. See also A. Lawrence Lowell to Graham Wallas, December 5, 1908; William James to Graham Wallas, December 9, 1908; Jane Addams to Graham Wallas, December 21, 1908; in Wallas Papers.

79. Abraham Flexner to Graham Wallas, August 17, 1909, Wallas Papers.

80. Wiener, *Two Worlds*, 172.

81. Ibid., 131, 169–72, 187–88; Ronald Steel, *Walter Lippmann and the American Century* (Boston, 1980), 26–28, 45–49, 67.

82. Wiener, *Two Worlds*, 169, 172–73.

83. *Men and Ideas: Essays by Graham Wallas*, ed. May Wallas (London, 1940), 175–85.

84. Ibid., 175–76.

85. Ibid., 176–78.

86. Ibid., 178–85. See p. 180 for quotation.

87. H. G. Wells, "Roosevelt in Europe," *Collier's*, June 18, 1910, 27–28.

88. The essay originally appeared in 1909 in *Harmsworth's Popular Educator* under the title "Social Conditions and the Social Future in the United States of

America." J. R. Hammond, *Herbert George Wells: An Annotated Bibliography of His Works* (New York, 1977), 88.

89. H. G. Wells, *Social Forces in England and America* (New York, 1914), 357–65. See pp. 360–61, 364 for quotations. By the late 1920s, as revealed in such works as *The Open Conspiracy* and *The World of William Clissold*, Wells had come to believe that the best candidates for the world's saving elite would come from industry, and even advertising.

90. Wells, *Social Forces*, 345–46, 365–70. See pp. 345–46 for quotation.

91. Ibid., 339, 371–76. See pp. 372–74, 376 for quotations.

92. Ibid., 379–82. See p. 379 for quotation.

4. The Global Stage

1. Wells, *Experiment*, 568–612; MacKenzie and MacKenzie, *H. G. Wells*, 297–320; Smith, *H. G. Wells*, 217–42; Wagar, *World State*, 34–38.

2. Wagar, *World State*, 31–39, 99–100, 179–82, 247–50.

3. In his autobiography Wells expressed his displeasure with *What Is Coming?* which he called a product of his early, crude thinking about the war. He stated that the newspaper articles that make up the collection date from 1915, but J. R. Hammond, the Wells bibliographer, wrote that they were all published in the first half of 1916. See Wells, *Experiment*, 580–82, 593–94; Hammond, *Wells Bibliography*, 90.

4. H. G. Wells, *What Is Coming? A European Forecast* (New York, 1916), 215–18. See pp. 217–18 for quotations. Wells's sentiments on America appear mainly in chapter 10, which originally was published as an article in the *Daily Chronicle*. See Hammond, *Wells Bibliography*, 90.

5. In the same year Shaw went even further in discussing the precariousness of the Anglo-American relationship. He was repelled by the "sentimental twaddle" that he had heard not long before at a Mansion House celebration marking a century of peace between Britain and the United States, for actually the relationship had been characterized by "a hundred years of nagging and squabbling, of dislike and ill-natured stories, of fits of temper just saved from actual violence by pettiness and prudence; in short, of the least cordial relations of any two independent free nations in the world." It was an "illusion," he wrote, to think that Britain and America would never go to war. See George Bernard Shaw, "G. Bernard Shaw on Anglo-American Relations," *New York Times Magazine*, October 22, 1916, 2.

6. Wells, *What Is Coming?* 219–21.

7. Ibid., 224–26.

8. Arthur S. Link, *Woodrow Wilson: Revolution, War, and Peace* (Arlington Heights, Ill., 1979), 21–53; August Heckscher, *Woodrow Wilson* (New York, 1991), 390–93.

9. Arthur S. Link, *President Wilson and his English Critics: An Inaugural Lecture Delivered before the University of Oxford on 13 May 1959* (Oxford, England, 1959), 6–16; Laurence W. Martin, *Peace without Victory: Woodrow Wilson and the British Liberals* (New Haven, Conn., 1958), 68–69, 80–86.

10. George Bernard Shaw, "Open Letter to the President of the United States of America," *Nation* (London), November 7, 1914, 166; Barry Feinberg and Ronald Kasrils, *Bertrand Russell's America, 1896–1945* (New York, 1973), 65–69.

11. H. G. Wells, *Mr. Britling Sees It Through* (New York, 1916), 367–72. See pp. 367, 370–71 for quotations.

12. Ibid., 371–72.

13. Bainbridge Colby to Joseph Patrick Tumulty, December 21, 1917, in *The Papers of Woodrow Wilson*, vol. 45, *November 11, 1917–January 15, 1918*, ed. Arthur S. Link (Princeton, N.J., 1984), 340; Wells, *Experiment*, 604–5.

14. Wells, *Experiment*, 605–11.

15. Ibid., 605.

16. Woodrow Wilson to Bainbridge Colby, December 26, 1917, in *Papers of Wilson*, 45:363.

17. Wells, *Experiment*, 605; Link, *Woodrow Wilson*, 72–84; Martin, *Peace without Victory*, 132–62; John Morton Blum, *Woodrow Wilson and the Politics of Morality* (Boston, 1956), 144–48. Although he makes no claims about Wells's letter to Colby, David C. Smith does believe that Wells may have exerted some influence on the preparation of the Fourteen Points through, for example, his connections to Walter Lippmann. See Smith, *H. G. Wells*, 238, 551.

18. Wells, *Experiment*, 605.

19. Ibid., 607.

20. Ibid., 607–9.

21. Ibid., 608, 611.

22. Henry Arthur Jones, *My Dear Wells* (New York, 1921), 81–82; MacKenzie and MacKenzie, *H. G. Wells*, 328.

23. Wells, *Experiment*, 612–16; Wagar, *World State*, 39–40, 135–49; MacKenzie and MacKenzie, *H. G. Wells*, 319–24; H. G. Wells, *The Outline of History: Being a Plain History of Life and Mankind*, 2 vols. (New York, 1920).

24. Wells, *Outline*, 2:284, 294–95.

25. Ibid., 279.

26. Ibid., 503–7.

27. Ibid., 543–44.

28. Ibid., 544–45.

29. Ibid., 546, 549–50.

30. Ibid., 550–62. See pp. 557–58, 560 for quotations.

31. See H. G. Wells, *Russia in the Shadows* (New York, 1921 [1920]).

32. H. G. Wells, *The Salvaging of Civilization* (New York, 1922 [1921]), 45.

33. Ibid., 49–53. See pp. 49, 52–53 for quotations.

34. Ibid., 53–65. See p. 64 for quotation.

35. Ibid., 64–65.

36. Ibid., 49, 62–64. See pp. 62–64 for quotations.

37. See Harry N. Scheiber, *The Wilson Administration and Civil Liberties, 1917–1921* (Ithaca, N.Y., 1960); David M. Kennedy, *Over Here: The First World War and American Society* (New York, 1980); Robert K. Murray, *Red Scare: A Study in National Hysteria, 1919–1920* (Minneapolis, 1955); and Paul L. Murphy, *World War I and the Origin of Civil Liberties in the United States* (New York, 1979).

38. G. Bernard Shaw to Frank Harris, January 4, 1918, in *Bernard Shaw: Collected Letters*, vol. 3, *1911–1925*, ed. Dan H. Laurence (London, 1985), 520–21.

39. G. Bernard Shaw to Frank Harris, March 10, 1919, in *Shaw Letters*, 3:598.

40. George Bernard Shaw, *Heartbreak House, Great Catherine, and Playlets of the War* (New York, 1919), xxii–xxiv.

41. Graham Wallas, "The 'New Virility' in the United States," *New Statesman*, January 31, 1920, 487–88; Murray, *Red Scare*, 98–102, 192–200, 235–38, 242–44.

42. Wallas, "New Virility," 488.

43. Wallas, *Men and Ideas*, 108–13. See p. 109 for quotation.

44. Harold Laski to Graham Wallas, January 7, 19[20], Wallas Papers.

45. This discussion of Laski's background and tenure in North America is drawn from Isaac Kramnick and Barry Sheerman, *Harold Laski: A Life on the Left* (New York, 1993), 9–121; Kingsley Martin, *Harold Laski (1893–1950): A Biographical Memoir* (London, 1953), 9–46; and Granville Eastwood, *Harold Laski* (London, 1977), 1–19. For the relationship between Laski and Holmes, see Mark De-Wolfe Howe, ed., *Holmes-Laski Letters: The Correspondence of Mr. Justice Holmes and Harold J. Laski, 1916–1935*, 2 vols. (Cambridge, Mass., 1953).

46. Several studies of Laski's political thinking have been published in a variety of nations, most notably India. A recent biography with an emphasis on Laski's ideas is Michael Newman, *Harold Laski: A Political Biography* (Houndsmills, England, 1993). This discussion of his early ideology is drawn from Herbert A. Deane, *The Political Ideas of Harold J. Laski* (New York, 1955), 13–74, and Kramnick and Sheerman, *Harold Laski*, 72–75, 101–7, 122–26. Also useful for understanding Laski's political philosophy in the late 1910s is Henry Meyer Magid, *English Political Pluralism: The Problem of Freedom and Organization* (New York, 1941), 47–62.

47. Harold J. Laski to Oliver Wendell Holmes Jr., December 21, 1916; Harold J. Laski to Oliver Wendell Holmes Jr., January 10, 191[7]; Oliver Wendell Holmes Jr. to Harold J. Laski, January 13, 1917; Harold J. Laski to Oliver Wendell Holmes Jr., January 15, 191[7] ; in Howe, *Holmes-Laski*, 1:44, 53, 55–56. Similar sentiments can be found in Harold J. Laski to Graham Wallas, May 17, 1917, Wallas Papers.

48. Harold J. Laski, "The American University," *Manchester Guardian* (Anglo-American Number), January 27, 1920, 63. Laski anticipated some of the

themes he advanced in this article a year earlier when he contributed to the *New Republic* a review of Thorstein Veblen's *Higher Learning in America.* Harold J. Laski, "The Higher Learning in America," *New Republic,* January 11, 1919, 317–18.

49. For Laski's criticism of Oxford, see Harold J. Laski to Oliver Wendell Holmes Jr., March 21, 1920, in Howe, *Holmes-Laski,* 1:253; Harold J. Laski to Oliver Wendell Holmes Jr., February 20, 1928, in Howe, *Holmes-Laski,* 2:1028–29; Harold J. Laski to Oliver Wendell Holmes Jr., July 23, 1928, in Howe, *Holmes-Laski,* 2:1077; and Clifton Fadiman, ed., *I Believe: The Personal Philosophies of Certain Eminent Men and Women of Our Time* (New York, 1939), 139–40.

50. Laski to Wallas, May 17, 1917; Harold J. Laski to Graham Wallas, June 27, 1918; in Wallas Papers.

51. Harold J. Laski to Oliver Wendell Holmes Jr., October 30, 1916; Laski to Holmes, January 10, 191[7]; in Howe, *Holmes-Laski,* 1:32, 53.

52. Harold J. Laski, "Woodrow Wilson after Ten Years," *Forum and Century,* March 1931, 129–33. See p. 131 for quotation.

53. Harold J. Laski to Oliver Wendell Holmes Jr., March 18, 1919, in Howe, *Holmes-Laski,* 1:190n, 191; Harold J. Laski to Graham Wallas, May 12, 1919, Wallas Papers; Kramnick and Sheerman, *Harold Laski,* 125–28.

54. Murray, *Red Scare,* 122–34. For a narrative account of the strike, see Francis Russell, *A City in Terror: 1919, The Boston Police Strike* (New York, 1975).

55. Richard Hofstadter and Walter P. Metzgar, *The Development of Academic Freedom in the United States* (New York, 1955), 495–503; Kennedy, *Over Here,* 73–74; Murray, *Red Scare,* 169–70; Henry Aaron Yeomans, *Abbott Lawrence Lowell* (Cambridge, Mass., 1948), 308–27.

56. Kramnick and Sheerman, *Harold Laski,* 134; Martin, *Harold Laski,* 38.

57. Fadiman, *I Believe,* 141–42.

58. Harold J. Laski to Graham Wallas, September 21, 1919, Wallas Papers; Harold J. Laski to Oliver Wendell Holmes Jr., October 28, 1919, in Howe, *Holmes-Laski,* 1:218.

59. Eastwood, *Harold Laski,* 17.

60. Kramnick and Sheerman, *Harold Laski,* 134–40.

61. Harold J. Laski to Graham Wallas, September 30, 1919, Wallas Papers.

62. Harold J. Laski to Graham Wallas, December 21, 1919, Wallas Papers.

63. Martin, *Harold Laski,* 39.

64. Laski to Wallas, December 21, 1919, Wallas Papers.

65. Yeomans, *Abbott Lawrence Lowell,* 316–17.

66. A. Lawrence Lowell to Graham Wallas, May 26, 1921, Wallas Papers.

67. Laski to Holmes, October 28, 1919, in Howe, *Holmes-Laski,* 1:218.

68. Kramnick and Sheerman, *Harold Laski,* 132, 140; Martin, *Harold Laski,* 39; Eastwood, *Harold Laski,* 17.

69. A. Lawrence Lowell to Graham Wallas, January 18, 1921, Wallas Papers.

70. Fadiman, *I Believe*, 142. Laski alluded to his Harvard experience in *The American Democracy* (1948) when he wrote, "President Lowell informed one of his faculty in 1919 that he himself would resign if dismissal was the penalty for utterance in a famous dispute of that year; but he also told the lecturer in confidence not to expect promotion from the university." See Harold J. Laski, *The American Democracy: A Commentary and an Interpretation* (New York, 1948), 357.

71. Dean G. Acheson to Graham Wallas, February 11, 1920, Wallas Papers.

72. Kramnick and Sheerman, *Harold Laski*, 140–42; Martin, *Harold Laski*, 31, 38, 40–41; Acheson to Wallas, February 11, 1920, Wallas Papers.

73. Harold J. Laski to Oliver Wendell Holmes Jr., January 4, 1920, in Howe, *Holmes-Laski*, 1:230–31.

74. Graham Wallas to Gilbert Murray, November 1, 1919; Gilbert Murray to Graham Wallas, November 12, 1919; in Wallas Papers.

75. Kramnick and Sheerman, *Harold Laski*, 142–46; Martin, *Harold Laski*, 44; Harold J. Laski to Oliver Wendell Holmes Jr., March 28, 1920, in Howe, *Holmes-Laski*, 1:255.

76. Laski to Wallas, January 7, 19[20]; Harold Laski to Graham Wallas, February 27, 1920; Harold Laski to Graham Wallas, March 21, 1920; in Wallas Papers.

77. Harold J. Laski to Graham Wallas, June 4, 1920, Wallas Papers. See also Harold J. Laski to Oliver Wendell Holmes Jr., [May 15?, 1920], in Howe *Holmes-Laski*, 1:263.

78. Harold J. Laski to Roscoe Pound, December 28, 1920, Roscoe Pound Papers, Harvard Law School Library, Cambridge, Mass.

79. Fadiman, *I Believe*, 141–43.

80. Apparently, the *New York World* took the lead in commissioning the articles, which in America also appeared in the *Chicago Tribune*. In Britain the *Daily Mail* was carrying the series until Lord Northcliffe, who objected to Wells's strong criticisms of the French position at the conference, began to edit the reports. Wells was outraged, and eventually Lord Beaverbrook bought from his rival the rights to publish the articles. See H. G. Wells, *Washington and the Riddle of Peace* (New York, 1922), v; MacKenzie and MacKenzie, *H. G. Wells*, 332; Smith, *H. G. Wells*, 274.

81. This discussion is drawn from Thomas H. Buckley, *The United States and the Washington Conference, 1919–1922* (Knoxville, Tenn., 1970).

82. Wells, *Washington*, 5–6, 10–11. See pp. 5, 11 for quotations.

83. Ibid., 166–71. See pp. 167–68 for quotations.

84. Ibid., 171–74. See p. 172 for quotations.

85. Ibid., 175–78, 186. See pp. 176–77 for quotations. Despite the reverential tone he employed to discuss the origins of the Washington Conference, Wells was not oblivious to gritty political realities. He realized that the conference was the Republican answer to the Democratic-inspired League of Nations. See pp. 181–82.

86. Wells contrasted this event with similar ceremonies in Europe, which tended to be more somber. The Americans who attended the funeral had not, for the most part, actually lost loved ones in the war, and the ceremony was tinged with a heroic spirit. See Wells, *Washington*, 59–64.

87. Ibid., 64–67, 70, 196–205. See pp. 65, 203 for quotations.

88. Ibid., 245–55. See pp. 247–48, 253 for quotations. Actually, Wells himself had been quite scathing in his depiction of Congress in *The Future in America*.

89. Wells, *Washington*, 34–50. See pp. 48, 50 for quotations.

90. Ibid., 230–31, 302–3. See pp. 302–3 for quotations.

5. Main Street America

1. There is an immense literature on Chesterton, much of it written by self-styled Chestertonians. The posthumously published *Autobiography of G. K. Chesterton* (New York, 1936) is interesting, but the material included was chosen very selectively and can be unreliable. A valuable source is the massive, family-authorized biography written by a member of the Chesterton coterie: Maisie Ward, *Gilbert Keith Chesterton* (New York, 1943). Ward interviewed many who knew Chesterton, and she was the first to gain access to the Chesterton papers, long excerpts from which she published in the book. Three of the most substantial modern biographies are Michael Ffinch, *G. K. Chesterton* (San Francisco, 1986), Dudley Barker, *G. K. Chesterton: A Biography* (New York, 1973), and Alzina Stone Dale, *The Outline of Sanity: A Biography of G. K. Chesterton* (Grand Rapids, Mich., 1982). Two more-recent biographies are Michael Coren, *The Man Who Was G. K. Chesterton* (London, 1989) and Joseph Pearce, *Wisdom and Innocence: A Life of G. K. Chesterton* (London, 1996). General studies of note include Garry Wills, *Chesterton: Man and Mask* (New York, 1961), and a work by a disciple of Chesterton, Christopher Hollis, *The Mind of Chesterton* (Coral Gables, Fla., 1970).

2. This discussion of Chesterton's ideology is particularly dependent on two studies dealing with his political and social thought: Margaret Canovan, *G. K. Chesterton: Radical Populist* (New York, 1977) and Jay P. Corrin, *G. K. Chesterton and Hilaire Belloc: The Battle against Modernity* (Athens, Ohio, 1981).

3. Press Clippings Album No. 13, G. K. Chesterton Papers, Top Meadow Cottage, Beaconsfield, England (now housed in the British Library, London); Ffinch, *Chesterton*, 266, 272; Barker, *Chesterton*, 246; Dale, *Outline*, 224, 227.

4. Brocard Sewell, *Cecil Chesterton* (Faversham, England, 1975), 224, 227.

5. Cecil Chesterton, *A History of the United States*, ed. D. W. Brogan (London, 1940), xxxv.

6. Ibid., xxv.

7. Ibid., ix–xxiv. See p. x for quotation. Although Denis Brogan began to examine the United States in the prewar era—his book *Government of the People: A Study in the American Political System* dates from 1933—he was not treated in this

work because he was really one of the first professional scholars of America rather than one of the last amateur observers. Brogan was an American specialist in a way that his fellow academic Laski was not. On the other hand, Brogan did address himself to many of the broad themes that had always interested the British observers of the United States.

8. This discussion is derived from the entirety of Chesterton, *A History of the United States*. See p. 118 for quotation.

9. Press Cuttings Album No. 13, Chesterton Papers; Ffinch, *Chesterton*, 268–75.

10. Press Cuttings Album No. 13, Chesterton Papers; G. K. Chesterton, *What I Saw in America* (New York, 1922), 284.

11. Ford Madox Ford pursued this point in a 1927 book titled *New York Is Not America*.

12. Chesterton, *What I Saw*, 33–35, 38–44, 63–74. See p. 44 for quotation.

13. In deference to Chesterton's convictions, in this chapter the term "England," which he himself invariably employed, will generally be used in preference to the more comprehensive "Britain."

14. Chesterton, *What I Saw*, 1–15. See pp. 4, 7–8, 10 for quotations.

15. Ibid., 176, 260–69, 276–79. See pp. 176, 263 for quotations.

16. Ibid., 114–17, 275, 279–81. See pp. 116, 279, 281 for quotations.

17. Ibid., 141–57, 161–75. See p. 167 for quotation.

18. Ibid., 170–72. He also attributed the fads and restrictive rules to the control exerted by women in American society, and not merely the feminists whom he adamantly opposed. See pp. 172–74.

19. Ibid., 214–16.

20. G. K. Chesterton, *Fancies versus Fads* (London, 1923), 167–69.

21. Chesterton, *What I Saw*, 215–16.

22. Ibid., 216, 219–22. See pp. 220–21 for quotations.

23. Ibid., 217–25. See pp. 217, 222–23 for quotations.

24. Cecil Chesterton made a similar statement in his *History of the United States* at the end of his chapter entitled "The Jacksonian Revolution": "In the Monarchy an aristocratic parliamentarism won, and the Crown became a phantom. In the republic a popular sovereignty won, and the President became more than a king." See Chesterton, *History*, 119.

25. Chesterton, *What I Saw*, 75–76, 118–28. See pp. 120–21 for quotations.

26. Ibid., 15–17, 195–97, 281–82. See pp. 16, 282 for quotations.

27. Ibid., 16–17, 44–45, 197–200. See pp. 16, 44 for quotations.

28. Ibid., 100–114. See pp. 100–101, 103, for quotations.

29. Press Cuttings Album No. 13, Chesterton Papers; Chesterton, *What I Saw*, 44–45, 68, 89–90, 240 (pp. 44–45, 89 for quotations).

30. Chesterton, *What I Saw*, 88–90.

31. Ibid., 86, 89–94. See pp. 89–92 for quotations.

32. Ibid., 284–97. See p. 293 for quotation.

33. Actually, in the early 1920s, Wells conceded that he still harbored patriotic sentiments, but, unlike Chesterton, he felt apologetic about such feelings. He expressed this patriotism when he wrote, "I love the peculiar humor and kindly temper of an English crowd and the soft beauty of an English countryside with a strong, possessive passion. . . . I find it hard to think that other peoples matter quite as much as the English. I want to serve the English and to justify the English." See Wells, *Washington*, 13.

34. Chesterton, *What I Saw*, 226–42. See pp. 230–33, 241 for quotations.

35. Ibid., 139, 243.

36. John St. Loe Strachey to Theodore Roosevelt, April 3, 1906, John St. Loe Strachey Papers, House of Lords Record Office, London. Also see John St. Loe Strachey to Theodore Roosevelt, March 19, 1915, Strachey Papers.

37. This discussion is dependent upon the entirety of John St. Loe Strachey, *American Soundings: Being Castings of the Lead in the Shore-Waters of America, Social, Political, Literary, and Philosophic* (London, 1926).

38. John St. Loe Strachey to Laura Harlan, May 26, 1923, Strachey Papers.

39. John St. Loe Strachey to Theodore Roosevelt, March 10, 1906, Strachey Papers.

40. John St. Loe Strachey to Theodore Roosevelt, November 24, 1916, Strachey Papers. Also see John St. Loe Strachey to Theodore Roosevelt, September 23, 1916; John St. Loe Strachey to William C. Edgar, April 6, 1916; in Strachey Papers.

41. John St. Loe Strachey to James M. Beck, January 4, 1918; John St. Loe Strachey to Frank Aydelotte, August 22, 1918; in Strachey Papers.

42. Transcript of remarks delivered at the "English-Speaking Union of the United States Luncheon in Honor of John St. Loe Strachey, Esq.," New York, November 12, 1925, Strachey Papers.

43. Strachey, *American Soundings*, 16.

44. John St. Loe Strachey to Walter F. Angell, January 11, 1922, Strachey Papers. Also see John St. Loe Strachey to William Howard Taft, June 27, 1922, Strachey Papers.

45. G. K. Chesterton, *Charles Dickens* (London, 1925 [1906]), 91–110. See pp. 104, 106 for quotations.

46. Press Cuttings Album No. 13, Chesterton Papers. In the cartoon Dickens is saying, "I spoke very kindly of the Neil House in Columbus," and Chesterton is saying, "America must have changed a great deal since then."

47. Chesterton, *What I Saw*, 245–56. See p. 248 for quotation.

48. Ibid., 245–48, 255–56. See pp. 246, 248 for quotations.

49. A. N. Wilson, *Hilaire Belloc* (London, 1984), 29–41, 65–71, 75–80, 94; Robert Speaight, *The Life of Hilaire Belloc* (London, 1957), 52–61, 100–104, 114–15. See Speaight, *Life of Belloc*, 115, for quotation.

50. Speaight, *Life of Belloc*, 446, 448.

51. Hilaire Belloc to Mrs. Reginald Balfour, March 9, 1923, in *Letters from Hilaire Belloc*, ed. Robert Speaight (London, 1958), 135.

52. Wilson, *Hilaire Belloc*, 273.

53. Belloc to Balfour, March 9, 1923, in *Letters from Belloc*, 134.

54. Hilaire Belloc to Mrs. Reginald Balfour, March 17, 1923, in *Letters from Belloc*, 139.

55. Hilaire Belloc, *The Contrast* (New York, 1924 [1923]), 3–15. See pp. 9, 12–13 for quotations.

56. Ibid., 26–44. See pp. 32, 37, 41–42 for quotations.

57. Ibid., 45–48, 52–62, 69–71, 76–82. See pp. 55, 57, 78 for quotations.

58. Ibid., 48–51.

59. Ibid., 62–68. See pp. 63, 66, 68 for quotations.

60. Ibid., 69, 71–75. See pp. 69, 71–72, 74–75 for quotations.

61. Ibid., 84–85, 96–104, 109–11. See pp. 84, 100, 110 for quotations.

62. Ibid., 114–28. See pp. 117, 119 for quotations.

63. Ibid., 147–49, 154–66. See p. 147 for quotation.

64. Wilson, *Hilaire Belloc*, 272.

65. Speaight, *Life of Belloc*, 455–56.

66. Belloc, *The Contrast*, 167–80. While Belloc took a tough line in *The Contrast*, in a letter he wrote to his friend Charlotte Balfour from the United States, he revealed a surprising sympathy for the Jews. The malice shown toward the Jews in America was "very hard" on them, he acknowledged, and the restrictions made them feel like "enemies" in their own land. He remarked, "What a life! Fancy some wretched man coming with his family from, say, Poland, and landing into this!" See Speaight, *Life of Belloc*, 454–55.

67. Leonard Dinnerstein, *Antisemitism in America* (New York, 1994), 78–104.

68. See Albert Lee, *Henry Ford and the Jews* (New York, 1980); and Neil Baldwin, *Henry Ford and the Jews: The Mass Production of Hate* (New York, 2001).

69. Chesterton, *What I Saw*, 135–38, Press Cuttings Album No. 13, Chesterton Papers.

70. Belloc, *The Contrast*, 242–63. See p. 244 for quotations.

71. Ibid., 69–70.

72. H. G. Wells, *A Year of Prophesying* (London, 1924), 115.

73. Ibid., 115–20. See pp. 117–18, 120 for quotations.

74. Gordon N. Ray, *H. G. Wells and Rebecca West* (New Haven, Conn., 1974), 128–30, 148–58 (see p. 130 for quotation); J. R. Hammond, *H. G. Wells and Rebecca West* (New York, 1991), 142, 149–50.

75. Rebecca West, "How America Strikes Me," *Sunday Times* (London), May 25, June 1, June 8, 1924.

76. Wells, *Prophesying*, 208–11.

77. West, "How America Strikes Me," May 25, 1924.

78. Rebecca West, "These American Men," *Harper's*, September 1925,

448–56; Rebecca West, "These American Women," *Harper's*, November 1925, 722–30. For West's impressions of the sights she saw in America in, respectively, New York and the rest of the country, see Rebecca West, "Impressions of America," *New Republic*, December 10, 1924, 65–68; Rebecca West, "Travelling in America," *New Republic*, December 24, 1924, 112–15.

79. Box on U.S.A. Visit, 1930–1931, Chesterton Papers; Ffinch, *Chesterton*, 321–26; Rufus William Rauch, ed., *A Chesterton Celebration at the University of Notre Dame: Commemorating the Fiftieth Anniversary of G. K. Chesterton's Visiting Professorship in the Fall Term of 1930* (Notre Dame, Ind., 1983), 1–6.

80. *St. Louis Globe-Democrat*, January 24, 1931, in U.S.A. Box, Chesterton Papers.

81. *Sidelights* contains a collection of essays on America Chesterton wrote for a variety of publications following his trip there, as well as several pieces on society in modern Britain and some literary criticism.

82. *Syracuse (N.Y.) Post-Standard* [no date], in U.S.A. Box, Chesterton Papers.

83. G. K. Chesterton, *Sidelights on New London and Newer York and Other Essays* (London, 1932), 85–91. See pp. 85–86, 88, 91 for quotations.

84. Ibid., 119–20.

85. G. K. Chesterton, *The Thing: Why I Am a Catholic* (New York, 1930), 1–11; G. K. Chesterton, *All Is Grist: A Book of Essays* (New York, 1932), 58–64; Fred Hobson, *Mencken: A Life* (New York, 1994), 189–92, 211–12, 283; Terry Teachout, *The Skeptic: A Life of H. L. Mencken* (New York, 2002), 125. See Chesterton, *All Is Grist*, 62, for quotations.

86. *Sidelights*, 148–52. See pp. 148, 150–51 for quotations.

87. G. K. Chesterton, *Come to Think of It . . . : A Book of Essays* (London, 1930), 210–14. See pp. 211–12 for quotations.

88. Ibid., 215–19. See pp. 215, 218 for quotations.

89. Chesterton, *Sidelights*, 153–58. See pp. 154–55 for quotations.

90. G. K. Chesterton, *Generally Speaking* (London, 1937 [1928]), 189–95.

91. Chesterton, *Sidelights*, 100–108.

92. Ibid., 103–4.

93. Chesterton, *Come to Think*, 200–204. See pp. 203–4 for quotations.

94. Chesterton, *Sidelights*, 167–69.

95. Ibid., 111–14. See p. 114 for quotation.

96. U.S.A. Box, Chesterton Papers.

97. Chesterton, *Sidelights*, 111, 115–17, 124–25.

98. H. G. Wells to Sinclair Lewis, September 13, 1922, Wells Papers (also in *Correspondence of H. G. Wells*, 3:110); H. G. Wells, *The Way the World Is Going* (Garden City, N.Y., 1929), 248–56.

99. *New York Times*, December 19, 1930.

100. Chesterton, *Sidelights*, 109–14. See pp. 110–11 for quotations.

101. Ibid., 125–35. See pp. 126, 128 for quotations.

102. Ibid., 159–63, 165–66. See pp. 159–60, 162–63 for quotations.
103. Ibid., 129, 166–67, 176–84. See pp. 183–84 for quotations.
104. Ibid., 169–74. See p. 170 for quotation.

6. The New Deals

1. For Laski's Harvard years, see chapter 4.
2. MacKenzie and MacKenzie, *H. G. Wells*, 374–76.
3. This discussion is based primarily on Deane, *Political Ideas of Laski*.
4. See Harold J. Laski, *Democracy in Crisis* (Chapel Hill, N.C., 1933).
5. Deane, *Political Ideas of Laski*, 146–49; Kramnick and Sheerman, *Harold Laski*, 295–302.
6. Harold J. Laski to Oliver Wendell Holmes Jr., July 28, 1925, August 15, 1925, May 29, 1927; in Howe, *Holmes-Laski*, 2:770, 776, 946.
7. See Harold J. Laski to Oliver Wendell Holmes Jr., July 23, 1928, October 27, 1931, June 4, 1932, October 30, 1932; in Howe, *Holmes-Laski*, 2:1077, 1333, 1390, 1412.
8. Harold J. Laski, "The American Scene," *New Republic*, January 18, 1928, 237–39.
9. Harold J. Laski to Oliver Wendell Holmes Jr., August 6, 1931, in Howe, *Holmes-Laski*, 2:1322.
10. Harold J. Laski to Oliver Wendell Holmes Jr., March 23, 1931, in Howe, *Holmes-Laski*, 2:1312.
11. Harold J. Laski to Oliver Wendell Holmes Jr., October 15, 1932, in Howe, *Holmes-Laski*, 2:1411.
12. Harold J. Laski to Felix Frankfurter, August 18, 1928, Felix Frankfurter Papers, Library of Congress, Washington, D.C. (viewed on microfilm at the Harvard Law School Library, Cambridge, Mass.).
13. Harold J. Laski, "President Hoover," *Living Age*, June 1931, 367–69 (reprinted from the *Daily Herald* of London).
14. Harold J. Laski to Felix Frankfurter, February 11, 1932, Frankfurter Papers.
15. See Harold J. Laski to Felix Frankfurter, October 29, 1932, November 12, 1932, Frankfurter Papers. Also see Harold J. Laski to Oliver Wendell Holmes Jr., November 12, 1932, in Howe, *Holmes-Laski*, 2:1416.
16. Laski to Frankfurter, October 29, 1932, Frankfurter Papers. Roosevelt won with a substantial 57.4 percent popular-vote majority, and Thomas garnered only 881,951 votes. See George Brown Tyndall, *America: A Narrative History*, 2nd ed., 2 vols. (New York, 1988), 2:A33.
17. See Laski to Frankfurter, October 29, 1932, Frankfurter Papers. Also see Harold J. Laski to Oliver Wendell Holmes Jr., October 15, 1932, October 30, 1932; in Howe, *Holmes-Laski*, 2:1412–13. Although he was pessimistic about the

prospects, Laski wished to see Frankfurter named solicitor general. Roosevelt, counter to Laski's expectations, did offer the position to Frankfurter, who turned it down. But through the 1930s Frankfurter remained a part of FDR's inner circle, and in 1939 he was appointed to the Supreme Court.

18. William E. Leuchtenburg, *Franklin D. Roosevelt and the New Deal, 1932–1940* (New York, 1963), 9–11.

19. Laski to Frankfurter, November 12, 1932, Frankfurter Papers.

20. Laski to Holmes, November 12, 1932, in Howe, *Holmes-Laski*, 2:1416.

21. Harold J. Laski, "Roosevelt, the Fighter," *Living Age*, January 1933, 386–87 (reprinted from the *Daily Herald*).

22. Ibid., 387–88.

23. Ibid., 386–88. See p. 388 for quotations.

24. Harold J. Laski to Oliver Wendell Holmes Jr., May 7, 1933, in Howe, *Holmes-Laski*, 2:1437; Kramnick and Sheerman, *Harold Laski*, 390, 393.

25. Harold J. Laski, "President Roosevelt and Foreign Opinion," *Yale Review* 22 (June 1933): 707–13. See pp. 707, 713 for quotations.

26. H. G. Wells, *The Shape of Things to Come* (New York, 1933), 115–22, 174. See pp. 115–16, 174 for quotations.

27. H. G. Wells, "Roosevelt's Place in History," *Liberty*, December 9, 1933, 20–22, 24. See p. 22 for quotation.

28. Ibid. See pp. 20, 24 for quotations.

29. Ibid., 21–22, 24. See pp. 22, 24 for quotation.

30. Apparently, Laski penned the article nine months after Roosevelt took office—that is, in December 1933. The piece was also published in Britain as one of Laski's Socialist League pamphlets. Harold J. Laski, "The Roosevelt Experiment," *Atlantic*, February 1934, 148; Kramnick and Sheerman, *Harold Laski*, 309.

31. Laski, "The Roosevelt Experiment," 143.

32. Ibid., 145–49.

33. Ibid., 148–52. See p. 148 for quotations.

34. Ibid., 144, 152–53.

35. Franklin D. Roosevelt to H. G. Wells, December 4, 1933, Wells Papers.

36. H. G. Wells to Franklin D. Roosevelt, April 14, 1934, Wells Papers (also in *Correspondence of H. G. Wells*, 3:524).

37. Wells, *Experiment*, 679. Hoover's secretary, Lawrence Richey, protested against Wells's description of the Hoover White House and his characterization of the president as "a sickly overworked and overwhelmed man." According to Richey, Wells never actually got into the White House on his October 1931 trip because Hoover would agree to meet with him only in the "executive offices," where they talked for no more than two minutes. See *New York Times*, October 28, 1934.

38. Wells, *Experiment*, 679–80.

39. Ibid., 680–82.

40. Ibid., 681–83.

41. Ibid., 672, 675–78. See pp. 672, 676–77 for quotations.

42. Ibid., 671–75. See pp. 674–75 for quotations.

43. Ellis W. Hawley, *The New Deal and the Problem of Monopoly: A Study in Economic Ambivalence* (Princeton, N.J., 1966), 84–85, 95–97; Leuchtenburg, *Franklin D. Roosevelt*, 67–68.

44. Wells, *Experiment*, 673–74. Actually, Darrow's position turned out to be more complex, or confusing, than represented by Wells. Darrow and his former law partner, William Thompson, issued a "supplementary report" advocating socialism as a viable alternative to monopoly capitalism. See Hawley, *New Deal*, 96; Leuchtenburg, *Franklin D. Roosevelt*, 67–68.

45. Wells, *Experiment*, 675, 682–83. See p. 675 for quotation.

46. Ibid., 667–68, 683. See p. 668 for quotation.

47. This discussion is based upon Wells, *Russia*. For quotation see MacKenzie and MacKenzie, *H. G. Wells*, 326.

48. *Stalin-Wells Talk: The Verbatim Record and a Discussion by G. Bernard Shaw, H. G. Wells, J. M. Keynes, Ernst Toller, and Others* (London, 1934), 4–8. See pp. 4–5 for quotations.

49. Wells, *Experiment*, 683–702. See p. 689 for quotation.

50. Muggeridge and Adam, *Beatrice Webb*, 234–36; Harold J. Laski, "Balance Sheet of a New Civilization," *Saturday Review of Literature*, March 7, 1936, 3–4.

51. *The Letters of Sidney and Beatrice Webb*, vol. 3, *Pilgrimage, 1912–1947*, ed. Norman Mackenzie (Cambridge, England, 1978), 405.

52. *Stalin-Wells Talk*, 21–27.

53. Pearson, *G.B.S.*, 51–52, 322–32; Michael Holroyd, *Bernard Shaw*, vol. 3, *1918–50: The Lure of Fantasy* (New York, 1991), 221–55; *Bernard Shaw: Collected Letters*, vol. 4, *1926–1950*, ed. Dan H. Laurence (London, 1988), 457–58.

54. *New York Times*, October 12, 1931.

55. Laurence, "That Awful Country," 282–84.

56. *New York Times*, March 12, 1933. Shaw denied making the comment, but Keller stuck to her story. See *New York Times*, April 9, 1933.

57. *New York Times*, March 25, 1933.

58. Laurence, "That Awful Country," 284–86.

59. Ibid., 286–89.

60. G. Bernard Shaw to Lowell Brentano, March 14, 1933; G. Bernard Shaw to Ethel Warner, March 14, 1933; in *Shaw Letters*, 4:327–329.

61. George Bernard Shaw, "The Future of Political Science in America," *Political Quarterly* 4 (July–September 1933): 313–40.

62. Ibid., 316–18.

63. Following the address there was some discussion in the *New York Times* as to whether there ever was an "Uncle Jonathan" or whether Shaw had confused "Brother Jonathan" and "Uncle Sam." See *New York Times*, April 13, 14, 17, 1933.

64. Shaw, "Future of Political Science," 313–16, 319, 322–23. See pp. 314–15, 319 for quotations.

65. Ibid., 319–20.

66. Ibid., 325, 335–36, 338–39.

67. Laurence, "That Awful Country," 289–91.

68. *New York Times*, April 13, 1933.

69. *New York Times*, April 14, 1933.

70. Shaw, "Future of Political Science," 336.

71. *New York Times*, April 13, 1933.

72. Laurence, "That Awful Country," 292–95.

73. *New York Times*, February 5, 1936.

74. *New York Times*, February 8, 1936.

75. G. Bernard Shaw to J. Unsworth, July 29, 1941, in *Shaw Letters*, 4:608. Shaw's attraction to Hitler and Mussolini declined during the 1930s; he particularly deplored the Nazi treatment of Jews. See *Shaw Letters*, 4:457.

76. Franklin D. Roosevelt to H. G. Wells, February 13, 1935, Wells Papers.

77. Leuchtenburg, *Franklin D. Roosevelt*, 146–48.

78. Hawley, *New Deal*, 130–46.

79. Leuchtenburg, *Franklin D. Roosevelt*, 146.

80. H. G. Wells, *The New America: The New World* (New York, 1935), 31–38. See pp. 31–32 for quotation. Actually, Wells exaggerated the faith he had invested in the Brain Trust in 1934.

81. Wells, *The New America*, 33–38. See p. 37 for quotations. Wells's assessment of the philosophical inconsistency within the Roosevelt administration was shrewd. The president's advisers were broken into competing factions: Brandeisians like Felix Frankfurter, central planners like Rexford Tugwell, and proponents of organized business leadership like Raymond Moley. See Leuchtenburg, *Franklin D. Roosevelt*, 35–36; Hawley, *New Deal*, 19–52, 132–35, 283–92.

82. Wells, *New America*, 25–30. See p. 27 for quotation.

83. Ibid., 28–30.

84. Ibid., 30–31, 42–43. Wells's refusal to dismiss Long, Coughlin, and the other "raucous voices" as merely villains or clowns but to view them as spokesmen for legitimate public sentiment comports with the conclusions of one of the more recent students of these figures. See Alan Brinkley, *Voices of Protest: Huey Long, Father Coughlin, and the Great Depression* (New York, 1982).

85. Wells, *New America*, 38–40, 76.

86. Ibid., 37, 40–42, 76–77. See pp. 37, 42, 77 for quotations.

87. Ibid., 50–54, 56.

88. Ibid., 56–58.

89. Ibid., 58–61.

90. Ibid., 10–20, 22, 74–75. See pp. 14–16, 20 for quotations.

91. Kramnick and Sheerman, *Harold Laski*, 326–30; Martin, *Harold Laski*, 93–94; Eastwood, *Harold Laski*, 48–51.

92. Kramnick and Sheerman, *Harold Laski,* 398–99.

93. Harold J. Laski to Felix Frankfurter, October 18, 1935, Frankfurter Papers.

94. Harold J. Laski, "America Is Waking Up," *Living Age,* September 1936, 69 (reprinted from the *Daily Herald*).

95. Ibid., 69–71.

96. Harold J. Laski to Felix Frankfurter, August 8, 1934, Frankfurter Papers.

97. Harold J. Laski, "Laski on America," *Living Age,* August 1935, 554–55 (reprinted from the *Daily Herald*). See also Harold J. Laski to Felix Frankfurter, December 28, 1935, Frankfurter Papers.

98. Harold J. Laski, "A Word to the Republicans: The Duty of an Opposition Party," *Harper's,* October 1935, 513–23.

99. Ibid., 517, 518, 520.

100. Harold J. Laski, "A Formula for Conservatives," *Harper's,* September 1937, 382–90.

101. Roosevelt himself made such a comparison after he heard about the Schechter decision. Harold J. Laski to Felix Frankfurter, May 28, 1935, Frankfurter Papers.; Leuchtenburg, *Franklin D. Roosevelt,* 145.

102. Laski to Frankfurter, May 28, 1935, Frankfurter Papers.

103. Laski admitted that in writing the piece, he was guided by the articles Thomas Reed Powell had recently published in the *Harvard Law Review.* See Harold J. Laski to Thomas Reed Powell, January 15, 1936, Thomas Reed Powell Papers, Harvard Law School Library, Cambridge, Mass.

104. Harold J. Laski, "The Crisis in the New Deal," *Manchester Guardian,* January 14, 1936, 9–10 (reprinted in *Living Age,* March 1936, 85–87).

105. Harold J. Laski to unnamed friend affiliated with the *St. Louis Post Dispatch,* undated but probably late 1936, Frankfurter Papers.

106. Harold J. Laski, "An Englishman Looks at the Court," *New Republic,* March 3, 1937, 104–5.

107. Harold J. Laski to Felix Frankfurter, August 3, 1937, Frankfurter Papers.

108. William E. Leuchtenburg, *The Supreme Court Reborn: The Constitutional Revolution in the Age of Roosevelt* (New York, 1995), 134–54; Barry Cushman, *Rethinking the New Deal Court: The Structure of a Constitutional Revolution* (New York, 1998), 11–25; Joseph Alsop and Turner Catledge, *The 168 Days* (1938; repr., New York, 1973), 71–76; Michael E. Parrish, *Felix Frankfurter and His Times: The Reform Years* (New York, 1982), 267–70.

109. *New York Times,* October 22, 28, 1937.

110. H. G. Wells, "New Americans," *Collier's,* February 5, 1938, 14–15.

111. Ibid., 15, 44.

112. H. G. Wells, *World Brain* (London, 1938 [1935]), 103–15. See pp. 103, 105 for quotations. Wells titled the appendix "The Fall in America 1937." Another appendix to *World Brain* consists of "Transatlantic Misunderstandings,"

an article Wells contributed to the January 15, 1938, issue of *Liberty*. In this piece he discussed the misconceptions that worked against the unity of the English-speaking community, such as the British failure to recognize the heterogeneity of American society and the American suspicion that "British propaganda" was pervasive. See Wells, *World Brain*, 116–23.

113. Leuchtenburg, *Franklin D. Roosevelt*, 256–57, 261–65, 272–74, 347; Alan Brinkley, *The End of Reform: New Deal Liberalism in Recession and War* (New York, 1995), 3.

114. Kramnick and Sheerman, *Harold Laski*, 390, 403.

115. The first five volumes of *The Public Papers and Addresses of Franklin D. Roosevelt*, edited by Samuel I. Rosenman, cover the years 1928 to 1936. Eventually eight more volumes were published.

116. Harold J. Laski, "The Public Papers and Addresses of Franklin D. Roosevelt," *University of Chicago Law Review* 6 (December 1938): 23–26.

117. Ibid., 23–24, 31.

118. Ibid., 31–35. See pp. 31–32, 34 for quotations.

7. The Businessman's America

1. Laski apparently disapproved of these organizations and, like Chesterton, of the notion of a special Anglo-American kinship. In a 1932 letter to Frankfurter concerning the conservative American jurist James Beck, whom Laski called "beneath contempt," he wrote, "I believe that the people who appointed Beck to give the George Watson lectures are much the same people as those who run the English Speaking Union and the Pilgrim. If, like Beck, you are one of the four best lickspittles in America, ever prepared to talk tripe about Anglo-American cousinship (which really means the ability to understand each other's insults) you can always be certain of honour in this country." See Harold J. Laski to Felix Frankfurter, July 26, 1932, Frankfurter Papers.

2. Harold J. Laski, "England, Meet America!" *Living Age*, September 1939, 86–89 (reprinted from *Time and Tide*). See pp. 86–87 for quotations.

3. Harold J. Laski, "America Revisited: I," *New Republic*, July 12, 1939, 267–69; Harold J. Laski, "America Revisited: II," *New Republic*, July 19, 1939, 295–97. See Laski, "America Revisited: I," 267, for quotation.

4. Laski, "America Revisited: I," 268–69.

5. Kramnick and Sheerman, *Harold Laski*, 405–7; Harold J. Laski to Franklin D. Roosevelt, March 12, 1939, Frankfurter Papers. The following year Bertrand Russell did not fare as well as Laski, when community opposition forced him to lose out on an appointment at City College of New York. Feinberg and Kasrils, *Bertrand Russell's America*, 126–67.

6. Harold J. Laski, "The Obsolescence of Federalism," *New Republic*, May 3, 1939, 367–69. See p. 368 for quotation. The kernel of this article can be found in Laski, "Public Papers," p. 29.

7. Martin, *Harold Laski*, 121; Harold J. Laski to Franklin D. Roosevelt, August 19, 1939, Frankfurter Papers.

8. See Laski, "Public Papers," especially pp. 26–30.

9. Martin, *Harold Laski*, 121. The dedication was included in the British edition of the book but for some reason omitted from the American edition, though Laski referred to the dedication in his preface. See Harold J. Laski, *The American Presidency: An Interpretation* (New York, 1940), viii.

10. Laski to Roosevelt, August 19, 1939, Frankfurter Papers.

11. Laski, *American Presidency*, vii.

12. Harold J. Laski, "The American Political System," *Harper's*, June 1928, 20–28. See p. 20 for quotation.

13. See Harold J. Laski, *Parliamentary Government in England: A Commentary* (New York, 1938), especially pp. 116, 118, 136–39, 184–89, 201–2 for the comparison between the British and American political systems.

14. Laski, *American Presidency*, 1–12. See pp. 4, 7 for quotations. Laski also wrote that Bryce consorted only with, and was heavily influenced by, elite, educated Americans, the same kind of people he mixed with in England. See pp. 6–7. Actually, Laski himself was accused of mingling with only one segment of American society, the intellectual left.

15. Laski, *American Presidency*, 8–9, 41–53. See p. 8 for quotation. Laski's opposition to Bryce on this issue was new. Until 1939 he substantially agreed with Bryce's assessment of the quality of American presidents. See Laski, "American Political System," 21; Laski, "Public Papers," 28–29; Laski, *Parliamentary Government*, 202–3.

16. Laski, *American Presidency*, 24, 111–65, 245–47. See pp. 24, 116, 123, 159 for quotations. Laski viewed foreign policy as the successful exception in American government. He approved of the fact that in this realm Congress followed the lead of the president. The Senate's obstructiveness in the ratification of treaties, he felt, had been exaggerated, and he believed that maintaining some congressional role in foreign relations was important. See pp. 166–207.

17. Ibid., 70–110.

18. Ibid., 11–16, 114, 121, 155–56, 237–40, 243. See p. 155 for quotation.

19. Ibid., 24–25, 158–59, 162–65, 270–75, 277–78. See p. 163 for quotation.

20. Ibid., 245, 247–60, 275–78. See pp. 249, 251 for quotations.

21. Kramnick and Sheerman, *Harold Laski*, 412–14, 426–28, 432–34, 469–70; Martin, *Harold Laski*, 138–55.

22. Harold J. Laski to Franklin D. Roosevelt, July 26, 1940, Frankfurter Papers.

23. Harold J. Laski to Felix Frankfurter, November 24, 1940, Frankfurter Papers. See also Harold J. Laski to Felix Frankfurter, November 4, 1940, Frankfurter Papers.

24. Harold J. Laski to Franklin D. Roosevelt, February 18, 1941, Frankfurter Papers.

25. Harold J. Laski to Felix Frankfurter, August 13, 1941, Frankfurter Papers.

26. Harold J. Laski, *The Strategy of Freedom: An Open Letter to American Youth* (New York, 1941). See p. 78 for quotation.

27. Harold J. Laski to Felix Frankfurter, August 16, 1942, Frankfurter Papers.

28. Harold J. Laski to Felix Frankfurter, September 16, 1942, Frankfurter Papers. At the same time Laski was urging Roosevelt to exert his influence on the course of world events, some Americans were concerned about Laski's influence over the president. Amos Pinchot, a progressive who had become a staunch opponent of FDR, charged that Laski was the "intellectual switchboard" of a group of New Dealers and British Labourites who were leading America toward socialism. He argued that Laski, despite his disdain for the American system, had easy access to the White House and influenced Roosevelt more than any other man except for Frankfurter. The "Roosevelt program" was really the "Laski program." See Amos R. Pinchot, "The Roosevelt-Laski Scheme," *Scribner's Commentator*, October 1941, 62–68 (pp. 63, 65 for quotations). A member of the House of Representatives from Massachusetts read Pinchot's entire article into the *Congressional Record*. See Martin, *Harold Laski*, 196n.

29. Kramnick and Sheerman, *Harold Laski*, 20–26, 434–43; Martin, *Harold Laski*, 149–62. Laski never did get to America during the war years, for he would go, even though he did not need such permission, only if he received authorization from the highest level of government. In August 1941, even before he was snubbed by Churchill, he complained to Frankfurter of the treatment he was receiving. "They practically boycott me on the B.B.C. service to America," he wrote. Furthermore, not only was the government uninterested in sending him to the United States, but he heard that "a great lady" said in fact "the main task of English visitors to the U.S. was to counteract the kind of picture I was drawing to Americans of the English future." See Laski to Frankfurter, August 13, 1941, Frankfurter Papers; Martin, *Harold Laski*, 153–54.

30. Harold J. Laski, "The Public Papers and Addresses of Franklin D. Roosevelt," *University of Chicago Law Review* 9 (April 1942): 389–92.

31. Laski to Frankfurter, August 16, 1942, Frankfurter Papers. See also Laski to Frankfurter, August 13, 1941, September 16, 1942, Frankfurter Papers.

32. Harold J. Laski to Franklin D. Roosevelt, December 27, 1942, Frankfurter Papers.

33. Kramnick and Sheerman, *Harold Laski*, 450–56.

34. Harold J. Laski, "Open Letter to President Roosevelt," *New Statesman and Nation*, April 10, 1943, 236–37.

35. Harold J. Laski to Felix Frankfurter, December 26, 1943, Frankfurter Papers.

36. Harold J. Laski to Franklin D. Roosevelt, December 5, 1944, Frankfurter Papers.

37. Harold J. Laski to Felix Frankfurter, April 1, 1945, April 14, 1945, Frankfurter Papers.

38. Harold J. Laski to Felix Frankfurter, June 4, 1945, Frankfurter Papers.

39. MacKenzie and MacKenzie, *H. G. Wells*, 421–24; Smith, *H. G. Wells*, 428–34.

40. MacKenzie and MacKenzie, *H. G. Wells*, 423–24; H. G. Wells, *The Rights of Man; or, What Are We Fighting For?* (London, 1940), 59–61, 102–8.

41. The Sankey Declaration is published in various works of Wells from the 1940s, including H. G. Wells, *Guide to the New World: A Handbook of Constructive World Revolution* (London, 1941), 49–54.

42. Wells, *Rights of Man*, 13, 19–22, 29, 55–56.

43. Roosevelt was one of the world figures to whom Wells sent a draft of the declaration as it was being constructed. See Smith, *H. G. Wells*, 432; Franklin D. Roosevelt to H. G. Wells, November 9, 1939, Wells Papers. The Sankey Declaration may have been one of the sources that the president drew upon in formulating the Four Freedoms. See James MacGregor Burns, *Roosevelt: The Soldier of Freedom* (New York, 1970), 33–34.

44. MacKenzie and MacKenzie, *H. G. Wells*, 424; A. West, *H. G. Wells*, 151; Wells, *Wells in Love*, 224.

45. *New York Times*, October 4, 1940. Also see *New York Times*, October 5, 1940.

46. *New York Times*, October 9, 1940.

47. *New York Times*, October 24, 1940. Also see *New York Times*, October 13, 1940; *New York Times*, October 17, 1940.

48. Phillip E. Buck to H. G. Wells, September 26, 1941; H. G. Wells to Phillip E. Buck, October 10, 1941; in Wells Papers.

49. Wells, *Guide*, 89–91.

50. *New York Times*, October 5, 1940; Wells, *Wells in Love*, 224.

51. Wells, *Guide*, 20, 91.

52. H. G. Wells, *'42 to '44: A Contemporary Memoir upon Human Behaviour during the Crisis of the World Revolution* (London, 1944), 88.

53. Wells, *Guide*, 91.

54. Wells, *'42 to '44*, 85.

55. Wells, *Guide*, 29, 80; Wells, *'42 to '44*, 88–89.

56. H. G. Wells to Wendell Willkie, October 30, 1943, Wells Papers (also in *Correspondence of H. G. Wells*, 4:458). For Willkie's response, see Wendell Willkie to H. G. Wells, December 3, 1943, Wells Papers.

57. Wells, *'42 to '44*, 89.

58. Burns, *Soldier of Freedom*, 357–61.

59. See Wendell L. Willkie, *One World* (New York, 1943), and Steve Neal, *Dark Horse: A Biography of Wendell Willkie* (Garden City, N.Y., 1984), 262–64.

60. Wells, *'42 to '44*, 88–90.

61. H. G. Wells to Florence Lamont, January 21, 1944, Wells Papers (also in *Correspondence of H. G. Wells*, 4:485). The idea that Roosevelt would put Willkie in his administration was not a farfetched notion thought up by Wells. By the spring of 1944, Roosevelt and Willkie had become such kindred spirits that the president was not only considering him for a cabinet post but for the number-two spot on the Democratic ticket in November. Furthermore, both men felt alienated from their parties, and there was indirect discussion between the two of them in the summer of 1944 about eventually establishing a new progressive party. Willkie, however, died in October. See Neal, *Dark Horse*, 308–24; Burns, *Soldier of Freedom*, 510–13. Also see Wells, *'42 to '44*, 90.

62. MacKenzie and MacKenzie, *H. G. Wells*, 421–47.

63. Wells, *Guide*, 79–82.

64. H. G. Wells, *Phoenix: A Summary of the Inescapable Conditions of World Reorganisation* (London, 1942), 105.

65. Wells, *Guide*, 88–89.

66. Wells, *Phoenix*, 176.

67. Wells, *'42 to '44*, 81–85, 89–90. See pp. 82, 89 for quotations.

68. Kramnick and Sheerman, *Harold Laski*, 479–90, 505–6, 516–62; Martin, *Harold Laski*, 168–205; Eastwood, *Harold Laski*, 120–55; Deane, *Political Ideas of Laski*, 202, 290.

69. Kramnick and Sheerman, *Harold Laski*, 451, 453–54, 490–91, 494–503. See p. 496 for quotation.

70. This discussion is dependent upon Alonzo L. Hamby, *Beyond the New Deal: Harry S. Truman and American Liberalism* (New York, 1973).

71. Harold J. Laski, "If Roosevelt Had Lived," *Nation*, April 13, 1946, 419–21. See p. 419 for quotation.

72. Harold J. Laski, "The American Political Scene: The Case of Harry Truman," *Nation*, November 16, 1946, 548–51. See pp. 548–49 for quotations.

73. Harold J. Laski to Felix Frankfurter, May 2, 1947, Frankfurter Papers.

74. Harold J. Laski, "The American Political Scene: The Return to Reaction," *Nation*, November 30, 1946, 609–12; Harold J. Laski, "America—1947," *Nation*, December 13, 1947, 641–44. See Laski, "Return to Reaction," 610–11 for quotations.

75. Laski, "America—1947," 641, 644.

76. Harold J. Laski to Felix Frankfurter, September 27, 1947, Frankfurter Papers.

77. Deane, *Political Ideas of Laski*, 310–29; Kramnick and Sheerman, *Harold Laski*, 507–9, 512–13, 559–64; Harold J. Laski, "My Impressions of Stalin," *New Republic*, October 14, 1946, 478–79; Harold J. Laski, "Civil Liberties in the Soviet Union," *New Republic*, October 21, 1946, 507–8; Harold J. Laski, "What Democracy Means in Russia," *New Republic*, October 28, 1946, 551–52.

78. Laski, "Civil Liberties," 507–8.

79. Laski, "America—1947," 642.

80. Laski to Frankfurter, May 2, 1947, Frankfurter Papers. See also Harold J. Laski to Felix Frankfurter, July 16, 1947, Frankfurter Papers.

81. Harold J. Laski, "The American Myth and the Peace," *Nation*, February 12, 1944, 181–82.

82. Laski, "America—1947," 642.

83. Harold J. Laski, "Socialist Europe vs. US Capitalism," *New Republic*, August 4, 1947, 6.

84. Laski to Frankfurter, July 16, 1947; Harold J. Laski to Felix Frankfurter, September 11, 1947; Laski to Frankfurter, September 27, 1947; in Frankfurter Papers.

85. Laski, "If Roosevelt," 420; Harold J. Laski, "The American Political Scene: The Bankruptcy of Parties," *Nation*, November 23, 1946, 582–84; Laski, "America—1947," 642–43. See Laski, "If Roosevelt," p. 420, and Laski, "America—1947," p. 642, for quotations.

86. Martin, *Harold Laski*, 261; Lindsay Rogers, "What We Must Do to Be Saved," *Saturday Review*, June 12, 1948, 13.

87. Laski, *American Democracy*, ix.

88. See Ibid., 348–60; Harold J. Laski, "The American College President," *Harper's*, February 1932, 311–20.

89. Laski, *American Democracy*, ix.

90. Ibid., 7, 27–28, 42–43. See p. 43 for quotation.

91. Ibid., 5–6, 33–34, 47–49, 53–54. See pp. 5–6, 48–49 for quotations.

92. Ibid., 11–13, 39, 42–43, 55–56, 715–16. See pp. 12, 39, 56 for quotations.

93. Ibid., 3, 8–9, 13, 17–18, 23–26, 40, 57, 61, 717–18. See pp. 8, 18, 25 for quotations.

94. Ibid., 3, 8–9, 17–18, 23, 40, 59, 717–18. See pp. 18, 23, 717 for quotations.

95. Ibid., 5, 13, 17–19, 25, 34, 52, 70–71, 167, 176–77, 732–33, 745–50, 753, 755–56. See p. 52 for quotation.

96. Ibid., 17–19, 52, 228, 745, 756. See pp. 17, 52 for quotations.

97. Ibid., 165–77, 185–99. See pp. 165, 170, 199 for quotations.

98. Ibid., 21–22, 35–36, 68–71, 77, 81, 177–78, 182, 188–89, 235, 437–40, 733–35, 748–55, 758–59. See p. 177 for quotation.

99. Ibid., 129–37, 178–82, 200–263, 735–36. See p. 258 for quotation.

100. Two prominent political scientists, Lindsay Rogers and Charles E. Merriam, were both essentially negative, while the distinguished historians Perry Miller and George Dangerfield were inclined to be more generous toward Laski. See Rogers, "What We Must Do," 12–13; Charles E. Merriam, Review of Laski, *American Democracy*, in *American Political Science Review* 42 (December 1948): 1211–13; Perry Miller, "Harold Laski on America," *Nation*, June 19, 1948, 689–91; George Dangerfield, "The American Experience," *New Republic*, June 14, 1948, 21–22.

101. Henry Steele Commager, Review of Laski, *American Democracy*, in *New York Herald Tribune Weekly Book Review*, June 6, 1948, 1–2.

102. Arthur M. Schlesinger Jr., "Laski and the Democratic Way," *New York Times Book Review*, June 6, 1948, 1, 32–33.

103. Oscar Handlin, "American Culture—The Socialist View," *Atlantic*, February 1949, 59–62. See p. 59 for quotations.

104. Handlin's *Atlantic* piece had not yet appeared, but Howe made specific reference to Schlesinger's review in the *New York Times Book Review*.

105. Mark DeWolfe Howe, Review of Laski, *American Democracy*, in *Harvard Law Review* 62 (December 1948): 338–44. See pp. 338–39 for quotations.

106. Kramnick and Sheerman, *Harold Laski*, 512, 571.

107. Harold J. Laski, "Truman's Task in Europe," *New Republic*, December 20, 1948, 10–13.

108. Kramnick and Sheerman, *Harold Laski*, 571.

109. Harold J. Laski, "America, Good and Bad: Power, Leadership, and Fear," *Nation*, June 25, 1949, 701–2; Harold J. Laski, "America, Good and Bad: Parties, Unions, Press," *Nation*, July 2, 1949, 8–10; Harold J. Laski, "America, Good and Bad: Fears and Opportunities," *Nation*, July 9, 1949, 34–35. See Laski, "Power, Leadership," p. 702, and Laski, "Fear and Opportunities," p. 34, for quotations.

110. Laski, "Power, Leadership," 701; Laski, "Fears and Opportunities," 33–34. Laski was very sympathetic to the plight of Alger Hiss, the former State Department official who was accused of having engaged in espionage for the Soviets and convicted of perjury in 1950. See Harold J. Laski to Felix Frankfurter, August 8, 1949, Frankfurter Papers; Deane, *Political Ideas of Laski*, 328.

111. Harold J. Laski, "Liberty on the American Campus: A Bill of Particulars," *Nation*, August 13, 1949, 149–51; Kramnick and Sheerman, *Harold Laski*, 572; Martin, *Harold Laski*, 247–49.

112. Harold J. Laski, "Liberty on the American Campus: Conditional Freedom," *Nation*, August 20, 1949, 181–82; Laski, "Bill of Particulars," 149–51. See Laski, "Bill of Particulars," 150, for quotation.

113. Martin, *Harold Laski*, 252.

Conclusion

1. See Fussell, *Abroad*, 37–50.

2. Mitford exposed the funeral industry in *The American Way of Death* (1963), and for decades Alistair Cooke broadcast his weekly "Letter from America" over the BBC.

3. See *The Moronic Inferno: And Other Visits to America* (1986).

4. Raban wrote *Old Glory: An American Voyage* (1981), an account of his journey down the Mississippi River, and *Hunting Mister Heartbreak: A Discovery of*

America (1990), which spotlights four geographically and culturally distinct American towns. He is also the author of a study of the settlement of the plains, titled *Bad Land: An American Romance* (1996).

5. For a sampling of American history written by British historians in the 1960s and 1970s, see David H. Burton, ed., *American History—British Historians* (Chicago, 1978).

Bibliography

Manuscript Sources

Andrew Carnegie Papers, Library of Congress, Washington, D.C.

G. K. Chesterton Papers, Top Meadow Cottage, Beaconsfield, England (now housed in the British Library, London).

Felix Frankfurter Papers, Library of Congress, Washington, D.C. (viewed on microfilm at the Harvard Law School Library, Cambridge, Mass.).

Henry Demarest Lloyd Papers, Library of Congress, Washington, D.C.

Passfield Papers, British Library of Political and Economic Science, London.

Roscoe Pound Papers, Harvard Law School Library, Cambridge, Mass.

Thomas Reed Powell Papers, Harvard Law School Library, Cambridge, Mass.

Albert Shaw Papers, New York Public Library, New York.

John St. Loe Strachey Papers, House of Lords Record Office, London.

Graham Wallas Papers, British Library of Political and Economic Science, London.

H. G. Wells Papers, University of Illinois Library at Champaign-Urbana.

Periodicals and Newspapers

Review of Reviews (London), 1890–1900, and selected issues thereafter.

New York Times, 1930–1940 (selected issues).

Published Primary Sources

Addams, Jane. *Twenty Years at Hull-House*. New York, 1910.

Amis, Martin. *The Moronic Inferno: And Other Visits to America*. New York, 1987 [1986].

Arnold, Matthew. *The Complete Prose Works of Matthew Arnold*. Vol. 10, *Philistinism in England and America*. Ed. R. H. Super. Ann Arbor, Mich., 1974.

———. *The Complete Prose Works of Matthew Arnold*. Vol. 11, *The Last Word*. Ed. R. H. Super. Ann Arbor, Mich., 1977.

Baker, Ray Stannard. *American Chronicle*. New York, 1945.

Belloc, Hilaire. *The Contrast*. New York, 1924 [1923].

———. *Letters from Hilaire Belloc*. Ed. Robert Speaight. London, 1958.

Brooks, John Graham. *As Others See Us: A Study of Progress in the United States*. New York, 1908.

Bryce, James. *The American Commonwealth*, 3 vols. 1888. Reprint, New York, 1973.

Burton, David H., ed. *American History—British Historians*. Chicago, 1978.

Carnegie, Andrew. *Triumphant Democracy: Sixty Years' March of the Republic*. Rev. ed. New York, 1893.

Chesterton, Cecil. *A History of the United States*. Ed. D. W. Brogan. London, 1940.

Chesterton, G. K. *All Is Grist: A Book of Essays*. New York, 1932.

———. *The Autobiography of G. K. Chesterton*. New York, 1936.

———. *Charles Dickens*. London, 1925 [1906].

———. *Come to Think of It . . . : A Book of Essays*. London, 1930.

———. *Fancies versus Fads*. London, 1923.

———. *Generally Speaking*. London, 1937 [1928].

———. *Sidelights on New London and Newer York, and Other Essays*. London, 1932.

———. *The Thing: Why I Am a Catholic*. New York, 1930.

———. *What I Saw in America*. New York, 1922.

Clarke, William. *William Clarke: A Collection of His Writings*. Ed. Herbert Burrows and John A. Hobson. London, 1908.

Commager, Henry Steele. Review of Laski, *American Democracy*. In *New York Herald Tribune Weekly Book Review*, June 6, 1948, 1–2.

———, ed. *America in Perspective: The United States through Foreign Eyes*. New York, 1947.

Dangerfield, George. "The American Experience." *New Republic*, June 14, 1948, 21–22.

Dickens, Charles. *American Notes and Pictures from Italy*. Oxford, England, 1978 [1957].

———. *The Letters of Charles Dickens*. Vol. 3, *1842–1843*. Ed. Madeline House, Graham Storey, and Kathleen Tillotson. Oxford, England, 1974.

———. *Martin Chuzzlewit*. Oxford, England, 1984.

Edel, Leon, and Gordon N. Ray, eds. *Henry James and H. G. Wells: A Record of Their Friendship, Their Debate on the Art of Fiction, and Their Quarrel*. Urbana, Ill., 1958.

"England and America: Contrasts: A Conversation between Bernard Shaw and Archibald Henderson." *Bookman* (New York), January 1925, 578–83.

Fadiman, Clifton, ed. *I Believe: The Personal Philosophies of Certain Eminent Men and Women of Our Time*. New York, 1939.

Hall, Basil. *Travels in North America, in the Years 1827 and 1828*. 3 vols. Edinburgh, 1829.

Handlin, Oscar. "American Culture—The Socialist View." *Atlantic*, February 1949, 59–62.

Howe, Mark DeWolfe. Review of Laski, *American Democracy*. In *Harvard Law Review* 62 (December 1948): 338–44.

———, ed. *Holmes-Laski Letters: The Correspondence of Mr. Justice Holmes and Harold J. Laski, 1916–1935.* 2 vols. Cambridge, Mass., 1953.

James, Henry. *The American Scene.* Ed. Leon Edel. Bloomington, Ind., 1968.

Jones, Henry Arthur. *My Dear Wells.* New York, 1921.

Kemble, Frances Anne. *Journal of a Residence on a Georgian Plantation in 1838–1839.* Ed. John A. Scott. New York, 1961.

Kipling, Rudyard. *American Notes.* 1899. Reprint, New York, 1974.

———. *From Sea to Sea: Letters of Travel.* 2 vols. New York, 1899.

Laski, Harold J. "America, Good and Bad: Fears and Opportunities." *Nation*, July 9, 1949, 33–35.

———. "America, Good and Bad: Parties, Union, Press." *Nation*, July 2, 1949, 8–10.

———. "America, Good and Bad: Power, Leadership, and Fear." *Nation*, June 25, 1949, 701–3.

———. "America Is Waking Up." *Living Age*, September 1936, 69–71.

———. "America—1947." *Nation*, December 13, 1947, 641–44.

———. "America Revisited: I." *New Republic*, July 12, 1939, 267–69.

———. "America Revisited: II." *New Republic*, July 19, 1939, 295–97.

———. "The American College President." *Harper's*, February 1932, 311–20.

———. *The American Democracy: A Commentary and an Interpretation.* New York, 1948.

———. "The American Myth and the Peace." *Nation*, February 12, 1944, 180–84.

———. "The American Political Scene: The Bankruptcy of Parties." *Nation*, November 23, 1946, 582–84.

———. "The American Political Scene: The Case of Harry Truman." *Nation*, November 16, 1946, 548–51.

———. "The American Political Scene: The Return to Reaction." *Nation*, November 30, 1946, 609–12.

———. "The American Political System." *Harper's*, June 1928, 20–28.

———. *The American Presidency: An Interpretation.* New York, 1940.

———. "The American Scene." *New Republic*, January 18, 1928, 237–39.

———. "The American University." *Manchester Guardian* (Anglo-American Number), January 27, 1920, 63.

———. "Balance Sheet of a New Civilization." *Saturday Review of Literature*, March 7, 1936, 3–4.

———. "Civil Liberties in the Soviet Union." *New Republic*, October 21, 1946, 507–8.

———. "The Crisis in the New Deal." *Manchester Guardian*, January 14, 1936, 9–10.

———. *Democracy in Crisis.* Chapel Hill, N.C., 1933.

———. "England, Meet America!" *Living Age*, September 1939, 86–89.

———. "An Englishman Looks at the Court." *New Republic*, March 3, 1937, 104–5.

——. "A Formula for Conservatives." *Harper's*, September 1937, 382–90.

——. "The Higher Learning in America." *New Republic*, January 11, 1919, 317–18.

——. "If Roosevelt Had Lived." *Nation*, April 13, 1946, 419–21.

——. "Laski on America." *Living Age*, August 1935, 554–55.

——. "Liberty on the American Campus: A Bill of Particulars." *Nation*, August 13, 1949, 149–51.

——. "Liberty on the American Campus: Conditional Freedom." *Nation*, August 20, 1949, 181–82.

——. "My Impressions of Stalin." *New Republic*, October 14, 1946, 478–79.

——. "The Obsolescence of Federalism." *New Republic*, May 3, 1939, 367–69.

——. "Open Letter to President Roosevelt." *New Statesman and Nation*, April 10, 1943, 236–37.

——. *Parliamentary Government in England: A Commentary*. New York, 1938.

——. "President Hoover." *Living Age*, June 1931, 367–69.

——. "President Roosevelt and Foreign Opinion." *Yale Review* 22 (June 1933): 707–13.

——. "The Public Papers and Addresses of Franklin D. Roosevelt." *University of Chicago Law Review* 6 (December 1938): 23–35.

——. "The Public Papers and Addresses of Franklin D. Roosevelt." *University of Chicago Law Review* 9 (April 1942): 379–92.

——. "The Roosevelt Experiment." *Atlantic*, February 1934, 143–53.

——. "Roosevelt, the Fighter." *Living Age*, January 1933, 386–88.

——. "Socialist Europe vs. US Capitalism." *New Republic*, August 4, 1947, 6.

——. *The Strategy of Freedom: An Open Letter to American Youth*. New York, 1941.

——. "The Temper of the Present Time." *New Republic*, February 18, 1920, 335–38.

——. "Truman's Task in Europe." *New Republic*, December 20, 1948, 10–13.

——. "What Democracy Means in Russia." *New Republic*, October 28, 1946, 551–52.

——. "Woodrow Wilson after Ten Years." *Forum and Century*, March 1931, 129–33.

——. "A Word to the Republicans: The Duty of an Opposition Party." *Harper's*, October 1935, 513–23.

Marryat, Frederick. *Diary in America*. Ed. Jules Zanger. Bloomington, Ind., 1960.

——. *A Diary in America, with Remarks on Its Institutions*. Ed. Sydney Jackman. New York, 1962.

Martineau, Harriet. *Society in America*. Ed. and abr. Seymour Martin Lipset. New Brunswick, N.J., 1981 [1962].

Merriam, Charles E. Review of Laski, *American Democracy*. In *American Political Science Review* 42 (December 1948): 1211–13.

Miller, Perry. "Harold Laski on America." *Nation*, June 19, 1948, 689–91.

Mitford, Jessica. *The American Way of Death*. New York, 1963.

Muirhead, James Fullarton. *America: The Land of Contrasts: A Briton's View of His American Kin*. London, 1902 [1898].

———. "Some Recent Books on the United States." *Atlantic*, October 1907, 553–68.

Nevins, Allan, ed. *America through British Eyes*. New York, 1948.

Pinchot, Amos R. "The Roosevelt-Laski Scheme." *Scribner's Commentator*, October 1941, 62–68.

Raban, Jonathan. *Bad Land: An American Romance*. New York, 1996.

———. *Hunting Mister Heartbreak: A Discovery of America*. New York, 1991 [1990].

———. *Old Glory: An American Voyage*. New York, 1981.

Rogers, Lindsay. "What We Must Do to Be Saved." *Saturday Review*, June 12, 1948, 12–13.

Schlesinger, Arthur M., Jr. "Laski and the Democratic Way." *New York Times Book Review*, June 6, 1948, 1, 32–33.

Shaw, George Bernard. *Bernard Shaw: Collected Letters*. 4 vols. Ed. Dan H. Laurence. London, 1965–1988.

———. "The Future of Political Science in America." *Political Quarterly* 4 (July–September 1933): 313–40.

———. "G. Bernard Shaw on Anglo-American Relations." *New York Times Magazine*, October 22, 1916, 2–3.

———. *Heartbreak House, Great Catherine, and Playlets of the War*. New York, 1919.

———. "A Nation of Villagers." *Everybody's Magazine*, December 1907, 861–65.

———. "Open Letter to the President of the United States of America." *Nation* (London), November 7, 1914, 166–68.

———, ed. *Fabian Essays in Socialism*. London, 1889.

Smith, Goldwin. "If Christ Came to Chicago." *Contemporary Review*, September 1894, 380–89.

Stalin-Wells Talk: The Verbatim Record and a Discussion by G. Bernard Shaw, H. G. Wells, Ernst Toller, and Others. London, 1934.

Stead, W. T. *The Americanization of the World; or, the Trend of the Twentieth Century*. New York, 1902 [1901].

———. *Chicago To-day; or, The Labour War in America*. 1894. Reprint, New York, 1969.

———. *From the Old World to the New; or, A Christmas Story of the World's Fair, 1893*. London, 1892.

———. "The Future of the English-Speaking World." *Cosmopolitan*, January 1902, 341–46.

———. *If Christ Came to Chicago! A Plea for the Union of All Who Love in the Service of All Who Suffer*. Chicago, 1894.

———. "Jingoism in America." *Contemporary Review*, September 1895, 334–37.

———. *Satan's Invisible World Displayed; or, Despairing Democracy*. New York, 1897.

———. ed., *The Last Will and Testament of Cecil John Rhodes*. London, 1902.

Strachey, John St. Loe. *American Soundings: Being Castings of the Lead in the Shore-Waters of America, Social, Political, Literary, and Philosophic*. London, 1926.

Trollope, Frances. *Domestic Manners of the Americans*. Ed. Donald Smalley. New York, 1949.

"Two Views of America." *Nation*, December 20, 1906, 537–38.

Wallas, Graham. "The American Analogy." *Independent Review*, November 1903, 505–16.

———. "The Eastern Question." *New Republic*, January 27, 1917, 348–49.

———. *Men and Ideas: Essays by Graham Wallas*. Ed. May Wallas. London, 1940.

———. "The 'New Virility' in the United States." *New Statesman*, January 31, 1920, 487–88.

Webb, Beatrice. *Beatrice Webb's American Diary, 1898*. Ed. David A. Shannon. Madison, Wis., 1963.

———. *The Diary of Beatrice Webb*. 4 vols. Ed. Norman MacKenzie and Jeanne MacKenzie. Cambridge, Mass., 1982–1985.

———. *Our Partnership*. Ed. Barbara Drake and Margaret I. Cole. London, 1948.

Webb, Sidney, and Beatrice Webb. *The Letters of Sidney and Beatrice Webb*. 3 vols. Ed. Norman MacKenzie. Cambridge, England, 1978.

Wellman, James. "A Nation's Will—The Future of America." *Harper's Weekly*, December 29, 1906, 1898.

Wells, H. G. *Anticipations of the Reaction of Mechanical and Scientific Progress upon Human Life and Thought*. New York, 1902 [1901].

———. *The Correspondence of H. G. Wells*. Ed. David C. Smith. 4 vols. London, 1998.

———. *Experiment in Autobiography: Discoveries and Conclusions of a Very Ordinary Brain (Since 1866)*. New York, 1934.

———. *'42 to '44: A Contemporary Memoir upon Human Behaviour during the Crisis of the World Revolution*. London, 1944.

———. *The Future in America: A Search After Realities*. New York, 1906.

———. *Guide to the New World: A Handbook of Constructive World Revolution*. London, 1941.

———. *H. G. Wells in Love: Postscript to an Experiment in Autobiography*. Ed. G. P. Wells. Boston, 1984.

———. *Mankind in the Making*. New York, 1904.

———. *Mr. Britling Sees It Through*. New York, 1916.

———. *The New America: The New World*. New York, 1935.

———. "New Americans." *Collier's*, February 5, 1938, 14–15, 44.

———. *New Worlds for Old*. New York, 1908.

———. *The Open Conspiracy: Blue Prints for a World Revolution*. Garden City, New York, 1928.

———. *The Outline of History: Being a Plain History of Life and Mankind.* 2 vols. New York, 1921.

———. *Phoenix: A Summary of the Inescapable Conditions of World Reorganisation.* London, 1942.

———. *The Rights of Man; or, What Are We Fighting For?* London, 1940.

———. "Roosevelt in Europe." *Collier's,* June 18, 1910, 27, 32.

———. "Roosevelt's Place in History." *Liberty,* December 9, 1933, 20–22, 24.

———. *Russia in the Shadows.* New York, 1921 [1920].

———. *The Salvaging of Civilization: The Probable Future of Mankind.* New York, 1922 [1921].

———. *The Shape of Things to Come.* New York, 1933.

———. *Social Forces in England and America.* New York, 1914.

———. *Washington and the Riddle of Peace.* New York, 1922.

———. *The Way the World Is Going.* Garden City, N.Y., 1929.

———. *What Is Coming? A European Forecast.* New York, 1916.

———. *World Brain.* London, 1938 [1935].

———. *A Year of Prophesying.* London, 1924.

West, Rebecca. "How America Strikes Me." *Sunday Times* (London), May 25, June 1, June 8, 1924.

———. "Impressions of America." *New Republic,* December 10, 1924, 65–68.

———. "These American Men." *Harper's,* September 1925, 448–56.

———. "These American Women." *Harper's,* November 1925, 722–30.

———. "Travelling in America." *New Republic,* December 24, 1924, 112–15.

Willkie, Wendell L. *One World.* New York, 1943.

Wilson, Woodrow. *The Papers of Woodrow Wilson.* Vol. 45, *November 11, 1917–January 15, 1918.* Ed. Arthur S. Link. Princeton, N.J., 1984.

Wright, Frances. *Views of Society and Manners in America.* Ed. Paul R. Baker. Cambridge, Mass., 1963.

Secondary Sources

Allen, H. C. *Great Britain and the United States: A History of Anglo-American Relations (1783–1952).* New York, 1955.

Alsop, Joseph, and Turner Catledge. *The 168 Days.* 1938. Reprint, New York, 1973.

Anderson, Stuart. *Race and Rapprochement: Anglo-Saxonism and Anglo-American Relations, 1895–1904.* Rutherford, N.J., 1981.

Bagwell, Philip S., and G. E. Mingay. *Britain and America, 1850–1939: A Study of Economic Change.* London, 1970.

Barker, Dudley. *G. K. Chesterton: A Biography.* New York, 1973.

Baylen, Joseph O. "A Victorian's 'Crusade' in Chicago, 1893–1894." *Journal of American History* 51 (December 1964): 418–34.

Baldwin, Neil. *Henry Ford and the Jews: The Mass Production of Hate*. New York, 2001.

Beloff, Max. "The Age of Laski." *Fortnightly*, June 1950, 378–84.

Bender, Thomas, ed. *Rethinking American History in a Global Age* . Berkeley, Calif., 2002.

Berger, Max. *The British Traveller in America, 1836–1860*. New York, 1943.

Blum, John Morton. *Woodrow Wilson and the Politics of Morality*. Boston, 1956.

Brinkley, Alan. *The End of Reform: New Deal Liberalism in Recession and War*. New York, 1995.

———. *Voices of Protest: Huey Long, Father Coughlin, and the Great Depression*. New York, 1982.

Buckley, Thomas H. *The United States and the Washington Conference, 1921–1922*. Knoxville, Tenn., 1970.

Burns, James MacGregor. *Roosevelt: The Soldier of Freedom*. New York, 1970.

Canovan, Margaret. *G. K. Chesterton: A Radical Populist*. New York, 1977.

Carrington, Charles. *Rudyard Kipling: His Life and Work*. London, 1978 [1955].

Chester, Edward W. *Europe Views America: A Critical Evaluation*. Washington, D.C., 1962.

Clarke, Peter. *Liberals and Social Democrats*. Cambridge, England, 1981 [1978].

Clinton, Catherine. *Fanny Kemble's Civil Wars*. New York, 2000.

Conrad, Peter. *Imagining America*. New York, 1980.

Coren, Michael. *The Man Who Was G. K. Chesterton*. London, 1989.

Corrin, Jay P. *G. K. Chesterton and Hilaire Belloc: The Battle against Modernity*. Athens, Ohio, 1981.

Cosgrove, Richard A. *Our Lady the Common Law: An Anglo-American Legal Community, 1870–1930*. New York, 1987.

Cronon, William. *Nature's Metropolis: Chicago and the Great West*. New York, 1991.

Cushman, Barry. *Rethinking the New Deal Court: The Structure of a Constitutional Revolution*. New York, 1998.

Dale, Alzina Stone. *The Outline of Sanity: A Biography of G. K. Chesterton*. Grand Rapids, Mich., 1982.

Deane, Herbert A. *The Political Ideas of Harold J. Laski*. New York, 1955.

Dinnerstein, Leonard. *Antisemitism in America*. New York, 1994.

Dizikes, John. *Britain, Roosevelt, and the New Deal: British Opinion, 1932–1938*. New York, 1979.

Downey, Dennis B. "William Stead and Chicago: A Victorian Jeremiah in the Windy City." *Mid-America* 68 (October 1986): 153–66.

Eastwood, Granville. *Harold Laski*. London, 1977.

Eckhardt, Celia Morris. *Fanny Wright: Rebel in America*. Cambridge, Mass., 1984.

Evans, J. Martin. *America: The View from Europe*. Stanford, Calif., 1976.

Feinberg, Barry, and Ronald Kasrils. *Bertrand Russell's America, 1896–1945*. New York, 1973.

Ffinch, Michael. *G. K. Chesterton*. San Francisco, 1986.

Forster, John. *The Life of Charles Dickens*, 2 vols. Ed. B. W. Matz. New York, 1911.

Fussell, Paul. *Abroad: British Literary Traveling between the Wars*. New York, 1980.

———, ed. *The Norton Book of Travel*. New York, 1987.

Gerlach, Murney. *British Liberalism and the United States: Political and Social Thought in the Late Victorian Age*. Houndsmills, England, 2001.

Gilbert, James. *Perfect Cities: Chicago's Utopias of 1893*. Chicago, 1991.

Ginger, Ray. *Altgeld's America: The Lincoln Ideal versus Changing Realities*. New York, 1958.

Gossett, Thomas F. *Race: The History of an Idea in America*. Dallas, 1963.

Graybar, Lloyd J. *Albert Shaw of the* Review of Reviews: *An Intellectual Biography*. Lexington, Ky., 1974.

Hamby, Alonzo L. *Beyond the New Deal: Harry S. Truman and American Liberalism*. New York, 1973.

Hammack, David C. *Power and Society: Greater New York at the Turn of the Century*. New York, 1982.

Hammond, J. R. *H. G. Wells and Rebecca West*. New York, 1991.

Harris, Frank. *Bernard Shaw*. New York, 1931.

Hawley, Ellis W. *The New Deal and the Problem of Monopoly: A Study in Economic Ambivalence*. Princeton, N.J., 1966.

Heckscher, August. *Woodrow Wilson*. New York, 1991.

Heindel, Richard Heathcote. *The American Impact on Great Britain, 1898–1914*. Philadelphia, 1940.

Higham, John. *Strangers in the Land: Patterns of American Nativism, 1860–1925*. New York, 1981 [1955].

Hitchens, Christopher. *Blood, Class, and Nostalgia: Anglo-American Ironies*. New York, 1990.

Hobson, Fred. *Mencken: A Life*. New York, 1994.

Hofstadter, Richard. *The Age of Reform: From Bryan to F.D.R.* New York, 1955.

Hofstadter, Richard, and Walter P. Metzger. *The Development of Academic Freedom in the United States*. New York, 1955.

Hollis, Christopher. *The Mind of Chesterton*. Coral Gables, Fla., 1970.

Holmes, Graeme M. *Britain and America: A Comparative Economic History, 1850–1939*. Newton Abbot, England, 1976.

Holroyd, Michael. *Bernard Shaw*. Vol. 1, *1856–1898: The Search for Love*. London, 1988.

———. *Bernard Shaw*. Vol. 3, *1918–50: The Lure of Fantasy*. New York, 1991.

Honan, Park. *Matthew Arnold: A Life*. New York, 1981.

Horsman, Reginald. *Race and Manifest Destiny: The Origins of American Racial Anglo-Saxonism*. Cambridge, Mass., 1981.

Hulme, Peter, and Tim Youngs, eds. *The Cambridge Companion to Travel Writing*. Cambridge, England, 2002.

Ions, Edmund. *James Bryce and American Democracy, 1870–1922*. London, 1968.

Jacobson, Matthew Frye. *Barbarian Virtues: The United States Encounters Foreign Peoples at Home and Abroad, 1876–1917* . New York, 2000.

Johnson, Edgar. *Charles Dickens: His Tragedy and Triumph*. Rev. and abr. ed. New York, 1977.

Jones, Howard Mumford. "Arnold, Aristocracy, and America." *American Historical Review* 49 (April 1944): 393–409.

Jones, Peter d'A . *The Christian Socialist Revival, 1877–1914: Religion, Class, and Social Conscience in Late-Victorian England*. Princeton, N.J., 1968.

Kammen, Michael. *In The Past Lane: Historical Perspectives on American Culture*. New York, 1997.

Kaplan, Fred. *Dickens: A Biography*. New York, 1988.

Keller, Morton. "Anglo-American Politics, 1900–1930, in Anglo-American Perspective: A Case Study in Comparative History." *Comparative Studies in Society and History* 22 (July 1980): 458–77.

Kelley, Robert. *The Transatlantic Persuasion: The Liberal-Democratic Mind in the Age of Gladstone*. New York, 1969.

Kennedy, David M. *Over Here: The First World War and American Society*. New York, 1980.

Kingsmill, Hugh. *After Puritanism, 1850–1900*. London, 1929.

Kloppenberg, James T. *Uncertain Victory: Social Democracy and Progressivism in European and American Thought, 1870–1920*. New York, 1986.

Knoles, George Harmon. *The Jazz Age Revisited: British Criticism of American Civilization during the 1920s*. Stanford, Calif., 1955.

Kramer, Paul A. "Empires, Exceptions, and Anglo-Saxons: Race and Rule between the British and United States Empires, 1880–1910." *Journal of American History* 88 (March 2002): 1315–53.

Kramnick, Isaac, and Barry Sheerman. *Harold Laski: A Life on the Left*. New York, 1993.

Laurence, Dan H. "'That Awful Country': Shaw in America." In *Shaw Abroad*, ed. Rodelle Weintraub, 279–97. University Park, Pa., 1985.

Lee, Albert. *Henry Ford and the Jews*. New York, 1980.

Leuchtenburg, William E. *Franklin D. Roosevelt and the New Deal*. New York, 1963.

———. *The Supreme Court Reborn: The Constitutional Revolution in the Age of Roosevelt*. New York, 1995.

Lewis, Arnold. *An Early Encounter with Tomorrow: Europeans, Chicago's Loop, and the World's Columbian Exposition*. Urbana, Ill., 1997.

Link, Arthur S. *President Wilson and his English Critics: An Inaugural Lecture Delivered before the University of Oxford on 13 May 1959*. Oxford, England, 1959.

———. *Woodrow Wilson: Revolution, War, and Peace*. Arlington Heights, Ill., 1979.

Lipset, Seymour Martin. *American Exceptionalism: A Double-Edged Sword*. New York, 1996.

Lockhart. J. G., and C. M Woodhouse. *Cecil Rhodes: The Colossus of Southern Africa*. New York, 1963.

MacKenzie, Norman, and Jeanne MacKenzie . *H. G. Wells*. New York, 1973.

Magid, Henry Meyer. *English Political Pluralism: The Problem of Freedom and Organization*. New York, 1941.

Mann, Arthur. "British Social Thought and American Reformers of the Progressive Era." *Mississippi Valley Historical Review* 42 (March 1956): 672–92.

Martin, Kingsley. *Harold Laski (1893–1950): A Biographical Memoir*. New York, 1953.

Martin, Laurence W. *Peace without Victory: Woodrow Wilson and the British Liberals*. New Haven, Ct., 1958.

McBriar, A. M. *Fabian Socialism and English Politics, 1884–1918*. Cambridge, England, 1962.

McCormick, Richard L. *From Realignment to Reform: Political Change in New York State, 1893–1910*. Ithaca, N.Y., 1981.

McKelvey, Blake. *The Urbanization of America, 1860–1915*. New Brunswick, N.J., 1963.

McNaught, Kenneth. "American Progressives and the Great Society." *Journal of American History*, 53 (December 1966): 504–20.

Miller, Donald L. *City of the Century: The Epic of Chicago and the Making of America*. New York, 1996.

Moore, R. Laurence. *European Socialists and the American Promised Land*. New York, 1970.

Morgan, Kenneth O. "The Future at Work: Anglo-American Progressivism, 1890–1917." In *Contrast and Connection: Bicentennial Essays in Anglo-American History*, 245–71. Ed. H. C. Allen and Roger Thompson. London, 1976.

Muggeridge, Kitty, and Ruth Adam. *Beatrice Webb: A Life, 1858–1943*. London, 1967.

Mulvey, Christopher. *Anglo-American Landscapes: A Study of Nineteenth-Century Anglo-American Travel Literature* . Cambridge, England, 1983.

———. *Transatlantic Manners: Social Patterns in Nineteenth-Century Anglo-American Travel Literature*. Cambridge, England, 1990.

Murphy, Paul L. *World War I and the Origin of Civil Liberties in the United States*. New York, 1979.

Murray, Robert K. *Red Scare: A Study in National Hysteria, 1919–1920*. Minneapolis, 1955.

Neal, Steve. *Dark Horse: A Biography of Wendell Willkie*. Garden City, N.Y., 1984.

Newman, Michael. *Harold Laski: A Political Biography*. Houndsmills, England, 1993.

Orde, Anne. *The Eclipse of Great Britain: The United States and British Imperial Decline, 1895–1956*. New York, 1996.

Pachter, Marc, ed. *Abroad in America: Visitors to the New Nation, 1776–1914*. Reading, Mass., 1976.

Parrish, Michael E. *Felix Frankfurter and His Times: The Reform Years*. New York, 1982.

Pearce, Joseph. *Wisdom and Innocence: A Life of G. K. Chesterton*. London, 1996.

Pearson, Hesketh. *G.B.S.: A Full Length Portrait*. New York, 1942.

Pelling, Henry. *America and the British Left: From Bright to Bevan*. London, 1956.

Perkins, Bradford. *The Great Rapprochement: England and the United States, 1895–1914*. New York, 1968.

Pierce, Bessie Louise. *A History of Chicago*. Vol. 3, *The Rise of a Modern City, 1871–1893*. New York, 1957.

Raleigh, John Henry. *Matthew Arnold and American Culture*. Berkeley, Calif., 1961.

Rapson, Richard L. *Britons View America: Travel Commentary, 1860–1935*. Seattle, 1971.

Rauch, Rufus William, ed. *A Chesterton Celebration at the University of Notre Dame: Commemorating the Fiftieth Anniversary of G. K. Chesterton's Visiting Professorship in the Fall Term of 1930*. Notre Dame, Ind., 1983.

Ray, Gordon N. *H. G. Wells and Rebecca West*. New Haven, Ct., 1974.

Rice, Howard C. *Rudyard Kipling in New England*. Rev. ed. Brattleboro, Vt., 1951.

Rodgers, Daniel T. *Atlantic Crossings: Social Politics in a Progressive Age*. Cambridge, Mass., 1998.

———. "In Search of Progressivism." *Reviews in American History* 10 (December 1982): 113–32.

Rotberg, Robert I. *The Founder: Cecil Rhodes and the Pursuit of Power*. New York, 1988.

Russell, Francis. *A City in Terror: 1919, the Boston Police Strike*. New York, 1975.

Russett, Bruce M. *Community and Contention: Britain and America in the Twentieth Century*. Westport, Ct., 1983 [1963].

Savell, Isabelle K. *Politics in the Gilded Age in New York State and Rockland County: A Biography of Senator Charles Lexow*. New City, N.Y., 1984.

Scheiber, Harry N. *The Wilson Administration and Civil Liberties, 1917–1921*. Ithaca, N.Y., 1960.

Schults, Raymond L. *Crusader in Babylon: W. T. Stead and the* Pall Mall Gazette. Lincoln, Nebr., 1972.

Scott, J. W. Robertson. *The Life and Death of a Newspaper*. London, 1952.

Sewell, Brocard. *Cecil Chesterton*. Faversham, England, 1975.

Shannon, R. T. *Gladstone and the Bulgarian Agitation 1876*, 2nd ed. Hassocks, England, 1975.

Smith, David C. *H. G. Wells: Desperately Mortal*. New Haven, Ct., 1986.

Solomon, Barbara Miller. *Ancestors and Immigrants: A Changing New England Tradition*. Chicago, 1972 [1956].

Speaight, Robert. *The Life of Hilaire Belloc*. London, 1957.

Steel, Ronald. *Walter Lippmann and the American Century*. Boston, 1980.

Teachout, Terry. *The Skeptic: A Life of H. L. Mencken*. New York, 2002.

Thomas, John L. *Alternative America: Henry George, Edward Bellamy, Henry Demarest Lloyd, and the Adversary Tradition*. Cambridge, Mass., 1983.

Tulloch, Hugh. *James Bryce's* American Commonwealth: *The Anglo-American Background*. Woodbridge, England, 1988.

Wagar, W. Warren. *H. G. Wells and the World State*. New Haven, Ct., 1961.

Wall, Joseph Frazier. *Andrew Carnegie*. New York, 1970.

Waller, P. J. *Town, City, and Nation: England, 1850–1914*. Oxford, England, 1983.

Ward, Maisie. *Gilbert Keith Chesterton*. London, 1944.

Watt, D. Cameron. *Succeeding John Bull: America in Britain's Place, 1900–1975*. Cambridge, England, 1984.

Webb, R. K. *Harriet Martineau: A Radical Victorian*. New York, 1960.

Weiler, Peter. "William Clarke: The Making and Unmaking of a Fabian Socialist." *Journal of British Studies* 14 (November 1974): 77–108.

West, Anthony. *H. G. Wells: Aspects of a Life*. New York, 1984.

West, Geoffrey. *H. G. Wells*. New York, 1930.

Whyte, Frederic. *The Life of W. T. Stead*. 2 vols. London, 1925.

Wiebe, Robert H. *The Search for Order, 1877–1920*. New York, 1967.

Wiener, Martin J. *Between Two Worlds: The Political Thought of Graham Wallas*. Oxford, England, 1971.

Wills, Garry. *Chesterton: Man and Mask*. New York, 1961.

Wilson, A. N. *Hilaire Belloc*. New York, 1984.

Woodward, C. Vann. *The Old World's New World*. New York, 1991.

Yeomans, Henry Aaron. *Abbott Lawrence Lowell*. Cambridge, Mass., 1948.

Index